HAWAII
SCANDAL

*This book is dedicated to
the remarkable people of Hawaii
who have triumphed over infamy
more than once.*

HAWAII SCANDAL

COBEY BLACK

Also by Cobey Black

<u>Books</u>
Bernice Pauahi Bishop Her Life and Legacy
with Kathleen Mellen

'Iolani Luahini
photographs by Francis Haar

<u>Play</u>
The Angel Club

ISBN 0-89610-389-7
First Edition, First Printing – 2002

Produced, designed and distributed
by Island Heritage Publishing

Address orders and correspondence to:

 ISLAND HERITAGE
94-411 Kō'aki Street
Waipahu, Hawai'i 96797
Orders: (800) 468-2800 • Information: (808) 564-8800
Fax: (808) 564-8877
Website: **www.islandheritage.com**

"...It has plagued Hawaii as no other event in the history of these Islands. It has brought in its wake one horrible event after another; filled the people of this happy country with sorrow and fear; sowed the seeds of hate and distrust where they never existed before; and threatened the very foundations of government with destruction by the wave of prejudice and passion that has been aroused among people thousands of miles away who do not understand our problems but still hold our fate in their hands.

"It will plague us from now until the end of time unless the complete truth is unfolded and justice is done."

–Honolulu editorial, May 9, 1932

ONE

As a child, I lived in a sheltered suburb of Washington, D. C., with houses set in sloping lawns and a few large estates, one of which had been the summer home of Alexander Graham Bell. It was called Twin Oaks, and our lawn in the back was separated from it by an easily surmountable hedge of honeysuckle. We children considered the Bell Estate our twelve-acre backyard. Although the gardener occasionally set off a shotgun blast when the apples began to ripen, we played unmolested because the mistress of the estate, a niece of the inventor, was not bothered by children and had even invited me to tea.

I went without my parents' knowledge. She and her daughter gave me cookies and real tea, I remember, not cocoa. I also recall that Mrs. Granville Fortescue was an aristocratic lady whose good manners could put a child at ease. She smiled more often than her pretty daughter, who was a grown young woman and married. Her daughter's name was Thalia Massie. They politely asked me to come again if I were playing near the house, but I never went.

My parents found out about the visit. I could tell it troubled them. My father was a Naval officer, and he said that Mrs. Massie, whose husband was also in the Navy, had been involved in a brutal crime that had taken place the year before in far-off Hawaii. Lieutenant Massie and Mrs. Fortescue had also been mixed up in the scandal. There had been a murder. My parents spoke in quiet, shocked tones, and told me to stay away from the manor house.

That was the first I heard of the Massie Case.

Not until 25 years later, when I went to Hawaii as a journalist and came across the bulging file of the "Ala Moana Case" in the morgue of the *Honolulu Star-Bulletin*, did I learn more of what happened in the fall of 1931 and the spring of 1932. That winter the Massie Case became a cause célèbre throughout the country, drew the legendary criminal lawyer, Clarence Darrow, from retirement to defend his last case, prompted the President of the United States to convene his Cabinet and rocked Hawaii with the threat of martial law.

One of the greatest crimes of modern time, it combined elements of mystery and violent death with political manipulation and social reform, entangling the lives of all the Island people in its web. The foolish whim of a bored young woman precipitated the reassessment of mankind's deepest problems: racism, militarism, corruption and sex.

All of what happened will never be learned. Only one person knew it, Thalia Fortescue Massie Uptigrove, the pretty blond matron on the lawn at Twin Oaks, who, in July of 1963, closed the bathroom door of her Palm Beach apartment and swallowed a bottle of sleeping pills.

For Thalia, this last sleep ended a living nightmare that began at 11:30 p.m. the evening of September 12, 1931.

TWO

The night was clear. In the velvet sky of the tropics there was no moon but the stars were out. They vied with the Saturday night illumination of lantern-spangled pavilions and the bandstand in Waikiki Park where the Order of Eagles was holding a public dance that enlivened the palm shadows. There was also dancing at the Ala Wai Inn, a teahouse frequented by military couples and local haoles, or white people. At a verandah table for six, three junior Naval officers and their wives ordered a second round of drinks.

Lieutenant Massie's 20-year-old wife drank only half of hers. Aloof and moody, she left her husband and the dancing couples, unnoticed, and walked out into the soft air of night. "I always leave parties when I'm bored or tired of them," said Thalia Massie later. "He knew that I had not wanted to go to the party."

She crossed the Ala Wai bridge, passed a lighted saimin stand and a barbershop, then slowly made her way under the remaining trees of an abandoned coconut grove. Traditionally, it was an area of laxity.

At one time, Hawaiian royalty had sported among the palms and built mullet ponds and beach cottages near the shore. Later, as word of Waikiki's beauty spread, pale tourists from mainland America mingled with the brown beach boys, and a large, white frame, turn-of-the-century hotel, called the Moana, was built on the oceanfront. In the mid-1920s it was joined by a pink stucco palace, as dome-bedecked as a rajah's redoubt, that replaced the royal fishing lodge and assumed the dignified title of the Royal Hawaiian Hotel.

The posh hostelry housed guests from the two Matson steamers that arrived alternately every fortnight, bringing from the West Coast a total of less than a thousand passengers. This modest semi-monthly influx did little to spoil the natural splendor of the quiet resort. Its scimitar of sand lay unmolested in the path of Pacific tradewinds that trailed long white combers into shore from the turquoise sea. Farther out, beyond the reef, where the blue deepens to cobalt, a stronger wind would catch the sails of small craft on Boat Day and send them skimming to meet the arriving *Lurline* or *Malolo*.

The length of beach stretched a mile from the yacht harbor toward Honolulu at its Ewa end, to the opposite horizon where the toe of Diamond Head tested the waters. Even into the 1930s there was a

lovely remoteness about the place. Traffic was still confined to weekend motorcars, hotel taxis and, now and then, a pony cart laden with
children from kamaaina families whose residences nestled in the cool
Manoa and Nuuanu valleys, but who had beach houses on the sands
beneath Diamond Head. A more common sight would be a gang of
brown boys, beach-bound and carrying elliptical surfboards as they
wove among the scattered tourists like a school of koa fish.

It all seemed an innocent idyll. In the corner of Waikiki nearest
Honolulu, however, life moved at a faster tempo and wild parties were
rumored at the Niumalu Hotel, a kraal of thatched cottages and jungle
gardens. For a while, a nearby area had been a quarantine station.
Before then, it was a former beach haven for Hawaiian alii, or royal
chiefs, and had belonged to an ancient noble family in the days of the
kingdom. High Chiefess Kaikilani-wahine-o-puna had inherited the
land from her inbred ancestors and passed it on to her half-caste son,
John Ena, who in turn sold it for resort development. An amusement
park had mushroomed on the site at the beginning of the century, when
it was considered the highlight of a weekend to take the trolley from
Honolulu across the duck ponds and rice paddies to Waikiki Beach.

The former cholera swamps that had bordered Waikiki on its
mauka, or mountain, side had been drained for the Ala Wai Canal and
new land along Ala Moana was formed of coral fill from the dredging
of Pearl Harbor by the Dillingham Corporation a few decades earlier.
Not far from where the canal emptied into the sea was the Ala Wai Inn.
Although prohibition had been in effect for more than a decade, it was
no secret that beverages stronger than tea could be had at the teahouse.
A jerry-built torii gate framed the entrance in an ersatz attempt at
authenticity, matching the pagoda-tiered tarpaper roof. Because there
was something slightly unsavory about the neighborhood, and because
the dance band was better than that at the public park, the teahouse
drew a young, racy crowd whose parents had tea-danced a generation
earlier at the staid Moana Hotel down the beach. They were regularly
joined by Pearl Harbor partygoers, who rented homes in the Manoa
Valley and served aboard ships at the Naval Base, Tommy and Thalia
Massie among them.

"I left alone," her version of the story began. Behind her, the teahouse was throbbing with bootleg abandon as the strong local whiskey,
okolehau, flowed freely in the packed rooms of the two-story inn. She
had stood for a moment on the bridge, built the year before to accom-

modate increasing beach crowds, and watched the exaggerated shadows of the dancers as they formed patterns on the canal, like figures reflected in a funhouse mirror.

Her path skirted the forsaken amusement park, in which the only active concession was the bandstand, and followed in the same direction the road eventually leading to the Niumalu cottages where it was rumored servicemen kept clandestine assignations with local women.

"I walked down Kalakaua Avenue and turned toward John Ena Road because it was better lighted. I walked to where the road turns to Fort DeRussy. I intended to walk back to the Ala Wai Inn. When I reached that point a car drove up and stopped. Two men jumped out. One struck me ...I screamed. The two men dragged me into the car and held me down in the back seat."

Thalia Massie spared no details when she later told her story of the night of violence. She remembered four or five dark men, young Hawaiians she thought, one of whom repeatedly struck her about the face. "I was struck a great many times with a closed fist." The car raced away from the lighted avenue. The frail girl struggled between her burly captors who laughed at her feeble thrashing and insulted her with lewd remarks. As the windows darkened with the shadows of dense foliage and the car swerved off the main road, the frightened girl realized her abductors were taking her to an area off the beaten track where her cries would be unheard. The car stopped and she was dragged from the back seat, over the rough ground to a clearing in the undergrowth.

"I started to cry," she remembered. Her tears antagonized her assailants. One struck her a fierce blow. "I think my jaw was fractured then. I told him it felt like one of my teeth had been knocked out. He told me to shut up." She was thrown to the ground with brutal force.

"I was assaulted four to six times in all." She was sure one of them raped her twice and that her abductors were with her at the deserted area of the old quarantine station for about twenty-five minutes; that she heard them speaking a foreign language; and that one of them was called "Bull." She also believed that she heard the names "Shorty" and "Billy" or "Benny."

"I struggled as hard as I could. They hit me so hard I was dazed...One of them said 'Hurry up, we have to go back out Kalihi Valley.' One of them helped me to sit up and said that the Ala Moana was over there. I saw the car and the number. I thought the number was 58-805...They drove off very fast."

"I was very much dazed and wandered about in the bushes. I came to the Ala Moana. I asked some people in a car if they would take me home. I didn't tell them what had happened to me because they were strangers. When my husband came home, I told him all about it...I didn't want to report it to the police. My husband reported it. Do you suppose I wanted to go through all this?"

But this was much later, this remarkable recollection of details. The blond girl, her hair falling over the bodice of her green evening gown, was bewildered as she staggered from the ironwood thicket to the highway. Briefly, she swayed in the glare of headlights as an approaching car slowed down. The two families in the car were aghast at the sudden appearance of such a bizarre apparition: a beautiful girl waving her arms and weeping by the roadside in the middle of the night.

All five passengers told the same story:

"We had been playing bridge at my home and were on the way to the Kewalo Inn to get something to eat when we saw a young woman standing in the road," said the driver, Eustace Bellinger. He and his wife had shared a quiet evening of cards with their neighbors, Mr. and Mrs. George Clark, and the Clarks' son, George, Jr.

"We stopped," continued Bellinger, who remembered the moment well. "She being on the right side of the car and our windows up, it was not possible to understand the first words spoken, and on lowering the window about the first thing I remember was the lady saying 'Are you white people?' We answered yes."

"Thank God," said Thalia, opening the car door and slipping in next to young Clark, who recalled that she was "sitting partly on my right leg as the car was narrow for the three of us in the front seat. I could see that her lips were swollen and she had a mark on her cheek; her hair was down."

It was apparent to all of them that their unfortunate hitchhiker had been roughly handled, although none of them noticed any injuries so severe as to cause active bleeding. "When asked what happened," continued Mrs. Clark, "she said some Hawaiian boys had beat her. Her face about the lips was badly swollen and she had a mark on her cheek which might have been caused by a ring," continued the housewife, who leaned forward from the back seat and confirmed her son's description of their passenger. "I suggested, or someone did, that we take her to the police station so she could report the matter."

"I don't want to go there," pleaded Thalia with a flash of ferocity. "Take me home, please, and my husband will take care of me."

"When I asked her if she had been hurt any other way, she said no," added Mrs. Clark, "and asked us not to ask her any more questions, as her jaw hurt her so badly. As we were strangers, she perhaps did not want to tell us what had occurred. My attention was drawn to her as she stood in the road waving her arms, as she looked like my daughter, Ramona, who was out that night. I had a good look at her from the light in the car, and could see she was badly hurt. I am sure she was not drunk, nor had been drinking, as I sat right back of her and was leaning forward and there was no liquor on her breath. We all noticed that her evening gown seemed to be in good condition, and after reading of the assault wondered how it could if four or five men assaulted her."

"We asked her what part of Manoa and she gave us her address," said Mr. Clark. "We took her to Manoa Valley and dropped her off where she lived." As the car neared the darkened house, Mrs. Clark asked her son to take the distressed lady to her door, but George, Jr., declined the suggestion. "I did not think it advisable as her husband might take a shot at me." His mother did not insist.

"After taking her home and leaving her, she assured us she was all right and thanking us, we went for our meal," continued Mrs. Clark. "On the way back, my son saw a purse in the road or on the side of the road, also a powder puff, a lipstick and, I think, a comb. This was somewhere near the place we picked her up. We read all sorts of articles about her being drunk and other things but she was not drunk nor did she smell of liquor." Mrs. Clark's perceptive memory also placed the hour of the encounter: "I would judge the time to be between 12:45 and 1 a.m."

At 1:48 a.m. a telephone call was received at the Honolulu Police Station. A man's voice said "A woman has been assaulted by men, please send an officer," and gave the address of Lieutenant Thomas H. Massie, in Manoa Valley. Officer William Furtado, on duty with Officer George Harbottle, received the radio call while cruising in their patrol car and went immediately to the address. En route, they were joined by the traffic officer, William K. Simerson, who was already in the neighborhood and during his routine patrol of the valley had picked up a drunk, whom he had in tow.

Detective John Jardine dispatched from headquarters two investigators, George Nakea and Frank Bettencourt. When Jardine learned of the seriousness of the situation, he also headed for Manoa Valley. With him went Officer William Seymour. Mingling with the swollen ranks of policemen on the small lawn of the Massie's home were half a dozen Navy friends who had planned to regroup at a neighboring shipmate's home after the Ala Wai Inn had closed. The sobering young couples conjectured in subdued voices the events of the evening since Thalia's disappearance from the dance. Their whispering gave way to a whoop of recognition when they spotted the drunk in the custody of Officer Simerson. He had been a member of their party. They wondered what on earth he was doing in a squad car.

Inside the lighted bungalow, the victim had little to say. An hour earlier she had staggered in the door from the Bellingers' car, brushing aside the wagging welcome of her setter, Prince. Except for the dog, the house was deserted. Her first instinct was to remove her clothes from her battered body and, feebly, she managed to change into her pajamas. She dragged herself to the bathroom and tried to collect her wits, realizing even in her hysteria that what had happened could have yet more disastrous consequences. She longed for her husband, hoping he would call before she lost complete control of herself.

Her hope was fulfilled: the phone in the living room rang. She collapsed on the sofa, sobbing like a madwoman when she heard his voice. She was still moaning on the couch when the police arrived. Her broken jaw hindered her speech; her mind was equally bruised. At the time she could remember nothing of her assailants nor their car, except that it had a torn top. This she remembered, and that she had prayed as they ravished her without mercy.

A pout of appraisal had been on Thalia's lips six hours earlier as she slipped into the evening dress of fragile green silk and smoothed its folds before the mirror of the Massie's three-bedroom cottage in fashionable Manoa. The color of the gown enhanced her fair complexion and brightened the blue of her large, almost protruding eyes. It was a lovelier dress than normally found in the closets of wives of junior Naval officers, with a touch of extravagance in the fur-trimmed sleeves. Her slippers, too, of softest snakeskin, were chosen for a foot accustomed to elegance. Thalia was well aware of her place outside the circle of convivial young married couples in the Navy, and on this evening she was determined to leave if the party lapsed into its customary dullness, stimulated by nothing more intellectual than Navy shop talk and coarsened by bootleg okolehau. Often before she'd forsaken Tommy's friends for the company of a good book.

The Massies dined alone. At about 9 o'clock, they were joined at their home by two other Navy couples, the Bransons and the Browns; Lieutenants John J. Branson and Thomas M. Brown were stationed with

Tommy Massie at the submarine base at Pearl Harbor. Theirs was a familiar social sextet, and Thalia joined in the first round of okolehau and ginger ale. However, she lingered over the glass, refusing a refill. Just out of her teens, she was still unaccustomed to the heavy drinking of the service.

As the party mellowed, someone suggested they go dancing in Waikiki. The orchestra at the Ala Wai Inn played till midnight. As she and her husband walked to their car, Thalia's mercurial mood dipped again and she told Tommy she would really prefer to stay home. It was not the first time she had backed down from a party, nor the first time that Tommy had persuaded her to come along.

Her despondency did not improve, however. As the night progressed in the screened-off rooms of the teahouse on the Ala Wai, Thalia idled over her drink at their verandah table as the others danced. The staccato beat of the Charleston on the packed dance floor set the tempo of the night's gaiety and depressed the bored wife as it increased in rowdiness. Couples wandered from booth to booth. Jerry Branson had joined a group of civilians in the next room and was telling them of the intricate workings of submarines. When Joe W. Stryker, also a lieutenant from Pearl Harbor, asked Thalia to dance, she made no effort to hide her scorn. Why, asked Joe, was she in the habit of making caustic remarks about people? Thalia replied, with a bluntness already painfully familiar to her husband's shipmates and their wives, that she had few friends in the Navy, and what's more didn't mind hurting people's feelings. Lieutenant Stryker found little warmth to kindle in this strange, cold girl whose beauty seemed in no way endearing, and as he left her at her table, he told her quite frankly that she was making enemies in the Navy, although he was not among them.

Joe's words had been meant as a kindly admonition, but they fell as added drops of gall in Thalia's bottled mood of bitterness. Tommy returned from the booth where he'd been with Branson and offered her another drink, which again she refused. Also, she wished to avoid the crowded dance floor where Jerry was now leading the orchestra; he and Tom Brown were having a glorious time and their wives seemed to share the carousing revelry which she considered banal. Without offering an excuse, Thalia left the booth. Trailing aimlessly through the drinking throng, she found her way to the second floor room where more Navy couples were being hosted by Lieutenant Ralph Stogsdall. She pushed wide the screen, attempting a smile of cordiality that froze on her pale face as she became aware of her unwelcome. She and Stogsdall exchanged words, the officer telling her that she had no backbone and was a clinging vine who couldn't stand on her own two feet. Once or twice she wandered away from the door, finally returning with the intention of joining the party. None of the men volunteered his seat. Susan Fish, a young Navy wife, made a sign to her husband that it was time to leave. Mrs. Stogsdall also indicated a desire to dissolve the company. Her husband, Ralph, still made no move to stand as Thalia's blue eyes reflected the intentional slight. She asked outright if he were not going to offer a lady a seat. With equal candor, Stogsdall, his tongue loosened by liquor, replied that he had no intention of doing so.

"You're not a gentleman," lashed Thalia, bringing the Navy lieutenant to his feet at last.

"And you're a louse," he retorted, adding that his party didn't want her around.

Thalia's eyes flashed. She slapped him across the face with all the force of her slender hand.

"Someone had better find Tommy Massie and have him come up here and take care of his wife." The command was directed to Lieutenant Fish, and the junior officer immediately headed for the lower floor of the teahouse. "Lieutenant Branson was in the booth, but not Lieutenant Massie," recalled Susan Fish, agreeing with the others in the party that Jerry seemed to be all over the Inn and having a whale of a good time. "We were about to leave and my husband didn't want to leave Thalia alone, so my husband went and got Lieutenant Massie to come back and look after his wife. It must have been near 11:30; we got home before midnight. The Stogsdalls left the same time we did. I saw them get in their car."

Although the heavy drinking had taken its toll on Ralph Stogsdall, Mrs. Stogsdall remembered seeing the Massies together in the upstairs room just before she and her husband left. She thought the time was 12:10 a.m. since her clock at home showed 12:30 when she walked in the door; but she later amended this hour, agreeing with the others that Thalia was last seen at 11:30 p.m.

When Tommy was next seen, it was downstairs with his crony, Jerry Branson, and not with Thalia. "Jerry, it's 11:55 p.m. and the last dance is announced," he told his friend. Jerry searched for his wife to share it with him. As Tommy and the Bransons headed for the dance floor, Jerry kicked off his shoes and in his stocking feet gave the applauding audience a ragged but not inept soft-shoe routine. He was in a mood that one of his companions described as "hilarious...He was half stewed."

With new life injected into the already roaring party, the dancers begged the orchestra not to stop. The floor was so crowded that ordinary dancing was impossible so couples joined hands and kept up the fun until the orchestra finally refused another note and packed their instruments.

Soon after, Lieutenants Massie and Branson sought out the telephone at the Inn, according to Tommy, who clicked the receiver and tried to place a call. A couple named Pringle, friends of the officers, jokingly asked Tommy what he was up to, telephoning at such a late hour. Massie told them he was trying to reach his wife, Thalia. He wanted to prove to her that he had looked for her, something she always accused him of not doing. The Pringles placed the time at 1:15 a.m., and as far as they knew, Tommy Massie's call went unanswered.

Mrs. Branson had also walked out on her husband since she could no longer find him, offering a ride to Lieutenant and Mrs. Brown without telling Jerry. She and the Browns were to join another Navy couple, the James V. Rigbys, at their Manoa Valley home for a nightcap after the dance. They'd all talked it over while Tommy was still on the phone, so it was to the Rigbys that Massie drove his car with a raucous Jerry Branson on the front seat beside him. They reached the Rigby home before the others and found the door of the dark house unlocked. Jerry made himself at home, Tommy recalled, unbuttoning his shirt, loosening his belt, and stretching out on the couch. He was asleep almost instantly. In the silent house, Tommy found his way to the kitchen and opened the refrigerator in search of eggs to scramble, but finding none, he awakened the maid in the children's room and asked for the Rigbys. They were still out, the sleepy maid told him. Tommy wondered if the party may have moved up the valley to his own home, not far away, and phoned the number of his house. The voice that answered was Thalia's and it was hysterical.

"Tommy, something terrible has happened!" she wailed. "Please come home at once!"

Massie hung up the receiver and dashed from the house. In the stupor of his sleep, said Jerry Branson, he heard a car start and grind out of the driveway. Rousing himself, he wondered at his friend's agitation and decided to follow on foot. He didn't bother to button his trousers, he later told the police, as he staggered out the door.

The cottage in Manoa Valley looked calm enough as Tommy Massie turned into the drive. "But as I went up the steps I could hear her crying. She ran to the door and collapsed in my arms. Although she had managed to change into pajamas, her condition was pitiful," he recalled,

"...blood coming from her nose and mouth, her legs crushed and bruised - and a large bruise on the side of her face." Her weeping was uncontrollable. "I thought a truck had run over her," Tommy said. He begged her to tell him what had happened.

The only reply that she could muster at first was, "It's too horrible!" She kept moaning and then told him that some Hawaiians had dragged her into a car, beaten her savagely and taken her to a lonely spot off the Ala Moana road and raped her again and again.

"Oh my God," sobbed Tommy, his head in his hands. He wandered about the room in a daze as his young wife, crumpled on the couch, kept saying, "I want to die. I hope I die."

"I tried to comfort her, but I couldn't," he said. Then he took a clean handkerchief from his pocket and gently wiped the blood from his wife's face. "She wouldn't even let me do that." He asked her if she had taken precautions to prevent conception or disease.

"Yes, I've done everything I can," whimpered Thalia. "I want to die." Her anguished husband called the police.

She had married at sixteen, a wide-eyed, wistful bride who seemed more a child playing dress-up than the wife of the slender Naval officer who stood at her side in the candlelight of the Bethlehem Chapel beneath the vaulted arches of the National Cathedral in Washington. It was Thanksgiving Day 1927, and the wedding was the social event of the season. Born into the social register, educated abroad and in the capital city, Thalia became attracted by the dapper, sensitive Kentucky midshipman at nearby Annapolis, and after his graduation in June, at the age of 22, the young couple became engaged. They were an appealing pair, part of their charm stemming from the fact that both were small, with delicate features. Thomas Hedges Massie had changed little since his plebe year at the Naval Academy, weighing a slight 133 pounds and standing five-feet-six inches at the time he was commissioned an ensign. His brown eyes, set wide in a high forehead under side-parted soft brown hair, complimented the fair coloring of his azure-eyed betrothed, who was an appropriate two inches shorter than he and of the gentle demeanor approved by his southern family in Winchester. The Fortescues also must have considered the match appropriate since Tommy was invited to the family's Long Island estate, known as "Wildhome," in Bayport.

It was the heyday of the reckless 20s and they were children of the age. One day, bored with a movie in Patchoque, a neighborhood less exclusive than Bayport, they saw an unattended baby in a carriage on the sidewalk outside a movie theater and wheeled it off on a whim. In all sincerity, teenage Thalia claimed she had temporarily abducted the wailing infant because it was neglected and wanted attention. She had meant no harm. The distressed mother was not in sympathy with this explanation and she had the young couple arrested. They were held on $100 bond, but the case was dropped in juvenile court.

Other pranks enlivened the courtship. Thalia, always on the lookout for adventure and enjoying the social immunity of her Olympian caste, had purchased a gross of pencils and with her fiancé had peddled them from house to house, dissolving in giggles when patrons slammed doors in their tender, well-fed faces. After her marriage, too, she displayed a headstrong streak in her generally phlegmatic temperament that created the impression she was "too highbrow." Fellow members of her service social world were baffled by her preference for the bookshelf to the bar.

Instead of joining the other wives in classes of flower arranging or hula dancing, she had enrolled as a part-time student at the University of Hawaii. A girl of refined sensibilities and keen intellectual curiosity, she was conscious of the inadequacy of her fragmented education, so abruptly curtailed by marriage. She had confided her self-doubts to a young assistant professor of education and psychology at the university, and his counseling had been a balm to the self-torture she suffered during recurrent bouts of depression. She agreed, with Tommy's encouragement, to a personality inventory for neurosis, and although the results were locked deep in her heart and enjoyed the safekeeping of the junior professor's confidential files, her husband noticed that the counseling sessions benefited his doll-wife's capricious disposition. Her father was an author and she harbored literary ambitions. She was interested in facets of life alien to her own and less pampered, yet many of her acquaintances considered her spoiled.

As a baby, Thalia's beauty had been breathtaking. Enormous eyes of clear china blue dominated a cherubic face appropriately haloed by fine golden hair. Her nose was pert and her complexion porcelain. She was much admired and a long succession of nannies and frauleins had paraded her proudly through Parc Monceau, the Serpentine Gardens and Du Pont Circle. Somehow this beauty had never fully matured as Thalia grew into her teens, so that the round eyes of childhood seemed slightly thyrotoxic in young womanhood. The dimpled chin became merely chubby but in keeping with a vulnerable softness that seemed to pervade all her body, and her personality as well. Nevertheless, she was still an appealing and lovely looking girl.

She gave a first impression of being submissive, an outward manifestation of her cowed admiration for two strong-willed parents. She lacked the fiber of her mother and the panache of her father, but had inherited to a high degree the latter's headstrong impetuosity. Major Granville Roland Fortescue had known a full and vigorous career before he married in 1910 at the age of thirty-five. An extremely fit and handsome man, he early acquired the nickname "Rolly" befitting his style of bravura. His stepfather was Robert B. Roosevelt, uncle of President Theodore Roosevelt, and the lad grew up in a military atmosphere. It was inevitable that he become a first lieutenant in the Cavalry, joining Colonel Teddy Roosevelt's Rough Riders. He was wounded at San Juan Hill, and in appreciation of this military feat, his former colonel appointed him as an Army attaché on the White House staff. It was during his tenure as aide to President Roosevelt that he met the beautiful Washington debutante Grace Hubbard Bell.

The legends about him began to grow while he was still at Yale and later at the University of Pennsylvania. Before graduation, he left college for a military career, resigning to become a war correspondent and eventually the author of half a dozen books and as many plays. None of his plots surpassed his life, however, since his adventurous spirit led him to the Philippines, the interior of Venezuela where he explored the headwaters of the Orinoco River, tracing the treacherous jungle waterway to its mouth, and finally into a major's uniform in France during World War I, where he was again wounded, this time in Mountfaucon. Having served with half a dozen foreign units as war correspondent for London newspapers, including the Spanish, Belgian, French, English, Russian and Turkish armies in the field, he had a scoreboard of medals. The left breast of his dress uniforms bristled with such diverse decorations as the Distinguished Service Cross, the Victory Medal with three stars, the Purple Heart, the Spanish War Medal, the Philippine Insurrection War Medal and the Order of the Rising Sun.

It would have been extraordinary if the children of such a man had been bereft of a romantic nature. Thalia had envisioned excitement in faraway places as the wife of a brilliant young Naval officer, and was rather disenchanted when Tommy left for sea on the newly commissioned U.S.S. *Lexington* soon after their marriage, thus restoring her to her virgin bed in the family home at Twin Oaks. She joined him when he was next assigned to New London for submarine training and was thrilled when news of his transfer to the Pacific was announced, with headquarters in Honolulu. But despite the glamour of Hawaii's beauty, the casualness of its good life and the deferential treatment she received from her husband's superior officers, who were aware of her social prestige and the influence of her family, she found that life could pall as rapidly in the tropics as in the confined atmosphere of an East Coast Naval base. Receptions and service soirees were anathemas to her and she seldom bothered to hide her distaste for them. When the cocktail chatter became too inane, she would put down her unwanted glass and wander outside to drink in the undiluted air of the night. There was a recklessness in these solitary excursions that exhilarated her. She gave no thought to danger nor to the concern of those who feared for her safety. Such conduct was ideal fodder for gossip and Thalia's name was often dealt with the cards over Navy bridge tables. Not the least of those who despaired of her vagaries was her husband.

As Tommy was telephoning the police about the catastrophe at his home, the officer on the Manoa beat, William Simerson, swung his police car hillward into the valley. He was on routine patrol duty and was amazed when his headlights impaled the figure of a man in a white linen suit just 200 yards from the Massie house. The disheveled pedestrian was walking with his coat over his arm, his shirt unbuttoned, necktie to one side, shoes untied and the fly of his trousers not fully closed. It was Jerry Branson, and he could swear more effectively than he could maneuver. In no uncertain terms, the Naval officer told the policeman what he thought of the accusing questions being leveled at him. "None of your damn business," said Jerry when Simerson persisted in his interrogation. "I'm a Navy Shore Patrol officer and I have as much right as anyone to be here." The policeman thought otherwise. As Branson became increasingly abusive, Simerson took him to the nearest patrol box and called for a police wagon. It was at this moment that Officer Furtado drove past, answering the call from Lieutenant Massie. He stopped and relayed the radio message to Simerson that a woman had been assaulted in the Manoa district and, owing to Branson's condition, he recommended the sooner the intoxicated suspect was taken to headquarters the better. Still objecting, Jerry Branson was hustled into Furtado's car and the policemen headed for the Massie home, their hostage now consigned to the backseat.

It had been a busy night at police headquarters. At 12:48 a.m., exactly an hour before Tommy Massie had picked up the phone and asked the operator for the police, an irate Hawaiian woman had stormed the receiving desk to report an accident in which she and her haole husband had been insulted and accosted. They had been drinking with friends and were on their way home.

"My husband and I proceeded to town by way of King Street," said Agnes Peeples to the sergeant at the desk. Still in high dudgeon, she gave the listening officer a blow-by-blow account of the angry altercation that had taken place only ten minutes before. "We got to King and Middle at 12:35 and at that point there were three cars proceeding to Kalihi on King Street. My husband blew the horn. One turned into Dillingham and the other proceeded to Kalihi, and when he got to the intersection of King and Liliha the car coming down almost collided with us. It didn't stop!

"It was going 45 miles an hour and it almost hit our car, and my husband, to avoid the collision, stopped in the middle of the street, and these boys stopped on the right-hand of our car, not parallel but behind, and so I says, 'Why don't you look where you're driving?' and one of the boys swore at me, and my husband stopped the car again to see who those boys were and a big Hawaiian fellow said, 'Get that God damn haole out of the car and I'll give him what he's looking for.'"

This insult to her husband was more than Mrs. Peeples could bear without active retaliation, and as the hulking Hawaiian approached her car, she opened the door and stepped into his path.

"I got out and pushed him away and when I saw that he was going for my husband's car, I got hold of him...and this Hawaiian boy hit me on the left ear. I staggered back to my feet again and choked him and hit him." A crowd gathered.

The other boys in the back car realized their big Hawaiian friend had met his match and one of them got out and shouted to Mrs. Peeples, "Get in the car."

"I got in my car," she continued, "He hit me with his clenched fist once. Then they got in their car and pushed off fast. They proceeded down King Street to Iwilei and we followed them and my husband turned down to the police station. It never took longer than five minutes to get here." A note of triumph tempered her anger, as Mrs. Peeples added, "We got the number of the car. It was 58-985. I thought it was a Chevrolet touring car, light tan or brown. There were four boys in it."

By the time the indignant Hawaiian woman had regained her composure, the sergeant at the desk had already broadcast an alert to the two patrol cars equipped with radios. The number of the car was given, the direction in which it was headed, and a description of its occupants. The report was also given to Detective John C. Cluney when he called in to headquarters a few minutes later, and he began tracing the owner of license number 58-895. Within the hour, the two radio patrol cars also received the second assault report: a haole woman beaten and criminally assaulted by a gang of young Hawaiians in Manoa Valley. The first reaction of the police was to connect the two assaults.

THREE

In Hawaii, night has a tactile quality and falls on the landscape like a curtain of silk. Its gentle shroud is deceptive, for even in the land of the lotus, human nature cannot be smoothed into flawlessness. In Honolulu as in any town when passion exceeds the law, rape and robbery choose darkness as their cover. So it came as no surprise to two members of Hawaii's police force when the radio of their squad car blared a countercommand to divert their course from Jack Lane, where a burglary had been committed in the early hours of Sunday morning, September 13, 1931, and ignore the fight reported by Agnes Peeples at King and Middle Streets. Their orders were to proceed at high speed to Manoa Valley, where the more serious crime of rape had been reported.

Officers Furtado and Harbottle were the first to arrive at the Massie home. They had picked up Officer Simerson and his suspect, Lieutenant Branson, 200 yards from the house.

"I met Lieutenant Massie at the door and explained my mission," reported Furtado. "He told me his wife had been beaten up and assaulted. Mrs. Massie was lying on a couch near the front door...there was blood dripping from her top lip. The only thing I noticed about Mrs. Massie's face was the busted lip, her hair was all mussed up and she was crying."

The police officer took notes as Thalia told, in broken sentences, her story of the abduction by a "bunch of boys who appeared to be Hawaiians, in an old model Ford or Dodge touring car."

"I asked her if she knew the number of the car in which she had been abducted and she told me she did not. I asked her if she could recognize the boys and she replied she could not recognize them, only by their voices. I then asked if she was unconscious at any time...and she said she was never unconscious at the time."

Furtado's notes were corroborated by Harbottle: "She said she could not identify the car...the top was flapping and it might have been an old car...Then he questioned her further and he asked if she really could identify the boys and she stated she could not."

The tearful girl reminded the police that it had been dark in the thicket, that she had been held down during most of her ordeal, and in her daze had overheard only one name, "Bull." She had no idea of the license number. When traffic officer Simerson asked her if she realized all Honolulu cars have five-number plates and any one or two numbers would provide a lead, she could not offer even one number.

"She said she was positive that they were all Hawaiian boys," added Simerson, "four or five, she was not sure. She did not attempt to describe any of the boys."

Other officers questioned her, with the same negative results. She lay on the couch, shaking her head as tears rolled from her frightened blue eyes. Policeman Frank Bettencourt and City Detective George Nakea noted that she was "more or less upset and was sobbing but talked rationally and did not rumble in her speech." Could she identify the car, its license or its occupants? Again she shook her head and distinctly whispered, "No."

Another whisper in the room was perhaps as portentious as that of the distraught girl: while Thalia wept on the couch, one of the officers took Lieutenant Massie aside, and out of hearing of the others told him another woman had been reported assaulted by a carload of local boys only an hour earlier and the police were broadcasting the license number. He gave the naval officer the number of the vehicle that had nearly collided with the Peeples' car.

Outside on the lawn of the Massie home, the milling crowd of friends, neighbors and policemen aimlessly congregated like the cast of an amateur melodrama on the first night of rehearsal; no one seemed to know the script and the director had not yet appeared. The lull was filled with backstage gossip.

Authority arrived with Lieutenant of Detectives John Jardine who took one look at the ravaged girl —"her hair was full of ironwood pine needles and she was so brutally beaten that it made me sick"— and told her husband that if she had lodged a complaint of criminal assault, she should be taken to the hospital immediately. Thalia pleaded with her husband to let her stay at home, but he followed Jardine's advice and led his weeping wife out to the detective's car. At the wheel was Officer William Seymour. Jardine told him to head for the City and County Emergency Hospital.

As she stumbled to the street between the parted lines of curious spectators, Thalia noticed Lieutenant Branson in the back of a parked patrol wagon. "Jerry, what are you doing here?" she asked, then added "Never mind, Jerry."

A voice in the crowd said, "She's goofy."

The entire cast of the roadshow moved to the grounds of Emergency Hospital. It included the half dozen chatting Navy couples who had

been invited to the Rigbys for a nightcap, an increasingly large percentage of the Honolulu police force and a Shore Patrol officer, Lieutenant
Commander Richard Bates. The doctor on duty, Dr. David Liu, made
his entrance at the emergency door and immediately ushered Thalia
into the examining room, refusing to discuss her condition with the
crowd gathering on the porch outside. Nurse Agnes Fawcett prepared
the patient for examination at 2:35 a.m. Thalia told the nurse that some
Hawaiians had assaulted her; it was dark and she could not recognize
them. She mentioned no other details. She repeated the same thing to
the doctor, who also remembered that she told him "it was about two
hours ago the thing had happened; that she went home and douched
herself and cleaned all up."

He did not examine her entire body, but he noted in his report that
her lips and cheeks were swollen, and that he made a pelvic examination. The vaginal examination showed that the "hymen was old, lacer-
ated at 5 and 7 o'clock position. No other abrasions or contusions
noticeable. Patient was raped two hours ago and douched herself before
she came into the Emergency Hospital."

Later, after consultation with Dr. R. B. Faus, City and County
Physician, Dr. Liu conceded, "this woman could have had four men and
not show any marks. One reason is because she had been a married
woman. The vagina opened quite a bit."

The doctor made some other interesting observations: Thalia was
fully conscious, "she got right up and walked and would have limped if she
were semiconscious." She had been drinking "I detected alcohol and she
was under the influence of liquor." She was "on the border of hysterics."

The doctor remembered one thing more, but had attached no significance to it: while the examination was going on, he overheard a
conversation beyond the open window, "not in the office, but they were
talking about some number on the porch outside. I heard them talking
but I didn't pay any attention to that part. Several people and officers
were there. I just stayed inside so nobody could talk to me."

The second radio patrol car, driven by Officer Claud Benton, had
arrived at Emergency Hospital and shortly thereafter a broadcast from
police headquarters announced that the car bearing license No. 58-895
had been picked up. The number was broadcast several times and could
be heard for some distance.

The murmuring among Thalia's friends on the porch increased in
volume in direct proportion to the sound of the broadcast over the
police radio in the nearby squad car. Everyone was talking at once and

rumors were rampant. The police evaded the questions of the Navy people, prompting one officer, Lieutenant W. A. McKecknie, to approach Dr. Liu for information.

"I tried to get information from the doctor; he also told me the case could not be discussed. Then Mr. Massie came out and told us what had happened and one of the deputies standing there said they had the number of the car they were looking for that had assaulted another woman...He said they had a Ford sedan or Chevrolet touring car...I thought he mentioned the actual number."

It was apparent that the reluctance of the police to discuss the case did not preclude a detailed discussion of the suspected car. Its description was common knowledge by the time Thalia and Tommy were taken with Jerry Branson to headquarters by Detective Jardine.

While the doctor was examining Thalia, Jardine had given Branson, whom he had requested be brought to the hospital for questioning, a cursory cross-examination. The young officer's mind had cleared enough to pinpoint his whereabouts during the night. Despite an evening of strenuous socializing, he was also relatively immaculate. His white suit, though rumpled from his nap at the Rigby's and with a tear at the corner of one pocket, was nevertheless spotless. His hands were clean and devoid of abrasions or blemishes. Jardine was convinced he had no part in the bloody attack. This opinion was confirmed by Massie, who termed Branson's implication "absurd." He told the detective "Jerry was with me all evening. He wasn't out of my sight for more than 10 minutes from the time we arrived at the Ala Wai Inn until we reached the Rigby's. I can vouch for his actions." No charges were placed against Lieutenant Branson, and after reaching the police station, he was released.

"What is your full name?"

"Mrs. Thalia Hubbard Massie."

Inspector of Detectives John McIntosh, a seasoned law officer with 30 years of experience in Australia and Hawaii, sat facing Mrs. Massie in his office at the police station. It was 3:30 a.m. The detective and the victim were alone. Thalia had just arrived from the hospital and it was her first formal interrogation. She had regained much of her composure and looked at the officer through swollen dry eyes.

"Will you relate to me what happened to you tonight?"

"I left home about 9 p.m. with my husband to go to the Ala Wai Inn...Around midnight, I decided to go for a walk and some air." Thus

again the young woman began her tale of terror. Every word was recorded, including a few new details. She identified the car that had carried
her to her fate as a Ford touring car, her answer being more specific than
her previous description of "an old touring car, Ford or Dodge, with a
flapping top." She also told McIntosh that its passengers included not
only "Bull" but also "Joe" along with two others.

"Do you think you could identify these men, Mrs. Massie?" the
detective asked.

"I don't know," said Thalia, for the first time qualifying her negative answer.

"What was the license plate, do you know?"

"I think it was 58-595," said Thalia softly and without hesitation. "I
would not swear to that being correct. I just caught a fleeting glimpse
of it as they drove away."

Inspector McIntosh wrote the number down on his blotter.

In another part of the city, Officer John C. Cluney checked a number written on his police pad. It was 58-895. The number had been
traced to a 1929 Ford Phaeton belonging to a geisha girl with the family
name of Ida, living on Cunha Lane. Cluney found the house and with
the help of his flashlight made his way to the garage and trained the beam
on the license of the parked car. It was the one, all right. He walked forward and put his hand on the radiator; it was still warm.

"I went to the house and rapped at the door," recalled Cluney, "and
a woman came to the door and asked who I was and I said 'Tantei,'
which is Japanese for detective and she opened the door and there were
two girls came, and I said I wanted to see the boy who operated the car."

"It is kind of late," said the older girl, "three o'clock in the morning."

"That doesn't make any difference. I want to see the boy," said the
tantei. "And then Ida came out and I asked him if he operated the car
and he said, 'No, he loaned it to a Hawaiian boy,' and I asked him if he
knew him and he said he knew his name, and I said, 'Who were in the
car?' and he said 'Four other boys,' but he didn't know them, and I said
if that is the case, I will place you under arrest."

The boy's two sisters stood wondering under the porch light. A
shadow of distress swept over their pretty, smooth Asian features. The
younger one drew back in fear behind her older sister.

"He is the only boy in the family and it will break the old lady up if
she finds there is anything wrong with the boy," said the sister who
worked as a geisha to help support the family.

The detective said he couldn't help it, the boy would have to come with him to the police station. As Horace Ida put on his leather jacket, his sister was told to follow.

"You can drive the car down, this 58-895, and I will take Ida with me," said Cluney to the girl.

After arriving at the Kapiolani Building, temporary police headquarters, Officer Cluney left Ida in the detective assembly room with a couple of fellow officers and went into Captain McIntosh's office to inform his chief that he had brought in the car and its suspected driver. He came out in a minute or two and took the boy over to a far corner of the room.

"I said to him that it looked pretty tough for him, or words to that effect. Then Ida said, 'I was driving the car. I'll tell you the truth!' Ida then went on to say, 'I was driving the car when the Hawaiian boy who was with me struck the black kanaka woman in the face, but I didn't know nothing about a white woman.'"

"At this moment I concluded talking to him," continued Cluney, aware of the significant mention of "a white woman." "The other officers in the room could have heard the conversation between Ida and me but I do not know if they did or did not and they did not tell me if they did."

Not a hundred yards away but out of sight in the maze of corridors, Tommy Massie sat waiting for his wife. She had been called into McIntosh's office without him. He talked easily with the one or two officers who stopped by his bench and their attitude toward him was one of sympathy. "He was a gentleman," remembered one.

"Captain McIntosh was in his office together with Mrs. Massie only a few minutes when he opened the door and called me in," said Officer Cluney, who had a clear recollection of the occasion. "As I entered the office, Mrs. Massie was still seated at the desk and Captain McIntosh was sitting a little to the right of Mrs. Massie. Captain McIntosh asked me the number of the car that I had brought in. I had this number written down on a card and I held it before me where the Captain could read the number himself without my telling him and without Mrs. Massie being able to see it.

"I had the number, 58-895, written in black lead pencil, and after Captain McIntosh glanced at the number which I had on the card he called my attention and pointed to the number that was written on the blotter of his desk. I glanced at this number and noticed that the number was off one cipher."

His chief then told the detective to wait outside. Cluney rejoined
the officers in the assembly room where Ida was still standing in a corner by the window. Soon the door to the detective office opened and
for a second time Cluney was beckoned.

"Captain McIntosh again came to the door and told me to bring in
the man. I called Ida and he walked toward me where I opened the door
to Captain McIntosh's office and we both walked in. I brought Ida within six or seven feet of Mrs. Massie and told him to stand there. I stood
at one side."

The blinking boy fingered the buttons of his leather jacket and
kept his eyes averted and his dark head bowed. Through heavy
lids and with her jaw still pulsing with pain, the blond girl faced
him directly.

"Look at your beautiful handiwork," barked the police captain, waving in the direction of the battered Navy wife.

The boy glanced up. "I didn't do it," he said quickly.

No one spoke for a moment.

"Mrs. Massie then looked Ida over carefully and at the same time
nodded her head several times as though to infer that Ida was one of
the men who had assaulted her," recalled Officer Cluney. "She started to question him, asking him if he knew a boy by the name of 'Bull,'
said something else that I was unable to get, but it was my opinion that
she was trying to get Ida to talk so as to get his voice and to learn the
identity of 'Bull.' At that moment I was excused from the room by
Captain McIntosh."

Ida's sister was taken home but the car with the incriminating
license was retained at headquarters. Officer Cluney also left for home,
neglecting to tell his chief that Horace Ida, inadvertently and without
prior knowledge of the Massie charge, had mentioned to him that the
boys in the car "had nothing to do with a white woman."

Thalia was driven home with Tommy in Lieutenant Jardine's squad
car. She was too exhausted even to weep and they drove in silence.
Later in the day, however, when she was being interrogated again, she
remembered for the first time that one of the boys who had raped her
was wearing a leather jacket.

The leather jacket, rolled with the chamois side out, served as Ida's
pillow in the city jail that night. Between snatches of sleep, he
answered police questions, explaining that he had at first denied having
the car because he was trying to shield his buddies from involvement in
the Peeples affair, but now that they were suspected of beating up the

blond haole woman, he was willing to tell all he knew of their night on the town.

He was told he could save the full story for the next day when McIntosh would question him further; meanwhile the important thing was to find his buddies. Did he have any idea where they were? At home where they should be, reasoned Ida. The police concentrated on the area between the Palama Settlement House and Alewa Heights.

FOUR

The lower slope of the once verdant valley between the Alewa and Palama rises of Honolulu had become by the early 1930s a dozen acres of waterfront blocks clogged with rabbit-warren tenements, haphazard shacks with corrugated roofs, bootleg bars and Buddhist temples. On the upper slopes, frame houses clung to the hillsides with the same tenacity that they clung to respectability. Proud Asian and Hawaiian families tended their small gardens, prayed to their God, saved their money for the education of sons, and kept their children clean, but it was a losing battle against encroaching slums.

As the valley dipped to the sea, it carried with it the silt of humanity: the drifters, the misfits, the mateless outcasts, the defiant youth who had broken away from the moorings of family ties. This derelict flotsam collected in the basin called Mosquito Flats.

Down near River Street, the weathered shophouses with flat wooden facades were festooned by sagging balconies that paralleled in symmetry the swayback rooftops overhanging the narrow streets. Valiantly, the Nippon Theatre plastered fresh billboards and drew the leading actors from Tokyo to add a note of probity to the corner of Aala Street and Beretania. Japanese families flew paper fish from bamboo poles on Boys' Day, and firecrackers sparked the crowds on Chinese New Year. A few of the Chinamen sitting at counters strung with pressed duck and dried shark fins still wore their hair in waist-long queues, and the most traditional among them had aging mail-order brides with bound feet.

The polyglot charm of the area was overshadowed, however, by the corruption it harbored. Prohibition had further festered the ghetto, turning pool halls into speakeasies. Near the docks in Iwilei, women were a cash commodity. In the hardened core of the slum—the plot known as Green Block—gambling tables filled the back rooms. Jobless plantation workers were the steady customers, their swarthy ranks occasionally counterpointed by white sailor suits, soldier khaki and the leather jackets of young toughs. Moral laxity overlooked acts of passion that were considered crimes in other parts of the city.

It was a quarter familiar to all port towns that face the Far East and had been worse before the great Chinatown Fire swept it temporarily clean a couple of decades earlier. Now the area spawned street gangs, such as the Kalihi Gang and the School Street Gang, shiftless youths who learned early the laws of the city jungle. The Territory of the School Street Gang, sometimes called the Kalani Gang after the nickname of its leader, was bordered by the Flats, Hell's Half Acre and Blood Town. On its southern boundary was Vineyard Street, where the Liberty Dance Hall, known as Shanka Barn in deference to the social risks involved in fraternizing with the hostesses, was run by Russian Nora.

The rugged neighborhood included Buckle Lane, the most crime-ridden street in Honolulu, yet honorable, hard working, law abiding families still lived there, and some community effort was made to help them. The National Guard encouraged athletics; a settlement house was built at Palama. But only the very old and the very young seemed to have made a decent peace with life. Japanese grandmothers, kimono-clad and wearing getas, played games in a square of sunlight no bigger than a back stoop with toddlers whose hair bristled like the black sea urchins on sale in the teeming open Kekaulike Fish Market at the foot of the street. Hawaiian tutus gathered strays to their ample muumuu bosoms. The dying generation sought solace in the temples, and when the youngsters were a little older they would find their recreation in the Palama Settlement House.

But for the older youth of Palama and Kalihi, a settlement house held as little excitement as a Buddhist temple. Many of them congregated at the Kauluwela playground, and it was there that the police found Horace Ida's companions the next day.

By sunset on Sunday, September 13, less than 24 hours after the crime, all five boys had been arrested. Besides Ida, there was David Takai, also of Japanese descent, the two Hawaiians, Joseph Kahahawai, Jr., also known as Joe Kalani, and Ben Ahakuelo, and Henry Chang, Chinese-Hawaiian. They were the nucleus of the School Street Gang. None had made any effort to conceal his whereabouts, Benny wandering onto the playground several hours after his friends had been apprehended. Without him, the others had been taken immediately to the Massie home for Thalia's identification, returning to detective headquarters where Inspector McIntosh interrogated all five of them at 6:55 that evening. Deputy City and County Attorney Griffith Wight was also present. Ida was brought in first.

Three of the boys, he said, had begun their Saturday night in a booze joint near his place. They borrowed his sister's car and drove to a wedding luau on School Street where they had a few more beers. They, too, were bored and in search of excitement. Hoping to find it in Waikiki, they headed for the public dance hall near the Ala Wai Canal.

"How many people rode to Waikiki Park in your car?" asked McIntosh.

"Myself, Chang and Kalani, three of us," said Ida.

"What time did you get to the park?"

"Half past eleven."

"Where did you park?"

"On John Ena Road. I parked inside the entrance."

"When you got inside, what did you do?"

"We could not go inside to the dance pavilion so we stayed outside. Mac Takai and Ahakuelo were dancing. We waited and when it was through we all went home."

"Who went home?"

"Five of us."

"How long before the last dance did you wait?"

"About five minutes."

"Then you drove down John Ena Road, down to Ala Moana?"

"No," denied Ida vehemently. They didn't go anywhere near Ala Moana. "We went down to Kalakaua Avenue, drove down Kalakaua and crossed King Street to Beretania."

"Why didn't you drive straight across?"

"I don't know," the boy hesitated. "We followed a car. Ben knew the boys in the car. We went back to the luau."

"Were all the boys sober in the car?"

"Yes."

"Were any asleep in your car?"

"No. When we got to the luau, it was pau - nobody was out in the yard but we heard music playing in the house and somebody singing 'Memories.' We stood by the window but didn't go in because we weren't invited."

"If you weren't invited, why did you go back?"

"Well, Ben Ahakuelo wanted to go."

"Who did you drop off first?"

"Ben. Then I took the other three boys down Liliha Street and stopped the car where Takai lives. I just made the turn into King Street when a Hudson car came along full speed and almost hit us. I tried to avoid the accident and I said to them, 'What's the matter with you?' There was a man and a woman in the car. He started cussin'. David got back in the car and we stopped alongside each other. This woman came out and started cussin'. We all jumped out of the car."

"What time was that?"

"About 20 after 12. When the woman started cussin' again, naturally the fellows wanted to fight and the Hawaiian boy came out and tried to shove her away and she shoved him away and they started to fight. Then there was a crowd gathering there and I told the boys let's beat it. So I drove off."

"How were you dressed last night?"

"I had my suspenders and white shirt, dark trousers and dark shoes."

"From the time you left Waikiki, at five or ten minutes after twelve, until you dropped these boys off at their various homes, you never lost sight of them."

"No."

"You're positively sure they never got out of your sight?"

"Yes. My sister came home the same time I came home."

The Chief of Detectives suddenly produced some green beads from his pocket and threw them on his desk blotter. "These beads were the ones picked up in your car," he said in a hard, flat voice, looking right at the boy.

"I don't know about them," said Ida, baffled.

Griffith Wight, of the City Attorney's Office, took over the interrogation as McIntosh slowly picked up the beads and returned them one by one to his pocket.

"What is your name?"

"Horace Ida, or Shomatsu Ida, also known as Shorty."

"Shorty, do you know where the old quarantine station is? Out on the Ala Moana?"

"Yes."

"Were you there Saturday night?"

"No."

"Were you on the Ala Moana road any time between Saturday night and Sunday?"

"No."

"Now Shorty, when you left the dance hall after twelve o'clock Saturday night, September 12, 1931, did you have your leather coat on, or when you drove to the luau?"

"No."

Inspector McIntosh lifted his head from the beads he still held in his hand and his eyes narrowed as he slowly asked the Japanese boy if he had his leather jacket with him or on him any time during Saturday night.

"No," said Ida.

"You did not have it in your car with you at all?"

"No."

The other passengers in Ida's car told the same story, explaining that if the driver's description of the route did not exactly coincide with theirs, it was because he had been on the mainland when some of the streets were changed. There was one other discrepancy. When Henry Chang was asked what Ida was wearing, he said "He had the same jacket on."

Benny was also shown Ida's coat. "I don't know whether that was the one," he said, "but he had on a skin coat like that."

Joe Kahahawai remembered it too. "He had a leather coat on, Shorty did."

Horace Ida, 24, a short, tightly-knit muscular man with sleek black hair brushed into a pompadour above his handsome broad features, was born on the island of Maui soon after his parents arrived there from Japan as plantation laborers. His father later became a fisherman and was lost at sea. Lost, too, in a sense was the boy. Typical of the post-immigrant generation of Asians in Hawaii, he was born an American citizen but was not yet accepted as one. Nor could he turn back for security to the old-country customs of his parents. Like most of his friends, he had no job, no high school diploma. He sought employment on the mainland and had returned just three weeks before from Los Angeles, still jobless. He gravitated to his old haunts, the pool halls, the bootleg bars, the playground oasis where the same games were being played by players now in early manhood.

Cast adrift by the collapse of family discipline and filial piety that had been the ethical framework of their heritage, many of this transition generation succumbed to an aimlessness sparked by aggressive animosity toward the haole caste system.

Descendants of the white missionaries, who had arrived in Hawaii a century before, determined the economic and social structure of the Islands, a structure they governed with a hand as unswerving as the one which formerly held the Bible. As the educated elite, with degrees from Ivy League colleges, their leading role was inevitable. "Honolulu is the only city I know where the money power is in the hands of the godly," said a minister of the day and a haole himself.

This power structure was dominated by a handful of corporations known as the Big Five. They were Castle & Cooke, C. Brewer, American Factors, Alexander & Baldwin and Theo H. Davies. All were Caucasian controlled.

Watchdog of the status quo in Hawaii was the military. The armed forces were inclined to see issues in black and white, and not in the subtler shades of brown and beige. The normal tensions of a port town were magnified by the Polynesian sun. The ingredients of the melting pot of the Pacific were still defined, their raw edges rubbing against one another, creating friction and exposing nerves. Increased instances of this friction had caused a bill, calling for reform of the outmoded Police Department controlled by an elected sheriff, to be introduced in the immediate past session of the Territorial Legislature. But hearty, hail-fellow Patrick Gleason, the lovable Irish sheriff, known as "Honest Pat," continued throwing torch-lit luaus and receiving loyalty in return for his prodigious hospitality, so the law had failed to pass, although the circumstances that prompted it remained unabated.

Alienated from moral support in other directions, the Islands' aimless youth often strayed in a direction free of morals: crime. Three of Horace Ida's four companions had records of arrest. Henry Chang, Benny Ahakuela and Joe Kahahawai, all in their early twenties, had already tangled with the police, the first two having served time in Oahu Prison on charges of attempted rape. Kahahawai, also born on Maui, had no prison record but had spent 30 days in jail for robbery. He was a member of the National Guard and competed as a boxer on the Guard team. "Mac" Takai, the fifth occupant of the car, had no police record, nor had Horace Ida.

Benny Ahakuela was also a boxer, one of the most promising in the Territory. A former football star, he competed regularly in the ring for the local Amateur Athletic Union, and only a few months earlier had represented Hawaii in the 1931 National Amateur Boxing Championship Tournament held in Madison Square Garden in New York.

His chances of winning the tournament might have been better had he not spent the previous three months in prison. Although the charge had been rape, Ahakuelo, and Henry Chang, with three other boys, were found guilty of assault with intent to ravish. The case, which had taken place in 1929, involved six youths of the average age of 18, who lived in the School Street neighborhood and frequented the Kauluwela playground. One evening a young teenage Chinese girl whose home was nearby watched them playing ball, and when one of the boys asked her to meet him behind the darkened buildings, she consented. The other boys followed.

The girl was late returning home and lied to her aunt as to her whereabouts, finally breaking into tears when the accusing guardian questioned her persistently about her soiled dress, disheveled hair and telltale stains. Beaten into submission by her aunt's threatening incriminations, she cried out that she had been raped, naming the six boys from the playground. The aunt called for court action.

Testimony disclosed, however, that the girl could have freely left the scene between acts, as she was alone while each boy went back to the playing field to call another for his turn. Evidence showed nothing but duplicate fornication. The jury recommended leniency for the boys and the judge imposed a minimum sentence of four months, which, with good behavior, would result in three months' imprisonment, the maximum sentence for the crime of fornication. The boys began their prison terms in the fall of 1930. The following months, Benny Ahakuelo sparred with other athletic inmates in anticipation of the Amateur Boxing Championships. In January, he met with the parole board and was personally interviewed by the Governor; having completed the minimum sentence for good conduct, he impressed them sufficiently to be recommended for release. The boy was not pardoned, but late in January, the warden, acting on the sponsorship of several estimable haole citizens, including the chairman of the local Amateur Athletic Union, recommended to the prison board that he be discharged. The discharge received the approval of the board and the Governor, and in February, Benny was free to represent the Territory at Madison Square Garden.

It was Benny who had insisted they return to the wedding luau, where Sylvester Correa, brother of the bride, saw them between midnight and 1 a.m. All the boys admitted they'd caroused during the evening, drinking before the dance and following a friend's car afterwards, one of them jumping between running boards. They admitted "trouble with a woman in a Hudson" that had turned into a "roughhouse," but with equal unanimity they steadfastly denied having been near the Ala Moana. All claimed to have slept at home that night, and soundly.

There was little sleep at the Massie home. Lieutenant Massie had taken his wife from the police station and put her to bed. Lieutenant Jardine of the detective force, who accompanied them to the house, picked up the clothes Thalia had worn earlier, including the ill-fated gown of fragile green silk. As soon as the police left, the exhausted girl collapsed again into incessant sobs that racked her abused body and kept her husband in a pacing state of torment.

"She kept asking me why they hadn't killed her," recalled Tommy later. "She was in a total state of collapse..." The next day, already dawning outside the windows of the Manoa cottage, offered no respite for the harried couple. During the morning, Chief of Detectives McIntosh drove Ida's car to the house, and led the weary girl out to inspect it. In the afternoon, the police brought four of the youths to the Massie home, Benny Ahakuelo still being at large.

Tommy, Lieutenant L.L. Pace, a neighbor and fellow submarine officer, Commander Bates of the Shore Patrol and a Marine M.P. helped the police simulate the darkened conditions of Thalia's midnight ride: they drew the curtains in the living room and lined the boys up near the couch so their alleged victim could hear their voices when she questioned them. One of the detectives went into Thalia's bedroom and told her that he had brought some suspects with whom he wanted her to talk, and that she should look them over but say nothing as to whether or not she recognized any of them. Mrs. Pace, who had been comforting Thalia, noticed that she had again begun to tremble and asked if she wanted anything before she went into the living room. "Yes, my glasses," said Thalia, taking them from the bedside table. The Marine M.P. motioned for her to come into the darkened outer room.

Thalia entered calmly and sat on the couch. She put on her glasses and talked with the boys, directing her questions to Kahahawai and Chang, avoiding Ida's gaze. She asked them their names and where they had been the night before, to which they replied in monosyllables that they had been to a dance in the amusement park on John Ena Road. The interview was over in a few minutes and when the boys were taken out, Thalia said she was positive of the two she had spoken with, but that she couldn't recall Takai. Ida, she said, reminded her of the man who was driving the car.

As the police car drove off, Dr. Paul Withington, the Massies' personal physician, arrived. He examined Thalia briefly and immediately recommended that she return to the hospital. She was taken to Queen's Hospital where Dr. John E. Porter made a more thorough examination. His report revealed that Thalia had indeed been badly mauled:

> Patient came into hospital with fractured jaw and contusions and abrasions. General condition, fair, except patient quite upset following accident. Fractured lower jaw at the angle of the right side near 3rd molar. Considerable displacement

> Contusion left elbow. Abrasion six inches long front leg, starting at ankle extending upward. Contusion right wrist. Leg below right knee front - bruise two inches, inner knee one inch. Bruise one inch front middle left thigh. Front right bruise one

inch. Outer left thigh 1-1/2 inches. Left shoulder bruise 1 inch.
Right upper chest 1-1/2 inches.

J.E.P

Dr. Porter called in a dental surgeon who recommended removal
under gas of the third molar, deeply impacted by the force of the blow
into Thalia's lower jaw. She was given sedatives, after which she asked
to be left alone with Tommy. He sat on her bed, holding her hand, as
she fitfully lapsed into a tortured sleep.

A few hours later, she was again aroused as the police brought Benny
Ahakuelo, the fifth suspect, to her bedside. Groggily, she looked at the
young Hawaiian as Tommy raised her head, but she failed to recognize
him. Calling on the sympathy of the police, the exhausted Naval officer, who himself had had no sleep for over thirty hours, pleaded that they
allow his wife to rest. However, they were back the following day with
Ahakuelo, who was taken into Thalia's room. She identified him this
time as being the one who sat beside the driver, particularly because of a
gold tooth in front which she had seen when he turned around and
spoke to the others on the way to the deserted animal quarantine station.

To Thalia's identification of the three of the boys was added an
impressive grab bag of evidence. Even while she was first questioning
the men who she claimed dragged her into the underbrush at the side of
the Ala Moana, the police were combing the area. Officer Claud
Benton found a mirror, a half-filled package of Lucky Strike cigarettes,
two match boxes, an old ginger ale bottle that smelled of whiskey and a
mildewed handkerchief. Near a level concrete slab, the grass had been
recently trampled and pressed down, and Benton claimed that he found
tire marks in the earth of three worn Goodrich Silverton Cord tires and
one Goodyear all-weather tire imprinted by a left rear wheel. They were
freshly made, and matched the tires of Ida's car.

On the heels of the first wave of inspectors came Assistant Chief of
Police William Hoopai and Officer George Cypher, who arrived on the
scene at 6 a.m. Their findings included a broken strand of jade beads
and a celluloid barrette. Before the day was out, the grounds had been
visited by more law officers than a Labor Day policemen's picnic and the
resulting devastation was complete enough to render any tire marks
inconclusive as evidence.

The mirror, however, as well as the beads, the barrette and the package of Lucky Strikes were positively identified as Thalia's. So was the
evening purse picked up by George Clark, Jr., when the Bellingers drove

back to the spot where they had met the pitiful girl as she stumbled from the dark shadows of the roadside bushes onto the Ala Moana.

Nor were the Bellingers and Clarks the only ones who saw the slender young woman in the green dress wandering in distress after she left the Ala Wai Inn. Several people on John Ena Road saw her pass the saimin stand, and the girl in the barbershop watched her wonderingly: "She was stumbling along with her head on one side."

"She was drunk," said another bystander. "Her hair was hanging down..." Those who saw her remembered her long evening gown of pale green silk. They agreed on another point: she was being closely followed by a white man.

FIVE

Already alarm was spreading through the "coconut wireless," just as on the reefs off Waikiki a thrust of the fisherman's spear disturbs the schools of fish in the coral heads a hundred yards away. The special sonar of danger had been set in motion. It reached Pearl Harbor at about the same time Thalia reached Emergency Hospital.

Although the day was Sunday and inactivity lulled the battleships of the U.S. Fleet tethered in their berths off Makalapa, the Commandant of the 14th Naval District was in his office. Rear Admiral Yates Stirling, Jr., his black shoes matching in high polish the shine of his brass buttons, was a conscientious officer, steeped in the proud tradition of the Navy. As recently appointed commandant, he intended to run a taut ship. But the old sea dog was not without a romantic streak and his memoir of Sunday morning, September 13, 1931, began on a bucolic note:

"The sun was shining, the cool trade winds were blowing, the flowers everywhere were giving off their delicious fragrance, the doves were signaling their mates with their melodious calls, the air station on Ford Island opposite my house was launching its planes for routine flights to various islands, and the little submarines were backing away from their piers to submerge in the blue waters outside the lochs. Life seemed just as joyous as ever with no change in the outlook.

"I had just arrived at my office when I was told Captain Ward Wortman was on the phone from the Submarine Base...his voice was choked with emotion and horror, so unlike this energetic, happy person.

"Admiral, something terrible has happened," said the sub-base commander. "I'm on my way over to see you immediately."

Admiral Stirling tried to envision the catastrophe as he hung up the phone. "For the life of me, I could not imagine. I thought of all the terrible things possible: the sinking of a submarine, an explosion in a submarine—almost everything but what Wortman was on his way to tell me. He burst into my office. His usual jovial face was white as coral sand on the beach outside and the hand holding the inevitable cigarette was shaking violently."

"My God, Admiral," exploded Wortman in a voice trembling with wrathful indignation. "Mrs. Massie, that kid bride of Lieutenant Tommy Massie, one of my officers, was criminally assaulted last night about midnight by a gang of half-breed hoodlums on the Ala Moana. She's in city hospital prostrated and seriously hurt. The police believe they have five of the criminals in the city jail."

The Admiral was stunned by the news. "I was aghast. I knew Thalia Massie as a friend of my daughters, one of the younger set, demure, attractive, quiet-spoken, and a sweet girl, minding her own affairs. I knew her to be the daughter of prominent people in the Eastern states, raised in a cultured American home. God, what an awful thing to happen to this delicate girl. Then my mind suddenly switched to the thousands of young officers, sailors, and marines on the Naval Base and in the ships, who as American youth had been taught to hold the honor of their women sacred. What would happen when they learned of this terrible crime against a defenseless woman of their own race by half-breed ruffians? Wortman seemed to have read my thought."

"I have stopped all liberty from the Submarine Base," said the enraged Captain. "I hope you approve. Of course, we can't keep it a secret. Rumors are out already in the city."

The Admiral indicated immediate approval of the Captain's action as he paced before the open window overlooking Pearl Harbor. Suddenly he turned to his subordinate and brought his fist down on the polished desk.

"Wortman," he said in a voice of uncompromising authority, "our first inclination is to seize the brutes and string them up on trees."

The Captain nodded in emphatic agreement.

"But we must give the authorities a chance to carry out the law and not interfere," continued his commanding officer. "The case must take the usual legal course. It will be slow and exasperating to us. We must all be patient."

Although it was not in the Submarine Commander's nature to be patient, his respect for star-spangled authority was as deeply ingrained as his loyalty to his service, and he agreed to restraint for the present. As Captain Wortman left for the hospital to see Tommy Massie's bride, the Admiral called for his staff car and ordered the driver to head, flags flying, for the governor's mansion. Governor Lawrence M. Judd was on another island, but Acting Governor R.C. Brown received the Commandant, and Acting Mayor Fred Wright was also called in for consultation. They immediately conferred with City and County Attorney James F. Gilliland, and Admiral Stirling learned that the case would not be investigated by the city's top legal officer but by Deputy City and County Attorney Griffith Wight. Familiar with the ways of

red tape and bureaucratic buck-passing, the Admiral felt the Navy was
already getting the run-around. His indignation mounted. "The
District Attorney was too deaf to conduct a trial," noted the Admiral
scathingly in his journal.

Yates Stirling was the prototype of an admiral: silver-templed,
tanned, with piercing blue eyes and a lean, weathered profile. Trim as a
spar, his figure commanded authority, an impression complimented by
the unfailing crease in his freshly starched, high-collared, immaculately
white uniform. The Navy meant more to him than a career; it was a
heritage, a sacred trust.

The son of an admiral, he had been born, nearly sixty years earlier,
in California while his father was on a tour of Pacific sea duty. The family home, however, was in Baltimore and young Stirling was reared in an
atmosphere that prided itself on a background of Anglo-oriented ancestors who became the founding fathers of America.

"George III forced us to sever our lands from British domination,
but he did not drain the blood from our veins," said Yates Stirling on
one occasion.

The Naval Academy at nearby Annapolis, at one time colonial
capital of Maryland, claimed many Southern sons who sought a service
career and who were proud to perpetuate a reputation of being members of the most aristocratic branch of the armed forces. There was still
much of British tradition about the American Navy. Even into the
1930s, Britannia ruled the waves as the leading naval power, setting an
admired example for other navies, including our own. Overtones of
British colonial paternalism, as well as a strong sense of class distinction, were reflected in the American officer corps. Stirling went so far
as to say after World War I that he felt "obligated to England for saving
us by holding out until we could get into it and I naturally became an
interventionist." He added: "There is no need for an alliance between
a mother and son."

He had graduated from the Naval Academy in 1892, a few months
after his 20th birthday. It was already evident to his contemporaries that
the fiery, red-haired ensign was destined for a colorful career. His outspoken, short-fused, explosive personality made him a maverick in a reg-
imented metier.

"All my life I have been called a stormy petrel," he confessed in his
later years. "I have never hesitated to use the pen to reveal what I considered should be brought to public attention, usually with the Navy, but
often to a wider public. I have always believed that a Navy man actu-

ally is disloyal to his country if he does not reveal acts that are doing harm to his service and show, if he can, how to remedy the fault. An efficient Navy cannot be run by 'yes-men' only."

Asked once to what he attributed his proclivity for getting into controversies, the salty admiral whose greying hair still showed traces of red, said, "I suppose it's just my cantankerousness."

It was more than that. It was a sense of duty instilled since his childhood as a Navy junior and an innate pride in the military way of life. Even in love, he was a traditionalist, marrying the daughter of an Army general killed in the Philippines.

Stirling himself was a hero during the First World War. He maneuvered the troopship under his command with such expert seamanship that more than 2,000 lives were saved. The vessel was formerly a ship in the German navy called the *Crown Prince Wilhelm*. After capture, it was converted to American transport service, evacuating wounded soldiers and American dependents from war-torn France. A German submarine commander recognized the former *Wilhelm* and maneuvered within firing range. Stirling himself sighted the advancing torpedo 700 yards off his starboard beam and due to hit midship any minute. Rather than lose priceless seconds in relaying the alarm to his engineers, the captain himself dashed to the engine room and rang up both engines full steam astern. As the ship's turbines ground into reverse, Stirling recalled "a miracle happened. The torpedo missed our bow by a scant few feet."

On another occasion, by working his full crew furiously all night, he was able to rescue more than 1,500 officers and men from a nearby transport shelled in convoy. By dawn all personnel from the sinking ship had been transferred to Stirling's transport without a single casualty.

He had gone into submarines himself in 1914, eventually assuming command of the submarine flotilla of the Atlantic Fleet. His first report to his superior officer was a blunt declaration that American submarine construction suffered many defects and that only one of the fourteen boats under his command was ready to submerge with safety in scheduled maneuvers. Told by the alarmed Navy Department to make a complete report, Stirling pulled out all stops on submarine security and torpedoed the underwater service with a barrage of criticism that set off a controversy in Congress, where he was called as a witness before the House Naval Affairs Committee.

Although throughout his career he was sporadically at odds with the Navy Department, he distinguished himself in the Spanish American War as commander of a flotilla of minesweeping launches, converted from whale boats, that survived the hazardous task of clearing Guantanamo Bay. He also served with honor in Cuba and the Philippine Insurrection and with the Yangtze River Patrol in China.

Sea duty along distant shores and contact with the abject poverty of yellow- and brown-skinned peoples in the slum ports of the Orient increased his pride in "the good Anglo-Saxon stock" of America. "I'm proud of being about three-quarters Scotch-Irish," he often said, and was suspicious of what he considered inferior races claiming the rights of United States citizenship that his Revolutionary ancestors, a dozen generations earlier, had risked their lives to achieve.

"In the last forty years, unhappily, many foreign persons, also seeking relief from oppressions of government, poverty and ignorance, came to America," he said in a speech delivered in Honolulu. "Many are willing to share our blessings without understanding our ideals, ideals the original settlers paid for in blood and hardships—the price of American liberty.

"In the last forty years, through immigration purposes for supplying labor, the leaven of Anglo-Saxon blood in America has dropped more than fifty percent. These immigrants in large measure were without knowledge of self-government and had not been given the opportunity of self-government. Yet according to our loosely formed laws, they were soon permitted full participation in the rights of American citizenship without proper understanding of liberty.

"What will be the American of the future? Will he comprise the blood of practically all the races of the world?" asked the apprehensive Admiral. "Will this amalgamation make him a virile, distinctive, outstanding individual, and will he spiritually express the highest principles and ideals of humanity?"

Never a man to equivocate, the Admiral left no doubt in his audience's mind as to how he would answer these questions. And what better proof of his point than the hoodlum element of Honolulu, reasoned the racist Admiral. A depraved product of mixed races who preyed on helpless women, the dark-skinned thugs accused of raping Thalia Massie, the wife of a Naval officer, were, he was sure, a threat to the very life blood of America. Not for a moment did Admiral Stirling question their guilt of the most heinous crime in civilized society.

The five Island boys, who were questioned without let-up for three days, maintained their innocence. Only details of the route taken from the dance to the luau and the question of what Ida was wearing varied; otherwise their alibis coincided and were unshaken. When Ida was again shown the beads from Thalia's broken necklace and told they were found in his car, he answered, "If that's true, then they were planted because there was no woman in my car that night." It was not true, however, merely a ruse on the part of the jittery police in their anxiety to break the case.

On Monday, September 14, Ida, Chang, Ahakuelo, Kahahawai and Takai were examined at City and County Emergency Hospital by Dr. Thomas M. Mossman. He looked for evidence of traumatism, presence of blood or genital semen, and telltale abrasions. His findings were negative. The clothes and underclothes claimed to have been worn by the boys the previous Saturday night were also examined for sperm, with the same negative results. It was noticed that a scab on the knuckle of Kahahawai's right hand had been recently split, just below his heavy school ring, but the boxer said it was from sparring at the National Guard Armory a few days earlier.

The next morning, an odd procession trailed through the gleaming white corridors of Queen's Hospital, founded by the gentle wife of King Kamehameha IV seventy years before as a haven for those of her people whose suffering required medical attention. The two Hawaiian boys, Ben Ahakuelo and Joe Kahahawai, passed the portrait of Queen Emma in the hospital foyer, oblivious to the gaze of the benefactress of their race, and with the three other suspects followed Detective McIntosh and Deputy City Attorney Wight to private room 235. In it lay Thalia, propped up on pillows and still under heavy sedation. Her face was more swollen than ever, and bruises, unnoticeable a day or two before, had reached their vivid bloom. Her blond hair, dark with fever dew at the hairline, spread unbound on the pillow and emphasized the childishness of her waxen, doll-like face.

"Aren't you proud of yourselves," said McIntosh sarcastically as he ushered the shuffling boys into the room.

"We didn't do it," said Ben.

"You know you did," whispered Thalia from the bed, her voice distinct with conviction.

"Oh yeah," said the suspect. "I don't know you and I don't know anything about it." He sneered as he said it.

Thalia turned her head toward Kahahawai. "You did do it. You can't deny it."

"I didn't do it," insisted the glowering Hawaiian.

Again the room was darkened and the boys were strategically placed at the foot of the bed to simulate the circumstances of the abduction

described by Thalia. Ida was made to sit on the end of the hospital cot
with his back toward the Navy wife, as though he was driving a car. The
police told him to put on his leather jacket and then asked Thalia to
touch it. The girl pulled herself up from her pillows and stretched out
her hand in revulsion, stating it was the kind of jacket worn by the driver of the car carrying her assailants.

"Ida was taken out into the corridor and sat on his haunches as a
catcher on a ball team squats behind homeplate, directly across from
Bennie Ahakuelo," said Detective Otto Stagbar, one of the police officers who accompanied the boys to the hospital. "It was at that time that
Ida made a motion or signal to Bennie Ahakuelo which I interpreted as
motions to designate the route they had driven from Waikiki Park to the
luau on School Street, as their stories had differed. And after leaving
the hospital I asked Ida what he meant by the signal and he told me that
some of the boys were mixed up as to which way 'we turned or the route
we took from the park that night.'"

Tommy Massie comforted his wife as the detectives and law officials
conferred in the hospital corridor, occasionally sending one of the boys
into the sickroom for further conversation. "She questioned them all,"
recalled the concerned husband, "but seemed to concentrate on
Kahahawai. After fifteen minutes, the detectives called me out and
said, 'Go back and see what your wife says.' I leaned over her bed and
she said 'They are the ones.'"

Thalia this time positively identified four of the five as her assailants.

"Don't let there be any doubt about it," said her husband. "Don't
you know if there was any doubt about it I never could draw another
easy breath," Thalia answered.

Tommy Massie was convinced of his wife's sincerity, as were most of
the police. One faction, however, questioned the justification of the
repeated trips to the hospital by the local boys if the victim was so sure
of their identity and they wondered why she had not reacted more violently to the sight of them when they were first taken to her home the
morning after the assault. They were in the minority, however, as the
authorities investigating the case proceeded exclusively on the theory
that the boys involved in the Peeples' fracas were the same ones who
abducted Thalia Massie. No other suspects were brought before the
Navy wife for identification.

Just prior to the lodging of charges against the five youths on the
Tuesday after the crime, the entire facilities at the disposal of the
Territorial government were offered by Governor Judd to the mayor

of Honolulu in the solution of the case. A quick trial was the wish of the day.

This wish was thwarted. Thalia was in no condition to appear in court; her wired jaw became infected; her temperature hovered at 104 degrees for many days and delirium ensued; she was under sedation for weeks. Five days after her jaw was broken, she was operated on by the dental surgeon who removed the third molar in the line of the fracture that was preventing healing. The fear of pregnancy plagued her day and night. Terrorizing dreams snatched her from sleep and left her sweating and screaming in the dark.

Despite the deterioration of her physical health, Thalia had remarkable moments of mental clarity. The more opportunity accorded her to view the suspects, the more identifying details she recalled of her assailants that corresponded to similar characteristics of the five youths.

By the time Chief of Detectives McIntosh and Deputy City Attorney Wight called on her again on September 21, she was enjoying almost total recall. Her answers to their questions, as she lay in the hospital bed, made a fascinating contrast to the negative monosyllables she had offered eight days earlier when her abduction was only an hour or two in the past. The trauma of hysterics no longer hindered her memory: names, faces, wearing apparel and even the clear after-image of the license plate beneath the glow of the tail light were readily recalled.

"Do you know what men of that crowd grabbed you and put you in the car?" asked Griffith Wight.

"Yes. Henry Chang and Joe Kalani," answered the patient, using the nickname of Kahahawai with unfaltering familiarity.

"The front seat was quite light, wasn't it, and you could see those two? Did they turn their heads and talk at all?"

"The one named Benny did."

"You could see he had a funny mouth?" pressed Wight.

"He had a gold tooth. In the back it was dark. As soon as I got in the car I went down and I couldn't see anything."

The calm dialogue continued as the fan above the white bed whirred in harmony with the dispassionate monotone of voices. The sick girl, helpless on the pillows, with her revitalized memory and the prop of drugs, heretofore a handicap, to compensate for her lack of physical strength, did not hesitate as she continued with her answers.

"When they grabbed me in the street, I saw both Joe and Henry."

"When you were in the car, did they bend forward so you could see their faces?"

"Yes. They were holding me down."

"That street is pretty well lit?"

"Yes."

"Now, this Mac," continued Wight, referring to Takai, whom she had failed to identify, "is he a short man?"

"I thought there was another short one there besides Chang—a lean, slight man."

"At any time that evening, before talking to Mr. McIntosh, did anyone mention the number of an automobile to you?" asked Wight, suddenly changing the subject.

Thalia opened wide her clear blue eyes and looked unwaveringly into those of her interrogator. "No," she said.

"Did you by any means whatever—from your husband, or any person, or over the radio—hear the number 58-895 mentioned?"

"No."

"And that number you told me was the number of the car—you got as they fled?"

"I said 58-805," replied Thalia firmly.

"Do you remember?"

The girl put her head back on the pillows and looked at the fan lazily turning overhead. The questioning seemed as endless as the rotations of the blades. She didn't wait for the Deputy City Attorney to finish his question. "I remember one officer asked me if it happened in the house," she said evenly, "and whether it was Lieutenant Branson." Her voice was tinged with derision. The attorney and the detective exchanged glances.

"Could you tell by any means when your jaw was broken first - do you think it was in the car or outside?" asked Wight, again on another tack.

"I think this side was broken first," answered Thalia, with a faint grimace, tenderly fingering the left side of her crushed jaw.

"Were you pretty much all in?" asked Wight gently.

"Yes, they hit me several times when I was in the car. After I got out of the car I remember they hit me once and I said, 'Look out, you've knocked a tooth out'—that's on this side." She turned her head toward the two men in the room and laid her hand on the right side of her jaw. "I got a lot of blows both places."

"You are absolutely positive you can identify these four men?"

"Yes."

"You remember you told Mr. McIntosh that one of the men's names was Joe?"

"Yes."

"You told him the same night, after you told him the number of the car?"

"Yes. I also remembered the name 'Bull' and another name that sounded like 'Billy'."

"Did you hear the name 'Shorty' used?"

"Yes. At the scene of the crime."

"It had been established by two members of the car that the driver had on a leather coat. You said later you felt the coat."

"Yes," said Thalia. A slight shudder shook her shoulders.

"And the car had a rear light so you could see the number?"

"Yes," said the girl, propping herself up on one elbow. She then told the officers that Joe Kahahawai was wearing a blue shirt and trousers. The shirt had short sleeves. Benny was in blue too; she remembered his blue trousers.

"How was Chang dressed?" asked Wight, then remembering that she had said Chang was wedged in the back seat with her, he changed his question. "How, if he was in the back seat with you, could you recognize Chang?"

"By his face and his build," she answered.

"You remember his face?"

"Yes."

"You couldn't forget Joe's face?"

"Never."

Thalia's increasingly calm ability to recall the events of her night of abuse did nothing to expedite either her recovery or the trial of her case. Because of her confinement the grand jury was unable to hear her testimony until six weeks after the assault. There was no other course possible in view of the circumstances than to present the case, which had as its basis and support the Navy wife's narrative and identification, to the Territorial grand jury.

During the investigation, City and County Attorney James Gilliland called on the Attorney General and a local law firm of prominent lawyers for assistance.

Gilliland, despite his premature deafness and Admiral Stirling's scorn, was an astute and conscientious barrister who had earned his LLB at Georgetown and his Master of Law at Harvard. No provincial advocate, he had served as secretary to a former Attorney General, a Solicitor General and other national figures in Washington. He was a large, bluff, good-humored man who showed a promising talent in federal service in Washington but chose to pursue his career in his native Honolulu. A wise choice, since he was not yet thirty years old when he was elected City and County Attorney three years before the Ala Moana trial. He directed his youthful energy to breaking the case. Some 200 pages of statements were taken. Many witnesses were interrogated more than once. It was pointed out that penetration alone constituted rape, and the presence of semen was not necessary to prove guilt.

On the evidence gleaned and the advice of the Attorney General and the local lawyers, the defendants were indicted. Late in October a true bill charging all five boys with rape was returned, and counsel for four of them was announced in the persons of two of the keenest legal minds in the Territory: William H. Heen was a Territorial senator and Chairman of the Judiciary Committee of the Senate; William B. Pittman, brother of United States Senator Key Pittman, had the reputation of being Hawaii's leading criminal lawyer.

The names of these public figures usurped the front pages of Hawaii's newspapers, while readers remained ignorant of the identity of the complainant. She was described by the press, which honored anonymity in rape cases, only as "a beautiful young woman, cultured and of gentle bearing."

Rumors filled the vacuum of delay. It was voiced in whispers that a socially prominent Navy wife was the victim. The rumors grew: was she the victim of a savage assault by brutal strangers or by someone whom she knew more intimately? What was a shipmate of her husband doing wandering near the Massie house, his trousers unbuttoned? Was it true that her marriage was not a happy one? Was she another one of those frustrated blond Coast haole housewives with a predilection for dark beach boys? Or perhaps she was just a neurotic notoriety seeker. The rumors became cruel gossip. It was inevitable that their echo should reach the ears of the authorities at Pearl Harbor.

Captain Wortman, Massie's commanding officer, became a daily visitor to the inner office of the Commandant of the 14th Naval District. Admiral Stirling was not above spreading rumors himself. As senior authority of the Naval personnel, he was responsible for the welfare of every Navy man in his district as well as the man's dependents. He felt this responsibility keenly and made every effort to unravel the twisted threads of circumstance that enmeshed the Ala Moana assault.

One day he told his submarine commander that police had confided in him soon after the crime "that roving bands of dark-skinned hoodlums in motor cars hijacked women as the latter made their way to bungalows at the end of John Ena Road.

"A hijacking gang was cruising that night in a car, and happened to turn into John Ena Road where Mrs. Massie was walking," reported the Admiral. "Preying upon women has apparently become a pastime of the gangster element, and the police are making little effort to stop it. Oftentimes, the women picked up are not unwilling, but, if they resist, it makes small difference, for the hoodlums are sure of police protection, having friends and relatives on the police force. As a rule, the women are of the Oriental races and from the 'red light' district in the city, and, if they prefer charges, they can be intimidated by a threat of deportation to the mainland."

That the delicate young Navy wife who was often at his quarters as a friend of his daughters should be manhandled in the manner of a prostitute made the old skipper's blue blood boil. He was even more incensed at what he considered apathy on the part of Territorial officials. When he learned of the high legal support the defendants were having, he called on Governor Judd and the Attorney General and demanded the best available legal talent be recruited to prosecute the case.

"The Territorial Government, I found, seemed convinced it was not necessary to obtain more expert lawyers for the prosecution," bitterly complained the Admiral later. "The answer when this, to me, vital question of legal talent for Mrs. Massie came up was: 'There are no funds.' This attitude more than any other aroused in me a maddening disgust for the way the case was being conducted.

"Quick action in my opinion was necessary, with prompt and adequate punishment, if the prestige of the white race in Hawaii was to be preserved."

If the Territory could promise him nothing more than a prosecution "in the sole hands of the Assistant District Attorney whose boss was too deaf to be of any help to him...pitted against two of the best criminal attorneys," the wrathful Admiral would seek help elsewhere in the community. He appealed to the controlling haole powers and to various civic organizations, including the Chamber of Commerce. "Vain promises were made to me...and it was before a meeting of such prominent men, who had gathered to discuss means of convicting the assaulters, I first learned of the vicious tale about the beach-boy." The Admiral was stunned. He was all too familiar with the rumors defaming Thalia, "stories that she was on her way to a rendezvous with a man, but that a dark-skinned Waikiki beach boy was the lucky one was the vilest of lies!"

His voice trembling with wrath, the Admiral rose before the assembled businessmen and, again pounding the table for emphasis, he said "Even if it were true, that would in no way mitigate the offense against society. It is a hideous crime just the same. Any woman whatsoever is entitled to protection from such wild beasts."

His tirade was followed by silence, confirming in the Admiral's eyes that there was no more to be said. It did not occur to him that among his listeners there may be those who considered the possibility of the boys' innocence, the girl's instability or even that race was not an issue in the case. The Admiral was absolutely correct in one assumption: "It is difficult to discover the source of these vile lies, but their circulation is rapid and far-reaching."

During these storm-gathering fall months, the names of Thomas and Thalia Massie never appeared in print—except once. This exception was prophetic. Buried among the social notes in the *Honolulu Star-Bulletin* on October 11, 1931, was a nugget of relevance:

> Mrs. Granville Fortescue of Washington, D. C., and her daughter, Miss Helene Fortescue, who will be one of next winter's debutantes in the capital city, arrived Friday morning for a visit with Mrs. Fortescue's daughter and son-in-law, Lieutenant and Mrs. T.H. Massie, USN.

> Mrs. Fortescue's uncle was Alexander Graham Bell, inventor of the telephone, and her husband, Colonel Fortescue, is a nephew of President Roosevelt. He was one of his Rough Riders and later was President Roosevelt's aide at the White House.

The information was brought in by a slim, young Naval officer who introduced himself as Lieutenant Massie. The society editor accepted the picture of the two handsome Fortescue women offered by the Lieutenant, but neglected to print it. She didn't give the matter a second thought.

Hawaii's newspaper readers also overlooked the inconspicuous society item, unaware that the names therein would become household words in the Islands a few months later. Instead the reading public concentrated on headlines that re-echoed the outcry of an increasingly incensed citizenry.

COMMUNITY AROUSED FOR PROTECTION OF WOMEN FROM ATTACK, blared one banner, calling for Hawaii's populace to stamp out the peril of rape.

"More and more it becomes apparent that public sentiment must be mobilized against vicious elements that are preying on the women of Honolulu," wrote the editor of The Honolulu Advertiser two days after the society note appeared in the rival paper.

"Womanhood must be safe from violence 24 hours a day...The honor of the community is at issue...we must reform present conditions. We cannot afford to admit to ourselves or the world that Honolulu is powerless to shield its women from the terror that presently menaces them."

While the press and public rallied to the defense of virtue, the fate of the Massie Case took another strange twist, one that might have eliminated irrefutable evidence. On the evening of October 13, a few days after her mother's arrival and exactly a month to the day from the time she first sobbed out her story of rape, Thalia entered Kapiolani Maternity Hospital. In the stillness of the darkening room, the dread-sick girl braced herself for nightfall. Her sleep had been unmercifully fraught with nightmares and alone in her bed she waited for the panic of depression to close in.

The next morning, Dr. Paul Withington, her family physician, performed a curettage to allay her fears of pregnancy.

SIX

A different stillness filled the courtroom of the Territorial Judiciary Building on the morning of November 16, 1931. It seemed an extension of the humming bees in the plumeria blossoms outside the open windows of Judge Alva Steadman's circuit court. Sunlight lay on the lawns, belying the dark unrest of the city. The stillness was one of tension.

The gathering throngs moved quietly along the outdoor corridors of the ornate Judiciary Building towering in two colonnaded tiers above them. The building was a reminder of the royal pomp which had endeared the proud Hawaiian rulers to their people during the previous century. It had been commissioned by King Kamehameha V, who proposed its name: Aliiolani Hale, House of the Heavenly Chiefs. At the death of this last of the Kamehameha line of kings, however, in 1872, the original plans were altered by the more practical superintendent of public works, and the House of the Heavenly Chiefs became the House of Parliament.

A few years later, in 1878, on the 100th anniversary of the discovery of the Sandwich Islands by Captain Cook, a statue was erected in honor of the mighty Hawaiian warrior chief who had united the Islands and become their first ruler, Kamehameha the Great, a contemporary of Cook.

It was Kamehameha I who promulgated the Mamala-hoe, the ancient Hawaiian Law of the Splintered Paddle, which proclaimed safety for the old and feeble, for women and children "that they may lie on the roadside and they shall not be molested."

The larger-than-life-size gilded statue, with its upraised hand of protection, seemed a fitting reminder to Hawaiian lawmakers of their duty to maintain the well-being of the Kingdom, and the bronze colossus was placed in front of the new Parliament House. The building served this purpose until the overthrow of the Monarchy in 1893, when it became the Judiciary Building. The open arches on both floors afforded access to the high-ceilinged chambers, and as the waiting crowds wandered in and out among the columns, many of them fanning themselves with palm fronds, they painted a deceptive picture of carefree Polynesia.

Beneath the brightly colored canvas a more sinister undertone was infusing the spirit of Hawaii-nei, as primitive as the insecurity that plagued the warring chieftains before Kamehameha. The roadsides were no longer free of molestation. No one entering the courtroom passed the commanding figure of the just and mighty King without being reminded that the safety of women and children was fast becoming a mockery. The very air seemed heavy with foreboding.

A spell of Kona weather had battened on the city a few days before, depriving Honolulu of its usual refreshing tradewinds and rendering it helpless in the grip of oppressive humidity. In the courtroom, the bailiffs had been instructed to keep the doors closed once the wooden benches were filled, and they anticipated a sweltering session.

There was not a seat left by 8:35 a.m., five minutes after the doors opened, and many people were turned away. Trials and elections were the favorite pastimes of a population cut off by lack of communication from the World Series ballgames, heavyweight boxing championships, Broadway musicals, tickertape parades and Barnum & Bailey Circuses that provided an entertainment outlet for their fellow Americans on the mainland. Election campaigns in Hawaii in the 20s and 30s, replete with luaus and dancing girls, rivaled as roadshows anything produced on the Chautauqua Circuit, and the Island people's craving for stage drama was sublimated by court drama, especially when the case involved a beautiful young heroine who had allegedly suffered a multiple rape. The entire community had become a participating audience, emotionally involved in the unfolding plot. As rabidly as any Yankee or Dodger fans in the heat of a play-off, the court spectators took sides. Opinions clashed and tempers ran high. There seemed to be a personal pride at stake that was evolving into a racial vendetta unlike any the Islands had ever known. All eyes focused on the stage of the Judiciary Building.

As the cast of the courtroom drama entered the sultry chamber on the first day of the Ala Moana trial, the spectators fell silent as though signaled by an opening curtain. A seasoned actor in Hawaiian political roles, Senator Heen had accepted the defense of the accused boys because he was convinced of their innocence, although he knew his fee from the families would be far from adequate. In agreement with him was his fellow defense attorney, William Pittman. He had been born in Mississippi, a tenth generation American of pre-Revolutionary ancestry and a descendant of Francis Scott Key, yet he felt the dark-skinned defendants, no matter how recent the naturalization of their forebearers, deserved the American right to plead innocent until proven otherwise. His fee, like Heen's, was far less than he normally received in a criminal case because the defendants' families had assumed all financial responsibility. A third lawyer, Robert Murakami, was appointed to defend

David Takai for a fee of $200. He, too, must have felt that innocence was its own reward.

Prosecutor Gifford Wight, the skilled young Deputy City Attorney, was, contrary to Admiral Stirling's assessment of his ability, a formidable match for the defense. Forty-one years old, a former officer in the U.S. Army where he had served for seven years as a captain in the Infantry, he held a Ph.D. from Yale and Bachelor of Arts and Doctor of Jurisprudence degrees from Stanford University. His record during the two years he'd served as Chief Criminal Deputy Attorney with the City and County Attorney's Office was impressive: of forty-one felonies tried, there had been twenty-eight convictions, four mistrials, one directed verdict, and only eight acquittals.

The judge was Alva E. Steadman, a product of Stanford and Harvard Law School appointed by President Coolidge as the first judge of the First Circuit Court of Hawaii. He had married into the kamaaina missionary Cooke family and was well thought of in the community, although he was only thirty-five years old. Among his virtues was a sense of humor, having stated to the press on the date of his swearing-in, Friday, January 13, 1928: "If I am a failure as a jurist, the calendar may be blamed." His impartial sense of justice, however, had prompted him to refuse a request from Admiral Stirling that the trial be closed to the public to spare the long suffering complainant additional emotional distress.

It was the glamorous young complaining witness whom the crowds had come to see, and as the stifling day wore on without her and the selection of the jury dragged into a second day, the tension temporarily slackened and the court guards opened the balcony doors so the spectators could file out in disappointment. Only a small audience heard the final selection of the jury: half were part-Hawaiians, two were of Chinese descent, two of Japanese, one of Portuguese, and one was a haole. Their occupations were as diverse as their birthrights: utility employees, iron-mongers, a retired police captain, a car salesman, an insurance agent and three clerks from three of the "Big Five" corporations that controlled Hawaii's economy.

The first witness to take the stand on November 18, however, was Thalia Hubbard Fortescue Massie. As word of her arrival spread, the courtroom refilled to capacity. The drama was to play to packed houses for three high-strung weeks, and Thalia was to be followed by sixty-three other witnesses.

Her entrance was modest, with her large eyes downcast in contrast to the defiantly proud demeanor of her mother, Mrs. Fortescue, who braced her on one side while the solid figure of City and County Attorney James Gilliland supported her on the other. She was demurely dressed in a dark suit with a white collar. "Her face was scarred," according to a reporter of the day, "her body bent and wracked by physical and mental anguish, and her voice shaking at times with emotion and fatigue as the girl bravely faced the ordeal of the crowded courtroom."

She walked to the stand unaided, and with admirable composure sat down in the witness chair. Though wan and weakened by two months of medication and relentless nights of sleeplessness, she maintained control of herself, her blue eyes unflinchingly returning the gaze of five pairs of brown ones.

"Where were you shortly after 11:50 p.m., the evening of September 12?" began the direct examination by her counsel, Griffith Wight.

"I was at a dance at the Ala Wai Inn and I left shortly after 11:30 p.m."

This was the first variation that was to punctuate her testimony, conflicting with her earlier conversations with the police. Two hours after the crime, she had told Captain McIntosh that she had left the Inn "around midnight" to go for a walk in the fresh air. During Heen's cross examination, she explained that any confusion immediately after the crime stemmed from the state of shock which gripped her senses and blacked out her mind. She told the court that her husband handled the police interviews those first few hours of the night of terror. She was too dazed to remember anything.

"Did the police ask you any questions?"

"I don't remember."

"Do you recall being asked by either Officer Furtado or Officer Harbottle what happened that night?"

"No. My husband explained it all."

"Do you remember whether or not you told the officers about that night?"

"I don't remember. I wasn't thinking about the boys or the police; only about myself."

"Do you remember saying on that same occasion something to this effect—that you didn't hear any names except 'Bull'?"

"No. That wasn't so."

"Do you remember making a statement that you were unable to identify the boys because it was too dark?"

"No. I don't remember making any such statement."

Senator Heen asked her if she remembered saying something about the car, that it was an old touring car, a Dodge or Ford, with a flapping top. She denied describing the car in any way until she saw it the next afternoon at 3 o'clock when Captain McIntosh brought it to the Manoa house.

"And did you recognize the car, Mrs. Massie, at that time?"

"It was just like the car I had seen the night before - just like it."

Outside the Judiciary Building, the Ida car was driven up King Street and parked at the courthouse door. The jury filed out to inspect it. It was a 1929 Model A Ford touring car in excellent condition with nothing loose or flapping about the top. It was testified by the defendants that the car was in the identical condition, except for a wash and polish, as it was on the night of the assault, and none of the police officers disputed this statement. No fingerprints nor blood stains marred its interior. The exterior was brown.

"What was the color of the car?" Heen asked Thalia on the stand.

"It was sort of brown," she said.

Nor was Thalia's the only testimony that was contradictory to earlier statements. Several members of the Police Department corrected themselves; their memories of what was said when Tommy Massie first called them to the house were as equivocal as his wife's. One officer, who in his report to the City and County Attorney had positively stated that the number of the car involved in the Peeples incident was mentioned to him over the phone at the Massie home and that he had conveyed the information to the Naval officer, refused to admit on the stand that he had gotten the number. No one seemed to be able to produce the original report.

Another officer said he distinctly heard the weeping wife tell a fellow detective that the license contained the numbers "55," but he had failed to mention this detail until he took the stand, much to the amazement of other officers who were with him at the Massie home and heard no numbers mentioned at any time.

Officer John Cluney, who picked up Ida, recalled in court that the boy had admitted "one of the fellas in his car struck Mrs. Peeples, but as far as striking a white woman, he said, he didn't know anything about it."

"At that time had you mentioned to him that a white woman had been struck?" the officer was asked on the stand.

"I had not."

"Did you know it at that time?"

"I knew."

"Had anybody else said it to him?"

"No."

"He just said that voluntarily?"

"Yes."

"Did you put it down in your report?"

"I did not."

"You didn't think it was important evidence?"

"I knew it was important evidence. I was instructed to keep it under cover. I had a conversation with Mr. Wight. He said it was good stuff."

"To hide?"

"I don't know what his intentions were."

"Did you tell McIntosh before you went home what Ida said to you before Ida went into his office?"

"I did not."

"Why didn't you, having good evidence involving Ida?"

"I didn't do it, that's all."

In fact, it hadn't occurred to him to mention it to Deputy City Attorney Wight until a month after the boy had said it, continued the witness. "I volunteered it."

"But you didn't volunteer it to McIntosh, your superior, before Mr. Wight?"

"Well, we just happened to be talking about this case and I remembered the exact statement Mr. Ida made to me that night," said Officer Cluney.

As casual with their evidence were the police officers who investigated the scene of the crime. Detective Claude Benton testified that he found tracks in the soft dirt at the old quarantine station soon after the assault and was able to identify the make of the tires responsible for them. On the following day Officer Benton drove the defendant Ida's car to the scene, taking with him Ida and Officer Samuel Lau, the latter for the purpose of photographing the tracks. Benton testified that they drove Ida's car alongside the fresh tire marks that he had seen and that they were identical.

There was a ripple of heightened interest in the courtroom. Senator Heen rose to cross-examine the witness, and as he hammered Benton for more details, the officer admitted that only one of the tire marks was visible by then, the others having apparently been obliterated by the influx of other investigators. The defense counsel called Officer Lau to the stand.

Lau testified for the defense that when he arrived with Benton the tracks were so thoroughly marred that it was not worth the trouble to

take a picture of them. He then brought out an astonishing fact that
had not been reported to the prosecuting attorney nor the Office of the
City Attorney: that Chief of Detectives McIntosh earlier that Sunday
morning, before dawn, had a mechanic start Ida's car without the key,
which Ida had in his possession, and without Ida's knowledge, and with
another officer had driven the car several times around the same road
within the quarantine station grounds. Benton arrived on the scene
soon after McIntosh left in Ida's car.

When Detective McIntosh was subpoenaed as a witness by the
defense, he admitted this was true.

Senator Heen dismissed the witness and let the sudden silence of
the courtroom absorb the full impact of this testimony.

Not at all confused was one piece of testimony: Thalia's recollection of the rape. On this the prosecution would ultimately rest its case,
and as quickly as possible, Prosecutor Wight directed Thalia's thoughts
to that violent span of minutes that would indelibly brand her memory
for the rest of her life. In a sympathetic tone, almost casual in its intimation of personal concern, the prosecutor leaned toward his witness.
The courtroom leaned with him, even the proud figure of Mrs.
Fortescue, whose remarkable composure throughout her daughter's testimony had gained the admiration of the gallery. There was not a sound
in the hushed chamber.

Gently, Wight asked the unblinking girl, as he would a bereaved
child, to tell the Court exactly what happened when the boys drove off
the lighted road into the bushes at the abandoned quarantine station.

"They stopped the car and jumped out," said Thalia quietly. "They
dragged me out of the car."

"After they dragged you out, did they drag you some distance?"

"About from here to where the courtroom ends," said Thalia, raising her hand in which a handkerchief was crumpled and pointing to the
end of the room thirty feet away. She then clasped her hands in her lap
with unaffected, dancing-class primness.

"When they dragged you to that spot, what did they do?" asked
Wight tenderly.

Pittman was on his feet immediately, objecting. He wished to know
which defendants were to be tried before this line of questioning continued. The objection was denied, exception noted.

"Chang assaulted me," said the witness, undisturbed. She lowered
her eyes.

"When you say assaulted, you mean he had sexual intercourse with you?"

"Yes," whispered Thalia.

"Objection!" shouted Heen. The objection was overruled.

Smoothly, Wight continued the direct examination of the girl whose hands were now trembling as she knotted the handkerchief between her fingers. She answered the prosecutor's questions in a soft, clear voice with no trace of fabrication.

"How do you know it was Chang?"

"Because he was holding me in the car and he dragged me over there. He helped the others drag me over there. He never let go of me."

"Did you consent to this act?"

Thalia's eyes widened and her pallid cheeks flushed with sudden color. "Certainly not," she said. "I tried to get away but I couldn't. I couldn't imagine what was happening. He just hit me; the others were holding me—holding my arms."

"And when Chang completed this act, what happened next?"

"Then one of the others did it—I don't know which one."

Senator Heen arose, motioning to strike the answer. His objection was overruled, and Wight ignored the interruption in his determination that the court should hear every detail of the atrocity recalled by his pitiful client.

"When you say 'did it,' do you mean have sexual intercourse with you?"

"Yes."

"Now what happened after that?"

"After that Kahahawai assaulted me."

"By that you mean have sexual intercourse with you?"

"Yes."

"How did you know it was Kahahawai?"

"Because he had been sitting beside me in the car and I recognized his face. He had a short-sleeved shirt on. He knocked me in the jaw; I started to pray and that made him angry and he hit me very hard. I cried out 'You've knocked my teeth out' and he told me to shut up. I asked him please not to hit me any more." Tears welled up in the large blue eyes and Thalia's lips quivered. "Then I prayed."

All eyes in the courtroom were uplifted to the girl and there was no motion, no sound. Only Mrs. Fortescue turned her gaze from the pale of oval of Thalia's face, the cheeks of which now glistened with tears. The tortured mother looked straight at the defendants, who were seemingly as hypnotized as everyone else by her daughter's moving recital.

"He hit you when you started to pray?" pressed Wight softly.

"Yes," whispered Thalia.

"You say your jaw was broken?"

"Yes."

"Was that the hardest blow struck?"

"Yes."

"During the short time you were in those woods with these men do you know how many times you were assaulted?"

Both Pittman and Heen were on their feet. "Objection to the line of examination," demanded the latter. Again Judge Steadman overruled the defense.

"From four to six times," said Thalia, her small voice filling the breathless courtroom. "I think Chang assaulted me twice because he was standing near me and he said he wanted to go again. The others said all right and a little later he assaulted me."

"Mrs. Massie, do you know any other individual besides these two men who assaulted you?"

"Ida."

"How do you know that?"

"I felt his coat against my arm."

"What was your physical condition when this was going on, as to strength?"

"They hit me so much that I was sort of dazed. I had no strength left. I had struggled as hard as I could." She seemed to crumple as she said the words, as though the hushed courtroom had drained her of all stamina and rendered her as helpless as she had remembered being as she lay panting on the ground at the mercy of the savage men above her. The court ordered a recess, one of several in its efforts to show the exhausted girl all possible consideration.

When the court reopened the testimony, Thalia was cross-examined by the defense, who asked if she were still dazed when the boys left her.

"I was very much upset," she answered, "but I could sit up and when they left me I could stand up alone."

"About how long were you down at this spot altogether?"

"I don't know."

"You have no idea at all?"

"Well, perhaps it was twenty minutes."

Thalia was asked to tell the court of the language used by her assailants.

"They said a lot of filthy things to me."

"You mean obscene things?"

"Yes, and they called each other by name. I heard the name 'Bull' used, and I heard the name 'Joe,' I heard another name, it might have been 'Billy' or 'Benny' and I heard the name 'Shorty.' One helped me to sit up and said, 'The road's over there', and then they all ran off and got away."

"Now when you got home, what did you do?"

"I took off my clothes and took a douche."

"You mean medical protection?"

"Yes."

"Were you successful?"

"No," confided the trembling witness, explaining that she had had no marital relations during the crucial month and had spent each day in mounting fear that she had conceived at the hands of the fiends who defiled her. For a full minute she wept gently. When her sobs subsided, she was asked "What happened?"

"A couple of weeks later I found I was pregnant."

"What did you do about that?"

"I went down to Kapiolani Maternity Home and had an operation performed by a doctor."

Thalia spoke as though it were all a dream, a twisted fairy tale told by a sad princess, as she sat on the edge of the straight koa chair, smoothing the skirt of her lovely suit and in a gentle voice describing a nightmare of rape and abortion which, as the scars on her tender face testified, had somehow happened to her.

SEVEN

The five defendants, playing Caliban to the plaintiff's Ariel, offered discordant counterpoint to Thalia's tremolo of testimony. Among people accustomed to the graces of life, shyness is disguised in a controlled poise that borders on hauteur, but among those for whom life is a grim daily battle, uneasiness wears a sullen mask. As Thalia chose her words with delicate care, the defendants glumly muttered theirs.

The two Hawaiian boys, dark and rugged, were but three or four generations removed from a culture that had not yet known the wheel, although the ethical system of their recent ancestors was as intricately effective as any of Periclean Greece or feudal Europe. It had been shattered a century before by the advent of Christianity, with its narrow disciplines alien to the pliable and embracing Polynesian personality.

Although the three Asians, fine-boned and of bantam stature, were of nationalities that had known centuries of culture when the inhabitants of America were also wheeless, they were sired by generations of rustic stock who had lived by the earth or sea. Like the Hawaiians, they were country boys whom a whim of history had thrust into city life. Gangs of their kind, bound by mutual inadequacy and the need for camaraderie, could be found beneath the green lampshades of any pool hall on River Street.

They sat stolid and expressionless in the courtroom and just as impassively maintained their story in pidgin English. Not one of them would admit to the nickname "Bull," although in the Islands it was a common slang appellation, like "Mac" on the mainland. Also in police files, with the moniker "Joe Kalani," it was listed as an alias of Joseph Kahahawai, Jr.

Witnesses at the dance pavilion, friends who followed their car to the intersection where they nearly collided with the Peeples, hosts of the luau who had honed the complement of guests to a core of intimates singing "Memories" and snubbed the boys' overtures to rejoin the party, the parole officer who policed the dance, and members of the defendants' families all testified to their sons' whereabouts during the course of the evening. Only briefly, during about twenty minutes before 12:30 a.m. and the first hour of September 13, they were not seen.

Had Thalia left the Ala Wai Inn at 11:35 p.m. on the fateful Saturday night, as she now believed, and walked directly to the vicinity of the dance hall, as she testified, she would have arrived on John Ena Road no later than 11:45 p.m. However, a couple who had attended the dance, George Goeas and his wife, were sauntering to their car parked on the Ena road when, at between 12:05 and 12:10 a.m., they saw a haole woman pass by with a haole man immediately following her.

George Goeas, a reputable employee of a kamaaina—or old Island family—firm and a completely disinterested person, unacquainted with either Lieutenant Massie or his wife or any of the defendants and not of the racial background of any of the accused boys, had read of the Ala Moana assault case soon after it happened and immediately reported to the Police Department the information he possessed. In view of the discrepancy of twenty to thirty minutes between the time the Goeases saw a woman of the general description of Thalia on John Ena Road and the time the prosecution had concluded that she, according to her own statement, would have reached the approximate point of abduction, Prosecutor Wight decided not to use the testimony of Mr. and Mrs. Goeas. As a result, they were used as witnesses for the defense. George Goeas's statement to Detective John Jardine at police headquarters was repeated as he took the witness stand:

He identified himself, giving his age as twenty-six, his address as Captain Cook Street, and his occupation as assistant cashier of the Dillingham Insurance Company.

"Tell us what you know in connection with the Mrs. Thomas H. Massie Assault Case," the young businessman was asked.

"I and my wife left the Waikiki Dance Hall about 12:10 a.m.," he began. "Before going home, she asked me to eat noodles with her. We took the entrance of John Ena Road when we left the park. I got my car, which was parked opposite the entrance of the park. We ordered some noodles and while waiting. I noticed a white woman walking down with her head bent down, and the way she walked seemed as if she was under the influence of liquor. About a yard behind her we saw a white man following directly in back of her. He kept this pace for about twenty-five yards and from there on I could not see as there was a store blocking the view."

"And what time was that?"

"About 12:15 a.m., Sunday, September thirteenth."

George Goeas remembered clearly what the couple looked like. "She was about five feet four or five inches tall, medium build, and she wore a green gown. He was a white man, about five feet nine inches tall, weight about one hundred sixty-five pounds, was bareheaded, and wore a dark brown suit. He looked like a soldier to me. I didn't see any cars following them from the time I first saw them to the time I last saw them. There were two cars parked along John Ena Road off the entrance of Waikiki Park...one looked like an Essex touring car and the other looked like an old Ford touring car."

It was the condition of the woman that most interested Defense Counsel Heen, and when George Goeas was on the stand, he asked him to tell the court what it was about the woman that drew his attention to her. "How did you happen to turn around and look again?" asked the Senator.

"I noticed the way she was walking at the time," said the witness. "It seemed kind of funny to see a white woman walking in that kind of condition and I thought she might be under the influence of liquor and noticed the way she held her head down, and it made me think they had a quarrel or something."

"Will you please step down and walk as near as you can the way she walked," asked Heen, "as you observed her that night?"

Dramatically, George Goeas walked to the jury box, turned and began slowly weaving back to the witness stand, his head bent low. Heen waited until he had been reseated for several silent seconds before he resumed the direct examination.

"Did you lose sight of them or just simply turn around?"

"When they passed me and the lady brought my noodles, we kept on eating and forgot about everything. A few days after that I went down to the police station on my own volition. I read in the papers where this case happened, so I wanted to do my bit and try to see if this was the right party, so I just wanted to say what I saw to help get the real party, so I went down and talked with Detective Jardine."

The witness had a straight-forward appeal that was very much to the advantage of the defense, and the defendants' lawyers saw to it that it was enhanced by appropriate histrionics. Still questioning the clean-cut young executive on the stand, Senator Heen casually walked over to the case containing exhibits and leaned on it.

"Did the police show you the dress at that time?"

"Yes, a few days later."

"We have here a green dress top and also the skirt part," said the defense attorney, stepping aside to reveal Thalia's gown to the jury. "Is that the dress they showed you?"

"That is."

"And do you recognize that as being the dress you saw on that woman?"

"It is. That is the very color I explained to them. Yes sir, that is the dress."

Mrs. Goeas's testimony confirmed that of her husband. She further noted that the woman had fair hair, "three quarter length, but it was tied in the back." As for the gown the girl was wearing, "when we first saw it, I couldn't tell more or less what it was until she got into the light and then I knew it was green. It had a bow in the back, at the waist," said Mrs. Goeas, adding that the man was wearing dark trousers and a buttoned sweater, also dark. She had not accompanied her husband to the police station, so later detectives questioned her at home, bringing Thalia's dress with them.

"Did you examine the dress at that time?" asked the defense.

"We looked at it when the policeman placed it in front of him."

"Including the top, like this?" asked the short, dignified senator, holding the long green dress and jacket up so that the hem brushed his shoe tops.

"Yes," answered Mrs. Goeas, sharing a smile that flitted across the face of the courtroom.

"Do you recognize that dress as being the dress this woman had on that night?"

"Yes."

The next witness was a shy lady barber, Alice Aramaki, who remembered very well seeing a woman in a green dress walk down John Ena Road on the night of September 12. Alice worked in her sister's barbershop next to the general store run by her father, and across the way from another of the family grocery stands whose waxen fruit, jars of sweet and sour seeds and trays of sushi were local staples that filled the crannies of Honolulu's side streets. They also served saimin, the hot noodle broth of shrimp stock, a Japanese snack that is the Asian answer to the Western hotdog. The young barber had just swept the floor and was closing the barbershop at about 10 minutes after midnight when she glanced over at Kimoto's Store.

"I see one woman," she told the court. "She had a green dress. Pretty long down to here," said the tiny Japanese girl, stooping to touch her ankle. "She was hanging her head down and walking slowly. She was a white woman, with blond hair. A man was walking maybe five or six feet away from her. Behind. He was a white man. He was shorter than the woman. She was big, weighs maybe one hundred fifty pounds.

He wears white shirt, maybe Navy blue or black pants, I can't tell. He was walking pretty fast."

"Do you recognize this dress as being similar to the one you saw on that woman?" asked Heen.

"The dress I seen was a little darker."

Regardless of the conflicting testimony of these eyewitnesses, they were the most effective the defense had produced and caused considerable comment in the courtroom. The press played up their stories and Thalia's gown became the most popular topic of conversation in the community. The scandalous rumors of drunken orgies, a secret paramour and a marital rift increased in volume. The Navy bristled under the onslaught of criticism, enraged that the Hawaiian people should so viciously bite the hand that protected them. "They are grasping at straws in their efforts to defame Mrs. Massie's character," said Admiral Stirling.

"Mrs. Massie appeared unconscious of the many evil eyes upon her from some parts of the courtroom," he commented later, "belonging to those who had been spreading almost unspeakable slanders of her to defame her character in the hope of destroying belief in her testimony to the jury. The cruel description she gave of her shame must have been a most nerve-racking ordeal, yet she bravely described the atrocious crime from the beginning to the end and told a story that could not be shaken."

EIGHT

In the pre-dawn hours of a rainy morning two weeks after Thalia's tragic ride had triggered a manhunt for witnesses that kept the Police Department working around the clock, Detective Lieutenant John Jardine, who had just gone off duty, sat down at the counter of the Green Mill and ordered a cup of hot coffee.

The Green Mill was an all-night grill that catered to fugitives from both sides of the law. On the stool next to Jardine was an army non-com, a well-known shadow in the world of shades who frequented that uncertain area of Honolulu known as Mosquito Flats. Familiar with most of the figures in the limbo fringing the underworld, Jardine recognized the sergeant as a gambler named Krassis, who had enlisted at Schofield Barracks but spent more of his time at downtown crap tables than on the drill field.

"Good morning," said the gambler to the detective. "How you making out with the Massie case? I think you got the right boys."

"I don't know," said Jardine warily. "How do you know?"

"Two or three days or maybe a week after the rape, Jimmy Low and I were talking about it here at the Green Mill," said the gambler. "Jimmy told me that you had the right ones. On the night the girl was picked up, he happened to be following in the car behind with two or three others and saw some men forcing a woman into a car. Do you know Low?"

"I do," said Jardine. James Low was a former member of the Board of Supervisors, from the Big Island of Hawaii.

"Well I don't want to get mixed up in it, but I thought you might want to talk to Low," said the erstwhile sergeant.

The detective returned to the police station and typed a memorandum for Chief of Detectives McIntosh, who later took the matter up with City Attorney James Gilliland. Detectives Jardine and Otto Stagbar were assigned to pick up Low and those who had been with him the night of September 12. They had no trouble finding the former supervisor and his companions. Eugenio Batungbacal, Charles Chang and Roger Liu.

The latter three were called as rebuttal witnesses for the Territory, while Jimmy Low, whose version of what happened to the girl on John Ena Road was totally different from theirs, testified for the defense.

Prosecutor Wight felt he had an ace in the hole when he produced these witnesses of Thalia's abduction. As it turned out, he also had a joker.

Eugenio Batungbacal, a small beetle-browed man of Filipino extraction and precarious occupation, was of the band of indistinguishable single males bound by a single purpose in an alien land: to earn enough money as contract canefield laborers to return as barons of their native barrios in distant Zamboango and Luzon. Most of them never made the journey home as they saw their common dream dissolve in gambling debts.

In faltering pidgin, Eugenio told of driving his comrades to the dance hall in Waikiki Park. "I stop by the saimin stand, I think between 11:30 and 12 o'clock," he said to the court.

"Could you get any closer than that?" pressed Wight, since the value of his witness's testimony hinged on the time he saw the girl walk past the saimin stand.

"Beg pardon," said the Filipino, his face furrowed in incomprehension. Wight tried a different tack: "What did you see?"

"I see about four or five mens with one girl; two mens, holding the woman with hands and one is following. They look like they force the woman into the car."

"What car?"

"I don't know what kind of car, but I am sure it is touring."

Senator Heen rose in exasperation. "We move to strike all this testimony, as this testimony should have been given in chief, and if they are trying to put this in chief, it is not rebuttal."

"Objection overruled," said Judge Steadman.

"You said four or five men?" continued Wight in triumph. "What color were their faces?"

"Four or five mens, I am not sure. I don't know what color these mens faces, but I think Japanese and Hawaiian; look like to me one Japanese, one Hawaiian. The rest I don't know. No haoles."

"After you saw this, what did you do?"

"I drive my car to Ft. De Russy and turned around because Chang's car is still at the Frozen Orange. I drive him down there to get his car. That's all."

On cross-examination Eugenio proved equally frustrating as a witness. When asked by the defense for the exact time he saw the woman near the saimin stand, he vaguely answered "Maybe 11:30, maybe about quarter to 12, something like that." And Thalia's dress, what about a green dress?

"I don't know what about a green dress, or what color, but I see one woman, that's all. I don't know what color is her dress. Night time hard to tell. There was light there but you can never tell. I am not interested to see what kind of color her dress. I just see her and I don't know what kind of dress, you know."

Heen was not sure he did. He asked what color hair the woman had; the witness did not know. "Did you see a man walking by her?"

"I see plenty, four or five."

"Did you see one walking by her first?"

"I never see one man. I saw four by her, four or five."

"You show us how she was walking when you first saw her?"

"How can I when there were two mens holding her and I am just one?" said the fiery little Filipino.

The frustrated defense counsel turned to Judge Steadman. "I move to strike the answer as unresponsive."

"Has the witness ever said he saw her walk?" asked the Judge quietly.

"Did you see the girl walking?" asked Heen.

"I saw the girl walking with the mens the first time," answered Eugenio with overdrawn patience, as exasperated with the apparent dullness of the lawyers as they were with him. "I thought they go together; just go with a party. The girl is just like drunk, you know. I don't think that the mens were—we don't pay any attention."

"Senator Heen, are you examining the witness?" interrupted the Court.

"He has answered my question," said the defense attorney. "I didn't ask him for all these things."

"What IS your question?" asked the Judge, not above confusion himself.

"Come down and show us how this woman was walking," insisted the defense to the witness. "You said she was walking like she was drunk."

"I can't show you how she was walking at that time," retorted the witness. "I think she was drunk because two mens held her arms and she tried to get away and that is what make me believe she is drunk."

"And they were all walking together?"

The little man on the stand gripped both arms of the chair, thrust his gnarled face forward and very slowly explained his part in the proceedings. "You asked me first if I saw one woman walking. Yes. She is walking with the mens. The mens hold her in both arms and some are following and some staying behind. I don't know about anything else. That's all I saw."

"And in front of them was a car standing?" said Heen lapsing into the patois.

"No."

"There was no car at all?" asked the lawyer in surprise.

"There was no car at all."

Heen threw up his hands in dismay. Muffled laughter sparked the courtroom. Even Judge Steadman's eye held a twinkle of sympathy for the cross examiner's dilemma.

"You are sure you didn't see any car there?" asked the defense.

"No," said Batungbacal. "Behind plenty. Behind, not in front."

"Aha, there was a car standing or parked near your car?"

"No. Oh, one touring car that looked like they forced the woman to bring to that car parking over there. And when I drive my car fifty feet, I think I saw the woman and I still looking till fifteen or twenty feet."

"How long did they have to walk to get to that car?"

Prosecutor Wight arose and added his voice to the tangled thread of interrogation. "Objected to as ambiguous," he said. The courtroom tittered. There was no ruling from the Court.

"When you saw these men walking that way, you were surprised, were you not?" persisted Heen, undaunted.

"What you mean?"

"You were surprised?" pleaded the defense attorney. "You know what 'surprised' means…"

Again Mr. Wight raised his voice, "Objected to as ambiguous." Again the court offered no ruling.

"Surprised to see that woman," continued the patient defense counsel.

"I don't pay no attention," said Eugenio, with a note of pity for the confused attorneys. He matched his patience to theirs. "The first time I think that woman go with these boys. I think she is drunk and those boys just help put her in the car. That is what I think the first time."

"This woman was a white woman that you saw?" asked Heen gently.

"I don't know if she is white or not. I don't know because she is not facing to me. If she is facing to me I tell you whether she is nigger or white or Portuguese."

Senator Heen's shoulders slumped in defeat. The witness was dismissed.

More articulate but no more specific was the testimony of Charles Chang and Roger Liu who, in essence, agreed with the story told by Eugenio Batungbacal. "We saw men talking with the lady and they grabbed her by the arm and pulled her into the car," said Roger Liu.

"She was fighting, moving her arms and tried to pull away. They made her get in. They pushed her in." He also noticed that the girl had blond hair. He thought the time was about midnight.

Liu remembered on the witness stand that the girl had on a long dress, "Something like that one," he said, pointing to Evidence C which was Thalia's gown, spread on the table containing exhibits. "I saw the lady was moving, struggling. I believe two boy were trying to push her into the car. I thought they were just a bunch of friends."

Charlie Chang, when asked if he thought the roadside roughhouse was just horseplay among friends, testified, "I can't say that. In my opinion I thought they were dragging her into the bushes."

"Were they doing anything to this woman?" asked Griffith Wight.

"Well, two—a couple of them was holding her arms and intended to—it seems to me they were intending to lead..."

"We object to any 'intentions,'" interrupted the defense.

"Well, they circled around her, about four to six of them, and I say I believe they were leading her—intended leading her somewhere. Seemed same as they were dragging her."

"Directing her?" cross-examined Heen.

"Dragging her," said the witness emphatically.

Although Jimmy Low was in the same car with Chang, Liu and Batungbacal, he remembered quite a different scene. "We went first to the dance pavilion at Waikiki Park, then we came out and turned down John Ena Road toward the sea. After we came out of the gate and passed the stores, I saw a lady who looked like she was drunk, intoxicated, and immediately behind her was a man following her, about two or three feet, and in front of her was a car along the curb, facing the sea. After we passed a little way on I asked Eugenio, who was driving the car, to stop and turn around."

"Did you mention anything to Eugenio about what you thought was going to happen to this woman?"

"If I did, I don't remember."

"Did you ever at any time discuss this case with anyone else outside of members of the City Attorney's Office?"

"No, sir," answered Low under direct examination. "I did talk to Krassis. I told him I saw the lady that night, and that if they got the people who did the crime it would be a good thing, and that if the police got somebody I hoped it was the right party."

"Did you or didn't you tell him that the police have got the right car and the right boys?"

"No, sir."

"What time was it when you saw this woman on John Ena Road?"

"A little after midnight, about ten minutes," said Low, pinpointing the time of the seizure as he saw it and leaving a discrepancy with Thalia's time of approximately half an hour.

"Mr. Low, what was your purpose in turning around and going back when you saw the man and woman?"

"To see what happened - what was going to take place, because in the car, before we made the turn, one of the boys mentioned that it looked as thought the man was going to grab her."

"Did he say 'they' or 'the man'?"

"The man."

"Thank you," said the defense. "That is all."

Griffith Wight sat tensely at the prosecutor's table. He was determined to destroy the value of the witness's testimony, as it affected the time factor in the theory of the prosecution, essentially based on Thalia's narrative. Wight's tactic was to discredit the politician's reliability as well as his character.

"You know it was through Krassis's statement that we learned you knew about the case," said the prosecutor.

"Probably so," said the former supervisor for the County of Hawaii.

"You didn't came to us voluntarily, did you?" continued the Deputy City Attorney.

"No."

"Why not?"

"I didn't think I had to do your work," said Low, not bothering to disguise the sarcasm in his voice.

"When we first asked you about this case, didn't you deny you were ever at John Ena Road?"

"No. First, last and always my statement has been the same," said Low evenly.

The prosecutor approached the witness stand and squarely faced the man sitting in the koa chair. "Did you plead guilty on March 10, 1931, to the charges of being present at a gambling game, and to being fined twenty-five dollars?"

"I did," said Low.

Wight then asked the witness if he had not, four days after the alleged rape, said to a man named Krassis, "the police have the right car," and furthermore, told City and County Attorney James Gilliland that he expected to run for the Legislature, in the Fifth

District, home of the accused boys, and that he didn't want to testify against them?

The witness flushed, and positively denied such conversation.

A record crowd of spectators overflowed the ground floor galleries of the Judiciary Building and gathered on the lawn the next day. The trades were up and a brisk breeze ruffled the feathery branches of the monkeypod trees in the Iolani Palace grounds across the street where mynah birds argued their own court. It was the first day of the last month of 1931, and the Ala Moana rape case was drawing to a close.

Again tension reigned as the cast assembled for the final decisive battle. The five boys filed to their seats in silence. The tallest of them, Joseph Kahahawai, a dark Hawaiian with the prominent features of the Polynesian race, entered first. He was followed by Ben Ahakuelo, shorter than Kahahawai and more alert, with quick eyes and a tight-muscled physique. Harry Chang, slim and lanky, was wearing an open-necked shirt and no tie, and his harmonious features testified to Hawaiian-Chinese extraction, the racial combination credited for creating Hawaii's most beautiful women. David Takai, quiet, compact and bandy-legged, was unmistakably Japanese, as was Horace Ida, but with Western overtones. The most dapper of them all, Ida was ostensibly living up to prevailing Occidental haberdashery; his cream-colored trousers were immaculate.

Thalia appeared more rested than at any time during the trial; her pallor had regained a degree of scar-blemished color. The blond girl in her customary ingenue costume seemed to have absorbed strength through her mother's presence, a presence that demanded respect in its self-assurance. Handsome Mrs. Fortescue, slender and elegant, carried herself like a flag to the front of the courtroom and with her daughter sat on the bench only a dozen feet from the defendants whose existence she now ignored.

The whisper that greeted the mother and daughter did not directly concern them. The spectators had anticipated the arrival of Lieutenant Massie, who had been promised as a witness by the defense. Since his presence had been conspicuously absent throughout the trial, it had been assumed he would be among the last to testify. It was explained to the court by Prosecutor Wight that Massie was on Naval maneuvers, a commitment of top priority that took precedence over an appearance in court. No white Naval uniforms had contrasted to the gallery of business suits and aloha shirts, due to an order from Admiral Stirling that

Naval personnel appear only in mufti to avoid possible antagonism. Nor was Lieutenant Jerry Branson present at the trial in any capacity. He had appeared before a closed session of the grand jury, been dismissed and was at sea.

As the prelude of murmurs subsided, Griffith Wight, in a conservative suit reminiscent of his New Haven undergraduate days and a mood of absolute assurance, stepped forward to continue the case for the prosecution. Already Judge Steadman had announced that unless last-minute witnesses were called and their testimony admitted, the jury would retire before noon.

The jury was not to be blessed with such expediency. Still in the wings of the drama were two witnesses whose role was unsuspected up to the eleventh hour. Even Wight, who would call them for the prosecution, was unaware of their existence as he opened his argument. He looked first in the direction of the defendants, causing them to shift uncomfortably in their seats, then let his gaze travel to the frail figure of the victim who returned his gaze with a hopeful uptilt of her chin. He turned and faced the jury.

"Gentlemen, this is one of the worst cases we have ever had in the history of Hawaii."

Appealing to his Island audience, and concentrating on the twelve men of mixed racial background in the jury box, half of them Hawaiians and only one of them a haole, the prosecutor reminded them that "one of the first laws passed under Kamehameha the Great was that women, little children and the infirm might have safety on the highways."

He asked their compassion. "You heard her say 'This is a terrible thing to accuse a man of lightly'...Do you realize the complaining witness is a young, inexperienced girl? You saw what a clean, straightforward way she told her story. She didn't want to go through with this: it was a horrible ordeal for her but she went through with it bravely and without exaggeration...

"I want you to notice that throughout this case, the defense had referred to the complaining witness as 'that woman,' as though she were an elderly person. In fact, she is very young, younger than these grown men to whom they refer as 'the boys.' Boys!" The prosecuting attorney made a mockery of the word.

"They're not angels, you know that. They are more like devils!" he cried, looking directly into the uneasy faces of the defendants and in a quieter tone describing again Thalia's memory of how they laughed when the young girl, trembling beneath their outrage, had prayed for mercy. Slowly the prosecutor's eyes again brushed over the figure of the girl, huddled now toward her motionless mother, then piercingly focused on the gallery of hushed spectators.

"These men are lust-sodden beasts!" he shouted, his voice subsiding as he reminded them that the abused girl was forced to undergo an operation to prevent having a child from her night of brutality.

"When she was picked up by a passing car as she struggled along the road after the assault, she didn't want to go to the police station. What decent woman would—to be marked for life. She wanted to go to her own home. That was right and natural." And as Griffith Wight described it, that was the way it seemed. Each woman in the courtroom seemed to identify herself with the tender-aged girl and agree with the prosecuting attorney.

Wight then pointed out that the young Navy wife remembered the license number and described it within one digit. "And unless you want to brand this girl an unmitigated liar, you must accept her immediate identification of two of the defendants. Her story told to Chief of Detectives McIntosh the night of the crime, before these men were apprehended, checks absolutely to the men and their position in the car with their own story...She later positively identified Benny and Ida."

Drawing his argument up short, as though hung on the name "Ida," Wight paused. "Ida told so many stories about his coat that you can't believe any of them. Ida lied. He lied first when he denied that he knew who had his car that night; he lied in the rest of his testimony." The attorney then pointed out that the defendants gave different versions of the route they took from Waikiki amusement park. "Their alibi was not prepared well enough; they did not talk it over enough. As for Mrs. Massie's not identifying Takai, he identified himself when he admitted he was with the boys all evening."

And certainly no one, not one man in the jury box, could deny the vicious evidence that corroborated the complaining witness's story: the telltale marks that scarred her broken jaw, the bruised thighs. Mr. Wight drew a vivid word picture of the pitiful appearance of the helpless assault victim.

"If any further corroboration of the girl's story of being outraged is required, it is seen in the fact that her barrette, her beads and her pocketbook were found at the scene of the crime that she was seen on John Ena Road, that these defendants were seen signaling each other in the presence of the police—is that the action of innocent men?"

The counsel for the government then argued on the importance of the first tire marks found at the Ala Moana quarantine station. "The car number seen by Mrs. Massie and the tire marks found there which corresponded with the tire's treads should prove to every man on the jury that Ida's car was there that night!"

"Do not be swayed by Mr. Pittman's eloquence or Mr. Heen's persuasion, but consider carefully the credibility of the witness and let the facts speak for themselves...Our streets must be made safe for our women; I hate to think of a member of my family undergoing such an ordeal as that to which this young girl has been subjected."

The prosecutor placed both hands firmly on the rail of the jury box and leaned towards its occupants with an urgent sincerity that rang in his quiet voice as he made a statement as apocalyptic as it was appealing: "Put yourself in the place of the husband of a twenty-year-old girl to whom this had happened and you would want to go down and shoot the men!"

It was only 9:15 in the morning as the prosecutor concluded his opening statement. The day was still fresh from a dawn shower the night before and the spectators stood briefly to stretch their legs and walk to the windows and breathe deeply before Robert Murakami, attorney for Takai, made the opening argument for the defense.

"I have listened to the prosecuting attorney tell you what a terrible crime this is," he began as the courtroom settled attentively, "and we all agree with him. But, gentlemen," and he directed himself to the jury, "we cannot be swayed by our passion and prejudice against the crime itself. It is probably true that Mrs. Massie was assaulted, either by a gang of boys or by a man. It makes little difference whether she was assaulted by one man or a group, because we have shown beyond a reasonable doubt that these were not the men who committed the crime."

The more devious and less impassioned appeal to the jury's reason had its effect in the atmosphere of the court as everyone strained to hear the softly spoken words of the Asian American lawyer. "I will go further and question that the prosecuting attorney as a reasonable man can honestly believe that these are the men."

Murakami then outlined the prosecution's theory based on Thalia's testimony of time, which placed the hour when she was picked up at 11:45 p.m. Yet both she and the boys were seen after midnight, pointed out the trial lawyer, she on John Ena Road and the boys at the close of the dance, at about 10 minutes past 12. Mrs. Peeples's testimony proved beyond doubt that the boys were at King and Liliha Streets at 12:35 a.m.

"According to testimony of the government, it would take twelve minutes to get to King and Liliha," continued Murakami. "That leaves about twelve minutes in which these men dragged her from the car and assaulted her from four to six times. Is that humanly possible?" The lawyer paused as though expecting an answer from the jury.

He then asked the men before him to consider why the officers who first investigated the case were not called by the government. "Were they afraid of the whole truth and nothing but the truth?" He paused again and sauntered over to the defendants.

"The prosecution says that Takai identified himself." He looked at his client, who returned the gaze, lowering his head. "Takai made one small blunder—he asked a friend for a lift home from the park. Now he must submit to the anxiety of this trial. Takai told the truth because he had nothing to be worried about." The defense counsel smiled at his client reassuringly, then returned to his place before the jury. "If you think Takai lied, then his statement is the only thing that links him to this case. On the other hand if you believe what the witnesses said, then he came home with the other witnesses. We have taxed your patience. I would not have said a word if it had not been a very serious crime. I leave in your hands the fate of David Takai. I know by your true verdict you will clear David Takai."

This argument, effective in it understatement, was an appropriate prelude to the main act of the drama, the address to the jury of the stellar counsels for the defense, William H. Pittman and William H. Heen. Pittman, lawyer for Ida and Kahahawai, arose next and faced the jury.

"Gentlemen, I urge you to appreciate the seriousness of this case. Not only the seriousness of life imprisonment but the brand of rapist that is lower than a reptile!"

The lawyer's Mississippi accent gave added emphasis to the odious comparison. He pointed the finger of guilt at city incompetence.

"These boys are innocent," the defense attorney declared. "They are entitled to justice. They should be acquitted promptly. If you believe they are guilty they should be sent to the penitentiary for life.

"This Police Department in establishing the identity of these boys followed a procedure that has been discarded for fifty years. They brought the boys before Mrs. Massie and said, 'We have the boys we suspect and we want you to identify them.' Imagine a Police Department so covered with cobwebs as to depend on that kind of identification!

The procedure followed by the Police Department permitted Mrs. Massie to identify the men as her assailants by mental suggestion.

"Mrs. Massie never lived before in a country where there are Orientals and Hawaiians. I want to tell you that I have practiced law here for fifteen years among Orientals and when men who were my clients came to my office, I was not able to tell them apart. We have it from the evidence of the complaining witness that she could not identify the men or the car.

"She must have been terrified," he went on. "Four or five men dragging this refined lady into a car and assaulting her—she must have been in no condition to identify anyone beyond a reasonable doubt. Identification was impossible, she herself said so.

"The most damnable thing in the history of the Territory is the fact that the prosecutor and police withheld from the defense the information they had," he said. "It was just as much their duty to shield innocent men as to find the guilty ones...It was Sheriff Patrick Gleason's duty to find out who was wrongfully accused and those who were guilty. What was done will ever be a blot on the Territory!

"It will take as strong men as ever sat on a jury to do their rightful duty in this case," he continued. "The government tried to frame these boys into the penitentiary. There is no man who hates a rapist more than I do. I was born in a country where they brand them or burn them alive!...But there is a worse crime, one more heinous, and that is sending innocent men to the penitentiary!" The strident lawyer gripped the jury rail, leaning toward its occupants, then shifted into a lower key.

"Poor Mrs. Massie! I wish she did really know who assaulted her, because if she did I should like to see them rot in prison!"

Pittman pointed to the testimony of police officers who testified for the defense. The complaining witness, when questioned by those officers, said she could not identify either the men or the car.

"A child knows how she got the car number," the attorney asserted. "It was in the radio patrol car at the emergency hospital. The poor little woman now actually believes that she saw the car number. The evidence of the defense that she did not know the car number and could not identify the men early that Sunday morning is impeccable. The question of identification by Mrs. Massie is in reality the identification of those officers who wanted to get a conviction by fair means or otherwise." Pittman brought a raised fist dawn into the palm of his left hand.

"This is a frame-up!" he boomed. "Remember when I asked Mr. Wight to see those statements of Mrs. Massie's first interview with the police immediately after the crime. He said 'I won't show you.' Never in the history of twenty-five years of practice have I witnessed such a spectacle in a courtroom!

"We knew from the beginning that they were framing these boys and we knew from the beginning that these boy are innocent. Thank God we have proved it regardless of the feeling against these boys... these boys were not there. They could not have been there. You cannot if you are honest and upright men convict these men, but you must on your manhood be brave and fearless and acquit them and do it promptly. If you convict them you have got to have no conscience, you have got to have no soul, you have got to be cowardly!" He paused. His voice quieted.

"In my opinion, the girl was outraged—but not by these men. That car was planted there, waiting for Mrs. Massie and the people who put her into it knew who she was.

"The defendants made statements that are practically the same, without having opportunity to confer. When Senator Heen and I heard that, we knew these boys were innocent, and so we are here...don't tell me these boys are guilty if you want another night's peaceful sleep.

"This poor girl, when she got up and testified, was in reality telling what the police drilled into her. She couldn't identify anyone after the terrible ordeal she had undergone. It is a wonder she had any mind left at all.

"And no confession has been obtained from the boys, not one. Poor old Joe," as he termed Kahahawai, "was in jail after the others were out on bond but still didn't confess. Takai was offered immunity, but didn't confess. Given immunity!" he shouted. "Why, if he confessed he would have been mobbed. This court wouldn't give him immunity. They promised something they couldn't do.

"The assault must have happened after 12:30. It was between 12:15 and 12:20 that she was put in the car, the complaining witness was under the influence of liquor to which she was unaccustomed and she did not know when she was put in the car. She did not scream.

"If it had not been for the Peeples incident, these youths would not be in court.

"The tire marks were a frame-up to show that Ida's car had been in the Ala Moana scene, and Officer Sam Lau, who refused to photograph them, should be commended for showing up this reprehensible frame-up. If the public cannot trust the guardians of the peace, what protection have people?"

The defense attorney paused dramatically, drew himself up to his full height, breathing deeply, and in his most positive voice said, "I know these men are innocent; that's why I'm here. Any lawyer would be a coward who would refuse to defend accused men he knew to be innocent merely because public opinion was against them...I know we have found them innocent. I know this jury will not swerve from its duty of acquitting them.

"In closing, I urge you gentlemen of the jury to be brave and calm and not brand the defendants with a crime that would mark them as so low that they are not fit to crawl with reptiles!"

Disquieted by the conflicting theories of the defense and prosecution, and made restless by three hours on the hard benches of the courtroom, people began to stir, many turning to look at the clock in the back of the room, the hands of which, they were surprised to see, indicated that the long morning was not over. It was 11:30 a.m. and Senator William H. Heen had yet to voice his plea. The attorney for Ben Ahakuelo and Henry Chang sensed the impatience of the courtroom and notified Judge Steadman that he would consume at least two hours in analyzing the testimony when he spoke for the defense. It might be a good idea to have lunch first. The Judge agreed and the court was recessed until 1:30 p.m.

Despite the exhausting morning session, the spectators returned twofold in the afternoon and many were turned away. Senator Heen, dapper in a flawless beige gabardine suit, appeared remarkably refreshed by the luncheon respite and launched immediately into his argument

"I do not propose to leave a stone unturned in my endeavor to prevent five innocent boys from being railroaded to jail," he declared. "Where is the man who followed Mrs. Massie down John Ena Road? There can be no question but what that white man who was following the woman that night could have explained what happened there. The police were diligent in the case but that man has not been produced. Why wasn't he found?

"Where did Mrs. Massie get her liquor, if she was sober when she left the Ala Wai Inn and drunk when she got to John Ena Road. That is a mystery that should be explained.

"How do we know that she had been assaulted between 11:35 p.m. and midnight, and beaten? Why was she walking with her head hanging down? That has not been explained. Why did she take a long walk when she was tired? She did not pass the stores on John Ena Road until after midnight. Her whereabouts from 11:30 p.m. to 12:10 a.m. is another mystery the prosecution has not explained."

Having aroused doubts, the wily defense lawyer next presented facts. "Only a few hours after the assault, Mrs. Massie told the police she could not identify the men who were her assailants. She thought they were Hawaiians, and she knew nothing about the car number. She thought the top of the car was flapping. Let me read to you gentlemen a copy of a report made by a police officer investigating the case, dated October 16, 1931." Heen read the report of Officer Furtado saying the girl could not identify her assailants but would know their voices. "Furtado was the first officer she talked to, but this was not the first report he made. Furtado's first report is in the possession of the prosecution and was not turned over to the defense. Is that a square deal?

"The significance of that is that there must be something in it tending to establish the innocence of these boys. It is not fair to the boys and it is not fair to the jury that the Deputy City and County Attorney has not seen fit to let you know the truth!

"Mrs. Massie was only the mouthpiece for some of these detectives. She studied her lessons from members of the police force who wanted to send the men to jail. The testimony of the physician shows that she was under the influence of opiates given to ease her pain as a result of the shock, and did not know what she was doing for four or five days. In this state she was rendered susceptible to suggestion. But how could she possibly have remembered the details of her assailants?

"I challenge you members of the jury to describe the apparel of witnesses who have appeared during this trial. I wager none of you, unless you were acquainted with the witness, could remember what they wore, although you saw them in normal circumstances with your full faculties and not under the stress of excitement.

"If you can't do this, how do you expect a woman, under great strain and excitement, to do so faithfully and truthfully?

"The police tried to get the defendants to confess by trickery, by planting the beads and tire tracks. If these boys were guilty, they would have confessed then. But they couldn't confess because they had not assaulted Mrs. Massie. And if the police were able to manufacture false testimony in regard to the tire marks, it was nothing to them to whisper a car number to her.

"The difference in the boys' stories also proves that they didn't agree on a made-up alibi. The strongest feature in this testimony is that they didn't get together to frame it up..."

Point by point, the defense tore into the theories of the prosecution. Heen, the political warhorse, was in his elocutionary element and the courtroom was riveted to the slight figure of the successful lawyer whose forebearers had also pioneered Hawaii as Oriental immigrants. The only movement in the quiet room was made by Detective Jardine who was standing near a rear door. He opened it quietly and slipped into the corridor.

John Jardine, a chain-smoker, was in need of a cigarette, and no smoking was allowed while court was in session. He walked to the foyer of the Judiciary Building and took out a pack of Luckies. As he lit his cigarette, a friend touched his elbow.

"I've been up there the last couple of days and heard Heen arguing about a woman in a green dress and a white man following her. People were giving testimony to the effect the dress was the same as Mrs. Massie's. That wasn't Mrs. Massie who walked down John Ena Road."

Jardine snapped out the match that had burned to his finger. He looked at his friend in amazement. "No? Then who was it?"

"Will you keep me out of this?"

"O.K.," agreed the detective.

"The couple they saw were Mr. and Mrs. George McClellan. The McClellans told me so themselves."

"How can I get in touch with them?"

"Mrs. McClellan's now a patient at Tripler Hospital and her husband hangs out around the Y.M.C.A.," said the friend. "I've got to be shoving off."

"Thanks for the tip," said Jardine. "I hope this will clear up once and for all the ugly rumors being circulated about Mrs. Massie and Lieutenant Branson." The detective had interviewed Branson within hours of the crime and was convinced of his innocence. Many other members of the police force did not share this conviction.

"Me, too," said the tipster. "Some of them cops you have down there are the cause of these rumors. They even told me the Lieutenant was the one who beat her up and raped her." He shoved off. Rumor was that Branson had been shipped out of town by the Navy to avoid being subpoenaed to testify.

Jardine took the stairs two at a time and walked quickly to the court bailiff standing at the closed door behind the bar. "Tell City Attorney Jim Gilliland I want to see him. It's urgent." Two minutes later Gilliland was in the hall and Jardine repeated to him what he had been told in the foyer only minutes before.

"Wait here," said Gilliland, and he reentered the courtroom. From the doorway, Jardine could hear Judge Steadman call for a recess. A few minutes later the detective was called into the Judge's chambers and in the presence of Judge Steadman and the lawyers for the defense and prosecution, he repeated again what he had heard.

"Who was your informant?" asked the judge.

"The information was given to me in confidence," said Jardine. "I cannot reveal the source." A deposition was taken and the Court instructed a police officer to serve the McClellans with subpoenas. The judge then ordered an unexpected adjournment for the day. An epidemic of speculation infected the startled gallery and immediately spread throughout the city.

NINE

Honolulu had been under siege by the Ala Moana Case for nearly three months and the tension was beginning to tell on a population that locked its doors, flinched at night shadows, whispered on street corners and suffered sudden silences when Asian clerks served haole shoppers. On Hotel Street, sailors closed ranks as gangs of local boys jeered from doorways and no kanakas were seen in Vic Boyd's Pantheon Bar or Johnny Welch's Porthole or Moose Taussig's Grill, which once again reverted to meccas for Navy men as in the days when sailors earned their brawn in square-rigging, giving them a brawling reputation in port. Now the belligerence was revived and with it an insidious hostility as Navy men saw in each dark local face a possible rapist who would prey on their women.

Christmas was approaching and already McInerny's and Liberty House, the large downtown department stores, had put up festive fronts with tinsel-trimmed windows and gift wares. Normally the incandescent days of December, so clear even into night that the brilliant evening star seemed appropriately near at hand, gladdened the hearts of Hawaii as a harbinger of the holidays. The land, its lavender sunsets laced with the silhouettes of palms and its sands wave-washed into dunes, at this time of year likened to that of the original Christmas where snow and pines were also alien. The cheerful anticipation that normally stirred the city around Christmas time had been replaced with apprehension. There was nothing holy about the season, nor jolly either, and the people of Hawaii prayed that within the next few days peace on earth and good will toward men would be restored to their islands.

The faithful haole spectators of the courtroom, whose unfailing attendance encouraged among them a familiarity as inbred as membership in the exclusive Pacific Club, greeted each other with smiles and exchanged bluff assurances that surely this would be the last day of the trial, this sparkling Wednesday morning of December 2, 1931.

The mixed gallery, as it had been for six weeks, was filled to capacity, and extra newsmen and photographers were assigned to the Judiciary Building in anticipation of the final arguments of the defense and prosecution, and hopefully a quick verdict by the jury.

As Griffith Wight walked briskly to the bar, the courtroom prepared for his closing plea. Instead, he turned to the court and addressed Judge Steadman: "Your honor, new evidence has been discovered. I wish to call George McClellan to the stand."

The name rippled through the gallery and triggered babel among the defendants. George McClellan was well known in sports circles as a referee; he'd worked at Honolulu Stadium in connection with the boxing matches as assistant manager, and briefly ran the fights himself. For a while he'd served as an official at barefoot league football games. Many people knew him by sight. He was now working as a civilian at Luke Field, he told the court as he took the stand, and living at the Y.M.C.A. while his wife was in Tripler Hospital, where she'd been confined for several weeks.

On the night of September 12, however, his wife had been feeling fine and they'd gone dancing at Waikiki Park. When the dance closed they walked down John Ena Road to the saimin stand and had a bowl of noodle soup before going home. His wife was wearing a long green evening dress and he was wearing grey trousers, a white shirt and a blue slipover sweater. He remembered passing the barber shop because it was still open. Later he read that the Japanese girl who was the barber in the shop had seen a couple whose description matched their own, and he remarked to his wife at the time that the girl had been called as a witness in the rape case that everyone was talking about.

"Did you think she might have been referring to you?" asked Senator Heen in his cross-examination.

"Yes, I remember speaking about it to my wife three or four weeks ago or maybe longer. I just passed it off after that. I may have mentioned it to some friends."

"Why didn't you report this matter to the authorities?"

"I didn't think it concerned me. I didn't want to get involved in the case. I didn't think it was anything, to tell the truth."

"Did you talk to anyone before, either defense or prosecution, about this case?"

"No."

"How did you happen to bring this clothing?" asked the defense, referring to McClellan's blue sweater and a light green evening dress that had been added to the wardrobe of exhibits.

"Jardine asked me to bring it."

"Did you talk to him about the case?"

"No. He told me he didn't want to discuss it."

The attorney asked the witness to slip on the sweater. George McClellan obliged, pulling the garment over his head.

"What color is your wife's hair?" asked Heen.

"Dark brown."

"How does she wear it?"

"Bobbed," said McClellan.

Heen indicated that the defense had no further questions and the court recessed.

"We shall reconvene at Tripler Medical Hospital to hear the testimony of Mrs. George McClellan, a patient there," announced Judge Steadman.

A strange safari set out across the city that afternoon, following very much the same route as that taken by the boys to Liliha Street. The procession of cars skirted Mosquito Flats, passed the intersection where the Peeples had been accosted, and followed Liliha to Dillingham Boulevard, which led to the highway beneath the hills of Ft. Shafter, the Army's headquarters in the Pacific. On a bluff across from the fort stood the low, porch-spanned frame buildings of the military hospital. The lead car pulled up at the entrance and Judge Steadman, flanked by the attorneys, alighted. They were followed by members of the jury who had been packed into Territorial vehicles. Several key witnesses were also in the train, as well as members of the press and a handful of law officers. It was a dramatic moment as the motley group of officials fell into place on the front stoop of Tripler Hospital with Steadman, still in his robes, commanding respect as their leader. To the astonishment of the hospital staff, the entire court nucleus then walked through the double doors of the main entrance, and in a phalanx proceeded down the white corridors and were ushered into the medical library.

Folding chairs were set up in a special section of two rows of six seats for the jury. Judge Steadman, his dignity unshaken, assumed his place behind the librarian's desk and called the court to order.

Mrs. McClellan, who had been under hospital care for a month, was brought before the circle of jurors in a wheel chair. She was attended by a white-uniformed nurse. Pale and calm, she sat with her hands folded in her lap and quietly answered the questions put to her by the prosecuting attorney, Griffith Wight.

"Were you at a Waikiki Park dance the night of September 12?"

"Yes."

"What dress did you wear?"

"A light green dress. It was my wedding dress and I had it dyed green a year ago."

"Ankle length?"

"Yes."

"When did you leave the dance?"

"It might have been at the end or near the end."

"Where did you go?"

"Across the street to a saimin stand, the one closest to Kalakaua Avenue. We left there at 12:10 o'clock."

"How do you know?"

"I looked at a clock hanging on the wall there."

"How did you walk as you left?"

"My husband walked behind me most of the way."

"Had you had any trouble?"

"A little."

"How did you carry your head?"

"Down. I always walk with my head down."

"How tall are you?"

"Five feet, three inches. Or near that."

"What type of sash do you wear with this dress?"

"With a bow in the back."

Defense attorney William H. Heen waived cross-examination. Before the jurors left the hospital, Mr. and Mrs. George Goeas were brought in and looked briefly at the wan patient in the wheelchair. Alice Aramaki was also called from the hall and for a moment she, too, gazed shyly at the invalid girl.

George McClellan was still wearing his blue sweater when court reconvened later that afternoon in the Judiciary Building. He sat among the spectators, regretting his involvement in the affair and the strain it had put on his wife. George Goeas was on the stand and Senator Heen was asking if he knew the McClellans by sight.

"I've seen Mrs. McClellan many times with her husband, and I've seen him at football games. I've never talked to him because he was officiating. I've also seen him at the boxing matches and many times with his wife at Waikiki Park dances."

"Can you pick him out of the crowd out there?" asked the defense lawyer, ever aware of the dramatic value of action in a testifying witness.

"Yes. There he is," said Goeas, pointing to McClellan.

"You testified you saw a lady in a green dress and a man behind her on John Ena Road: was the coat he wore like Mr. McClellan's sweater?"

"It was not."

"Was this the kind of dress the lady wore?" asked the defense attorney, holding up the dyed wedding dress.

"It was a little darker."

"This couple you saw on John Ena Road, were they Mr. and Mrs. McClellan?"

"They were not."

"Thank you, Mr. Goeas."

The tiny lady barber, Alice Aramaki, was then called to the stand and dismayed both defense and prosecution by reiterating that the woman she saw stumble past her barbershop was "almost six feet tall, and the man about five-feet-four."

Wight, addressing the jury, said it was perfectly clear that the woman Miss Aramaki saw and the woman the Goeas' saw were totally different women and that they were followed by different men.

"There were two women at least seen there in green dresses," he said, "and it may have been that there were three or maybe four women in green dresses there in the course of half an hour...Whoever the women were, seen on the road that night, there still remained ample time for the commission of the crime," pointed out the prosecutor, reminding the jury that about half an hour of the evening of September 12 still remained unaccounted for by the five defendants.

He then turned to the blushing barber, sitting wonderingly in the witness chair, and told her there would be no more questions.

She was the last witness of a total of sixty-four who had been testifying for thirteen days. There was still a possibility that the case could go before the jury before the day was out. "My ruling is that you shall make such argument relating to this supplemental evidence as you would have made had this evidence been at the time you made your opening arguments," Steadman told the counsels.

The court recessed for dinner. It had been a grueling day, unrefreshed by the ride in the country, but its climax was still in store. The courtroom was as jammed at nightfall as it had been twelve hours earlier. The final scene of the Ala Moana drama was about to take place. The actors resumed their places and the spotlight again fell on William Heen, whose dialogue had been interrupted by the McClellan subplot.

"I want to say that whatever I was saying earlier still stands," Heen told the jury. "What did this new evidence amount to? Nothing, so far as the prosecution is concerned. If anything, it helped the defense. Mr.

and Mrs. Goeas viewed the new witnesses and were able to state definitely that the McClellans were not the ones they saw.

"The prosecution thought they had found something to pull them out of the mire. I told you yesterday that the prosecution was sunk. They were sunk deeper than ever today," he declared. "The prosecution states there are two or three theories of the case. I accuse the prosecution of gambling with theories. If that's what Mr. Wight wants to do, let's shorten the case and get a pair of dice!"

Griffith Wight glared from his chair and a fresh current of hostility recharged the weary courtroom.

"There can be only one theory in this case," continued Heen. "That woman was seized after midnight. We have evidence that the defendants were at the dance until after midnight. William Ah Sing, son of the clerk of the board of health, testified he saw Ben Ahakuelo at the dance and saw him come out after it was over," said the lawyer, referring to one of the defendant's friends who had confirmed their alibi. "They haven't denied that.

"The question of identity is of the utmost importance in this case. The witness was not under opiates when she first talked to Officers Bettencourt, Nakea, Furtado, Harbottle and Simerson. Dr. Liu and Miss Fawcett corroborated the policemen's testimony. Are we going to disregard the testimony of these witnesses because they are Portuguese and Hawaiians and Chinese?" shouted Heen, for the first time fanning the ugly flame of racism so long smoldering beneath the case.

The defense questioned the ability of the girl to see her assailants on a moonless night. He repeated his charge that testimony was manufactured against the defendants. He brought up Officer Cluney's failure to report Ida's reference to a white woman.

"Or so he said. That was the first intimation, gentlemen of the jury, that they were framing these defendants. And now I want to tell you about Officer Benton, the star witness for the prosecution and a bogus expert on tires. The whole thing's a bluff! Why didn't he include the tire marks in his first report, and when he did make a statement he said he found the tire marks at 3 o'clock in the morning? That was before the girl was even taken to the police station! Why didn't Benton mention them earlier? Because there weren't any tire marks! He thought of them later. Lau refused to become a party to this scheme. He has a heart and a conscience. Will you believe Benton or Lau?"

At this point the jury, as well as the courtroom, didn't know whom to believe. So much conflicting evidence, given under oath, had

clogged the case and their thinking. With a gravity that surprised even
the defense attorney, they pondered his question. He took full advantage of their bewilderment to press his point.

"The prosecution was caught red-handed in framing the tire evidence to send innocent men to jail. I charge Officer Benton with committing perjury on the witness stand...I say there are some unscrupulous
officers on the force. I agree with Pittman that the Police Department
is full of cobwebs. I urge a verdict of acquittal as a refutation of manufactured evidence. The defendants have not confessed. If these boys are
guilty of this crime, they should be hanged. I have a great prejudice
against this crime. But these boys are innocent! I urge the jury to return
a verdict of not guilty! I firmly believe an Unseen Power—
Providence—is protecting these boys. The public clamor is to crucify
them on the cross of prejudice and sentiment. Be honest and courageous in reaching your verdict and return a verdict of not guilty on your
first ballot!"

As Senator Heen returned to the counsel table, authoritatively
stacking the scattered papers of the defense into a neat pile as though
the case were already closed, Griffith Wight walked to the bar, turned
quietly to the jury and offered his rebuttal.

"Gentlemen, it is this lovely girl who crucified herself to protect
other women of Honolulu," he said in the voice of a friend, a husband,
a father, a brother. "I cannot praise Mrs. Massie enough for her bravery
in coming forward to testify in court. The assault will leave its stigma
with her throughout her life." No one could question the truth of these
words and the prosecutor continued his final argument in the same key
of confidence.

"Death is preferable to such an assault as was perpetrated. Mrs.
Massie were better off dead than to go through life in the condition in
which she was left by these lust-sodden beasts," he declared. "And she
knows it!" He looked at the trembling girl who flushed so that the scars
became livid in her face. Her mother beside her covered the girl's hand
with her own firm one. It was a moment of supreme anguish. All eyes
were on the victim.

"It is absurd to expect the prosecution to show which route was
taken by the boys. They were down there with this poor girl, and of
course they used names," continued Wight. "They were drunk and
drunken men talk too much...The minute Mrs. Massie saw these men,

she recognized them. If they had confessed they would have been lynched. They didn't break down because they were afraid to do so!"

Wight then walked to the jury rail and looked up at the twelve men, telling them of the care with which the lawyers of the Territory had investigated the case, and called their attention to Senator Heen's plea that the prosecution witnesses be disbelieved as against "a little bunch in the police force that has tried to double-cross the Territory." He, too, posed a question for their most serious consideration: "Which type of witness can you believe? The whole force of the Territory or these double-crossers?

"Have you ever heard lawyers in a case make such an attack as that which has been made here on the young girl who is the complaining witness and on me? I never have. They have not presented facts; they have resorted to attacks because they are desperate in their defense of these hoodlums?"

Heen and Pittman were on their feet, incensed and imposing an objection. They were overruled by the court.

"The defense attorneys object to my remarks because they hurt," said Wight.

Pittman objected again, and again was overruled.

"Senator Heen did a peculiar thing when he asked the jury not to believe what the prosecution might read from the transcript of evidence, then proceeded to do that very thing himself.

"If the complaining witness had not been able to identify her assailants, all she had to do was say so and she would have escaped publicity and humiliation that must follow her through life. It is absurd to suspect that she had undergone the torture of this trial to abet 'a frame-up!'"

Analyzing the testimony of witnesses, he pointed out that there was plenty of time that the defendants could have been with "this poor girl" at the old quarantine station, time enough for such bestial young hoodlums in the prime of their virility "to accomplish their purpose."

"Objection!" shouted Heen.

"Overruled," said Steadman.

"The Ford car driven by Ida is three years old, although the defense insists on referring to it as 'new.' And the top of a car that old will flap," Wight pointed out, adding that Thalia's memory was not to be underestimated. "Do you think this girl can ever forget the faces of the men who outraged her? Do you think she can forget the face of the man who struck her and broke her jaw? Senator Heen has asked you gentlemen of the jury if you could describe a witness who had been on the stand just a few days before. That is true. You couldn't describe him. But if you saw him again, you would know him—and he didn't assault you!

"And speaking of Mr. Heen, there's another thing he can't explain away: Why did the defendants tell three different stories about the route they took when they went downtown from Waikiki Park? They hailed their friends in another car simply for the purpose for attracting attention to themselves and establishing an alibi. The testimony of the defense shows that the defendants left Waikiki at about 12 o'clock," Wight pointed out, not specifically at 12: 10 as intimated. "How could they have followed a car that is shown to have left there at 12:30?" he asked, referring to testimony made by one of the defendants' friends. I repeat, there is half an hour that has not been accounted for by the defense, that they cannot account for." Wight lowered his hand firmly on the rail of the jury box. "They are desperate in what they will resort to! And shameful is the attempt of the defense to make it appear that the assaulted girl was drunk when she was seen on John Ena Road. Imagine adding a charge of drunkenness to the outrage that had already been imposed on her!"

As for planting the beads, Wight went on to point out that there was a lot of other evidence—Thalia's purse, mirror, cigarettes, barrette—all found at the site that could have been planted in the car, too, had the police considered such a thing. "And Officer Benton's testimony that the tire marks he saw the morning of the assault were those made by Ida's car still stands unchallenged! I also challenge Pittman's assertion that the defendants didn't have a chance to compare notes: they ate together every day in the jail yard...The defense asks you to disbeliev all our witnesses! They ask too much!"

Wight then told the jury that he asked them merely to consider the logical summing-up of the case for the prosecution. "Gentlemen, you have these points:

"The men admit their presence at Waikiki on the night of September 12 between 11:30 and soon after midnight.

"The plaintiff saw the car number.

"Eugenio Batungbacal and his companions saw the struggle.

"Some members of the gang were identified at the dance.

"The touring car was described.

"The girl immediately identified two of the men. She can never forget them.

"The defendants' story of how they were seated in the car is exactly the same as the girl's original story.

"She was badly beaten, outraged. And her possessions were found at the scene of the crime."

The prosecution continued to appeal to reason. "Think of Officer Lau, a fingerprint expert who couldn't find one single fingerprint on that car! Why? He did not want to find any! He wanted to rush to Mr. Heen's office. And Mr. Pittman has referred to the defendants as human boys with hearts. What of Kahahawai who rushes about beating defenseless women with his huge fist? Think of this frail woman suffering blows that broke her jaw while she prayed to God for deliverance...Mr. Pittman has urged you not to disgrace these men by sending them to jail. Jail is too good for men who have committed this crime, but unfortunately rape is not a hanging offense in this Territory.

"What we call on you gentlemen of the jury for is to vindicate Hawaii, to show that you will protect your women. Could you go home and look your mother or your wife or your daughter in the eye if you failed to do your duty in this case?

"I can see no reason for an acquittal, but should you acquit these men you will announce to the world that our women must be kept at home, that we must go armed to protect ourselves from gangsters. Gangs will run rampant. Which type of gangsters are worse? Chicago's liquor gangsters who kill men, or cowardly gangsters who outrage women?

"Gangsters can only be stopped by juries."

The prosecutor walked to the window of the courtroom and gazed for a moment from the window. Below, the street lights shone on the outstretched hand of the gilded statue of Kamehameha the Great. The Hawaiian courtroom was well aware of what had caught the lawyer's gaze.

"We expect you gentlemen to bring in a true Hawaiian verdict," said Griffith Wight, returning to the center of the bar, "and show the world that here is a place where above all things, we protect our women. The evidence in this is enough to convict these men. You all know that. Not one of the defendants who took the stand denied that Chang and Ahakuelo committed this crime. Certainly that is significant!" Again the prosecuting attorney looked in the direction of the open window at the soft Hawaiian night and, raising his arm in the gesture of Kamehameha, reminded the Island people in the courtroom of the halcyon days of justice under the great chief who brought peace to the Kingdom of Hawaii.

"Consider what he would have done in a case like this."

TEN

The long day was over, the long trial ended. Weariness pervaded the corridors of the Judiciary Building as the curtain of night closed the windows of the courtroom. The fate of the five boys and the justification for Thalia's months of torment were at the mercy of twelve men who were strangers to all of them.

"It has been a long day and I know you are tired," said Judge Steadman to the members of the jury. "You have listened with alert attention and I want to express my appreciation for the manner in which you have heard this case."

The jurors retired at 8:42 p.m. the evening of Wednesday, December 2. At midnight they had reached no decision, and the Judge called a halt to deliberations and excused them for the night. They would stay in rooms at the Alexander Young Hotel, three blocks from the courthouse, in the charge of two court bailiffs.

"You are to have no conversation with anyone, except the hotel people with reference to your needs there, and are to read no newspapers. If anyone attempts to communicate with you, you are to inform the court. If you have any communications to make, make them to me," said the Judge. "I do not wish, however, to interfere with any communications that may be necessary to your families." The court then ordered that spectators and others in the courtroom remain seated until the jury retired. They had waited for sixteen hours that day, they could wait a little longer.

A clear, beguiling morning greeted the men of the jury the next day as they took the shortcut through the Iolani Palace grounds from their hotel to the Judiciary Building. They had slept well, breakfasted heartily and were crisply linened in home-laundered shirts brought by their solicitous wives and families to the hotel in the early hours of morning. The brisk trades prevailed and seemed to augur clean-sweeping action, so it was with a light step that the twelve men mounted the staircase to the jury room and joked as the doors were locked behind them.

That evening they emerged rumpled, dispirited and undecided. Friday also dragged into another day of inconclusive deliberation. For the first time since the opening of the trial, interest among the gallery occupants flagged and vacant benches appeared. The five defendants wandered in and out under bailiff escort. They asked for a newspaper and divided it, a couple of them reading an account of the trial, while the two Hawaiians, Ahakuelo, and Kahahawai, pored over the sports pages. All of them laughed at the comics, noted a reporter, and they were relaxed, more so than anyone else concerned with the case, whispering among themselves and seemingly unconcerned that by now the entire city was speaking in whispers.

The grim specter of distrust haunted Honolulu, slashing out in overt threats of reprisal among the sailors jeered at by local boys, and offering lip service to the dissemination of scandal. Only the Japanese language papers had made Thalia's name public, but it was common knowledge that the society wife of Lieutenant Thomas Massie was the victim and many of the more vicious gossip-mongers thought she had it coming to her. The circle of senior officers and their distaff elite were now familiar with the lurid details of Thalia's violation as well as Tommy Massie's concern to the point of almost total distraction over his wife's condition. Against the doctor's advice, he had taken Thalia home from the hospital a week after her operation, assuming all responsibility for her welfare. It had also been against his better judgment, but Thalia had pleadingly convinced him that her own bed would halt the nightmares that still plagued her, and she needed him by her side when the thief of terror robbed her of sleep. As a result, Massie had become a night nurse to the demanding patient, sacrificing his own rest and arriving for duty each morning at the Sub Base hollow-eyed and shaken.

There was widespread pity, too, for the young wife whose childhood had been sheltered by the insulating comforts of high social position. Her hothouse upbringing and budding age made the outrage seem much worse. Massie's superiors were concerned by the erosion of the promising officer's morale: bringing a pampered Ruth into the alien com of service life was difficult enough, but to have his bride molested, brutally so, by a gang of native hoodlums could destroy the career, health, marriage and perhaps life itself of the attractive young couple. It would be for the good of everyone, Admiral Stirling decided, if Lieutenant Massie were on maneuvers during the trial. Meanwhile in the wardrooms there was talk of nothing else, and the submarine commander, Captain Ward Wortman, became increasingly alarmed. He was not a man to stand by in the face of what he considered his duty, and if the situation worsened, he resolved to take action himself.

The latent resentment toward the free-spending sailors increased among the shiftless, dark-skinned youth of midcity Honolulu and blos-

somed into bitter animosity on those night streets where bootleg okolehau released pent-up hostility.

Leaders of the haole community whom business had entwined eco-
nomically as well as socially with the high brass of the services and who
had heretofore prided themselves on their racial tolerance found they
were taking sides against the non-Caucasian people of the Islands with
whom they'd previously enjoyed a reserved working compatibility. The
more outspoken of this power block agreed with the reactionary cries
from the mainland press, confirmed by the Navy's vestige of colonialism,
that Hawaii was not yet ready for statehood and wished to delay the day
when haole supremacy would be in jeopardy. Fomenting forces were at
work to break the grip of the Big Five, those controlling corporations
that had begun a century earlier as mercantile and sugar factors and
developed into agency companies dominating the pineapple and sugar
industries, as well as the freight and passenger services between the mainland and Hawaii. They owned the largest hotels catering to the growing
tourist trade, ran the best stores and managed an impressive chunk of the
wholesale and insurance businesses. Ancestors of the haole executives of
the Big Five had worked hard, they reasoned, supplying ingenuity and
capital to develop the Islands' economy and bring Hawaii into the 20th
century. They feared the established order would be wrecked if power fell
into the hands of the ambitious Asian element so steadily growing in
Honolulu, and agreed with the Navy that the tide should be checked
that was bringing with it inefficient law officers, corrupt politicians and
cold-blooded rapists. That the heterogeneous heritage of the Islands had
also produced outstanding professional men, civic leaders, business
tycoons and civil servants who were riding the wave of progress, as well
as a blended society unique in America, became irrelevant. Opposed to
statehood because of the mixed-racial majority of voters, reactionary
haoles found themselves on the horns of a dilemma since statehood
would also promise better government and less opportunity for local corruption.

For the majority of the community, however, including responsible
legislators and middle-class wage earners of mingled races, the setback
to statehood was a serious threat to the future development of Hawaii,
and they deplored the dark cloud of racism that the Massie affair had
cast over their sun-filled land. Nearly everyone agreed, too, that the
tropical Islands were ripe for political reform and that the Police
Department, especially, could stand a thorough airing.

The restless undercurrent, triggered by the trial, had rocked the status quo and created a force of mounting violence that could engulf the city with the inexorable devastation of a tidal wave. Even in the sealed jury room this apprehension permeated the chamber.

Toward noon on Friday, December 4, Moses Kaululaau, the bailiff attending the jury of the Ala Moana assault case, slowly paced the corridor outside the closed door of his charges. As he passed near the door, he was astonished to hear the violent sounds of a chair being thrown against the wall, a wild scuffle amid muffled admonitions and threats. He unlocked the door and threw it wide, encompassing the scene in a single glance, then dashing on the double down the hall, he called to his fellow bailiff on duty to send word to Judge Steadman to hurry to the jury room immediately.

"I was sitting in my chambers about 12:20 when a Mr. Manuel Cabral, a pensioned police officer who has been assisting around the court, came to me and requested that I go to the jury room at once without telling me why," recalled the Judge. "I requested Mr. Wight and Mr. Heen to accompany me, and they did so. The door of the jury room was open and all the jurors were standing when we arrived there."

The astonished judge and the two lawyers stopped short and gazed at the scene: ten of the jurors, in their shirt sleeves and disheveled, were standing in a ring around two of their colleagues who had stripped to their undershirts and, with fists cocked, were circling each other belligerently at ten paces, scowling and tensed to strike out. Furniture had been pushed to the wall and the room vibrated with animosity. The Judge immediately dashed between the combatants.

"Attire yourselves correctly, gentlemen," he ordered sharply. Sheepishly, they complied as the other jurymen also put on their coats and straightened their ties.

"I can appreciate that during a long trial and prolonged deliberations, personal feeling can be aroused," said Steadman. "It is of paramount importance, however, that every juror restrain and control his passions and endeavor to behave in a calm, judicial manner."

"But he called me a bastard," said one of the belligerents.

"I can only repeat the importance of every juror's controlling himself." The jury listened with chastised attention and acquiesced to the Court's suggestion that they all go calmly to lunch and forget the scene and what motivated it.

Calm prevailed well into the next day and still no verdict. In the late morning, defense counsel Heen arose and asked recognition of a motion. "We of the defense submit that the jury, after prolonged session, has reached a point where at least two of the jurors have shown by their actions that they were about to resort to physical violence and are no longer capable of relying on the process of reasoning in determining their verdict. On behalf of all the defendants, I now move that in view of the facts stated that the jury be called in from the jury room and discharged and that a mistrial be entered."

"Motion opposed," shouted Prosecutor Wight, on his feet. "On the grounds in part that there was no showing as to what caused the commotion."

"Motion overruled," said Judge Steadman. "The commotion transpired in the presence of Mr. Heen without objection from him and nothing more has happened now, twenty-two hours later. Since the court has observed the jury as it has gone to meals and been given evidence of the jury's now being calm, and since that time the jury has asked for evidence, indicating to the court it is still considering evidence, and moreover, since the jury has not indicated to the court that it's unable to agree and there's no reason to believe that the altercation has not been smoothed out, the motion is denied. I believe it was a momentary flare-up occasioned by a word."

Everyone had the jitters. Many wives in the city's suburbs slept with loaded pistols under their pillows. Such spunk delighted Admiral Stirling, who himself had the nickname "Two Gun Stirling."

"In all the seriousness of the situation, the women showed a rare sense of humor when they decided they would carry revolvers for their own protection," wrote the Admiral later about the dynamite-packed period. "Authorities did not dare refuse licenses, and gun shops did a thriving business selling miniature automatics small enough to go into a woman's handbag. It was not an uncommon sight to see ordinarily timid women proudly display their weapons to each other and challenge each other to pistol matches on the beach." Rare humor indeed.

Less amusing was the epidemic of hysteria mounting among the women whose husbands were at sea. Although Thalia calmly walked her dog each day, many of her neighbors would not go out of their houses. At Shore Patrol headquarters at Pearl Harbor, a report came in from Mrs. Pace, the Navy wife who comforted Thalia the night of the rape, that she had received mysterious phone calls on two consecutive nights. On the third night her husband arrived home and the calls ceased abruptly. Mrs. Rigby, also a close friend and neighbor of the Massies, whose home was to have been the scene of the nightcap rendezvous after the party at the Ala Wai Inn, awoke one night to hear the voices of two men whispering beneath her bedroom window. Although paralyzed with fear, she managed to telephone the Navy Patrol, which immediately dispatched two shore patrolmen to the Manoa address, but Mrs. Rigby told them the men had disappeared into the adjacent weeds and they found nothing. Another night, a nearby wife rose screaming from her bed at the sound of voices. Again nothing.

From behind drawn curtains, Navy wives watched suspicious cars roving up and down the streets. "The Japanese driver stopped and two girls of the geisha type wrote down the number of my mail box," raved the wife who had reported the ominous phone calls, pleading for protection by the Shore Patrol. The same day, yet another Navy wife, next door to the Massie home, saw the same car pass "with two Oriental women eyeing the house carefully." The panicked women were beginning to see in every dark-skinned male a potential rapist.

"My car was forced to the curb on Pensacola Street by a fat Hawaiian who said, 'You damned haoles think you own this place!'" wailed a distressed female voice over the Navy patrol phone. She identified herself as Mrs. Clinton Brian, wife of a lieutenant commander, and their home was across the street from the Massie house. A few days later she called again, this time to report that as she picked up her children at school with two other service wives, another car "filled with Hawaiians put on the brakes just in time to prevent a collision, and backed off laughing."

"Did you get the license number?" asked the man on duty.

"Of course not," bemoaned the distraught wife. "What good would our word be against that of half a dozen natives?" The harassed sailor on the other end of the line tried to calm her, assuring her that her home was under protective surveillance, and asking her to call if another incident plagued her. She called within a couple of days. She had seen the car again. "The driver was a big Hawaiian who scowled at me in passing." But this time she had collected her wits and told her son to write down the number. Triumphantly, she passed it on to the Shore Patrol. She would keep in touch, she promised. It was apparent she suspected that she had been singled out as a target of persecution by predatory toughs, and shortly thereafter, she called to say this suspicion was confirmed: one of her persecutors had been so brazen as to come to the very door of her house. "Ostensibly, he was selling brooms," she confided over the telephone. "He had only two brooms, where the usual peddler has a number of them when he comes around. That man was very dark," she continued, her voice close to terror. "He looked Hawaiian or mixture, slim, medium height. When no one answered the doorbell, he circled the house twice, and even went down toward the garage and servants' quarter!" The Navy Patrol comforted the hysterical woman and promised to report all these incidents to higher authorities immediately.

Defenseless wives were not the only alarmists. Several sailors in the motor pool at Pearl Harbor reported threats from gangs of local roughnecks. The driver of a Navy commissary vehicle had just picked up provisions at American Factors and was on the way back to the Navy Yard when three men jumped on each side of his truck and forced him to the curb in front of the Aala Market. "Here he saw a policeman. The hoodlums—six men of mixed blood—ran behind some buildings on the waterfront; there was no attempt made to follow them," read the Shore Patrol report, adding: "The driver asserts that they were evidently intending to beat him, and requests an armed guard on his future trips."

An enlisted mail clerk from Pearl Harbor was chased from Rogers Airport intersection for a couple of miles by four "large and dark men ... Japanese or Chinese, with some Hawaiian blood" in a Studebaker touring car. "I drew my '45' on them with my right hand as I attempted to keep my car clear of them with my left. On seeing the gun they took off again at full speed and turned down Moanaloa Garden Road, while I proceeded to the Honolulu Post Office with funds and mail." Later in the day, when the sailor was off-duty and driving his own car, the same Studebaker tailed him. He was able to elude his pursuers, but the experience left him unhinged and he requested further protection.

Daily, Lieutenant Commander Bates of the Shore Patrol compiled the mounting complaints, and copies of the reports were sent by hand messenger to the desks of Captain Wortman on the Submarine Base and Admiral Stirling at 14th Naval District Headquarters. Stirling kept a cool head in the face of the storm, still counting on the justice of the courts despite an inner wrath that kindled increasingly with the course of events, but Wortman's fuse shortened with each incident and when one day the Shore Patrol commander brought to his office a scrawled letter delivered to the Chief Petty Officers' Mess at the Sub Base that ended with the threat: "WE HAVE RAPED YOUR WOMEN AND WILL GET SOME MORE," signed "THE KALIHI GANG," the hardboiled submariner exploded in fury.

There was no doubt in his enraged mind that this last straw was not the joke of a prankster, but the culmination of a campaign of terror aimed at the white families of his officers by a native gangster element at large in the city. That Shore Patrol officers should share these suspicions with a conviction as great as his own served to bolster his determination to reveal the scandalous situation in Hawaii to the ultimate authorities in Washington should one more incident threaten the Navy in Honolulu.

The jury of the Ala Moana Case was out ninety-seven hours in futile deadlock, the longest deliberation in Hawaiian court history. More that one hundred ballots were cast. In the intensity of their struggle for a verdict, the jurors had come to blows but to no decision. At no time had they reached a greater majority than seven to five for either conviction or acquittal. On Sunday, December 6, Judge Steadman declared a mistrial.

Thalia walked unflinchingly out of the courthouse between Admiral Stirling and Mrs. Fortescue, calm as the eye of a hurricane in the raging forces whirling about her. "I stand ready to testify again whenever the Ala Moana Case may come up for trial," she told the press with more maturity than she had yet shown. She then opened wide her guileless blue eyes and said, "It is not vengeance I want but justice. I want justice not only for myself but for all the women of Honolulu. Not until all rapists are convicted, can we, the women of this city, feel safe at all times in our homes and upon our streets." She then took her mother's arm, as though absorbing its strength, and walked quickly through the silent, parting throng of spectators on the lawn beneath Kamehameha's statue.

The five defendants were jubilant at the outcome, greeting the mistrial with smiles and rib-punching, and accepting with alacrity the invitation of a former police lieutenant and ardent supporter of their innocence for a couple of beers at a speakeasy on Kukui Street. No one else in the city of Honolulu felt like celebrating.

As hopelessly split as the jury was the community. The melting pot of the Pacific seethed. Civilian was pitted against military, race against race. A cry for law and order welled up from the stricken heart of Honolulu. An angry wave of indignation rolled in from Pearl Harbor. "A stupid miscarriage of justice!" ranted Admiral Stirling privately. "The criminal assault of a white woman by five dark-skinned citizens of the Territory, the victim being the wife of an officer of the defense forces of the United States, has gone unpunished in the courts!

"It could have been avoided if the Territorial government had shown more inclination to sympathize with my insistence upon the necessity of a conviction. I feel that a stronger will to convict those guilty—for it was evident to me and many others that the defendants were guilty—would surely have brought justice. I was informed reliably that the vote of the jury began and remained to the end, seven for not guilty and five for guilty, the exact proportion of yellow and browns to whites on the jury," continued the admiral, speaking off the record and with more vehemence than accuracy.

"Hawaii has changed! It has become the Orient!"

Little did the Commandant know that the Governor had also been informed reliably that the fight for conviction was led by a pure blooded Japanese, a pure blooded Chinese and a part Hawaiian; that three part-Hawaiians voted at all times during the four-day deliberation for conviction, and two others on some ballots. Even had Admiral Stirling known, he was in no mood to believe it.

There were rumors that the Navy would take action in the next prosecution of the alleged assailants of the wife of one of their own kind. Admiral Stirling publicly denied the rumors, but only half-heartedly. He was to admit: "In my mind and the mind of the Navy people, there was a belief that all the dark-skinned people, together with the civilian authorities, were on the side of the defendants and against the complainant and the Navy."

He confided to friends and later for publication, "we must consider the question of support of these five men. The two Japanese could count upon support from their race in the Islands, for the Japanese in Hawaii are known to be both proud and clannish. We must remember that two were of Hawaiian blood. It was a foregone conclusion that the acknowledged head of the Hawaiian race, a princess of the blood, would aid them in the trial." He was referring to Princess Abigail Kawananakoa, descendant of royalty and political leader of the Hawaiian community. He seemed unaware that Hawaiian indignation at the course of justice matched his own.

The proud Polynesians deplored the threat of anarchy in the land made peaceful by their ancestors and famous by its reputation of integrated aloha. As Republican National Committeewoman, Princess Abigail showed an enlightened magnanimity that her critics lacked. "The energies of all persons, regardless of race, color or creed should be concentrated in bringing about peace and safety in Honolulu. The guilt or innocence of the defendants must be determined by due of process law," she stated to the press. With compassion, the niece of the consort of Hawaii's last king asked her people to "prevent disturbances which defeat the purpose of law. Such disturbances serve only to arouse prejudice and other agitations which have been absent from these Islands since Kamehameha the Great evoked the Mamalohoe Ke Kahawai (the Law of the Splintered Paddle): 'Let the aged and the weak pass unmolested along the highways.' Meanwhile, I stand in utter sympathy beside the woman who is still being sacrificed on the altar of merciless publicity."

Also standing at Thalia's side was another woman of forceful character; her mother Mrs. Fortescue had been stunned by the outcome of the trial, which she considered a farce and a travesty. She had seen her firstborn, a gentle girl just out of her teens, undergo the most brutal suffering that could befall a woman. As Thalia, well suited by temperament to play the role of a sacrificial lamb, calmly accepted the fact of a new trial, Mrs. Fortescue was appalled at the prospect of her daughter's replaying the sordid courtroom drama. She found a champion for her sentiments in her son-in-law, Tommy, who felt the misery endured by his tortured wife had not been justly avenged. Even as Griffith Wight blasted the defense after the mistrial was entered, calling for a new trial in January, the young Naval officer and the society matron contemplated with dread the days that lay ahead. Like all their Navy friends, they were convinced of the defendants' guilt. A single confession could resolve the case. While Thalia dozed over a book in a corner chair of the Manoa cottage, Tommy and his mother-in-law talked into the night.

The day after the mistrial an editorial in the morning paper voiced the hope that the new trial would be expedited as far as possible in the cause of prompt justice:

> "In the meantime, the stern duty is laid on police and community generally to see that the truth of this revolting affair be brought to light. Until that is established Hawaii cannot hold up its head to the world. At a time when the Territory is asking for Statehood and is otherwise largely in the public eye, it is imperative that the criminals be brought to justice."

The editor called for the offer of a reward leading to the conviction of the guilty—"$10,000 not being an excessive figure." No sooner were the newsboys on the street than a lodge of Odd Fellows offered $500, which was promptly matched by Wortman's Submarine Squadron Four at Pearl Harbor. A "mother" donated $25. Anonymous contributions poured in from all over Honolulu. As the shamed city valiantly made an effort to raise its head, the Navy fired a salvo that reverberated all the way to Washington: On December 12, Rear Admiral George T. Pettengill, commander of minecraft forces on maneuvers in the Lahaina Roads, wired the Pacific Fleet commander on the mainland that Honolulu was not a safe place for wives and families of the fleet. The city reeled under the blow. The order went out to increase the Shore Patrol, and Captain Wortman called an emergency meeting of his staff.

Also in jeopardy was the safety of "dark-skinned people." Even as the irate fleet admiral in Hilo was framing his cable, lesser members of the fleet were framing plans for more direct retribution. Action, they felt, was worth a thousand wireless words.

ELEVEN

The headlights of four speeding cars cut through the midnight rainforest of the Nuuanu Pali. The Pali, a wild and haunted place on a dark night, is the crest of Oahu, major island of Hawaii. It was reached, in the thirties, by a winding road that threaded through valleys of lush vegetation spangled with waterfalls. Long before and still shrouded in legend, Kamehameha the Great forced the doomed battalions of his last enemies up the Nuuanu Valley to the Pali precipice in a disastrous retreat that ended in their mass death as the resisting warriors plunged two thousand feet to the crushing rocks below.

Born of nature's fury and baptized by the blood of vengeance, the Pali was the perfect place for perpetrating violence and it was not by chance that the four cars chose its lonely track as their route on a cloudy Saturday night a week after the Ala Moana trial. Outriders clung to running boards, while within men sat closely packed. In the lead car, between the driver and the man by the window, rode Horace Ida with a gun in his ribs. Against a posse of twenty men, he knew he had no chance and he sat trembling and silent as the sinister caravan carried him to his fate.

An hour later the vigilantes returned without him and the four cars again threaded their way through the tropical maze down the mountainside and became lost in the Honolulu traffic. It was with deep satisfaction that one of the passengers wiped blood from the buckle of his belt. Meanwhile, Ida lay in a pasture gully on the windward side of the Pali.

He could hear the lowing of dairy cows nearby but otherwise the land was silent and the sound of the receding motors had long since been swallowed up by the night. Soon he would have to move because the ground was growing cold under the damp blanket of mist, but his body ached and he was reluctant to try to put on his shirt over the raw welts that laced his back. His sister had ironed the shirt just before they left their house together, four hours earlier.

"I had taken my sister out to a teahouse where she was to entertain as a geisha," he told Captain McIntosh later, as he sat gingerly on the edge of a chair in the police station and through battered lips recounted what had happened to him that night.

"After dropping off my sister, I drove around town looking at the crowds on the streets until about 9:30 o'clock when I saw a crowd of fellows I knew on the sidewalk on Kukui Street, near the Hosei Undertaking Parlor," said Ida.

The corner was a favorite hangout for the School Street Gang. A bootleg joint operated behind a blacked-out shop front and it was there that Ida declared he recognized one of his assailants, a sailor called "Primo" whom he had met in the bar just the week before when former policeman Eddie Ross, had taken him there with the four other defendants for a beer on the Sunday night after the mistrial had been entered.

"I stopped and got out of my car and talked to my friends there. I don't know who was in the crowd. We had talked about five minutes when a car passed with a bunch of men in it. I think they had been trailing me all evening.

"The car was traveling Ewa. Pretty soon four cars came back and stopped where we were, and a lot of men jumped out of them ... The other fellows ran, and I would have run, too, but they surrounded me. A man got out with a gun in his hand and stuck it in my ribs. Another one said 'That's the guy.' ...It was a fellow they call 'Primo.' I was in the Kukui place with Takai getting some beer and we were discussing the case. This fellow Primo butted in—he was feeling pretty good—and told us he was a fighter. He wore a sailor's blue uniform. He said he was a French Canadian...We didn't say much to him. He wanted to talk and told us who he was...I saw him again in the gang that took me across the Pali. He wasn't in the car they took me in, he must have been in one that followed, but he was in the crowd over there when they beat me...

"Four men grabbed hold of me, and a fifth man stuck his gun in my ribs...The man with the gun acted like he was in command. He ordered the others around. He had on a black suit, and wore no hat. He had a small mustache. I think his hair was combed on one side. His hair was dark brown, I should say. He was a man about thirty years old. They put me in the front seat of a roadster that had a rumble seat. I think it was a Chrysler. I was between the driver and the man with the gun. I didn't pay much attention to the driver, I was watching the man with the gun, but I think the driver was in his shirt sleeves. Most of them didn't have their coats on. When they got out on the other side of the Pali, I saw some of them wore dungarees but it was too dark to tell exactly how they were dressed.

"I didn't fight when they grabbed me: I couldn't fight with a gun in my ribs. The car they put me in, followed by the other three cars, drove up Kukui Street to Nuuanu and then turned up toward the Pali. On the way the man with the gun put me through a regular third degree. He asked me if my name was Ida and I told him it was. He asked me if I was one of the men that assaulted that woman; that she had identified me, and told me to confess. He told me he would blow my brains out and throw my body over the Pali. There were some men in the rumble seat—three I think—and one on the running board. The one on the running board said they had a rope and were going to string me up. I didn't see a rope but I heard them talking about it. I told them they had nothing against me and asked the man not to hold a gun on me. I won't run away, I told him, but he choked me and told me to shut up...

"We went on across the Pali and where the road turns off to Kailua, near the dairy there, they turned off the road and the cars stopped. All the men got out. They told me to take off my sweater. I did. Then they made me take off my shirt. I stood there bareback. One of the men took off a small belt and began to beat my back with it. That didn't hurt much, so two others took off big belts and beat me with the ends that had buckles. They beat me until I was down. Then they kicked me and hit me on the head with the butt of a gun. They thought I was unconscious, then they left me. I don't know how long they were beating me, I think it must have been ten or fifteen minutes. It was dark but I think I could identify two or three of those who were in the gang. I had seen them before. I would know the man with the mustache and I would know Primo.

"I lay there for a while because I didn't know whether they had gone away. I was afraid they would shoot me.

"When I thought it was safe I dragged myself out on the road and started towards Kaneohe. Some people came along, picked me up and took me to the deputy sheriff at Kaneohe. He had them take me to the police station in Honolulu. After I had made my report at the police station I was taken to the Emergency Hospital. From there I went home."

The examining physician was amazed at the young man's stamina. "Ida was severely handled," he said. "He's lucky to be alive."

Admiral Stirling coldly commented, "It was to be expected. I was surprised that Ida came off with nothing worse than a severe beating." He claimed a confession was obtained.

Absolutely not, said Ida's family, proud that their only son had shown true *yamato damashii*, or Japanese spirit, by enduring a near fatal beating rather than confess to a crime he did not commit.

There were no fewer then eight riot calls turned into police head-quarters during the night. Sheriff Pat Gleason doubled the usual num-ber of police officers patrolling the city in anticipation of citywide violence and cruising patrol cars were ordered to break up all gangs con-gregated on streets.

Three men were arrested after a fight between Filipinos and sailors at a pool hall near the speakeasy on Kukui Street, and two suspects attached to the Pearl Harbor Sub Base were taken to police headquar-ters in connection with the abduction of Ida and turned over to Naval authorities. Police guards were stationed in the Alewa district along School Street near the homes of the five defendants, and Admiral Stirling brought into the city a special detachment of Marines.

While fighting and rioting erupted in downtown streets, Ben Ahakuelo and David Takai were dancing in the public pavilion in Waikiki Park. Admiral Stirling himself, with Commander Bates of the Shore Patrol and Sheriff Gleason, drove to the park and ordered that the defendants be escorted to the police station. Reluctantly, the boys reported to headquarters, where Joe Kahahawai had already turned him-self in for his own protection. All three members of the gang refused the offer of overnight police asylum and preferred to sleep in their own homes. Henry Chang had been contacted earlier and told the officers that he had in no way been threatened and also that he preferred not to seek safety at the police station.

The police had trouble enough on their hands and let the boys go. Groups of men in dungarees were launching pitched battles with civil-ian gangs as shore patrols rounded up 200 men and sent them back to Pearl Harbor. All shore leaves were canceled.

Late into the night, Stirling of the Navy and Gleason of the Honolulu Police kept their vigil throughout the seething community. Now and then "Honest Pat" Gleason glanced anxiously at his watch; within a matter of hours he was expecting close to a thousand guests at an all-day political luau to be held on the spreading lawn of his beach home at Lanikai. There wouldn't be much sleep for those members of his force whom he had assigned as a special corps to direct the flood of traffic that would pour over the Pali the next day for the Sunday picnic.

Pat Gleason's fears as a host proved groundless. More than eight hundred guests from all over Oahu streamed to his bountiful lawn where lauhala mats had been spread near the sea to accommodate the delicious feast of kalua pig, lomi salmon, chicken hekka and poi. Calabashes of island fruit were refilled with fresh regularity and gallons of lilikoi and guava punch were quaffed by the laughing friends of the beloved sheriff. Floating up to his ears in leis of orchids and sweet-smelling plumeria blossoms, "Honest Pat" drifted among his guests, entertaining them with jokes and joining in the singing of the strolling groups of Hawaiian musicians. No one clapped louder than the Sheriff for encores from the hula dancers, whose slender bodies flickered on the green lawn with the lengthening shadows from the flaming luau torches. Policemen and politicians, including Senator Heen and William Pittman, the defense attorneys, mingled with long-haired ladies in flowered muumuus, and a glorious feeling of unbound affection that is the essence of Hawaiian aloha pervaded the party. Only one speech punctuated the festivities: politician "Sunny" Cunha arose to praise the host and request of the lounging guests three rousing cheers. Happily, the guests not only complied, but tossed in a half dozen extra hurrahs that could be heard all the way to Kailua, where the Sheriff's special contingent of traffic officers had come directly from the quieting city to help handle the overflow of Gleason's guests, pouring in and out of the sprawling country home.

Meanwhile in a small frame house on Cunha Lane, on the other side of the island, Horace Ida nursed his wounds. In the downtown office building of Castle and Cooke, largest of the Big Five companies, the Chamber of Commerce called an emergency meeting of Honolulu's civic leaders, and in the governor's office at Iolani Palace, Admiral Stirling met with Acting Governor Brown, then framed a cable to Washington. As the powers of authority conferred and the politicians of Hawaii rejoiced, the city held its breath,

Trailing his last guests from the rousingly successful luau, Sheriff Gleason went straight from his duties as host to those of top lawman, and arrived at his desk in police headquarters Sunday evening to find Admiral Stirling, Chief McIntosh and Lieutenant Commander Bates of the Shore Patrol awaiting him. Also anxiously waiting for word of the course chosen to reestablish law and order were half a dozen members of the local press, who had been alerted to Stirling's cable to Washington. The Admiral, immaculately starched as for a command review, met behind closed doors with the Sheriff, whose aloha shirt was still rumpled from its recent burden of leis. The course chosen was one of restraint.

"I made no recommendation in my cable to Washington," said Admiral Stirling with a military calm unusual for the "stormy petrel" of the Navy. "I made a simple report of the situation in connection with the attack on Ida. While the situation here is quite serious, I do not believe it is serious enough to trouble Washington. I do not feel there is any need to call for drastic action."

The Admiral added that he did not contradict the recommendation made by Rear Admiral George Pettengill, who warned Admiral Richard Leigh, Commander of the Battle Fleet in the Pacific on the coast, that Honolulu was not considered a safe place for wives of officers of the fleet. "I was asked by the Acting Governor to make official denial, which I refused to do," revealed the Admiral later. "I told him that, in fact, I subscribed to that belief and until I could see some evidence that the rotten police situation had been cleaned up, I would publicly give that as my opinion."

This was not the public opinion given by the salty old sea dog, however. He announced to the newspapers that "The Navy feels that the burden of securing justice in this case and stamping out a known condition belongs to the residents of the community. To that end the Navy stands willing to cooperate with the civilian authorities."

The Admiral was a man of as many contradictions as he was of convictions. While publicly commenting on the lack of racial feeling created by the attack on Ida—"The feeling is not racial, in my opinion"—he was writing in his journal that "quick action, with adequate punishment for the criminals in the Ala Moana Case, was mandatory for the preservation of the prestige of the white people of Hawaii!" While vehemently denying that the Navy had anything to do with Ida's abduction, he was saying privately that "the civil authorities tried to prove that Navy men were involved, without success, but I believed they had been. It was said that a confession was the object of Ida's seizure and that one had been obtained."

Meanwhile even the fiery Commandant was aware that the order of the day was peace at any price, and as he emerged from his conference with the civil authorities, he spread oil on the troubled waters by announcing, "I feel that the feeling is against the five defendants in the case and not against any particular race or races. The Navy anticipates no race riots or any general disturbances."

It was difficult to tell if the Admiral's thinking was positive or wishful.

On Monday, December 14, the day after the luau and two days after Ida's kidnapping, The *Star-Bulletin* ran a two-inch banner headline: CHAMBER DIRECTORS OFFER A REWARD OF $5000 IN ALA MOANA ASSAULT. The lead story revealed that "A stream of wireless messages passed between the Navy in Honolulu and Delegate Victor S.K. Houston's office in Washington, D.C." In slightly smaller type was another headline, covering a boxed story also on the front page: SHERIFF GLEASON'S LANIKAI LUAU A GRAND SUCCESS AS PARTY WAR HORSES GATHER.

But it was too late to reassure the populace with parties, pleas of restraint or promises of rewards. Nervously, the people of Hawaii sat on their volcanoes. No eruption had ever echoed with such deep rumblings in the hearts of the islanders. "Honolulu stands shamed in the eyes of the world, her reputation blackened, her good name smirched," cried the *Honolulu Times* in a conscience-stricken orgy of self-flagellation. "Word has gone out that women are not safe alone at night on the streets of our city; that if they venture forth they run the risk of being assaulted and foully raped by gangs of lust-mad youths. And that word is true. WOMEN ARE NOT SAFE." A front-page editorial in the same issue deplored the "utter collapse of police protection" that made it necessary for the Navy to triple the Shore Patrol while officers at sea were away from home, and their wives made to rely for safety on pocket pistols. Pent-up emotion burst forth in print. Unplanned, unconsciously, the dividing city was preparing to join battle. The Japanese paper, Jitsugyo-no-Hawaii, deplored the racial friction that Admiral Stirling's public statement had sought to soothe.

> "The kidnapping of Horace Ida and the flogging of him by 20 unidentified men to near death Saturday night is an outrage of the rawest sort, unprecedented in Hawaii, and the Japanese community is incensed...Ida and four other boys were tried before a fair-minded jury and a mistrial entered. It is the first time in Hawaii that such an outrage has been committed. The men who attacked Ida should be brought to justice."

From the Hawaiian community came a cry of anguish as the Sons and Daughters of Hawaii, descendants of the Polynesians who had established a paradise in the Pacific, called for a restoration of order such as that enjoyed under the firm hand of their ancient warrior king, the great Kamehameha, who had tolerated no violation of women in his land:

> "An admiral of our Navy has wired his chief in Washington, D.C., that Honolulu is an unsafe port for the wives of Naval officers, that a Naval officer's wife has been ravished by five beasts. What can we, the Daughters and Sons of Hawaii, say in defense of

our city and our gentlemen after that broad statement, when the constituted officials of our community are so casual in their attempt to run down the culprits of this gross outrage?

"Is there no way to impeach these men that we have placed in office? For it seems that we are heading at a very fast pace for a government by commission when we cannot enforce the law."

Inevitably a scapegoat emerged, and it was the fun-loving, honest, slack Sheriff Patrick Gleason. The buoyant politico-policeman bobbed on the surface of the storm, an easy target for all troubleshooters, while below the sinister currents of far deeper turmoil, of racism, militarism and corruption, continued to simmer. Among those taking potshots at the popular vote-getter in the sheriff's office was the editor of the *Honolulu Advertiser*, who titled his Monday morning editorial with the snide caption, "And Nero Fiddled at His Luau." Even in the scathing excoriation of the lax Police Department there was an inevitable accompaniment of Hawaiian humor:

"Nero fiddled while Rome was doing a spontaneous combustion ... so it fell out that Sheriff Patrick Gleason of this city was entertaining his police force, the attorneys for the defense and the political standard bearers with a gigantic luau while the whole island of Oahu awaited possible wholesale rioting throughout Sunday.

"In the security and serenity of his Lanikai luau, the Sheriff and his guests were far removed from danger and all alarms. There was an abundance of food and other refreshments; there was much slapping of backs, much exhilarating talk as to who will be the next sheriff, and such simple and gay bandiage that fairly set the tables in a roar. It was a grand luau, everybody agrees, and our courageous, resourceful, hospitable Sheriff outdid all his past performances.

"Far from the crowd's ignoble strife, far from such annoyances as guarding the city from possible anarchy—far, far away from all trouble—the Sheriff and his police and other guests threw cork and care aside and enjoyed a Sunday of sheer delight.

"It was a red letter day for the great custodian of the city's peace, a good bit of absolutely all right. And there wasn't a single flash of lightning to write disturbing letters on the wall."

The writing on the wall was there, however, and it foretold more ominous news than the downfall of Patrick Gleason and his outmoded office of elected sheriff. As the Navy steered its course into the troubled waters of Hawaii, it created a wake of hysteria that washed the shores of the West Coast. Screamed the headlines of the *Oakland Tribune* a few days after Ida's abduction:

RACIAL WAR FEAR GRIPS ISLAND CITY

The entire nation was becoming fascinated by idyllic Hawaii's threat of mass violence sparked by sex and colored by race. Hearst tabloids ran lurid cartoons of milk-skinned maidens being carried off to tropical lairs by brown brigands, bare-chested and slant-eyed.

The situation was ideal grist for the Time Magazine mill. In a late December issue of 1931, under the section RACES, was a subhead: "Lust in Paradise." In full-blown Timese the calumny unfolded: "Honolulu, paradisiac melting pot of East and West, was tense with trouble last week. Yellow man's lust for white women had broken bounds. Short, sharp orders brought the tramp of soldiery through the streets. A tremor of apprehension ran through Hawaii's motley population..."

The tremor was one of apprehension, indeed, as such misrepresented facts flooded the mainland. From the highest brass in Washington came further alarm: "...unless justice is done at the coming trial and hoodlum conditions thoroughly cleaned up...the fleet will not go to Honolulu this winter." Such a crucial threat struck fear into the heart of the community. The security of Hawaii's economy was in danger as well as that of its women.

Amidst the furor, the city was hushed. Dinner conversations lapsed into head-shaking silence. Holiday shoppers viewed the tinseled store windows in a mood of irony rather that gaiety. Gossip drowned out the song of Christmas carols. Quietly, the five boys, free on bail, reported each day to the Judiciary Building. At Waikiki, seasonal guests from Long Island and Pasadena continued to check into the new Royal Hawaiian Hotel and its dowager elder, the Moana, greeting their favorite beachboys with customary aloha.

But deep in the valleys of Oahu, the old Hawaiians heard the beat of ghostly drums, the ancient harbinger of disaster. Had more haoles of the community shared these same intuitive powers, they might have read a forewarning into the dispatch from the Chief of Naval Operations: "Americans will not stand for the violation of their women under any circumstances. For this crime they have taken the matter into their own hands repeatedly when they felt that the law of the land had failed to do justice..."

Only a Protestant minister, Reverend Galen R. Weaver, publicly recognized the portent of this thinly-veiled threat, and told his Sunday congregation that "of all the public statements,this is the most devilish and dangerous ... "

Tensely, the following week stretched from one day to the next.

TWELVE

Captain Ward Wortman, Commander of Submarine Forces at Pearl Harbor, known as COMSUBRON FOUR, sat at his desk at the Submarine Base and smoked one cigarette after another. A senior veteran in the most hazardous branch of the Navy, he was about to make a decision more momentous than any he had ever made in a career that looked on danger as a way of life. He stubbed out his cigarette and reread the cable that lay on his desk. At his instigation and with his personal guidance, it had been compiled by a member of his staff. The flushed submariner turned the report over to the radioman standing by and barked out the order that it be coded and sent without delay to Washington. It was addressed to the Secretary of the Navy, and it was stamped PRIORITY. A copy was sent to Admiral Stirling.

From: COMSUBRON FOUR

TO: SECNAV

Assault on wife of submarine officer occurred twelve September. Horribly beaten. Repeatedly raped. Necessitated operation for pregnancy. Six weeks hospitalization. Five defendants brought to trial late November. Despite recognition of two men and admission of the five being in a car whose number was taken by victim at time, a mistrial was entered after jury out four days. Defendants out on bail...boasting openly in the city. On ninth December letter received in this command: "We have raped your women and will get some more. Signed, Kalihi Gang." Letter submitted postal authorities for action. On twelfth an unidentified mob of about twenty kidnapped and beat one of defendants, a Japanese. This man accuses Navy personnel but investigation discloses no one connected with this command involved. Since this occurrence Navy mail clerk on duty forced to curb by natives in heavy car. Mud obscured license. Later followed him off duty. An official truck of radio station interfered with by six men who fled at sight of police. Officers wives have been driven to curb and vilely insulted while driving alone. These events occurring on streets of city in broad daylight. Other disturbances after dark. Prowlers, gangs...Navy patrol increased by forty men...This force for protection of Navy homes. Complaining witness ill. Husband at sea. Data compiled by member of staff 1215.

As soon as the cable reached the Navy Department in Washington, D.C., the alarmed Secretary of the Navy cabled Admiral Stirling at the headquarters of the 14th Naval District at Pearl Harbor. An accompanying cable was also sent to the commandant from the Chief of Naval Operation.

From: SECNAV
TO: COMFOURTEEN

Reference COMSUBRON FOUR. If the facts are as stated, it represents a very serious condition existing in the Islands, one of the most serious of which is the breakdown of the power of the civil authorities to see that the law is properly administered. You will confer with the Governor and the proper civil authorities and find out what steps are to be taken to prevent the occurrence of such acts and what degrees of protection can be expected from the constituted authorities. You will cooperate with the civil authorities in every way possible in order to prevent any acts of lawlessness taking place either on our own part or on the part of civilians where the Navy is concerned, but you should make it clear that we expect proper protection against lawlessness and if the constituted civil authorities cannot give it, that they must accept the responsibility for the position we may be forced to take in the protection of out own personnel from the lawless acts of others. You will also confer with the Governor as to the advisability of the fleet coming to Honolulu this winter, for it would be extremely inadvisable to send it there if the conditions pictured by COMSUBRON actually exist, for it would be beyond the limits of human nature that some acts of personal violence did not occur. Show this dispatch to the Governor and report the results of your conference.

A brief addendum to the Secretary's request, from Chief of Naval Operations Admiral Pratt, requested the commandant to submit by dispatch and amplify by airmail letter a full report of the essential facts in the Hawaii affair.

Admiral Stirling was awakened by an urgent early morning call from his communications officer saying that a priority cable had just arrived from the Secretary of the Navy in Washington concerning the Massie case. The officer read the message to the commandant over the phone. "Bring it over immediately," fired the Admiral. He quickly donned the fresh uniform laid out by his orderly, brushed aside the breakfast tray, stopping only long enough to gulp a cup of hot coffee, and dashed downstairs in the imposing commandant's quarters on the landscaped slopes of Makalapa, to his waiting staff car. A radio-signal-man delivered the Secretary's message as the Admiral picked up his briefcase at the door. Briefly, he scanned the decoded cable, then ordered his aide to call the Governor of Hawaii at his residence at Washington Place and arrange to meet him in the Governor's office in half an hour. As he stepped into the Navy blue sedan, flying the double star insignia of his rank, Admiral Stirling directed the driver to pick up Captain F.J. Horne, his chief of staff. "Then head without delay for Iolani Palace." The chauffeur snapped a salute and swung the staff car out of the curving driveway.

At the time of his appointment as seventh governor of Hawaii by President Hoover in 1929, Lawrence McCully Judd's family had been in Hawaii over one hundred years. Scion of one of the most prominent missionary families, the fruit of whose tree had supplied the Islands with some of its outstanding leaders, the thirty-nine-year-old statesman had for fifteen years been a director of one of the Big Five corporations.

His civic background was as impressive as his heritage: director of the Chamber of Commerce; charter member of the American Legion; trustee of Palama Settlement; twice chairman of the Republican Central Committee; four years a Territorial senator, two of them as president of the Senate; member of the Board of Supervisors of the City and County of Honolulu, and colonel in command of all troops of the Hawaiian National Guard.

A soft-spoken, bespectacled, dark-haired, brown-eyed man who wore a watch chain in his vest, he was respected for a kindly tolerance and resilient mastery of thorny situations, an ability brought on no doubt by the fact that he was the youngest in a family of nine children, seven boys and two girls. It was a remarkable family.

Probably the most numerous of all the families connected with the early mission days, the Judd clan was founded in Hawaii by Dr. Gerrit Parmelee Judd and his capable wife, Laura Fish Judd, herself the mother of nine children. Dr. Judd, grandfather of Governor Lawrence Judd, was a young surgeon and physician of the American Board of Missions who sailed from his home in Oneida, New York, with his bride of less than a year aboard the mission barque "Parathion," arriving in Honolulu on a Sunday morning in March 1828. He was an outstanding man in a unique era, toiling for more than a dozen years among a remote populace to whom the white man's diseases were a devastation without immunity, before becoming the first missionary to resign from the board, assume Hawaiian citizenship and accept an active post in the government of the Hawaiian Kingdom where he educated the ruling alii in the modern craft of statesmanship. He was advisor to Kamehameha III at a time when Hawaii was the center of a vortex of conflicting foreign ambitions in the Pacific. That the tiny island kingdom was able to maintain its independence despite the threatening overtures of colonial powers during the grasping middle years of the nineteenth century is a tribute to the mission doctor-turned-diplomat.

A man of fathomless energy and spiritual zeal, he worked unceasingly throughout those troubled years for the improvement of the Hawaiian people and their royal government. So great was King Kamehameha III's confidence in his haole advisor that in 1849 he entrusted Dr. Judd with the official care of the kingdom's two heirs, Prince Alexander Liholiho and Prince Lot Kamehameha, later to become Kamehameha IV and Kamehameha V, on a trip to Europe which also afforded the astute guardian the opportunity to negotiate treaties with Great Britain, France, Belgium and the United States for the guarantee of independence of the Hawaiian Kingdom.

One of Dr. Judd's sons became Chamberlain to King Kalakaua, last King of Hawaii, and another, Albert Francis, became Attorney General under King Lunalilo and later Chief Justice of the Kingdom. A worthy son of his father, Albert Judd was also the ideal prototype of the second generation missionary citizen of Hawaii. He was educated at Punahou, the already established seat of early haole learning, which his father helped to found, the oldest private secondary school west of the Mississippi. He was then sent to the mainland for his higher education, receiving a diploma from Yale and a law degree from Harvard. Thirty years later, in recognition of his services to Hawaii, he was also honored by Yale with a second doctor of laws degree, a distinction he fully deserved, having contributed his services to the last four monarchs of the Hawaiian Kingdom.

Scholarly and well-versed in the Hawaiian language, he often occupied pulpits of Hawaiian churches when he visited Island hamlets in his circuit duties as a judge of the Supreme Court, for the missionary blood still flowed strong in his veins and he was proud of being chosen president of the Hawaiian Mission Board. There was a strong and benevolent paternalism, too, among the Judds for the Hawaiian people, and it was not by chance that Albert's wife, who shared this love and sense of obligation towards the Islands, became universally known as "Mother

Judd." She maintained a large, sprawling home on the hillside of Nuuanu Valley where the lawns, shadow-laced with the tracery of vaulting monkeypod trees, were alive with the laughter of children.

Little Lawrence managed to hold his own among his spirited siblings, and by the time he had stretched into his teens, a tall, friendly, handsome boy, he was leading his own gang, which became known in Nuuanu Valley as "Lawrence's Army," a corps of barefoot brigands whose raids regularly depleted the Judd pantry. He and his fellow suntanned troops daily piled into a horsecart and rolled down the green hills to Punahou School. It was a good life, with frequent luaus and occasional horseback trips over the Pali to Kualoa Ranch, where the older boys could join the paniolos, or cowboys, in a cattle drive or goat shoot. Lawrence could look back on a blessed childhood, framed by strict but devoted parents and filled with memories of inviting valleys, family outings, a beloved mule named George Dewey that was his personal charge, of learning to play the ukelele and guitar and singing Island songs on tropical nights when only the buffo frogs helped break the soft Hawaiian stillness.

When Lawrence was thirteen, his father died, and soon after he was sent to the mainland, to Hotchkiss School in Connecticut. There he distinguished himself as an athlete and leader of the glee club. He went on to the University of Pennsylvania, and in a matter of months had made up his mind that he was wasting time in college that could be spent more profitably in business. Starting out as a laborer in the Carnegie Steel Company in Pennsylvania, he soon rose to a job in management that enabled him to make an easy transition to a responsible position with one of the Big Five companies in hometown Honolulu. It was inevitable that he should become involved in civic endeavors and eventually in politics. No one was surprised when the well-liked leading citizen was appointed governor of the Territory that his family had helped mold over the past century into a prosperous and peaceful community.

Governor Judd put in a call for Attorney General Harry Hewitt, then walked briskly down the broad steps of Washington Place, the white clapboard mansion built a couple of generations before by a wealthy sea captain whose son had married the future Queen Liliuokalani, sister and successor of King Kalakaua and last of Hawaii's monarchs. The handsome home with its French doors opening onto columned verandahs, held many fond memories for the young governor whose parents and grandparents had been royalists. It represented an era of gracious living in the lulled island kingdom and was one of the few buildings in Honolulu to make a felicitous transition from the monarchy to the modern age of Territorial Hawaii. Judd had played in the fern gardens as a boy and wandered cautiously through the formal salons, still filled with Victorian antiques and elaborately carved Chinese bric-a-brac garnered by the original seafaring chatelain, unaware it would one day be his home.

Another building that had gracefully survived the overthrow of the kingdom was Iolani Palace, across the street from Washington Place, an ornate miniature of those picturesque palaces of lesser European duchys that later were to inspire the scenic designer of *The Student Prince*. Right out of a Romberg operetta, it still waltzed within its wrought-iron trappings to bygone music on an unmolested carpet of velvet lawn in the center of the fast-paced city. The former throne room now housed the Legislature when it was in session, and the royal bedroom, up a burnished flight of koa stairs, had been converted to the governor's office. It was here that Judd awaited the impatient admiral.

Although he had been off Oahu during the final weeks of the Ala Moana trial, the Governor had been daily informed of the darkening situation during his official visit to the other Islands and had become increasingly perturbed by recent developments. He and Admiral Stirling had always enjoyed a friendly relationship; they shared an enthusiasm for deep-sea fishing and had frequently trolled away an afternoon together on a mutual friend's sampan. Such relaxed rapport had enabled them to hold many informal and constructive conversations on the defense needs of the Islands. As the Governor looked from his balcony window across the greensward of the palace grounds and saw the commandant's sedan pull up sharply to the portico, he wondered how long their association would remain compatible.

Immediately on confrontation, the Governor and the Admiral sensed they were at loggerheads. Briefly, they reviewed events, each from his own point of view, then Captain Horne handed Governor Judd copies of Captain Wortman's dispatch to Washington and Secretary Adams's reply. The Governor was dumbfounded, asking Admiral Stirling if he shared the alarm so vehemently indicated by the submarine commander, whose bias in the case obviously colored his cable.

"It is my opinion that Captain Wortman either deliberately sought to mislead the Secretary of the Navy as to the facts surrounding this case," said Governor Judd, withholding anger from his voice as he addressed the Admiral, "or that he was grossly misinformed by the member of his staff who compiled the data for his dispatch. As to this latter alternative I cannot believe that he should have sent this dispatch without having read these reports on which it was based and am therefore strongly inclined to the first alternative. His charges are wholly unjustified and what is worse, they are responsible for much of the misunderstanding of the local situation in Washington."

The Admiral did not flinch at the Governor's blunt words, but said instead that he too considered Wortman's dispatch most unfortunate. "I would never have made such charges, and would have attempted to prevent the sending of such a message had I been apprised of it in time," admitted Stirling, adding that, in fact, he had recommended to the Navy Department that the submarine squadron in Hawaiian waters be coordinated under his command, but the Navy Department had not acted favorably to his suggestion.

"As for incidents listed by Wortman as threats against Navy personnel and Navy families, they're pure imagination," conceded the Commandant. "There have been reported several cases of rudeness and discourtesy to Navy men and women on the streets which in themselves may have been perfectly harmless."

It was apparent the Commandant regretted this latest flare-up ignited by the submariner's rash fire, but he informed the Governor that he, as senior Naval authority in the Pacific, would nevertheless be compelled to present the facts to the Secretary of the Navy as he saw them. He hoped a close cooperation would continue between Iolani Palace and Makalapa. The men shook hands and expressed a mutual resolve that order be restored, after outlining a course of action.

As soon as the Admiral left, Judd ordered the Attorney General to make a thorough investigation of each of Captain Wortman's charges and compile them in a report that would be sent as soon as possible to Delegate Houston and the Secretary of the Interior, presenting the facts as the Governor saw them.

Back in headquarters, the Admiral picked up a copy of the day's paper. On the front page of the *Honolulu Advertiser*, dated December 20, 1931, in a small box several columns removed from the wire service headline, NAVY DEPARTMENT MAKES REQUEST FOR ALL FACTS IN CASE, was an inconspicuous news item that the editor had evidently considered of minor importance. Over and over again Stirling read the lightly-treated words. Their impact on the Commandant couldn't have been more appalling if they'd announced a declaration of war:

40 Assault Cases Here in 11 Months
City Physician Reports Examinations Made in Hospital

Forty cases of criminal assault were investigated by the physicians at the Honolulu Emergency Hospital in the first eleven months of this year, a report made by Dr. R.B. Faus, City and County Physician, shows.

The article did not elaborate on these findings, but the brief paragraph was all Admiral Stirling needed to convince him that Ward Wortman was not so far from the truth as the Governor would have the world believe. He ordered that a photostatic copy be made of the item, and of all local news stories and editorials deploring corruption and crime in Hawaii. If Washington wanted all the facts in the case, he was ready to give them. He then called his yeoman secretary and began calmly dictating a cable to the Naval Department.

From: COMFOURTEEN
TO: SECNAV OPNAV

-Replying to Secnav dispatch of eighteenth and OPNAV dispatch of nineteenth. On night of twelve September the wife of a Navy officer was raped by a group of men of mixed blood. Alleged assailants apprehended within twelve hours. Woman made positive identification of four men. Trial of five defendants began sixteen November, continued three weeks, resulted in mistrial. During the investigation of case Naval authorities rendered every possible assistance.

Commandant conferred with Acting Governor in effort to obtain best criminal lawyers available for prosecution. However, case went to trial with two most experienced criminal lawyers for defense, and prosecution only in hands of Assistant District Attorney...

Navy's cooperation with civil authorities has apparently aroused hostility among certain elements...and liberty of five defendants on bail has produced an effect upon Naval personnel which has caused overemphasis on occurrences possibly harmless in themselves. However several occurrences seem to show hostility and desire for revenge.

Police Department consisting of vast majority of Hawaiians and mixed bloods is divided in allegiance, in several cases in direct opposition to legal and police authority and friendly to criminal element. This force has shown itself inadequate to cope with gangs of hoodlums.

Sheriff who is a political appointment informed Commandant his inability due to decision of courts to break up gangs unless in overt violence...Commandant organized extra patrols for protection of Naval families left unprotected by inadequate police force.

On night of twelve December, one of defendants was beaten by large group of unidentified men. This defendant stated he knew five of his assailants. Upon being confronted by all possible suspects among Naval personnel he could not identify any one. No real basis for suspecting our men any more than citizens.

On same night groups of Naval personnel on liberty were reported to police, who fearing trouble called on Navy patrol. Commandant directed all men on liberty be returned to their command. Done without any disorder. Commandant in company with Sheriff of Honolulu observed condition.

Most serious aspects of situation are inefficiency of police force due to system of political appointments; people of mixed blood juries rendering justice doubtful in cases involving rape because of apparent apathy toward crime of rape.

Hospital records during last year show forty cases of women examined charging rape. Several cases convicted of rape were recently released by authorities on parole after four months Imprisonment.

Commandant has had several conferences with Governor and Attorney General and Chamber of Commerce. All are much concerned over situation.

The Commandant's cable went on to say that the conscious-stricken community, headed by the civil authorities, was doing everything in its power to clean up the mess, including the dismissal of ineffectual policemen, the hiring of the city's most eminent lawyers by the Chamber of Commerce to pursue the case, the offer of rewards, and the efforts of the City Attorney and the Chief of Detectives in conducting an all-out investigation. Governor Judd had arranged to call a special session of the Legislature to pass a new police bill that would take the Police Department out of the realm of politics. Also, steps were being taken to insure a better jury list in time for the retrial. The Governor certainly did not feel the situation was serious enough to cancel the visit of the fleet. Admiral Stirling endorsed this statement:

> Commandant strongly feels fleet maneuvers already planned for February in Hawaiian area should not be affected by existing situation ... expert police force, under responsible leadership, plus cooperation of Navy should bring security to community. Commandant is cooperating with civil authorities in every way.

Instead of being reassured by the Commandant's report, the Chief of Naval Operations was stunned by it. In wrathful indignation, he fired off a thundering reply to Pearl Harbor the next day, December 21, 1931:

From: OPNAV
TO: COMFOURTEEN

> The department is entirely in sympathy with the efforts to clean up conditions in community and directs you to cooperate in every way; HOWEVER, the fact remains that during the past year forty rape cases have been charged, and what is worse is that several men convicted of rape were released after four months confinement only. The last rape case, that of a naval officer's wife, resulted in a mistrial and failure by jury to convict after positive identification of four men.

> American men will not stand for the violation of their women under any circumstances. For this crime they have taken the matter into their own hands repeatedly when they have felt that the law has failed to do justice.

> The matter has gone beyond the realm of promise and intention and has passed into that of action and result. Consequently unless justice is done at the coming retrial and the police and hoodlum conditions thoroughly cleaned up by local authorities themselves, it will be unsafe to send the fleet there, for acts of violence which might result in bloodshed are most certain to take place.

Little did the incensed and misinformed admiral realize that within his own cable were the seeds of bloodshed and violence.

As word spread like wildfire through Washington and over the wireless to the nation that Hawaii had been reduced to chaos, that rape was rampant in the city of Honolulu, that a state of lawless interregnum gripped the Island paradise, Delegate Houston cabled Governor Judd:

"Admiral Pratt in bird's eye view of conditions in Hawaii is quoted as saying 'best criminal lawyers defended rapists, paid extraordinarily large fees...police officials made reports to defense attorneys instead of City Attorney...forty similar cases reported in previous eleven months...city not safe for Navy wives and American men take matters into own hands when law fails.' Congress up in arms."

Houston also expressed distress at the adamant refusal of the Navy to consider any view other that its own. He quoted the Chief of Naval Operations as saying, "The Governor has sent us word that the situation is exaggerated. This does not agree with the reports rendered me by Admiral Stirling."

It was the mild-mannered Governor's turn to explode. "Absolutely and unqualifiedly false!" he branded Navy reports. He immediately called in defense attorneys Heen and Pittman, showed them the charges from Washington, and accepted their sworn affidavits that their fees were comparatively small and paid entirely by relatives of the defendants. A prompt investigation proved that only two police officers made reports to defense attorneys and that they were called as defense witnesses as to facts already reported to the prosecutor. But it was the grossly misinterpreted statistic of annual rape cases in Honolulu that ultimately incensed the harassed Governor. Admiral Stirling had picked up the figure of "40 similar cases" in an incomplete news item and not bothered to check it out.

"The Ala Moana Case is unprecedented in the history of Hawaii," blasted Governor Judd, explaining in his counter-report that records from which such rumors grew were taken from physical examinations of females at the city's emergency hospital and an investigation by Attorney General Hewitt and City and County Physician Faus revealed that of this total, only two cases involved violence, and only one had been brought before the 1931 grand jury as rape—the Massie Case. All other cases involved such acts of nonviolence as incest, sexual intercourse with a minor, lascivious conduct, and for the most part "consent between unmarried parties."

The Governor also explained, with masterful patience considering his violent indignation, that never had a rapist in Hawaii been released after only four months in jail; in fact, the case to which Admiral Stirling referred did not even involve rape, but multiple fornication with consent of the victim. It was the case of the willing teenager who submitted to the boys at Kauluwela Playground.

"It must be borne in mind that we, in Hawaii, have various races of girls maturing unusually young, some of whom begin their sex life early and carry on until pregnant when often, fearing parental action, they raise the charge of rape. The result, however, is that such groundless charges are more often made in Hawaii than in purely Caucasian communities on the mainland.

It is submitted that the records place Hawaii very high in comparison with other communities of similar population as far as sex crimes are concerned.

The Ala Moana assault case stands unique and unprecedented in Hawaiian history, and it is largely because of that fact that the entire community has been so incensed and aroused over it.

It is unfortunate that the Navy personnel has apparently considered this case in any way a community threat against the Navy. The alleged assailants could have had no idea their victim was in any way connected with the Navy.

The Governor then pointed out an interesting fact: that one of the listed assault cases involved the indictment for rape of an aged Hawaiian woman, a grandmother, by a sailor in the United States Navy who was turned over to Naval authorities for trial. "There was no disposition at that time on the part of the Hawaiian community nor any other portion of the community to raise any point of Navy personnel being a menace to the civilian population, and no more justification exists for the Navy Department to construe the assault upon Mrs. Massie as a threat by any portion of the community against Navy women. No other instance is on record which has in any way impaired the safety of Navy women in Hawaii," pointed out Judd.

Restraint and an overwhelming desire to settle differences as expediently as possible prevented the Governor from mentioning also that a thorough investigation of all law infringements in Hawaii during the past year had turned up over 300 charges against Navy personnel, most of them cases of disorderly conduct and drunkenness. Judd did, however, include in his report a quote from Hawaii's most eminent historian, Professor R.S. Kuykendall:

"During at least a hundred years after the modern discovery of Hawaii, there is, so far as I am aware, no authentic case of a consummated assault by a Hawaiian man upon a white woman. There is only one case of attempted assault; this in 1821, when an intoxicated native (a former priest) threatened Mrs. Thurston, the missionary wife. It is stated that the King would have put the offender to death, but Mr. Thurston restrained him."

A very grave and dangerous injustice was being done the people of Hawaii, Judd felt, and he implored his superior, the Secretary of the Interior, to consider the true facts of the Hawaii affair as viewed from the Palace. "To assert that the citizens of Hawaii of every race and condition, except the limited criminal class, are not as law abiding as citizens of any other American community is to recklessly malign the people of this Territory. Comment of this character is the expression of persons who, themselves, demonstrate a lack of self-control and balance."

The Governor did not bother to disguise this slap at the Navy. "It is appropriate for me to state at this juncture that the very first laws printed in Hawaii in 1822 were made for the purpose of stopping the disorders caused by foreign sailors—sailors other than native Hawaiians."

Then, patiently and point by point, the leader of the Territory listed the contradictions to Captain Wortman's derogatory dispatch, as painstakingly tracked down by the Hawaii Attorney General: the identification of the assailants and the license number were open to question; there was no lawful means of preventing the defendants from being out on bail; the claim that they were boasting openly in the city was "absolutely baseless and with no possible justification"; after all, such boasting would have offered a clue worth a reward of several thousand dollars and no clue was forthcoming. As for the threat from the "Kalihi Gang," even the Postmaster of Honolulu conceded it was the work of a crank with a perverted sense of humor. The other incidents were admitted by the Commandant himself to be "pure imagination." They were a result of hysteria and "cannot justify the vicious conclusions and charges based thereon by Captain Ward Wortman." Nor had the complaining witness been ill at any time during her husband's absence at sea. The Attorney General himself called on her and "found her living alone and totally unafraid, despite the fact that her mother, who is now in Hawaii, had insisted she come and live with her during Massie's absence."

On the other hand, the Governor readily admitted that Admiral Stirling's assessment of the ineffectiveness of the Police Department was "undoubtedly fair," and a large element of the community agreed with him. Judd, himself, had just appointed an Advisory Committee on Crime to lead the way for reform legislation. But an outmoded Police Department did not necessarily mean all Hawaii had gone to hell in a lauhala basket.

To restore a sense of balance to the tottering community, the Governor also sent the Attorney General to the Chamber of Commerce to help clear up what he considered the Navy's falsification of facts. Hewitt met with the Citizens Committee and told them of the thorough investigation he had made. 'I discussed the situation with the civic leaders of the community," reported Hewitt to Governor Judd, "and we all believe that when taken in account the preponderant number of males to females in Honolulu, the large number of unmarried men in the Army and Navy stationed here, the number of different races living here and further fact that this is a seaport in semi-tropical surroundings, the foregoing facts do not indicate an alarming situation."

But the alarm had already been sounded abroad and no reasoning, no rectifying reports, no efforts at reconciliation could silence it. The mainland press had spread Admiral Pratt's assessment of a sordid situation in Hawaii, and the once royal bedroom of Iolani Palace was deluged with newspaper articles of vilification and editors' requests for clarification. Governor Judd, who had been keeping the Interior Department abreast of his version of events, cabled Secretary Ray Lyman Wilbur:

> "Tonight's dispatches indicate mainland press printing colossal and unforgivable falsehoods regarding local conditions and causing such tremendous injury to Hawaii and consequently to the Federal Government as will require years to overcome. Fairness and mutual welfare demand immediate and thorough investigation in order that Hawaii not be further defamed."

Trapped by machinations of fate as inexorable as the denouement of a Greek tragedy, a tragedy ironically triggered by the whim of a young woman named for the muse of comedy, the course of events continued to lead in the direction of disaster despite the Governor's frantic efforts to divert them. Slowly, the awful truth was unfolding: a gross, insidious misunderstanding had undermined the Islands. A strange assortment of social ills—of festering police corruption, of poisoning outside prejudice, of plaguing yellow journalism—had combined to create a community cancer, made malignant by the catalyst of racism.

Meanwhile the Secretaries of the Navy and of the Interior both asked their subordinates in Hawaii, Admiral Stirling and Governor Judd, respectively, to submit complete and separate appraisals of what had transpired in Honolulu since the night Thalia Massie had become bored with a dancing party. These reports, with all other correspondence concerning the Hawaii affair, would be submitted to the White House.

Surely, reasoned the Governor, when the two assessments were compared the truth would be revealed. With equal sincerity, the Admiral was certain the facts would uphold his version of events, and as though a sign from the ruthless muse of tragedy, fate played into his hands. On New Year's Day, two hardened criminals, both of Hawaiian blood, escaped from Oahu Prison and one of them raped a white woman in Honolulu. The "Stormy Petrel" of the Navy was not surprised when the news bulletin flashed the latest atrocity over his radio. Now the world would know that the Navy's concern was justified, and with blistering accuracy for detail he dictated a dispatch, the gist of which painted a black picture of sun-filled Hawaii.

From: COMFOURTEEN
TO: OPNAV

During morning baseball game at Territorial Prison, one January, Daniel Lyman, murderer, and Louis Kaikapu, burglar, escaped at 0900. Escape not discovered until 1930; not reported to city police until 2130. At 0715 January two, Kaikapu entered home in city, bound, gagged, raped young white American woman who was sleeping in bed after husband had left for work. Woman now in hospital as a result, wounded and bruised condition, face and body.

Kaikapu apprehended, but Lyman, believed more dangerous, still at large. Governor organized emergency Territorial police force of selected members of National Guard under Major Ross, appointed Deputy Chief of Police, and regular police force still functioning as separate organization. Naval Shore Patrol increased to eighty men for protection Naval Families. Men of American Legion, volunteers to police, Federal prohibition agents have joined manhunt. Commandant conferred with Governor. Emergency Territorial police force will continue to function after capture of Lyman until local vice conditions are cleaned up and new police law in operation.

New police law and completion of retrial should be conditions insisted upon by Navy Department before liberty is granted men of the fleet on next visit to Oahu.

On January 5, 1932, the Commandant cabled Washington that his complete report had been put aboard the last steamer and should arrive from the West Coast by airmail in a matter of days. The Admiral was unaware that by the time it reached its destination, yet another strange turn of events would render it out of date, and make the preceding months a mere prelude to pandemonium.

On the seventh of January, 1932, Admiral Stirling received Washington's reaction to the latest report of rape in the city his superiors now considered second only to Sodom in licentious crime:

From: OPNAV

TO: COMFOURTEEN

Inform Governor and all interested organizations that it will be inadvisable this year to plan any entertainment at Honolulu for officers or men of fleet. Unless informed by Commandant that local conditions are cleaned up definitely and thoroughly before arrival of fleet...This has been stated already as being the only safe policy for the Department to adopt and there is no intention for changing this policy unless there is a radical change in the situation in Honolulu.

The very next day, the already untenable situation changed radically, and for the worse. In sheltered Manoa Valley, where at dawn, rainbows rise and stretch before the respectable citizens of Honolulu stir from their beds, the innocence of morning was shattered by a shot.

THIRTEEN

The day, Friday, January 8, 1932, had begun like any other for the neighbors of the rented home on a side street in Manoa Valley. The sun had emerged sparkling from an early morning shower and by nine o'clock many of the housewives or maids already had their laundry on the lines. Few of them heard, and none of them heeded, the report of a pistol, or the later sound of an automobile starting, of a motor running at high speed, or the screech of brakes as a car careened around a curve and entered Waialae Road, racing toward the sea.

Thus the Massie Case shifted into high gear, carrying with it one of the most unlikely gangs of murderers in the annals of crime. At the wheel was an elegant socialite who could have been type-cast as the heroine of a drawing room drama, but hardly as the heavy of a murder mystery.

Grace Bell Fortescue was born into one of the oldest and proudest families of America. Her father Charles J. Bell, had been president of the American Security and Trust Company, Washington's leading bank. He once said of his dynamic daughter, "Grace would have been President if she had been a man." The fair-haired girl grew up in a stately mansion on Connecticut Avenue, and her childhood summers were passed at Twin Oaks, the rolling estate on Klingle Road, bordering Rock Creek Park.

The original patriarch of Twin Oaks had been her grandfather, Gardiner G. Hubbard, the Boston financier. It was he who gave Alexander Graham Bell the backing necessary to put the first telephone on the market. Even in a day of rugged individualism, Gardiner Hubbard was an outstanding man whose vision helped found the National Geographic Society and whose encouragement financed talent in scientific and artistic fields. His spacious country house was a center of enlightened hospitality during the Gay Nineties. On summer evenings a steady stream of liveried carriages passed beneath the porte cochere of Twin Oaks. One of his most prominent houseguests in 1897 was Queen Liliuokalani, deposed monarch of the Hawaiian Kingdom, who had been living at the Shoreham Hotel while appealing for support from solons in the Capital in her effort to regain the throne. Always a wholehearted supporter of a cause he felt just, Gardiner Hubbard acted not only as host to the unhappy Queen but also as friendly advisor, aiding her to the utmost of his ability in presenting her pleas for restoration of the monarchy.

Grace Bell Fortescue had been a teenager at the time, and the story of the Queen's visit was a highlight of her childhood. Hawaii tradition-ally held interest for the family; her cousin, Gilbert Grosvenor, editor of the National Geographic Magazine, made a special trip to the Islands in 1926 to gather material and photographs for a stunning all-Hawaiian issue that was to be acclaimed throughout the world and do more to put Hawaii on the map than anything since Captain Cook's arrival.

When Gardiner Hubbard built Twin Oaks, he patterned it after the Victorian seaside manses of the North Shore, outside his native Boston. But it saddened the otherwise successful man that his young daughter, Mabel, could not hear the song of the orioles in the oak trees of their new home, nor the laughter of the other children, since she was deaf. About the time of Mabel's eighteenth birthday, in 1877, a young Scotsman, 30-year-old Alexander Graham Bell, became a frequent visi-tor at Twin Oaks and spent many long summer evenings walking through the gardens with the slender girl whose affliction was dear to his interest in audio therapy. Inevitably, among the roses, love blossomed. Within the year, the first telephone organization was announced in the form of a trusteeship called the Bell Telephone Company with Gardiner Hubbard as trustee. Two days later Alexander and Mabel were married and Twin Oaks became their favorite retreat.

She was not the only Hubbard to marry a Bell. Ten years later her sister, Grace, married Charles James Bell, Irish-born cousin of Alexander, who was the general manager of the National Telephone Company before becoming a banker and establishing his own banking house in the nation's capital. Charles and Grace Hubbard Bell also lived off and on at Twin Oaks, entertaining there the tightly-knit social aristocracy of the East Coast and enhancing the comfortable estate's rep-utation of hospitality. Their children, a boy, and a girl named for her mother, grew up under the wide protective branches of oak trees. A lily pond was dredged below the sward of lawn and an apple orchard was planted in a corner of the property on Woodley Road. The lovely old summer home, so removed from strife and want, was a paradise for chil-dren of a carefree era. Young Grace enjoyed a happy childhood.

At fashionable Mt. Vernon Seminary, the slim, blue-eyed beauty was at the head of her class and many of her schoolmates were grateful for the coaching she found time to give them. She grew into a "courageous, able, brilliant and lovable woman," according to her friends, who admired her abilities as a golfer and a bridge player. As a member of the international set of the early 1900s, she was at home in Europe, speaking Spanish, French, German and Italian. She excelled as a horsewoman.

A mutual love of riding and the thrill of jumping created a bond of interest between the graceful post-debutante and dashing young Major Granville Fortescue, the adventurer-author who was a wounded hero of San Juan Hill and a familiar figure at the White House. Their brilliant wedding, the most elegant in the capital during June of 1910, was followed by a romantic honeymoon in Latin America, the first of many worldwide excursions together. Later they were to take their children with them, for the marriage produced three pretty blond daughters, of whom the first-born, a dimpled child, was named Thalia for the muse of mirth. When in turn Thalia announced her engagement, it seemed in accordance with family tradition that she should be chosen by a Navy man who would take her to the far corners of the globe. That her mother should join her in remote Hawaii for a winter visit also seemed natural.

At forty-eight, Grace Bell Fortescue was still a handsome woman. Her tall, erect figure had retained its athletic grace and she weighed the same trim 126 pounds she had weighed as a bride. Her blond hair was streaked with grey, but her eyes were bright blue and there was a youthful flair about the fashionable way she dressed. She had many loyal and amusing friends who treasured her company, but only an inner circle of intimates knew why she had so suddenly left the pleasant mid-Victorian house of the Roosevelts at Bayport, Long Island, in September 1931, after a cable from Honolulu.

By nightfall of January 8, 1932, her name was on the lips of shocked society's elite from Bar Harbor to Palm Beach. Newsboys shouted it in the streets.

At 7:45 that morning, Mrs. Fortescue had driven her Whippet sports roadster into downtown Honolulu and parked in front of the Judiciary Building. Several of the court clerks recognized her and wondered why, for the past couple of mornings, she had pulled her car to the curb near the Kamehameha Statue, as though waiting for someone. At 8 o'clock Joe Kahahawai arrived with his cousin, Eddie Ulii, to make his daily report to the probation officer. At the same time a large blue Buick sedan drove up and a man alighted. He was short and stocky with a rolling gait that suggested he might be a sailor. He walked casually over to the colonnade of the building, leaned against a column and lit a cigarette. A second man, who had a moustache and was wearing dark gasses and gloves, kept the motor running as he sat in the driver's seat.

The blue-eyed, gray-haired matron in the sports car pointed to Kahahawai as he came out and said, "That's the man." The waiting man ground out his cigarette and stepped forward, handing the boy a folded paper bearing a large gold seal.

"Major Ross wants to see you, Joe," said the stranger, referring to Major Gordon C. Ross, recently appointed Commander of the Territorial Police. "Come along with me."

"All right," said the strapping Hawaiian, cowed in the face of authority. He got into the back of the sedan and the two men sat on either side of him. His cousin asked if he might go along, but received a curt "No." He ran to the running board as the driver quickly put the car into low gear and asked where they were taking Kahahawai, but the Buick sped off, followed by Mrs. Fortescue's Whippet. Joe's cousin dashed back into the Judiciary Building, calling to the clerk of the court for help. In the speeding car, Kahahawai also wondered what was going on.

"What's the idea?" he asked apprehensively.

No one spoke as the car buffeted town-bound traffic wending down from the residential valleys, then turned left on Punahou Street and headed for East Manoa Drive. In front of Mrs. Fortescue's rented cottage on a quiet street, both cars stopped, and again the big Hawaiian, his features set in a sullen mask of distrust, demanded to know what his escorts wanted of him. Again the driver mentioned Major Ross.

"I'm going in to get him now," said Tommy Massie, slipping out from behind the wheel. Instead, he entered the house and got a pistol from the kitchen table, then called from inside the doorway, "All right, come in. Mr. Ross is here."

Kahahawai entered the living room, where another stocky man was waiting; he was not Major Ross. The strangers led their captive to the far end of the room and seated him in a chair. Massie, who was no longer wearing a moustache and had removed his dark glasses, came out of the kitchen and turned the gun on the startled Hawaiian. What happened next is Tommy's version:

"I threw back the carriage and let it slip into place," said the Navy lieutenant later. "I wanted to scare him as much as possible and said, 'You know who I am?' He looked and leaned back a little and said, 'I think so.'

"I have you up here to tell a complete story of what happened in September," continued Massie.

Mrs. Fortescue entered the front door and told one of the two enlisted men to close the door and stand guard, and then told Kahahawai to sit on the chaise lounge. Massie drew up a chair next to it.

"Then I put the gun on him and said, 'You did your lying in the courtroom but you're going to tell the whole truth and you'd better do it now!'" He looked nervous and trembled.

"I don't know nothin'," said the Hawaiian as his eyes dilated in terror.

An inquisition followed. The slight, white-faced Naval officer unleashed a volley of questions as Kahahawai winced under the sharp thrust of a gun nudging his ribs: Where was he the night of September 12? When did he beat up the woman? How did he drive home? Who kicked the woman?

"Nobody kicked the woman," moaned the Hawaiian. Beads of perspiration stood out on the dark, shaking head.

"Now I know you're lying," snapped the Naval officer, his southern drawl clipped with fury. He jabbed the gun into Kahahawai's side,

From where she sat on the settee, Mrs. Fortescue said, "There's no use fooling with him any longer." She arose, standing undauntedly erect. "He will stay there and lie all day. Let's carry out our other plan." Her son-in-law wanted to ask a few more questions.

"You were once a prizefighter?"

The Hawaiian nodded.

"That explains to me exactly how you hit the woman with one blow and broke her jaw!" Massie watched his victim wet his lips and noticed his whole body was trembling. "All right, if you're not going to talk, we're going to make you talk. You know what happened to Ida?" Still shaking, the boy said nothing. "All right, Lord, go out and get the boys and he will talk," bluffed Massie, turning his head toward one of the sailors. Then he riveted his gaze on the twitching face before him. "If you don't talk, they'll beat you to ribbons. Go ahead and tell your whole story." He pressed the gun against the wet shirt and repeated his threats.

"Yes. We done it," whispered the terrified Hawaiian. A shot rang out.

"The last thing I remember," recalled Massie, "was the picture that came in my mind of my wife he had assaulted, her prayer for mercy and his answer with the blow that broke her jaw." He did not remember pressing the trigger.

But the boy was dead. There was a moment of frozen silence. The four culprits watched a crimson pool spread beneath the slumped figure, as the two sailors, Edward J. Lord and Albert O. Jones, moved into frantic action. They dragged the bleeding body through the bedroom into the bathroom, stripped it of its gory clothing, wrapped it in sheets and trussed it with a length of rope. A high oleander hedge outside the kitchen door shielded them as they carried the limp, mummy-like burden to the waiting Buick that Mrs. Fortescue had pulled into the driveway, and stuffed it onto the floor of the back seat. One of them dashed back into the house, grabbed the dripping clothing, balled it into a sodden bundle and tossed it onto the floor in front. Someone ordered Jones to stay behind and clean up the mess.

"I stood by like a bump on a log," said Massie later. He also remembered that one of the enlisted men said he had acted like a damned fool and he resented it. Then they were speeding down a country road toward Koko Head beyond which the Blow Hole sucks a fountain of spray back into the surging sea.

Irony, which had stalked the case from the moment the young white woman named Thalia left a drinking party of haoles and ventured into the dark tragedy of night, again overtook the scene: the dangerous murderer, Daniel Lyman, who had escaped from Oahu Prison, was still at large, although his companion, the rapist, had been captured and reincarcerated. The entire community was teeming with an island-wide manhunt for Lyman, spearheaded by an alerted radio patrol squad under orders to report to headquarters every half hour. The regular police force was greatly augmented by the National Guard and members of the military police and Shore Patrol. A tightly woven police net had been thrown over Oahu and into it hurtled the killers of Kahahawai.

At midmorning, Officer George Harbottle, from his lookout station on the busy corner of Waialae Avenue and Isenberg Road, noticed a suspicious Buick with its back shade drawn weave through the traffic and speed toward Koko Head. Harbottle gave chase, pushing his accelerator to the floor and passing the heavy sedan while flashing his police badge at the grim occupants who ignored him with a fresh spurt of speed. A woman was driving and she nervously kept her eyes straight ahead. There was a man beside her on the front seat and another man in the back. The police officer's suspicions increased as he tried unsuccessfully to force the larger car to the side of the road, finally pulling over himself and firing three shots at the fleeing Buick, one of them hitting its tail light.

As he jumped back into his own car, a radio patrol officer drove past in the other direction and Harbottle shouted to him to join the chase. Close on the heels of the police, and all but smothered in the smoke-screen of dust from the country roads, was a reporter from the morning paper. He had spotted the darkened sedan as it cut carelessly through the drowsy suburb of Kaimuki and instinctively followed it. As the pursuers streaked across the wilderness of Isenberg Ranch, past mullet ponds, piggeries and taro patches, their ricocheting ranks were increased by another patrol car, three motorcycle police and an army vehicle filled with soldiers from the Hanauma outpost—all alerted in the search for the escaped convict. The barren wastes of Koko Head echoed to the sharp crack of police pistols and the walls of the crater vibrated with the wail of sirens. The caravan careened along miles of shoreline sideroads, stirring a serpentine trail of dust as the blue sedan attempted to throw off its followers, then disappearing and reappearing where mountain passes sliced the pursuit. Tenaciously, for ten miles the Buick hugged the trail. When at last it swept into the crater curves, flashing past sudden blue vistas and clinging dizzily to the rocky face of the extinct volcano, it lost momentum and the police cars gained, forcing it against a steep bank on the seaward side of the road above Hanauma Bay in the bowl of the crater.

"It was a grim scene witnessed by this reporter," wrote the newsman an hour later, "out there on the barren side of Koko Head, with the azure sea, flecked with dancing spots of sunlight, pounding the rocky cliffs several hundred feet directly below the spot where the cavalcade had stopped. Tight-lipped and pale, but showing no sign of nervousness, two men and a woman were ordered to raise their hands and get out of their car...A thrill of horror ran through the detectives and motorcycle officers as the body of a man, wrapped in a sheet and bound with rope, with blood soaking through by the head and chest, the bare feet showing from the other end, was discovered in the rear of the sedan."

The police separated the prisoners, ordering a man to sit in each of the two radio squad cars. When asked for his identity, the slighter of the two answered tersely, "Lieutenant T.M. Massie, of the U.S.S. S-43." The sailor identified himself as E.J. Lord of the Submarine Base and was promptly handcuffed. There were no handcuffs available for Massie. He was asked if the woman was his mother-in-law, Mrs. Fortescue.

"You'd better ask her about that," said Massie.

But no one dared. Mrs. Fortescue, wearing a stylish suit of navy blue serge and a jaunty hat of matching felt stepped lightly from the car, her head held high, and disdainfully surveyed the police from clear blue eyes beneath lowered lids. Sensing her dignity, the officers made no effort to restrain her as she strolled across the dusty road with all the casual grace of a fashionable woman crossing a marble foyer. She chose a rock over-looking the sea and nonchalantly sat down. "She appeared calm, sur-veying the car with its gruesome burden without moving a muscle of her face," continued the reporter. "She seemed detached, often looking over the sparkling sea and never saying a word."

Undoubtedly, her thoughts were also ironic. Was she thinking of her child, Thalia, the exquisite baby of mirth? Of her own childhood imbued with a sense of justice, in which the honorable thing was done without hesitation, regardless of personal consequences? Of the irony of life itself, that placed an heiress of one of America's most prominent families in the position of accomplice in the murder of an underprivi-leged native boy? Grace Fortescue had a penchant for irony. It was she who had composed the false summons which had been handed to Kahahawai only two hours before. On a sheet of plain white writing paper, she had printed a "warrant" which included a newspaper clipping pasted on the center of the page. The first line was misspelled:

> Teritorial Police
> Major Ross Commanding
> Summons to Appear
> Kahahawai, Joe
> "Life is a mysterious and exciting
> affair and anything can be a thrill if
> you know how to look for it and what
> to do with opportunity when it comes."

To the folded summons had been affixed the gold seal of the Chemical Warfare School, Edgewood Arsenal, Maryland. It was from one of Tommy Massie's military diplomas.

Tommy and the enlisted man had been frisked, but no weapons were found. In the upper left pocket of Lord's vest, however, was also a recent clipping from a local paper: a photograph of Kahahawai. As the two men sat between their guards, another police officer approached the patrol car in which Tommy Massie was being held and leaned on the window. "Good work, kid," he said.

"Are you speaking to me?" answered the pale Naval officer. Before the policeman could answer, Massie shook hands with himself and said, "Thank you very much."

"I was speaking to Detective Harbottle," said the policeman. Massie turned away, his face ashen.

Meanwhile a crowd gathered as the police and their captives awaited the arrival of the coroner and the Chief of Detectives. No one was allowed to touch the body, which still lay with its bare feet protruding from the back floor of the Buick. More reporters reached the scene and cameras snapped as Mrs. Fortescue retained her dignified poise and made no effort to shield herself from the photographers and the curious onlookers. One newsman braved her formidable aloofness and asked her name.

"I'd rather not say," she answered coldly, her voice thin and forced. These were the only words she uttered as all about her activity increased in frenzy with the arrival of Deputy Sheriff William Hoopai, identification officers Sam Lau and Albert Fraga, Chief McIntosh and the coroner. The wet, grisly sheet, from which all laundry marks had been clipped, was unwound from the still limp body and a bullet hole in the left breast was revealed. The body was identified as that of Kahahawai, and his three abductors were also recognized by McIntosh. The dead man's clothing was found in the front of the car, damp and bound up with towels bearing blood stains. A basket litter was brought to the sedan and the body was removed by Officer William Seymour and placed on the floor of a patrol wagon. The three prisoners were told to stand by until a thorough search was made of the kidnap car.

While awaiting the loading of the patrol wagon, Grace Fortescue might well have been waiting for the rising curtain of the opera. She gazed toward the Blow Hole throwing its plume of spray over the distant rocks as she would have at a white-maned conductor raising his baton, and she dismissed the stares of the morbid crowd and the flash of cameras with the disdain of a grande dame being photographed for the rotogravure page of the society section. As Massie and Lord were hustled into the idling paddy wagon, Mrs. Fortescue accepted the hand of a nearby police officer and fastidiously mounted the rear step. There was no room for her legs, however, in the compartment with its screened sides, now crowded to capacity with three husky Hawaiian police guards, so the composed matron, her son-in-law and their accomplice sat tucked in a crouched position in order to avoid resting their feet on the macabre basket that filled the floor between them. In this manner, the strange trio of murderers, proud as caged hawks in the wire net of the wagon, retraced the route of their wild ride as the Black Mariah carried them to jail.

FOURTEEN

Even as the Buick tonneau was racing toward Koko Head, other cars were dashing to other destinations in the city. The broadcast of Kahahawai's kidnapping had released a reckless current of traffic. To the home of Thalia Massie streaked a press car, arriving before it was learned that Thalia's mother and husband were involved in the crime. The police had not yet contacted the Massie house, although a newsboy was yelling "Extra" in front of the cottage as the press car drove up.

Again there had been inefficiency in the pursuit of law enforcement; as soon as Bailiff Bettencourt in the Judiciary Building was told by Eddie Ulii that Kahahawai had been seized, the court official sent him to find Major Ross, who in turn ordered the young witness to go immediately to the Police Station and give a first-hand account of what had happened. Instead, the frightened boy went home and changed into a clean shirt before appearing at headquarters. Valuable time had been lost as the police sought details of the abduction and attempted to answer calls from the local newspaper, which had been apprised of Kahahawai's disappearance by courthouse reporters promptly after Ulii's call for help. An "extra" was on the streets as the police swung into full action.

Detective Chief McIntosh grabbed the phone on his desk. "Put in a call to Mrs. Fortescue!" he barked at the operator. A man answered, stammered that Mrs. Fortescue was down at the Massie house, then abruptly hung up the phone. "Let's get up to Manoa Valley," ordered McIntosh to the officials who'd gathered in his office. But once more the press had scooped the police; the reporter was already on Mrs. Massie's doorstep.

"A woman of charm and beauty answered the doorbell," reported the newsman. "Her eyelids were reddened, but she showed perfect poise."

Through the closed screen door, he asked for an interview with Mrs. Massie, thinking the woman at the door was a neighbor or friend.

"I do not believe I have anything to say," answered Thalia, admitting her identity. She was silent but not surprised when the reporter told her that Kahahawai was missing. Wasn't she worried?, the newsman wondered; surely she had some opinion of what was happening in Honolulu. "Just a couple of words?" persisted the reporter.

With a little persuasion, she made a brief statement: "I have not been worried. I have been protected at all times by the Shore Patrol and have carried my revolver constantly as I do not think this town is safe for any woman."

Behind Mrs. Massie in the living room was a young girl, and a man who had obviously been drinking. Thalia left the door and wandered over to the man, who was reading an "extra," and lit a cigarette, then returned to the door.

"I am very sorry for the poor girl who was raped at Wilhelmina Rise, for I know just what she went through and I am glad Kaikapu was caught and put in jail, and I hope the rest of those who assaulted me will be put into jail as soon as possible. I have not been worried because I was confident the people of this city would see that justice was done."

The reporter attempted to look past the mistress of the house into the living room in an effort to identify her companions, but the charming young woman closed the door in his face before he could ask any more questions.

Rushing beneath the embracing bower of monkeypod trees on Manoa Road, a police car pulled into a side lane and screeched to a halt in front of the Fortescue bungalow. Out jumped a hierarchy of Honolulu lawmen: Chief McIntosh, Attorney General Harry Hewitt, Deputy City Attorney Wight and their driver, Detective Lono McCallum. On finding no one home, they piled back into the patrol car and headed for the nearby house of the Massies, passing the returning press car en route.

Thalia admitted them with submissive courtesy and introduced them to her younger sister, Helene Fortescue, and to Albert Jones, who arose unsteadily and held out his hand.

"You're drunk," said McIntosh.

"I'm always drunk,' admitted Jones. His voice sounded similar to the one that had earlier answered the phone at Mrs. Fortescue's. The sailor identified himself as a machinist second class from the S-22, a submarine at Pearl Harbor. As the officers were questioning Jones, another sailor entered the house and told police he was also from the submarine flotilla. He was an eighteen-year-old seaman named D.E. Gilkey, and he admitted it was he who had gone to the Rosecrans Service Station the night before and rented a blue Buick sedan. Afterwards he went to the fights, then proceeded to get drunk. "I was called at the base early this morning and told to report to the Massie house."

"And where were you last night?" the police officer asked the weaving Jones.

"Right here," said the sailor, his words slurred, "guarding Mrs. Massie."

Thalia and her sister corroborated Jones's statement, but McIntosh heard a different story from the Japanese maid in the kitchen. "There was no man when I arrived this morning at 8 o'clock. The man named Jones didn't get here until 9 o'clock."

"Did anyone bring a big Hawaiian, Joe Kahahawai, to the Massie house?"

"No," said the girl. Nor had she heard any shots.

The officials returned to their car, leaving Jones to continue his bleary watch over the Massie household. They had not yet learned that Kahahawai was murdered. The news hit them as they reentered headquarters. Headlong, McIntosh raced toward the Blow Hole, sirens screaming.

Downtown sped an old-model Chevrolet. Its occupants were also ignorant of the boy's violent end. The mother of Kahahawai and her second husband had been told her son was kidnapped and that he would be brought to the police station as soon as he was found. They were sitting in headquarters when word of his death came over the radio. Grief-stricken, they walked over to the morgue to await identification of young Joe's body.

Official cars converged on Iolani Palace. Conspicuous among them was the polished navy blue sedan flying the two-star flags of the Commandant of the 14th Naval District. The day before, Admiral Stirling had made a 10 o'clock appointment with Governor Judd for Friday, January 8. It was to be the third straight day that the Commandant, the Governor and the Attorney General had conferred to discuss the retrial of the Ala Moana Case, and the imperious Naval officer felt progress was being made. As he left his quarters that morning, he was determined to do all within his power to hasten the retrial so that Thalia and Tommy Massie could leave the Islands that had proved to them such a source of sorrow.

"I walked briskly across the wide lanai of my house and down the steps to my car," recalled the Admiral. "It was one of those beautiful Hawaiian days that awakened in one a delightful sense of the joy of living, and made one forget the very existence of sordid people whom a trusting Providence had permitted to exist on these heavenly islands."

The Commandant took a deep breath of the fresh sea air and stepped into the sedan. Before the door was closed, his orderly rushed out of the sentry box and called to him excitedly:

"Admiral, the patrol officer, Lieutenant Commander Bates, says it's most important he speak to you immediately. Something has happened that you must know before you leave!"

Stirling stepped from his car and hurried to the phone. "What is it, Bates?" he asked.

"Admiral, Kahahawai has been kidnapped by white men in a car from in front of the courthouse scarcely an hour ago. The police are on their trail. I think it was done by Massie," said the Chief of the Shore Patrol.

"I'm on my way uptown," snapped the Admiral, hanging up the phone and ordering his chauffeur to disregard speed limits and drive headlong to the palace. As the staff car threaded through traffic, the Commandant mused on the latest development in the tense drama: "I felt in my bones that something must break. In fact I wished for anything that would give me cause to take an active part in bringing these criminals to justice, whom we all knew were guilty. Tension was mounting higher and higher. Something was bound to break and now it was breaking with a vengeance. Had Massie the nerve to snatch Kahahawai from under the very nose of the trial judge? It didn't seem like him. To me he seemed so mild and self-effacing."

The old admiral was proud of his junior officer, and it was with buoyant reassurance that he stepped from his car and mounted the koa staircase to the former royal bedchamber now bearing the governor's seal. He stopped abruptly in the doorway of the office, taken aback by Judd's appearance. The Governor's face had been drained of all color and his body was shaking with emotion. Horror transfixed his gaze.

"They've killed one of my people!" he exclaimed in fury. "Lieutenant Massie and Mrs. Fortescue have been arrested in a car with the dead body and they are now in the office of the City Attorney." He raised his hollow eyes and looked squarely into the piercing blue ones of the Admiral. "That's a result of a disregard for our laws!"

The Commandant smiled. "I've been expecting something of this kind," he said steadily. "You would insist upon letting these criminals loose instead of keeping them locked up for their own security." Then he added, as Judd's livid face contorted with anger, "The killing of one leaves four for the trial. That's what I came to see you about."

"They have murdered Kahahawai!" enunciated the Governor, control strangling his words. "I'll bring the murderers to trial immediately."

"But Governor," said the Admiral, "Mrs. Massie did not kill Kahahawai and she deserves consideration and justice first. There are four attackers left, and I suggest you now lock them up." As a parting shot, Stirling added: "It may save their lives."

It was apparent to both the Admiral and the Governor that from now on there could be no friendship between them. Their viewpoints were irreconcilable. The Commandant coldly moved to the door, assuring the stunned Governor that the Navy could still be counted on for cooperation.

"I'll have to do some fast working," he thought as he descended the staircase, "if the Navy people who have killed this accused rapist are not to be confined for a long term of years in a disgusting and revolting Hawaiian prison...a prison where they would live at hard labor with Orientals and other dark-skinned criminals."

Later, when he recorded these thoughts, the Admiral added that it was too "abhorrent to even contemplate. It must not happen." He stepped out again into the unsullied sunlight of the beautiful Hawaiian day, his face now furrowed with determination.

In his squad car, on the way back from Koko Head, Detective McIntosh picked up Albert Jones at the Massie home and placed him under arrest as a suspect for murder. The sailor was searched and on him, secreted beneath his underwear, was the magazine of a .32 automatic pistol, with one cartridge missing. It was wrapped in the spurious summons crudely drafted by Mrs. Fortescue. There was also a slip of paper with the penciled telephone numbers of Mrs. Fortescue and the Massies. In the watch pocket of the sailor's trousers was an empty .32 caliber cartridge, similar to those contained in the magazine.

The teenage Gilkey was also taken to the station for questioning, although later released, and a more reliable guard than the drunken sailors was left by the police captain to see that no harm befell Thalia Massie. The detective chief had already relayed word to headquarters that the Fortescue house be searched and a detachment of officers was heading up the Manoa Valley as McIntosh descended.

The policemen found the bungalow unlocked "I opened the door and noticed all the shades and windows closed," recalled Luciano Machado, one of the detectives who entered through the front of the house with fellow officer Sam Kahanamoku. "I noticed a bullet lying on the dining room table and left it there. In the meantime, Sam Lau and Lono McCallum came in the back door and Sam picked up the bullet. It was a steel jacketed .32 caliber bullet. I also found on a settee a loaded .45 automatic stuck in the cushions and a woman's purse. While

McCallum unloaded the gun, I opened the purse and the first thing I saw was a picture of Kahahawai.

"I entered a bedroom and noticed the bathroom floor had been mopped recently. A wet mop was in a corner, the blankets were thrown back from the beds and some of the sheets had been torn off. There were bloodstains on the floor. I opened a closet and found a hand towel with blood on it and a shirt still reeking of sweat, a white shirt with torn sleeve. All the other garments were women's wear, including a torn wrapper. In the living room, I found a rope under the cushions of the davenport. It was new with a purple thread through it. There was also a cap on the davenport. In a trunk there were masquerade outfits, men's and women's, different kinds of make-up, black clothes."

Officers Lau and McCallum searched the kitchen. On the stove was a pot of coffee and a frying pan with two partly cooked eggs in it. They noticed the kitchen table had been set for two. Lono McCallum discovered a bottle of okolehau on a shelf, and in the living room two half-filled glasses. He sniffed the homebrew appreciatively. "Not bad," he commented to his companion. Lau had made an even more exciting discovery. On top of the refrigerator he found a basket of eggs. Nestled among them was a .32 caliber pistol.

The pistol shot that killed Kahahawai reverberated throughout Honolulu and unloosed a seething hornet's nest of hysteria. Few American cities had witnessed such an emotional conflagration sparked by the killing of one individual. Hundreds of people wandered from office buildings, grabbing each new "extra" as the newsboys rushed them from the presses. The sensational headlines and sketchy news stories agitated speculation, and rumors of mutilation and torture were rampant. Word spread that the alleged rapist had been brutally castrated before he was murdered. Crowds collected at police headquarters and fear laid a cold hand on the sunlit city. Just before noon, the tocsin on the Aloha Tower gave a militant blast. Five blasts of the alarm was the signal to mobilize the National Guard and the milling population paused, awaiting the next four blasts. Honolulu lay hushed beneath the tower as the single wail of the siren rent the pall of suspense.

Smiling Hawaiian faces, young and flushed with the joy of victory, lined the rail of the inter-island steamer *Waialeale* as it pulled into the pier at the foot of the Aloha Tower. The champion football team of the Kamehameha Schools was returning home from Hilo with their record for an unbeaten season intact. The siren from the tower gave the traditional long, welcoming whistle and the jubilant boys cheered their appreciation as they waved at the unusually large crowd gathering below. Their smiles faded, however, as they noticed the preoccupation of the mob. The siren had indeed been sounded for the victorious team but there was no air of celebration and the boys soon learned that a fellow football hero and member of their race, the notorious Joe Kahahawai, one of the alleged rapists in the Ala Moana trial, had just been murdered and that Honolulu was in a state of siege. As newsboys hawked the third "extra" to be published by *The Advertiser* that morning, the team was hustled into a waiting bus and whisked through traffic laced with police cars to their campus on the outskirts of the city. A report circulated through the throng beneath the Aloha Tower that there would be no more blasts of the alarm. This news spread further confusion.

No sooner had the siren subsided than telephone bells sounded en masse in Iolani Palace, clogging the frantic switchboard and prompting Secretary of the Territory Raymond Brown to advise all operators that martial law had not been declared, that the palace was unsure of the reason for the alarm and that all callers should be told to stand by for a press release from the Governor as soon as he emerged from an emergency conference with top officials,

At noon, Governor Judd issued a statement that was broadcast throughout the city: "This is the time when everyone must remain calm. The present situation requires the closest cooperation of all concerned. The executive forces are exerting every effort possible. The public will be informed from time to time of the steps being taken."

From the Governor's Office, Major Ross also sent out a bulletin that explained the purpose for blowing the tower whistle, and announced that of the 250 National Guardsmen who had turned out, only 100 men and officers would be needed to help patrol the city that night.

The Governor then drove to Oahu Prison and fired the deputy sheriff, who was the warden, and appointed in his place two officers of the Hawaii National Guard.

While outside, chaos plagued the streets, within the operating room of the morgue there was no sound save that of the click of surgical instruments. Dr. R.B. Faus, City and County Physician, performed an autopsy on the body of Kahahawai. He discovered that the boy had bled to death.

"Kahahawai was shot at the base of the left lung by a .32 caliber steel-jacketed bullet," reported the physician, who removed four liters of blood from the chest cavity. "The bullet entered near the nipple and passed through the lower portion of the lung, penetrating the pulmonary artery and lodging in the back to the right of the spine near the seventh rib where it was found against the skin and removed. The only other mark on the body was a small abrasion above the left eye which might have been made by a blow." No signs of mutilation were found.

There was a wristwatch on Kahahawai's right arm, and beneath the broken crystal, the hands had stopped at 9:45. On the ring finger of the left hand of the body was a gold ring from the class of 1928 at St. Louis College, the Catholic secondary school where Kahahawai had distinguished himself as a football star. The jewelry was brought out to the boy's weeping mother, who, at the sight of the ring, shook with quiet sobs.

She had never considered him a bad boy and regretted the day she and his father, Joseph Kahahawai, Sr., had left the country town of Lahaina, on the island of Maui, and with their infant son moved to Honolulu. The baby had been born on Christmas Day, a blessed child, she was sure, and because he was so large and healthy even as a toddler, she delighted in him and was proud when friends said "Esther, you and Joe have one fine keiki." For a while, she didn't like the dirty, crowded city but Big Joe had gotten a steady job as a motorman with the Honolulu Rapid Transit and three more children were born, only one of whom survived infancy. The family found a place to live in Iwilei near the waterfront. It was the rough redlight district and Joe, Jr., was raised in streets where pandering, prostitution and opium traffic were a part of everyday life.

After the marriage broke up and Esther met Pasqual Anito, she took the two children—Joe and his younger sister—and moved to the house of her second husband on Kamakela Lane, also in a neighborhood of slums, off School Street. It was there Joe became involved with a gang of young delinquents and eventually was arrested for robbery and convicted of assault and battery, although he'd never received a prison sentence. Because he was her first-born, just twenty-one years old two weeks before his death, she'd had great plans for him when he was growing up and insisted he have a Christian education. With his father's help, they'd been able to send the husky boy, grown into a muscular six-foot teenager, to the highly regarded parochial school noted for its outstanding athletic teams. He starred in several sports and was well-liked, but he wasn't much of a scholar and had dropped out when he was fifteen and still in only the seventh grade. He'd taken odd jobs for a couple of years, working around auto garages, but when he was eighteen, his parents convinced him he should go back to school. He reentered St. Louis College and again became a varsity football player. But when the fall season was over and the other students buckled down to serious studying, he dropped out again, and no amount of persuasion could make him go back.

He soon joined the National Guard, appearing on the Guard boxing team for three years as an amateur heavyweight, but for the most part he drifted with the shiftless youth of the slums surrounding him and occasionally flirted with the more dangerous sport of crime. After leaving school, he'd found that there was no market for athletes on the shrinking employment rolls, and with the Depression closing down many of the pineapple factories, there were more able-bodied men than jobs. He found work for a while as a machine operator. When he was laid off again, he gave up the idea of earning a living and preferred keeping in shape on the basketball courts of Kauluwela Playground. Larger than most of his companions, he became their leader. Also, in the full-featured way of Polynesians, he was handsome, with a large nose, generous mouth and high forehead that were typically Hawaiian, as was his devotion to his parents, although he outwardly scorned family ties and spent most of his time away from home. He was popular among his fellow guardsmen as well as his School Street buddies, and the one thing that had hurt him more than any other—more even than the break-up of his parents or the Ala Moana tragedy—was his dishonorable discharge from the National Guard after being charged by the grand jury of rape.

The shame of it all had shocked his mother and she'd wept every day of the trial, wondering if any further misery could befall the family at the hands of her only son. Softly sobbing in the cold corridor, she held the ring and tried to think of the days when young Joe Kahahawai, dashing down a cheering field, was the hero of the hour.

The four living members of the School Street Gang had reported to police headquarters when they heard of Joe's kidnapping and were put in a cell for their own safety. In another part of the station, the abductors of their ringleader were being led to police court in answer to the complaint warrant issued by Chief of Detectives McIntosh against Mrs. Fortescue, Lieutenant Massie and E.J. Lord on the charges of first degree murder in the killing of Joseph Kahahawai. A police matron held the arm of Mrs. Fortescue, more in sympathy than support, and as the two women approached the court, she turned to the proud prisoner and asked gently how her daughter was getting along since the grueling ordeal of the trial. For the first time that day, tears clouded the clear blue eyes and the socialite gripped the arm of the policewoman gratefully and said that although her daughter's jaw had not healed perfectly, she was thankful for a successful recovery.

After the charges were sworn to, the prisoners were taken by Deputy Sheriff Duke Kahanamoku to the City Hall office of City Attorney James Gilliland, where a conference was already in session. Among those attending were Sheriff Gleason, Attorney General Hewitt, Mayor Fred Wright, Lieutenant Commander Bates and Captain Ward Wortman. The two Naval officers, making no effort to hide their rabid disgust with the inefficiency of the Police Department and infuriated by the handling of the Navy captives as common criminals, had demanded a complete rundown of the events that led to the arrest of Mrs. Fortescue and the men from the submarine base. Griffith Wight was questioning the two policemen who had made the arrests in an attempt to piece together the story of the capture, when Admiral Stirling burst into the room. He quickly surveyed the scene, noting that Mrs. Fortescue, who was seated defiantly straight on a hard wooden chair, was almost at the end of her physical endurance. Massie and Lord were standing, both in civilian clothes, with the latter still wearing hand cuffs. This enraged the Admiral.

"Take off those irons!" he shouted.

His order was obeyed, and he then walked over to Mrs. Fortescue and put his arm about her. "My heart went out to this brave mother," he recalled. "Mine was a gesture of sympathy. I had daughters of my own. She understood, and I saw a tear travel dawn her pallid cheek, then she looked up and smiled, and I read in her strong face that she was undefeated and would fight for justice to the end."

The Admiral turned to the Assistant City Attorney, "There will be no more questioning of these people until they can be represented by their lawyer." Griffith Wight agreed to this. "He seemed to realize that a new element had been introduced into the situation. As the representative of the Navy, he knew I was there to insist on the rights of Naval people," said Stirling later. He then told the assembled officials that the Navy was assuming custody of the three prisoners. A complaint issue against Jones was to be filed later, when he was sober.

"They will go to the courthouses in my car and not to the jail," said the Admiral. It was an order.

As the assemblage in Gilliland's office broke up, an exited secretary slipped through the crowded doorway and told Sheriff Gleason that there was a radiophone call for him from New York.

The caller was an editor of the Universal News Service, a Hearst organization. The news of Kahahawai's murder had just reached Manhattan by wireless. "To what cause do you attribute the kidnapping of the Hawaiian?" asked the newsman.

"The kidnapping was caused by the playing up of the crime situation daily by Honolulu newspapers...in an effort to secure a special session of the Legislature to create a position of Chief of Police and oust the Sheriff from office," explained "Honest Pat."

"Is there an uprising among the natives because of the kidnapping?" asked the New York interviewer, as though Hawaii were darkest Africa.

Pat Gleason couldn't restrain an ironic smile. "The city is policed to take care of any emergency and there has been no uprising."

"If a Chief of Police position is created, will a native be appointed to office?" asked the newsman.

"I cannot say who will be appointed in that event," said Gleason flatly, then he continued to enlighten the Hearstling with an explanation of crime in Hawaii. "Due to the large number of servicemen of the Army and Navy stationed in Hawaii, the crime racket is fairly divided among servicemen and civilians. Crime distribution among racial groups is also evenly divided. Crime in Hawaii is not confined to Hawaiians. The Hawaiians are a group of law-abiding people."

"Are you Hawaiian?" asked the editor suspiciously.

"No, I'm not a Hawaiian. I'm half Irish and half Spanish."

"Thank you," said the newsman.

The conversation had lasted 10 minutes. It was the first interview by radiophone in the history of journalism in Hawaii. "Reception was excellent," announced Pat Gleason, proud of his role in the scoop.

"I insist the accused be given over to the custody of the Navy," said Admiral Stirling with authority. "They are in danger of mob violence, and I have no confidence in the police to protect them."

Judge Albert M. Cristy sat patiently in his chambers as the three Naval officers pressed their case for transferring the culprits into the safekeeping of Pearl Harbor authorities. After an hour, the Judge issued a statement to the waiting press:

"In view of the psychology of the people of Hawaii at this time in connection with the prisons available for safekeeping the defendants in the case arising today, I am considering an offer made by Admiral Stirling of putting at the disposal of this court the facilities of the receiving ship at Pearl Harbor to safely keep and produce from time to time these defendants for any orderly procedure which the jurisdiction of this court may require.

"The Court will appreciate the cooperation of the residents and citizens in keeping cool-headed."

The judge turned to Captain Ward Wortman. "As special officer of this court and custodian of the defendants, you have authority to keep the trio under lock and key and will be required to produce them at any time the court demands their presence."

"Yes, sir," said the Sub Base commander.

"I hereby appoint you an officer of the court and I place the defendants in your custody without bail." Triumphantly, Wortman and Admiral Stirling exchanged smiles. It was the first bright note in a dark week for the Navy.

"Heretofore I had intentionally kept myself in the background," wrote the Admiral in his journal, "but now I knew most bitterly that Hawaiian justice could be obtained in these two cases only through some strong method of intimidation. It was up to me to take an active part, using all the power I could wield to head off a justice that would delight to send these four white people to a long term of hard labor in a Hawaiian prison, while the four remaining rapists, whom all knew had committed the crime, and one far worse than the mere killing of a degenerate sex criminal, would go scot-free."

The Commandant arranged for attorneys Frank E. Thompson and Montgomery Winn, partners of a leading Honolulu law firm, to be retained temporarily as counsel for the trio. None of the accused had made any admission of guilt. Meanwhile seaman Albert Jones was being held incommunicado in a jail cell of the police station, close by the cell of the Ala Moana defendants. The sailor was primed to the gunwhales on bootleg oke and too drunk to face charges until he sobered up the next day. Also incommunicado from the press were Massie, Lord and Mrs. Fortescue. Frustrated and maddened, the reporters attempted to break the police cordon placed around the prisoners as they left for the receiving ship U.S.S. *Alton* at Pearl Harbor. One nimble newsman hurdled a desk in the police station and was promptly strong-armed back into line, another brazenly addressed Mrs. Fortescue as she passed through the door.

"Where were you this morning, and what were you doing, Mrs. Fortescue?" the reporter called with feigned innocence.

Grace Fortescue looked the young man in the eye and with equal sangfroid replied: "I was downtown shopping."

Downtown Honolulu was crowded but there were few shoppers. People wandered aimlessly as though dazed by disaster. One hundred and sixty-seven territorial policemen were on duty under the direction of Major Ross, who also welcomed the services of thirty men with a dozen cars furnished by the American Legion. Three new radio patrol cars recently ordered by the City and County were authorized by Assistant City Attorney Wight for immediate use as an emergency move in coping with the situation. The addition of the new cars doubled the size of the radio patrol. At 5 p.m., the Governor issued his second official statement of the day to the public: "I reiterate the necessity for calmness and the exercise of self-restraint at this time. The administration is taking all necessary measures. The Attorney General, at my request, is conducting a thorough investigation into the event of this morning. Oahu Prison has been placed under the control of Colonel W.A. Anderson of the National Guard."

Other measures to improve the demoralized state of affairs were being taken throughout the city. An order restricting enlisted men to Schofield Barracks was issued and a ruling decreed, "all cars entering the post containing Orientals will be stopped at the gate, unless the car bears Schofield tags, and the purpose of the visit be investigated by the gatemen. This order is in effect until further notice." Pearl Harbor immediately issued a similar order.

The newly formed Honolulu Citizens' Organization for Good Government called a meeting for 7:30 p.m. on the roof garden of the Alexander Young Hotel. Nearly a thousand people showed up. "Action to get united community support for a program of promotion of law and order is our purpose," announced socialite Mrs. H.A. Kleugel, chairman of the two-day-old organization. Mrs. Kleugel was an ardent club woman and personal friend of Grace Fortescue.

From the President of the Senate, Robert Shingle, on Molokai, came a wireless message to Governor Judd announcing the appointment of a committee of senators to confer with the Governor on the proposal to call a special session of the Legislature as soon as possible. Out at Waikiki Park, following a conference with Sheriff Gleason, members of the Veterans of Foreign Wars announced that the dance they were sponsoring on Saturday night at the public pavilion was called off.

A committee of the League of Women Voters made up of Mesdames George P. Cooke, Henry Damon, S.A. Baldwin, Walter E. Wall and A.N. Campbell proposed that the death penalty be established for the crime of rape.

The manager of Consolidated Amusement Company issued a news flash: *The Public Enemy*, advertised as a gangster picture to start a week's run at the Hawaii Theater, had been withdrawn and *Shipmates*, a comedy with a Naval background, had been substituted in its stead.

A radiant sunset behind the western ridge of Palehua contrasted to the dark mood of the city. The citizens of Honolulu watched the sun go down on the most infamous day they had yet known, and the foreboding in their hearts deepened with the approaching night.

At 8:58 p.m., the city was paralyzed by another blast of the Aloha Tower siren. This time there were five strident peals, each a minute and a half in length. Before the first alarm had dwindled to a plaintive sigh, telephone circuits were jammed at police headquarters, the Governor's mansion, the National Guard Armory and newspaper switchboards, causing a standstill in communications. The entire National Guard was mobilized, guardsmen scurrying to their duty stations, leaving their dinner tables, homes and families. Radio patrol cars raced once again through the streets and along country roads. People poured to the police station and a mob of several thousand packed the streets around headquarters as far as the waterfront. Military and municipal authorities of the Territory hurriedly reconvened in conferences as the population threatened to panic and the station was barricaded for fear of mob violence. Everyone begged to be told what it was all about, but no one knew.

Deputy Sheriff William Hoopai and two other officers stormed the locked Aloha Tower. Inspector Kam Kwai, with a well directed blow of a heavy sledge hammer, shattered a pane of glass in the door, and with other police and authorities, including the Harbor Master, dashed to the top floor where the desk of the night watchman was located. They found the watchman, Ben Dole, frantically answering telephone calls. The man was desperate and blurted out that he had received a call from a major with an unintelligible name, giving him orders to sound the five-blast signal. As the police pummeled him with questions, the harried watchman received another call.

"This is Lyman Bigelow," said the acting Chairman of the Board of the Harbor Commission. "Who gave you the order to blow that siren?"

Again Dole told his story.

"Well don't ever blow that siren again unless ordered to do so by the Governor, myself or Major Ross," roared Bigelow in a paroxysm of rage. Again it was all a terrible mistake, the work of a morbid prankster. Governor Judd promptly gave a stern warning against playing practical jokes in a time of community crisis, but the fearful crowds refused to disperse until finally police officers wearing gas masks and carrying tear gas bombs and sub-machine guns ordered them to return to their homes. The mob quickly melted into the night.

A pale moon, caught in an ice floe of clouds, floated over Manoa Valley as the city tried to sleep.

FIFTEEN

During the tense days that followed, the people of Hawaii walked with trepidation on the brink of martial law. From the mainland came the battle cry for action, swelled by the sensation-mongering Hearst press. A boxed editorial from the *New York American* had widespread and dangerous dissemination:

MARTIAL LAW NEEDED TO MAKE HAWAII SAFE
FOR
DECENT WOMEN

The situation in Hawaii is deplorable.

It is becoming or has become an unsafe place for white women.

Outside the cities or small towns, the roads go through jungles and in these remote places bands of degenerate natives or half whites lie in wait for white women driving by.

At least forty cases of such vicious outrages have occurred and nobody has been punished.

In the most recent case a white woman was attacked by five natives, knocked down, her jaw broken, terribly outraged and injured.

The perpetrators of this crime against pure womanhood, against society, against civilization, were freed on bail after a disagreement of a jury of their kind.

The husband of the abused and violated woman took the law into his own hands, since there was no other administration of either law or justice, and stands accused of killing one of the assailants.

Truly the situation in Hawaii is deplorable, and the most deplorable thing about it is that the perpetrators of the other forty outrages on virtuous white women were not duly executed.

Lieutenant Massie is wrong in not having his case submitted to a Naval court.

The whole island should be promptly put under martial law and the perpetrators of outrages upon women promptly tried by court martial and executed.

Until such drastic measures are taken, Hawaii is not a safe place for decent white women and not a very good place for self-respecting civilized men.

On the same day, *The Mirror*, a Hearst tabloid, editorially declared that the situation in Hawaii was the result of a Japanese plot to create anti-American hostility and incite the Japanese to an arrogant attitude against the American community.

In answer to the irresponsible scandal sheets, Lorrin P. Thurston, publisher of *The Honolulu Advertiser*, the local paper most in sympathy with the Navy point of view, stated: "No matter how disappointing it may be to those who want to believe otherwise, I make the following statements relative to conditions in Hawaii and full impartial investigation will prove them correct. There has been no rioting, racial or otherwise...The attempt to inject racial prejudice into the picture is deplorable and will lend nothing to the solution of the problem, which is not racial. There is no need for martial law."

Thurston then pointed out that the need was for remedying the inefficiency of the Police Department.

Another cool head in Hawaii was that of Riley Allen, editor of the *Honolulu Star-Bulletin*, whose editorial the day after Kahahawai's murder was a sobering antidote to the Hearst hysteria: "People who take the law into their own hands always make a mess of it," said the dean of Hawaiian newsmen. "Especially is this true when the misguided ones are from the ranks of those sworn to protect the Constitution and laws of our country." He called on his readers for self-control and preservation of dignity.

"We have before us a horrible example of what hysteria and lack of balance will do. That ought to be enough to arouse the sober judgment of every responsible citizen in support of orderly law."

A dozen leading wire services and newspapers throughout the country cabled Governor Judd for "five hundred words collect analyzing the situation and measures being taken." Conscientiously and immediately, the distraught Governor fulfilled every request, emphasizing that the situation was well in hand and as exactly as it would be in any other American community unaccustomed to crimes of violence.

The Governor was particularly disturbed by the grave lack of understanding of Hawaii in the continental United States. "Perhaps regarded as a semi-barbarian colony, it is a civilized Territory governed by substantially the same laws as any state," he cabled in a 500-word wire to the International News Service. "Shocked and grieved," he described Honolulu, "but meeting conditions with exemplary American calm."

It was the calm on the eve of eruption, and more than one newspaper on the mainland called for the impeachment of the rumbling Islands' governor.

Locally, fresh waves of criticism swept over the Navy as the top brass attempted to ride out the tempest of an antagonized citizenry. Admiral Stirling had immediately cabled Washington with a straight and accurate account of the killing, making no apologies. In response, Navy Secretary Charles Francis Adams ordered that Massie not be turned over to the court without his permission, but indicated that there would be no objection to a civilian trial for the three Navy men. Admiral Pratt's first reaction was to ask for a change of venue in the Massie trial, fearing a fair trial was not possible in Hawaii, "with its mixed jury of various racial origins," and favoring a transfer to a California court. The Navy also felt it would be unwise to try Lieutenant Massie in a city where there was "high feeling between lawless elements and the Navy."

The blasts from the big guns were returned with local fire: Pastor Galen Weaver demanded from his pulpit that Admiral Pratt be relieved, styling his statements "devilish." The preacher pointed out, "the Polynesian race is not on trial, nor is the white race or Navy on trial. It is a question of individual sin and personal crime, not a racial issue. There is a vast amount of dangerous propaganda of a racial nature in circulation which we need to counteract. Unfortunately...Admiral Pratt adds fuel to the flames."

In the lull of bewilderment that gripped Hawaii, the people of the sun-blessed islands asked themselves how such a misfortune could have befallen them. This soul-searching brought many answers:

"We have an education problem," said Dr. Dai Yen Chang, a Chinese dentist educated at Northwestern University. "Children going to public school grow away from their families. They are taught to want the very best...and they cannot buy. Whenever there is crime, there is much hysteria. Conditions are very much worse on the mainland...The races work together here."

The view of the Japanese was much the same, according to Dr. Harada, Yale graduate and history professor at the University of Hawaii. "I think it is unfortunate that the situation has received so much attention. There is a lack of law enforcement, especially by the police force. There has been no friction between civilian and military people until now."

The editor of the local Japanese newspaper agreed that exaggeration had spread on the mainland "chiefly through rather hysterical reports sent by local Navy people."

The more subtle complications of an island society of mixed heritage escaped the military and mainland critics. Honor killing did not meet with the Hawaiian sense of justice any more than missionary standards of sex relations met with Polynesian standards. Many dark-skinned boys went to prison with a profound resentment of the white man's injustice because they were convicted of something called criminal assault when all they were doing was loving a willing girl. This interpretation of the law in the context of custom had penetrated to some degree into the administration and was the cause for much of what outsiders called laxity of law enforcement.

The Hawaiian or Asian did not countenance rape or brutality any more than the Caucasian. Under the ancient Hawaiian law, a man found guilty of rape and sentenced by the kahunas, or priests, was taken to sea, cast adrift at sunset and forbidden to return.

Speaking for the Hawaiians, Reverend Akaika Akana of Kawaiahao Church, built under the direction of the Christian missionaries, defended his people: "I think the Hawaiians are absolutely capable of governing our situation...Hawaiian women have suffered at the hands of foreigners throughout history. Liquor was forced on them at the mouth of French cannon. And the attitude of the Hawaiians toward the whites has been one of unqualified friendship..."

Such brave sentiments of tolerance also served to blind Honoluluans to a basic cause of their problems: timidity and lack of executive ability, concluded John P. Marquand, who had been sent to Hawaii by the North American Newspaper Alliance: "A stranger here is confronted by the spectacle of a city bewildered by half-organized groups of street loafers tolerated by lenience and incompetence of officials."

Indeed, despite the open enmity in some quarters toward the military, it was the long-smoldering indignation of the Navy, due to the inefficiency of the civilian Police Department, the drawn-out method of conducting the rape investigation and trial—more slipshod than ship-shape—and the 97-hour indecision of the Ala Moana case jury that focused national and world attention on the social conditions of Honolulu and finally jolted its leading citizens and politicians into the necessary action for reform.

The most forceful local voice to demand a prompt clean-up was that of Walter F. Dillingham. "I consider the situation of Hawaii...more serious than at any time in all the years I have lived here," deplored the fifty-seven-year-old business tycoon. The Islands' most prominent haole, president of a dozen companies and on the boards of as many more, he had been a local "Rough Rider" in the overthrow of the monarchy, pioneered the Hawaiian railroad and dredged Pearl Harbor. He was also a staunch supporter of the Navy and had been a Harvard collagemate of former Assistant Secretary of the Navy, Franklin D. Roosevelt.

Now chairman of the trouble-shooting citizens' committee organized by the Chamber of Commerce the day after the lynching, Dillingham addressed its members: "You businessmen...pay 90 percent of the taxes and the time has come for you to demand a 90 percent voice in control of the government (otherwise) you must be prepared to go to Washington and obtain commission rule for Hawaii." There was enthusiastic applause from the committee.

Dillingham then met with the Governor, offering an ultimatum from the business community in the guise of a choice: either the Legislature convene at once and the amendment of police administration be given precedence over all other legislation, or the civic leaders of Hawaii would seek commission government. "We had a very satisfactory meeting," reported the kamaaina industrialist on leaving Judd's office. "We want the Governor to know he has the backing of the business community, but that immediate steps must be taken...I will submit to any kind of government rather than let conditions remain as they are today...We want action and if we can't get action here, we are prepared to take it to Washington and let Washington solve our problems."

Even as the two conferred, another meeting had taken place at the country's highest level.

SIXTEEN

Washington was already giving Hawaii's problem priority consideration. On the morning of January 12, 1932, the Cabinet Room of the
White House echoed with the shot fired in Manoa Valley four days
before, and the President of the United States pondered the matter with
his topmost advisors.

Earlier that day, the General Assembly of Kentucky, Lieutenant
Massie's home state, had wired the White House, urging the
Commander in Chief to use the military forces of the U.S. government
to wrest the defendants from Hawaiian soil. It was but one of many messages that had flooded the switchboards and in-baskets of the Executive
Offices as news of the alleged rapist's death at the hands of his avengers
stirred the heart of the nation and turned the spotlight of public attention on Hawaii's mounting turmoil. Sentiment in the States for the
most part was sympathy for the husband of the battered girl, but from
Hawaii came a counter cry of anguished injustice.

Now thoroughly apprised of both points of view, the gentle man of
moderation, President Herbert Hoover, entered the silent room in the
East Wing and faced his Cabinet secretaries. "Gentlemen, please be
seated," he said. "Our first business today will be the Hawaii matter."
He listened quietly while Secretary of Interior Wilbur and Secretary of
Navy Adams presented their versions of the situation. The Navy
Secretary reviewed his complete file of correspondence with the Naval
officials of the Fourteenth Naval District, adding that copies of the file
had been distributed to the pertinent committee chairmen in Congress
and to the Justice Department. Secretary Wilbur presented the dispatches from Governor Judd. This file was not yet complete, since the
Governor's preparation of a detailed report had been interrupted by the
most recent tragedy of the lynching.

It was to avoid just such lynchings and others acts of violence in the
largest military concentration of America—Hawaii—that the Navy felt
a change of venue for the forthcoming Massie trial had merit, pointed
out the Navy spokesman.

"I emphatically do not favor bringing the defendants to the mainland for trial," countered Secretary Wilbur, whose office was responsible
for the civilian government of the Territory.

Attorney General Mitchell commented that extradition was out of the question, since no law existed under which persons arrested for offenses committed in Honolulu could be tried on the mainland. It was to Mitchell that the President finally turned, ordering that the entire machinery of the Justice Department cooperate in compiling a report on "the Hawaii affair" at the earliest possible date, and that a special agent from the department make an investigation of the Islands, visiting officials, businessmen and all other authorities involved, in order that the situation be thoroughly comprehended and promptly remedied.

As a result of the Cabinet meeting, the Attorney General ordered Assistant Attorney General Seth Richardson, with five government sleuths, to Honolulu to conduct a sweeping investigation of crime and law enforcement in Hawaii and to make a report to the President and the Congress of the United States.

Meanwhile, Congress was reeling from the shock of the Navy cables and practically every agency in the federal government was directing attention to what Time Magazine called "Hawaii's raucous medley of race and sex."

On the Senate floor, Tennessee's incensed Senator Kenneth McKellar presented a resolution calling for a Congressional investigation. Senator Hiram Bingham of Connecticut, who had been born in Honolulu and whose ancestors had led the first missionary contingent in Hawaii, called for an early session of the Territorial Affairs Committee, of which he was chairman, to consider the McKellar resolution and spearhead the investigation. Senator Arthur Vandenberg, a member of the Territories Committee, backed the resolution with "a keen sense of responsibility in this matter," adding that during his recent visit to Honolulu, his observation was that Governor Judd was a conscientious and efficient official.

In the House, Representative James V. McClintic of Oklahoma, appointed chairman of the House Naval Affairs Subcommittee to investigate the Honolulu situation, rose on the floor of the House and made a blistering attack on the manner in which the trial of the defendants of the Ala Moana Assault Case was conducted.

"A study of Navy files indicates the situation is so serious that the committee will have to give much further study before making any recommendations."

On the afternoon of the Cabinet meeting, Admiral William V. Pratt, Chief of Naval Operations, was called to testify before the House Naval Affairs Committee. Cablegrams received just that morning from

Governor Judd in Hawaii denied the reports of widespread vice and violence and refuted certain aspects of the Navy files. The latest news
broadcasts mentioned that the Islands were calm enough for sailors to
enjoy a weekend of shore leave.

Navy Department officials confirmed the news dispatches, that
Naval personnel in Honolulu were indeed being granted shore liberty,
but only under strict supervision of blue-jacket patrols.

"The Department is gratified over this improvement in the situation," came the Navy answer, "but the general opinion is that unless the
President should order the fleet to Honolulu next month, the revised
schedule will be carried out, with the visiting ships boycotting that city."
The Department also revealed that Admiral Pratt had received several
messages from patriotic organizations and civilians in the country, congratulating him on his vigorous stand. He had also received some criticism from Hawaiian sources, but generally public reaction supported the
Navy.

It was not generalizations the committee was seeking, Chairman
Carl Vinson pointed out, but specifics, and the Chief of Naval
Operations was asked to present the facts of the Navy's stand.

"Yes, sir," said the dignified CNO, and as the hushed committee
room gave its undivided attention to his words, Admiral Pratt summa-
rized the Navy case. His statement was later made available to the press.

"The Department, about December 13, took official cognizance of reported disorders in Honolulu. On that day we
received a dispatch from Rear Admiral Stirling relative to an
attack on one of the five defendants at large on bail, following mistrial in the case of assault on a young Naval officer's wife.

Press reporters had indicated something amounting to internal
turmoil in Honolulu, and as a result the department asked Admiral
Stirling if he thought conditions warranted cancellation of the
fleet's visit to Honolulu in February. Admiral Stirling's reply indicated that efforts were being made, apparently successfully, to control the situation.

On December 17, further official reports from the Islands indicated that a tense feeling was developing. What appeared to be a
gang of hoodlums was insulting Naval personnel and their families,
and a message had been sent personnel at the submarine base at
Pearl Harbor further threatening to 'get' Naval women...

On December 21, I radioed Admiral Stirling that we were
fully in sympathy with efforts being made to clean up conditions in

the community, and directed him to cooperate in every way. I pointed out, however, that in view of the number of assault cases on white women, the apparent light punishment for several such cases and the mistrial in the case of Naval officers wife, the matter was one that demanded action rather than promises."

At one point in his presentation, the senior Naval officer was interrupted. A stir among the select listeners focused attention on a man who stood and addressed the Chief of Naval Operations. It was Delegate Victor Houston of Hawaii. A former Naval officer himself, Delegate Houston was the first person of Hawaiian ancestry to graduate from the Naval Academy, and he had enjoyed a successful career in the Navy. He had been appointed to Annapolis as an outstanding student and had many friends in the Navy and in Congress.

"Admiral, would you be certain to include in these papers all evidence that there have been forty similar rape cases? This figure was given by the Navy and we are distressed beyond measure by the disturbance it has created. We are determined that there shall be no exaggeration and a calm judicial approach to the problem be taken."

"The figure 'forty' appeared in a report from Admiral Stirling, Commandant at Hawaii," answered Admiral Pratt, "as well as in newspaper dispatches from Honolulu."

"But Admiral, this case is unprecedented so far as we know. There has been only one other case of attempted rape on a white women." The Hawaiian Delegate resumed his seat, his expression one of deep concern.

Admiral Pratt stuck to his guns. This time the Navy's salvos were being fired past the United States Congress:

"I advised Admiral Stirling to point out to the Governor that it would be unsafe to send the fleet there unless police and hoodlum conditions were thoroughly cleaned up, for we believed that American men would not stand for violation of their women under any circumstances, and had taken the law into their own hands repeatedly in the past in such cases where justice was not meted out.

Admiral Stirling informed us on January 4 that another rape of a white women had been committed, that the Islands were aroused and that although a conference had been held by the Governor to establish corrective measures, little had been done...

On January 6, I advised Admiral Stirling that until the situation was cleaned up, of which the Ala Moana case was but one incident, the entire fleet schedule would be changed, not only for the present but also in the future, as no gain in business to Honolulu could offset the grave dangers existing in Honolulu...

On January 8, we received word from Gov. Judd that the reports of the Honolulu situation were exaggerated and that efforts to clear the situation were meeting with success.

On the same date we were advised by Admiral Stirling that Kahahawai had been killed. This canceled the fleet's visit to Honolulu automatically and caused the entire matter to be made public; for we knew that with the fleet there and feeling undoubtedly running high, it would be unsafe not only for the Islands but also for our men to grant liberty at Oahu."

The Admiral leaned back in his chair and thanked the committee for the opportunity to discuss the matter with members of Congress.

It was an impressive and precise presentation of the facts as the Navy saw them.

When Secretary Wilbur was asked his reaction to the Navy spokesman's testimony, he replied to the press that he placed his faith in a Justice Department investigation to reveal the true facts.

"Are you going to take any action in connection with the Navy order keeping Lieutenant Massie in Navy custody?" asked the reporter.

"I have no intention of tying to interfere with the running of other departments," answered the Cabinet member. "I have enough trouble with my own."

In Hawaii, the reaction to the crucial day in Washington was one of relief. When told that the U.S. Senate had adopted a resolution calling upon the Attorney General to conduct an investigation and the President had ordered the facilities of the Justice Department be made available, Governor Judd brightened for the first time in many bleak days and wired Delegate Houston: "If this is correct, I urge the Attorney General immediately send an investigator, as it is most important to all concerned that the true facts be known."

Lieutenant Massie, too, reacted positively. When approached at the receiving ship by his lawyers, he announced that he had definitely decided to waive any rights to be tried by the Navy or in the federal courts and that he was willing to be judged by a jury of Honolulu citizens in the territorial courts, the same courts in which the Ala Moana assault case defendants were tried.

"I notified my superior this morning not to request a change of venue," said the slender Naval officer, standing pale and calm at the rail of the U.S.S. *Alton*.

Below decks, the receiving ship had been remodeled overnight to accommodate its latest and strangest passenger complement. The rigid comfort of the wardroom where once Naval officers played cards was now a restful prison. Tight-lipped Marines guarded the gangplank in place of the sideboys who years before had piped aboard visiting dignitaries when the Alton was the sleek cruiser Chicago and knew the surge of deep water beneath her keel. The once crack ship had long since gone aground on the mudflats of Pearl Harbor where she was stripped to a hulk and refurbished as a bachelor officers quarters. Although she would never again cut the ocean swells, the *Alton* was shipshape, with her brightwork polished and her decks as trim and trig as the proudest battleship.

Electric fans, call bells and all the conveniences of hotel service, including meals from the officers' mess, were available to the defendants, who were being held incommunicado by Captain Wortman. Off the quiet wardroom was a small cabin with a single bunk and adjoining bath for Mrs. Fortescue. Beyond was Tommy Massie's cabin, while the crew's quarters accommodated Jones and Lord. In the passageway, pictures had been hung on the bulkheads, one of them an original of a cartoon that appeared in the early humor magazine *Life* of an elderly man in a rocking chair listening to strains of Hawaiian music on a phonograph with eyes closed and visions of hula girls dancing in his head while his wife glowered at the smile on his face. The view from the hastily curtained portholes looked out on blue Hawaiian sky and tranquil hills. Music, books, cards were available—everything but freedom.

Within a few days after Kahahawai's death, the entire topside of the Alton was covered with flowers. Hundreds of letters and radiograms poured into the ship, addressed to Mrs. Fortescue, and bouquets by the truckload were delivered to the gangplank. Soon the harried Marine guards had to turn away the florist wagons, announcing that it was impossible to receive any more flowers: every available inch of space was fragrantly filled to capacity. In rooms, corridors, and even the basins of heads, were great banks of blossoms. The bloom-bedecked ship, heretofore an outcast of the fleet, resembled a float in the Rose Bowl Parade.

Included in the radiograms were messages from every state in the union. Friends in Hawaii sent baskets of fruit. No sailing of the Matson liner *Malolo* could match the homely grey cruiser, high and dry on the mudflats of Pearl Harbor, as a recipient of colorful aloha. The scene lacked only champagne. Messages of sympathy and encouragement flooded the transoceanic wires. The signatures on the cables were a roster of *Who's Who* and the *Social Register*.

From the Main Line, Philadelphia, wrote Mrs. Eva Stotesbury: "Dear Gracie, this brings you my love and heartiest sympathy and also my admiration and respect for your magnificent courage in this overwhelming misfortune. I would have done the same thing in your place and so would any other good mother. If there is anything I can do for you or yours, count on me."

Mrs. Breckenridge Long of Baltimore wired "Love and Sympathy."

Turner Johnson McKenzie, of the exclusive capital suburb of Chevy Chase, cabled: "Read of your trouble this morning. My father, Representative Johnson, is doing all he can at the Navy Department. Is there anything else I can do? If so please cable immediately. Will be glad to help in any way."

From the New York newspaper publisher Joseph Patterson came "Admiration and sympathy." And from New York's Four Hundred, Mrs. Cornelius Bliss sent "Dearest love. Thinking of you constantly."

Katherine McCook Knox of Washington, daughter-in-law of Philander K. Knox, statesman, asked Grace Fortescue to "Watch the sun break through the clouds. Browne and I send our love."

The owner of the Hope Diamond, Mrs. Edward McLean, a neighbor of the Fortescues in Washington, wired: "Dearest Grace, you have all my love and sympathy. If there is anything in the world I can do, don't hesitate to call on me. Devoted love."

Gilbert and Elsie Grosvenor, of the National Geographic Society and the exclusive inner circle of Washington society, assured their cousin of "Dearest love and sympathy. How can we help?" Prominent magazine illustrator May Wilson Preston, of Manhattan, sent word that "Love and sympathy is very strong here. Keep your courage up, dear."

From Honolulu, one of the most sympathetic messages was signed "A Japanese Mother," and from a hospital bed in New York, Granville Fortescue, who had collapsed in the Army and Navy Club at word of the tragedy and been rushed to a midtown hospital, where it was discovered he was suffering from pneumonia, sent a cable assuring his wife of his faith in her actions and enjoining her to keep her chin up.

It was more than Grace Fortescue could bear. When Thalia boarded the vessel, bringing yet another bouquet, the mother of the assaulted girl at last gave way to her strained emotions. "She was unable to carry on a long conversation without breaking into tears," reported her attorney. No one was permitted to board the ship without a personal pass from Admiral Stirling. A nervous breakdown confined Mrs. Fortescue to her bunk.

The mother of the murdered boy silently controlled her grief. At the funeral of Joseph Kahahawai, the father sadly said, "He was always a good boy, a boy who was well-liked by everyone...I asked Joseph to take an oath before God and he said 'Daddy, I swear before God that I never did anything wrong."

Rivaling the receiving ship in its profusion of flowers, the funeral was the largest ever held for a Hawaiian not of royal blood. A crowd of two thousand people overflowed the Catholic Cathedral of Our Lady of Peace. Candles flickered on the plain coffin and the vaulted nave was suffused with a sigh so subtle it no more than thickened the air as the mourners refrained from the ancient funeral chants reserved only for their alii. The Polynesians have a predilection for funerals; the ceremony of death is a source of wonder as great as the celebration of birth for a people whose lives for hundreds of generations were intimately involved with the ebb and flow of nature. A steady stream of softly weeping Hawaiians passed the bier, where the young man lay with an ilima lei around his neck.

His four companions of the Ala Moana case, released for twenty minutes from the custody of the jail, stood and gazed into the open casket. None of them uttered a word. Relatives kept an all-night vigil and Joe's cousin, Eddie Ulii, brought a wreath of fresh maile from the mountains. People of all races viewed the body until Requiem Mass on Sunday morning, when at 11 o'clock, many of them followed on foot the funeral procession as it wound through the city to Puea Cemetery on School Street. The hearse was preceded by honorary pall bearers, the Reverend Robert Ahuna and two motorcycle policemen, while immediately behind was a limousine carrying the family.

The cortege of cars circled the block of the burial ground. In one corner, the graves were well-kept and graced by trim stones, but for the most part the cemetery bore the pathetic vestiges of lives which had finally lost the struggle with survival and been pursued even in death by the anonymity of poverty. Weeds filled the sunken plots under toppled, home-made markers. On a few crumbling concrete crosses, names and dates had been crudely scratched; other graves were distinguished by only a circle of lava rocks. On a hillside of high grass, beneath tangled keawe trees, the coffin of Joe Kahahawai was lowered into the raw red earth as the multitude sang Ka Lani Kui Home, Hawaiian for "Angel's Welcome."

The priest opened the Bible and read from Genesis:

"And Cain talked with Abel his brother: and it came to pass when they were in the field, that Cain rose up against Abel, and slew him.

And the Lord said unto Cain, Where is Abel, thy brother? And he said I know not: Am I my brother's keeper?

And he said, What hast thou done? The voice of thy brother's blood crieth unto me from the ground."

Reverend Ahuna, speaking in Hawaiian, compared the vengeful killing of Kahahawai with that of Abel. Then he recalled the youth's athletic glory and his compliance with the law in reporting to the Judiciary Building, "Ignorant of the act that would cost him his life." He looked out over the solemn throng and continued in English, "I am happy to see this demonstration of sympathy for the parents of him who lies here, who was the son not only of his parents, but of Hawaii and the Hawaiians." The brief burial service was followed by hymns and the singing of the Hawaiian anthem, Hawaii Pono'i.

As the silent crowd dispersed, wading through the grass and brushing aside brambles, the strains of Aloha Oe filled the cemetery.

Kahahawai had been in his grave only a week when the special session of the Legislature opened at Iolani Palace on January 18, and the Police Chief Bill and Public Prosecution Measure were laid before the local lawmakers. These and other bills calling for changes in law enforcement were introduced in both houses. Within two days, the Police Bill passed the House twenty-five to four and was sent immediately to the Senate, where it passed the first reading with only one senator voting against it.

On January 22, Governor Judd signed a bill creating a Police Commission of five prominent business leaders. Six days later, Charles W. Weeber was appointed the first Chief of Police in Hawaii by unanimous vote of the newly organized Police Commission. Weeber had an outstanding record as a non-commissioned officer in the Army until he resigned to become the private secretary of Walter F. Dillingham, a job he had held for ten years. His first act of business as Police Chief was to order a thorough housecleaning of his department. The long overdue

Hawaiian police reforms were underway. It had taken a world-shaking pair of crimes—an alleged rape and a murder—to launch them.

By the last of January, Grace Fortescue had regained her composure and the four defendants appeared before the judge for arraignment. Hours before they were scheduled to arrive at 9 o'clock, the courtroom had been filled with spectators, the majority of whom were Hawaiian men and women. Their dark faces, somber and large-featured, were framed in wide-brimmed woven lauhala hats bedecked with blossoms and feather leis. Mushrooming in this floral field were the close-fitting chic clothes of society women who had turned out en masse as representatives of the Citizens' Organization for Good Government. A detachment of twelve uniformed guards policed the overflow of crowds in the corridors, through which often passed the "blues" of Navy enlisted men or the "whites" of line and petty officers.

Promptly at nine, Mrs. Fortescue entered the courtroom, followed by Lieutenant Massie. "Spectators saw a rather frail, middle-aged women to whom poise seemed as natural as breathing," wrote a witness to the scene. "She made her way through the ranks of uniformed police guards, stepping lightly, confidently. Her attire was subdued and smart. A wine-colored tri-corn felt hat, decorated with a bit of bright feathers matched in color a tailored knitted suit. Mrs. Fortescue was pale, her grey hair showed a little beneath the snug hat. Her eyes were clear and blue; her mouth was lipsticked...Smart details of her apparel were reflected in harmonizing shoes and gloves, yellowish-tan in color."

During the reading of the indictment on the charges of second degree murder by Barry S. Ulrich, Special Deputy Attorney General for the prosecution, Grace Fortescue calmly faced the court. Sitting next to her, Tommy Massie slumped in his chair and did not take a direct interest in the proceedings. He was wearing a light grey civilian suit and seemed more unhappy than disturbed as he gazed at the floor. The two enlisted men wore conventional blue suits and listened alertly to the arraignment, reaching out with curiosity to accept their copies of the indictment distributed to the defendants by the court clerk. Clean-shaven and crisp in their freshly creased blouses, they seemed typical carefree sailors. Edward J. Lord had been born in Milford, Massachusetts, twenty-one years before, and gone to sea as a teenager, having left school after the seventh grade. Blue-eyed, with light brown hair and a stocky physique, he was well-developed for his five-feet-five inch frame which was all muscle, the result of training as a boxer. He was still unmarried, as was Albert Orin Jones, also a native of Massachusetts and also well known in boxing circles. Jones held a second's license, but at twenty-seven, he was a veteran drinker and his short, thick body carried more flesh than his companion's. Both young seamen managed to maintain a spirit of levity despite the seriousness of the situation in which they found themselves.

The grand jury had voted against a true bill of first degree murder in their first report to Judge A.M. Cristy; no bill of kidnapping was returned. The Judge then charged the jury to consider second degree murder and a true bill was rendered. Even this charge raised the ire of Admiral Stirling.

"The grand jury, composed of many men of the white race, showed strong reluctance to bring in a true bill against the killers of Kahahawai," stormed the Commandant, not disclosing his source of information. "The Jury's first report to the Judge on the charge of first degree murder was twelve to nine for no true bill. Judge Cristy released one juror who had been appointed a police commissioner and who had voted for no true bill. The next vote was eleven to nine for no true bill. Twelve agreeing votes are necessary for any action. If the Judge had accepted the first vote, which would have been legal, there would have been no trial...Having been brought home the absolute necessity of obtaining the most experienced legal talent, I advised the defendants in the Kahahawai case to obtain the best lawyers possible."

After the reading of the indictment, Ulrich brought up the question of bail. "The government wants to make this a fair and orderly procedure," said the prosecution attorney, anxious at the outset to avoid the calamitous criticism of the Ala Moana trial. "We want to give the defendants every advantage to prepare their defense. The bail is already low, but in that regard I want to refer to another case, which has no connection whatsoever except insofar as the penalty is concerned. I refer to the Ala Moana Assault Case: the charge was rape, this is second degree murder—the maximum penalty is life imprisonment in both cases."

The prosecutor pointed out that in the Ala Moana case the bail at the outset was $10,000 for each defendant but was lowered to $2,000 with the understanding the defendants report daily to an authorized officer of the court. "The Territory is willing to consent to an identical arrangement in this case in the event that the same watch and guard is kept over the defendants."

It was suggested that if Admiral Stirling could get the permission of the Naval authorities in Washington for such an arrangement, the defendants could remain in Captain Wortman's custody on a lower bail. The Commandant immediately left for his headquarters and cabled the Navy Department for instructions. This delay meant that Mrs. Fortescue, Lieutenant Massie and the two enlisted men would spend a night in the Honolulu jail awaiting bond.

As word of the murder indictment reached the Capitol, Tennessee's Senator Kenneth McKellar arose in the Senate chamber and called for the immediate impeachment of Judge Cristy. His fellow senators kept cooler heads. Assistant Attorney General Seth Richardson was already preparing to leave for Honolulu, and the majority of the Senate wished to withhold further action until an unbiased appraisal of Hawaii arrived from the Justice Department.

Never had the Honolulu jail enjoyed the pleasure of such distinguished company as the overnight guest Grace Fortescue. The four walls of the bare cell became the salon of an embassy as Mrs. Fortescue removed her gloves, folded them neatly on a wooden table beside the copy of the *Woman's Home Companion* she had brought with her, and extended her hand to the flabbergasted police matron.

"Won't you join me for coffee," said the prisoner graciously, settling onto the iron cot that was the only other piece of furniture in the cell.

The matron was delighted, ordering coffee from the guard, and sitting next to Mrs. Fortescue. As the two of them chatted amiably, the prisoner suggested a game of cribbage, and again the matron accepted with a dignified thank-you befitting the invitation. The cook himself brought the coffee and Mrs. Fortescue enjoined him to stay awhile, probing him with courteous interest about his experience as a doughboy in France during the War. It was a convivial evening and time passed quickly.

The next morning the prisoners agreed to a press conference, arranged by their attorney, and met the newsmen in the bare receiving cell where sunlight filtered through the iron bars and fell on a littered table filled with empty coffee mugs, a metal pitcher, magazines and Mrs. Fortescue's chic leather overnight bag. She greeted the pressmen with a smile and a handshake.

"Oh, I'm glad that bond has been arranged," she said. "I shall be very happy to get back to the Navy Yard. Of course I don't know where I shall live there, but I shall do whatever Admiral Stirling tells me to do." She seemed eager to share with others her experience of lodging for the night in the city jail.

"I've never been fined before, not even for a parking ticket," she continued. "The first part of the evening was perfectly fine," her smile faded briefly into a charming frown as she added, "but I can't say that I had an altogether good night. Sheriff Gleason, the matrons and the guards were more than courteous and gave me every facility the jail affords. But you can imagine trying to sleep in a place where intoxicated persons are singing ribald songs, where drunks are swearing and cursing and the pandemonium of a place where such people are brought."

A murmur of sympathy welled from the press corps.

"I shall never understand why we were not permitted to return to the custody of the Navy, where we were brought by the court's previous order, instead of being sent to the city jail," she said with a small sigh, picking up the *Woman's Home Companion* in her gloved hand and tucking it under her arm.

As the prisoners prepared to leave, Tommy Massie offered cigarettes to their visitors. "I found an old shipmate here," he told them. "The cook. He made the best coffee for us that I've tasted in a long time."

"And the other cook," his mother-in-law added, "was gassed in the war. My husband, Major Fortescue, was gassed also, so we talked about that. And I had a pleasant game of cribbage with the matron, but she beat me!"

The jail matron registered a beaming smile.

"Everybody's been very kind," Mrs. Fortescue went on. "We appreciate greatly the attitude of the newspapers toward us. My friends in the East have sent clippings."

Just as she was entering the sheriff's automobile to go to Pearl Harbor, Mrs. Fortescue was asked to pose for news photographs.

"Would you mind waiting just a moment?" she asked the driver, Duke Kahanamoku of the Sheriff's Office. The tall handsome Hawaiian nodded his consent, as his charge stepped from the machine and called her son-in-law to her side.

"Now, where do you want us to stand?" she asked the obliging press. "Just a minute, where are the boys?"

Jones and Lord, who had already entered the radio patrol car, were hailed and all four of the defendants posed for a group photo. When the photographers were satisfied with the number of pictures, Mrs. Fortescue and her companions reentered the cars and with a wave from the window, departed for the Navy Yard.

"She was the personification of elderly charm," reported one of the smitten newsmen.

The extent to which Grace Fortescue had captured the imagination of the press was revealed in a boxed article that appeared on the front page of the Advertiser when she attempted to call her mother in Rome:

"Mother!"

It is the cry of the ages—the cry for help, broken by a sob.

All of us have used it—and Mrs. Fortescue whose motherhood has been trampled upon and desecrated in the person of her beautiful young, defenseless daughter, turns to her mother in her hour of ordeal. Across continents and oceans she would hear the voice of comfort.

"Daughter, I understand—my heart is with you!"

John A. Balch, president of the Mutual Telephone Company is working with Walter Gifford, president of American Telephone and Telegraph Company, a family friend in the East, and doing all in his power to bring this modern miracle about and has promised to make connections half way around the world so Mrs. Fortescue can hear her mother's voice.

It is fitting for the niece of Alexander Graham Bell. Could it have ever crossed his mind that two near and dear to him so widely separated, would find solace by means of his genius? But in the age of wonders it has come to pass.

Even Mrs. Fortescue's fortitude, the traditional bravery of Southern women, that has carried her through weeks of long-drawn agony at the trial of her daughter's ravishers, failed briefly when she received word her husband had collapsed. It was then the wish to hear her mother's voice became overpowering...With her husband fighting for each breath, herself and her son-in-law in a perilous position, her married daughter marked for life...where else could she turn for comfort?

So the telephone has come into its own.

Another call to another mother enabled Mrs. William S. Massie, in Winchester, Kentucky, to hear her son's voice for the first time in two years. She told reporters in Tommy's hometown that she was "so pleased to hear his voice that we did not talk about the case."

"Then what did he say?" asked a reporter.

"He said, 'Mother, I think of you all the time. Please do not worry.'"

SEVENTEEN

As the U.S.S. *Alton* and its crew of prisoners rode calmly in drydock, a fever of activity spread among Honolulu's judiciary circles. The cast for the second act of Hawaii's greatest legal drama was assembling. This time the spectators would include the entire nation. The eyes of the world were on the small courtroom in Honolulu. News items describing the troubles of Hawaii appeared in papers as far away as Budapest, Hungary. The mainland press sent out its front-line reporters, including William H. Ewing of the Associated Press, Russell Owen of the New York Times and Philip Kinsley of the Chicago Tribune, while in the heart of America, Don Blanding, poet laureate of the Islands, was defending the name of Hawaii Nei to packed houses in Mason City, Iowa, and points midwest.

The first leading player to be announced was newly-appointed public prosecutor John Carlton Kelley, forty-seven, an aggressive and astute trial lawyer with the reputation of being the most brilliant criminal analyst in the Honolulu bar. He was a native of Montana and had been born in that rugged part of the country that is the heart of America's great copper mines, a bleak, challenging land that early separates the men from the boys. Both John and his brother, Cornelius, had thrived on the rough outdoor life and enjoyed the jobs they held part-time at the mines during their school days. While Cornelius continued with the Anaconda Copper Company, eventually moving to New York and rising to its presidency, young John chose the law as his profession, graduating with distinction from the University of Michigan Law School. But the wild hills and wide-open spaces were in the blood of the young attorney and he grew restless in the confinement of a law office; his spirit rebelled at the cage of weighted bookshelves. Hopping freighters and taking odd jobs, he traveled for years in China, Fiji and Australia, arriving in Hilo, Hawaii, in the early 'twenties. He fell in love with the lambent land and its easy way of life, and was able to take up successfully his truncated career as a lawyer. He moved to Honolulu after a year, and in 1923 became Deputy City and County Attorney under William H. Heen, who was then City Attorney, an office to which Kelley aspired in 1926. His approach to politics was the same as that he applied to life and the law: honest, head-on confrontation. His first campaign speech jarred Honolulu voters with its bluntness:

To you honorable citizens, I present this issue: is a political brand or meritorious service the primary qualification justifying the individual to seek and hold public office? I have no promises to make. I have no undated resignations to tender. To handle the legal affairs of the City and County efficiently and to suppress vice vigorously will be my aim. My record is open to the public. My hat is in the ring.

He did not get elected. However, during the reforms following Kahahawai's lynching, the legal department was divided into civil and criminal branches, and John Kelley was appointed the first Public Prosecutor in charge of criminal matters. Governor Judd signed the Public Prosecutor Bill on February 9, 1932, and approved Kelley's appointment the next day. "The first task is to eliminate gangs and gangsterism," the new prosecutor told the press at City Hall.

An enterprising reporter followed Kelley to his office at police headquarters, and jotted down impressions of the man who would become known as "Fighting Jack."

"Handsome, blue-eyed Irishman. Chubby faced, kind of pink complexion found on baby talcum powder ads. Grey temples, receding hairline. Guards his girth carefully. Diets on milk for lunch. Keen legal mind. Hands of a surgeon. Gives hands excellent care, keeping nail file in a drawer for that purpose. Proud that once worked with his hands— meat packer in Australian slaughter house. Even became member of local meat packers union.

"Don't enter his office and start pounding his desk demanding this or that. Won't get you anywhere with him. In addition to quick wit and ready sympathy, has trigger temper. Likes cats and won't admit it even to the cat. Roughhouses his own pet cat to cover up fondness for it and gets scratched for his pains. Modest. Few aware he's brother of Cornelius Kelley, copper tycoon. Never mentions it. Can get very hard-boiled and frequently does but not for long. With characteristic Hibernian compassion, had been known to dab eyes at movies when hero getting the worst of it."

John C. Kelley also had a penchant for white linen suits, bright ties, good whiskey and the truth.

The last week in February, it was revealed that negotiations had been entered into with Clarence Darrow, the greatest criminal lawyer in America, by friends of the defendants. From the minute he decided to make his services available, the legendary Darrow began playing the leading role with the deft timing and honed empathy of the true professional of courtroom dramas. His legend was undimmed by years. Although a septuagenarian. "his eyes are sharp and keen," said a local announcement of the offer to Darrow. "It is said that in court he usually sits motionless with his eyes closed while a witness is being examined; he takes no notes but ten minutes later in cross-examining, he can accurately recall every statement of the witness, and is then anything but motionless with rapid fire questions and withering manner."

With this notorious technique he had defended the McNamara brothers, accused of bombing the Los Angeles Times in 1911, and by his own admitted skill spared the lives of the thrill-killers Loeb and Leopold in Chicago in 1924. A year later it was the great mouthpiece who championed the cause of evolution in the famous Scopes trial in Tennessee, his opponent having been the oratorical fundamentalist William Jennings Bryan. Darrow's brilliant reputation was not tarnished by the fact that he lost.

For eight days the dean of defense lawyers weighed the rewards of retirement against those of a final fling in the legal spotlight. The courtroom won. Even Prosecutor Kelley was pleased, stating he would welcome the opportunity to meet Clarence Darrow on the battlefield of the local Circuit Court. "It will be an interesting experience," he said, foreshadowing the restraint which would be his foil against the fustian Darrow.

With his seventy-fifth birthday less than a month away, Darrow said he felt "topnotch" as he walked down the gangplank of the Matson liner *Malolo* the morning of March 24, 1932. Brisk tradewinds further ruffled his ever-tousled dark hair, lightly streaked with grey. His blue eyes sparkled and he gave the appearance of a rumpled retired businessman unaware of the weighty work that lay ahead of him, with the freedom of four people resting on his massive shoulders, now burdened with a fragrant yoke of leis.

"Let's get rid of these jingle bells," he said, laughingly trying to disentangle the ropes of flowers. His objections were promptly overruled. "I look like a decorated hat rack," said Darrow, waving at admirers who thronged the ramp.

Meeting him as he landed were Commander Bates, Captain J. D. Wilson, Commander of Pearl Harbor Navy Yard, on hand as Admiral Stirling's representative, Mrs. Fortescue's brother and sister, who had arrived a few weeks earlier from New York, and local lawyers Frank

Thompson and Montgomery Winn, defense assistants. With Darrow were his pretty, vivacious wife and George S. Leisure, a brilliant young Wall Street attorney who had been chief of the U. S. criminal division of New York and was now a partner of William Donovan. Lieutenant L.C.H. Johnson, assigned by the Navy to aid in the defense, also accompanied the Darrows from San Francisco.

"Why did your husband take this case?" a reporter asked Mrs. Darrow.

"You ask him and then tell me," she answered with a bright smile. "I'd like to know myself."

The embattled old warhorse was delighted to give his reasons for accepting the Massie case. "I retired four years ago but here I am back in harness because this case gives me the opportunity to see Hawaii, the plight of the defendants appealed to my sympathy, and friends of the defendants urged that I take the case. Incidentally, the fee I shall receive was another incentive."

There were rumors that the retired legal hero had come on lean times with the Depression. In New York, the son of Mrs. Stotesbury had sent out letters to wealthy friends of Mrs. Fortescue, asking their help in raising the $30,000 anticipated in legal costs. Already, sailors at the shipyard had been assessed for a $7,000 fund to defend the two enlisted men. The stars of the legal drama would required a much higher fee.

An hour after he disembarked, Darrow conferred with local attorneys for the defense, and by 2 o'clock he was able to announce that the line of defense had been planned. What the defense would be, Darrow declined to say, but it had been indicated that a plea of "alarm clock" insanity would be its basis. Was this true? reporters asked.

"No comment," said the amiable attorney, showing his willingness to cooperate with newsmen by agreeing to a press conference that afternoon. Reporters trailed him from the Alexander Young Hotel to the downtown offices of Montgomery Winn, where he settled behind a desk and gazed with twinkling, humorous eyes at the roomful of respectful correspondents. He didn't let them down; the venerable court veteran was as outspoken on other subjects as he was silent on the honor killing of Kahahawai.

"What do you think of our race question?" asked a reporter.

"I didn't know there was a race question. I doubt if anybody really knows what a race is," said Darrow.

"Do you think there is an increase in lawlessness throughout the world?"

"People don't pay much attention to laws when they are hungry," said the great humanitarian, mellowing to his favorite subject. "To keep

any animal quiet, you've got to feed him. We've got too many laws anyway. Too much law and too little order. People haven't time to obey all
of them."

"Any comments on prohibition?"

"I think it will be changed—probably by repeal of the Volstead
Act."

"What will the effect of that be?"

"It will make it much easier to get a drink," said the smiling sage,
prompting a laugh from his interrogators. The smile disappeared with
the next question; his shoulders hunched, his head thrust forward and a
flash of fire extinguished the twinkle in his blue eyes when he was asked
his opinion of the death penalty for rape.

"Only damned fools would pass that sort of law any place in the
world. It simply makes it necessary to murder the woman to prevent her
giving testimony in court. and promotes blackmail and persecution.
Yes, they have those laws in the South, but I don't remember any white
man being executed under them. I have an abiding conviction that a
law should apply equally to all persons!!"

A spontaneous burst of applause broke from the press corps, as
reporters commented among themselves on the likelihood of fireworks
at the coming trial.

"Now, gentlemen, if you'll excuse me, I'd like to see my clients," said
the famous trial lawyer, scarcely pausing at the end of his 5,000-mile trip
before plunging into preparation of his case. A car was waiting to take
him to Pearl Harbor. "I can't work day and night—although I have
done that. But we are as anxious as anyone for a speedy trial, and while
we will require some time to prepare our defense, we want no more time
than necessary."

"What are your client's chances?"

"You never see a good looking woman convicted of murder or
manslaughter—or refused alimony," cracked Darrow, avoiding a reply
when asked whether Mrs. Fortescue answered that description.

"One more question, sir," pressed a reporter as Darrow hauled himself from his chair and nodded at the young newsman. "Have you any
other plans while you're in Hawaii?"

"As a matter of fact I do, son," was the answer. "I may become a
beach boy."

The city settled down. Somehow Darrow's relaxed presence was a
reassurance. The positive action of the Legislature helped restore com-

munity equilibrium, and the knowledge that a trouble-shooting team from the Justice Department was at large in the Islands prompted Honolulu to assume its best behavior. The citizens lapsed again into the easy pace of the tropics, and Shore Patrol guards were withdrawn from their stations among the officers' homes in Manoa Valley. The day after the murder, Thalia and her sister had left the valley and moved in with Navy friends quartered at Pearl Harbor, where she was able to see Tommy and her mother every day. Only once had she returned to Manoa: to pick up the family dog, Chris, which neighbors had found in the rumble seat of the Massie roadster after the excitement had subsided and sheltered until his mistress's return. Except for the grim irony of the circumstances that brought them together, the family of Mrs. Fortescue was enjoying an almost pleasant reunion, their first since Thalia and Tommy's wedding. The prisoners were permitted to leave the Alton for an evening of bridge or an informal dinner party with friends in the Navy Yard. Although they saw no people outside the Navy crowd except their attorneys, and talks for publication had been taboo, Mrs. Fortescue and Lieutenant Massie granted an exclusive first interview to Russell Owen, of *The New York Times*, aboard the prison ship.

"They seemed glad to talk," he reported, "and there were few reservations in their manner or conversation except as to the actual manner in which Kahahawai was killed. Their attitude could not be described as one of indifference, but it was certainly not marked by trepidation or a feeling that they had done something for which they should be ashamed or sorry. The seriousness of their predicament apparently affects them scarcely at all. Mrs. Fortescue's chief concern seems to be that the affair was bungled."

She was waiting for the correspondent in the Navy Yard, wearing a tailored cherry-red suit and a smart cloche of the same color. Extending her hand cordially, she guided the newsman over the boardwalk which bridged the mudflats to the dismantled old warship and led the way to her quarters in the stern.

"Would you like some coffee?" she asked, offering her guest a chair.

"I would indeed," said the charmed reporter as his hostess ordered a steward to bring refreshments. She then turned to Mr. Owen with a frank smile and awaited his questions. "How do you feel?" he asked in a tone of sincere sympathy.

"How do I feel?" she repeated, the inflection in her voice betraying her Southern upbringing. "Mostly that I am glad it is all out in the open. Those days when my daughter's name was suppressed, when it was not known whether or not she had been the victim of an assault, and when people looked curiously at us and wondered—those were worse than these last few weeks. There is a great sense of relief."

The coffee arrived and with the perfect poise of a social doyenne, Mrs. Fortescue poured a cup for Mr. Owen, asking him his preference for cream and sugar. She then poured her own, dismissed the steward and, leaning her arms on the table while gracefully cupping her chin on her clasped hands, continued the conversation.

"Thalia had a bruise on her cheek, you know, and people asked questions about it and it was awful. Now that the worst is over, I feel more at ease than I have in months," she admitted with an expression of lively candor, settling back on the bunk without compromising her perfect posture. "I have slept better since Friday, the eighth—the day of the murder—than for a long time."

"You certainly appear to be standing it well," complimented Mr. Owen.

"My mind is at peace," replied Mrs. Fortescue. "I am satisfied, and I am not worrying." She smiled again at the reporter and offered him more coffee.

At this point Tommy Massie entered the wardroom in his shirt sleeves, and his mother-in-law apologized for his informality, explaining that he had not been feeling well and was resting. Tommy also smiled, extended his hand at being introduced, and seemed perfectly at ease. "I've been enjoying my sleep too," he added, having overheard the last of the conversation. He joined them for a cup of coffee.

"If you don't mind my asking, I'd like to know your immediate reaction when you were overtaken in the car," continued the correspondent, turning again to Mrs. Fortescue. "How did you feel and what were your mental experiences?"

"I think the strongest impression was being dumbfounded that they wanted to know my name, that I could not keep it quiet," she said. "They had not mentioned my daughter's name in the first case, and I could not understand why they wanted mine or why it was made public."

"But did you not realize the danger of driving through city streets in that way?" asked the wondering newsman. After all, he mused silently, the car was carrying the body of a murdered man.

"No," said his hostess. "I did not know that they knew the car number, and it never occurred to me that we would be followed. Now, of course, I realize we bungled dreadfully, although at the time I thought we were being careful. I can see now that we were not. I made the mistake of pulling the shade down in the car."

Russell Owen put down his cup and looked at Mrs. Fortescue in amazement. His incredulity was tinged with marvel.

"I should not have done that," she went on. "We did not know we were being fired at. We heard something but thought it was the car back-firing or a tire blowing out. I was dumbfounded when we were stopped."

She paused briefly, aware of the reporter's own bewilderment, then leaned toward him sympathetically. "You must realize we had been under a terrible strain; as we had all suffered as I did not know it was possible to suffer. There had been terrible slanders, and everything had been done to blacken my daughter's reputation."

For the first time the correspondent heard bitterness in the cultured voice, as Thalia's mother indignantly described the "mishandling" of the assault case. "Her indignation might have been but the natural feeling of resentment by one who feels she is fundamentally in the right," concluded Owen. "The possibility that she had not done the right thing appeared to be far from Mrs. Fortescue's thoughts."

His hostess promptly controlled her condemnation and expressed the feeling that her thoughts of Hawaii and Hawaiians were not all negative, that the better class of Hawaiians do not condone any type of sexual assault. However, the danger for white women had not been exaggerated, she made it clear to the Eastern newsman, and there had not been the highest police efficiency in the Islands.

"I have talked to many women," she said, "who asked me if I carried a pistol when I went out at night. I have not done so, but I know there are some sections of the city where it is not wise for a woman to go alone at night, no matter what her nationality is. On the other hand, I have never questioned the safety of some districts, including that in which my daughter was walking on the night she was attacked. That is a fairly well lighted neighborhood, and the road she was on was the direct road to the fort and to our home. I would not, before last fall, have considered it dangerous. But there is certainly some danger now; that has been abundantly proved."

She stood up straightening the jacket on her suit, and asked Mr. Owen if he would like to visit the two sailors, Lord and Jones, who were also quartered aboard the *Alton* while on bail.

"Thank you. I would like very much to meet them," said the reporter. Mrs. Fortescue and Lieutenant Massie led the way past the officers' mess, where a group of officers looked up from their meal in unconcealed curiosity, a couple of them hailing Tommy by name. The trio walked along the abandoned gun deck, past forsaken gun emplace-

ments and beyond the galley, where the cooks also eyed them with obvious interest, momentarily neglecting their pots and pans. In the seamen's quarters, Lord and Jones promptly stood erect and grinned as Mrs.
Fortescue stooped to enter the portal. As she sat on the edge of a cot
and the sailors waited for conversational overtures, Owen scanned the
quarters. He noted an unused ping-pong table in one corner and that
the two sailors' cots were unmade. The inhabitants, however, seemed
very much at home and in the best of humor. Jones smiled broadly when
Mrs. Fortescue turned to him.

"Show them your scrapbook," she said to the sailor in a kindly tone.
Jones promptly withdrew from a shelf a thick album in which newspaper clippings relating to the case had been carefully pasted, and turned
the pages slowly for the benefit of the reporter.

"Show him your favorite article," said Mrs. Fortescue to Jones as
Tommy joined in the ripple of laughter. The sailor turned to the page
describing the statement he had made after his arrest, in which he said
he was drunk and that anything anybody said he did was probably true,
because he could not remember it.

Tommy Massie playfully poked him in the ribs, and Mrs. Fortescue
called good natured farewells as they stepped back into the passage.
Jones was still holding the scrapbook, and proudly told the departing
reporter that he'd just pasted some more clippings in that day.

"I ought to date them," said the sailor. "I've been thinking about
that. Gosh! I never got my name in the newspaper before!"

Russell Owen made sure it was on the front page of *The New York
Times* the next day.

High above the mudflats that landlocked the *Alton*, the white frame
building of the headquarters of the Fourteenth Naval District dominated Makalapa Crater. The overgrown bowl of the extinct volcano was
located at the mouth of the sweeping Ewa plain between the Koolau
Range to the east and the Waianae Range to the west, and had served
in ancient times as a natural fortification for warring Hawaiian chiefs.
As early as 1840, only twenty years after the arrival of the missionaries,
an American Naval officer had appreciated the strategic value of the
area that overlooked the outstretched palm of Pearl Lochs, a hand of
water that spread protective fingers into the fertile valley. Lieutenant
Charles Wilkes, Commander of the U.S. Naval expedition that made
the first geodetic survey of the Islands, had found fifteen feet of water
over the entrance to the lochs and suggested the coral bar be dredged to

provide passage into the deep inland harbor for the world's largest ships. Thirty years later, another American military man, Colonel John Schofield, recommended the United States acquire the rights of the harbor from the Hawaiian Kingdom and that a channel be blasted. This concession was granted and work was begun at the end of the century, when the Spanish American War awakened the United States to the value of the magnificent Naval port.

Even the keenest of American military minds and the latest in American engineering technology had not reckoned, however, with the deep-rooted superstitions of the ancient Hawaiians. Called Puuloa in primitive times, the harbor was believed to be the sacred home of the benevolent shark god Kaahupahau, who dwelt in the grotto on the Honolulu side of the inlet. The chief guardian of her majestic cavern was a huge brother shark who guarded the entrance of the lochs from a pit beneath the reef. The queen of the sharks was revered as a protector of the human race and had commanded her brother to be on alert against those marauders from the sea who would molest the inhabitants of the Islands.

As the work on the U.S. Navy drydock at Pearl Harbor neared completion in 1913, disaster struck and the foundations of the imposing structure gave way, injuring several workmen. The consternation of the Navy was great, but the Hawaiians in the valley smiled knowingly and kept their silence. When the Naval engineers began the actual dredging of the harbor, which involved the destruction of a sacred fish pond and several shrines dedicated to the great god Kane, the Navy had learned its lesson, ceremoniously removing the fish-god stones and taking them out to sea, where they were reverently lowered into the ocean depths. Work continued after that without incident, and by the 'twenties, Pearl Harbor was among the most important Naval installations in the country. As an instrument for national security, it was of inestimable value.

Indeed the concentration of military forces in that small corner of the Pacific, including the Army Air Corps base in Pearl Harbor, known as Luke Field and later to be changed to Ford Island, and the large cavalry barracks at the foot of the Koolaus, named for Colonel Schofield, plus a perimeter of coast artillery embattlements, made Hawaii the largest assemblage of military installations in the United States.

No one was more acutely aware of this than Rear Admiral Yates Stirling. The strategic importance of the Hawaiian Islands and the danger of their being sabotaged by local corruption and an influx of Asians was the basis of the Navy's smoldering concern over the Massie Case. It was this point that he strove to impress on the mind of the Assistant Attorney General during the investigations by the Justice Department.

Impatiently, he awaited the conference with Seth Richardson, who had arrived by steamship in March 1932. The trim, volatile Admiral paced the clapboard bridge of his headquarters and with a deep feeling of responsibility scanned the 300-degree vista that spread out before Makalapa. Below, the silver-fingered lochs of Pearl Harbor held a fleet of warships, seeming to duck in their berths beneath the flights of planes from nearby Luke Field. Far off to the right, beyond the moving carpet of sugar cane, could be discerned the fortifications of Schofield Barracks. Midway through the canefield rose the chimney spires of the sugar mill at Waipahu, beneath which nestled the feudal town of Asian plantation workers.

Assistant Attorney General Richardson settled into the leather chair offered by the Commandant. The articulate Admiral had carefully prepared his briefing.

"I'm sure you're well aware that the mission of the Navy here is of a rather complex nature," began Stirling as he seated himself behind his desk, on which lay a complete report. "A large amount of money already has been expended in the development of Pearl Harbor as a base for the fleet. There exists in this vicinity a large quantity of valuable war material such as fuel oil for the warships, mines and ammunition and stores of all kinds.

"Structures completed or in process of construction include a dry dock, marine railway, piers, slips, storehouses, hangars, radio stations, etc., aggregating a very sizable outlay of money by the United States government, and they constitute only a part of the necessary preparedness for a possible war in the Pacific.

"This material and, in addition, our internal and external lines of communications, our water supply, etc. are all practically unprotected from local sabotage..."

The intense Admiral rose from his desk and walked to the windows overlooking Pearl Harbor, then turned abruptly to the investigator from Washington and said with low-pitched force, "An acute threat of sabotage or anti-American actions by hostile elements in the local population before or during a war is a danger that would weaken the defense of the Islands to an extent that is scarcely appreciated in time of peace!"

He then resumed his station behind the desk and explained that the men in his command had duties enough without assuming control of an antagonistic population. "The large number of aliens in the Hawaiian

Islands is a matter of grave concern to our national government and years of study by civilian, military and Naval authorities of the probable attitude of certain Island-born Orientals has led to the conclusion that but doubtful reliance can be placed on their loyalty to the United States in event of war with an Oriental power."

"Is there any positive proof that their loyalty is to be doubted?" asked the assistant cabinet officer, impressed by the Admiral's concern and glad for the opportunity to hear the Navy point of view straight from the veteran mariner's mouth. Richardson had already had the first of several conferences with Governor Judd and police officials, and he was determined to maintain the unbiased point of view absolutely necessary for the effectiveness of his investigation.

Admiral Stirling assured his visitor that there was more than ample proof. "The presence of Oriental language newspapers, Buddhist temples, Oriental schools, Oriental organizations for various purposes are indicative of the methods by which many Island-born Orientals are being educated to consider themselves primarily subordinate to the country of their racial origin and tends to lessen to a considerable degree the so-called ties that might bind them to America.

"Racial feelings are strong among all Oriental races and there can be little doubt that the so called dominant white race is cordially disliked by all these races. No very great provocation would be required to cause these sparks of dislike to be fanned into active race hatred in time of war.

"What is also disturbing is the intermixture of races that has been going on in the Hawaiian Islands for many years," continued the Admiral, again rising and this time pacing the floor as he waxed eloquent on his favorite theme of miscegenation. "Scientists have stated that these intermixtures tend to produce types of lower moral and mental caliber than the pure blooded types of each race, and this intermixture is increasing to an extent that will tend to make each new generation of mixed bloods, with the continual introduction of a greater proportion of Oriental blood, contain a majority of individuals of lower intellect and increasing degeneracy.

"The present system of self government tends to increase the number of voters and consequently of politicians and potential office holders from among racial mixtures, bred for centuries with ideas of government, social and living standards so diverse from our American ideals, that social and political conditions in these Islands will have a tendency to drift further and further from such ideals and thus make the Islands more and more difficult to control in time of emergency.

"There appears to be a tendency among those who have spent their lives in Hawaii to forget that the major importance of the Hawaiian Islands to the United States lies in their situation as an outpost in the Pacific and not in their agricultural or industrial wealth. Their value to the United States as a commercial port depends entirely upon their security.

"Some of the people seem to feel that their individual rights as citizens should not be subordinated to national security..."

Behind the Admiral's desk hung a plaque bearing the seal of the United States Navy. Circling the rampant eagle was a strong anchor chain. Inscribed within the margin of the emblem were the words "Commandant, Fourteenth Naval District." Admiral Stirling glanced at the American eagle and the chain forged by his ancestors. The commander resumed his chair beneath the outstretched wings, and explained to Secretary Richardson that the unique situation in the Islands required remedies generally foreign to American ideas of government for civil populations. What was needed in Honolulu, he felt, was an emergency control until the people of Hawaii were capable of governing themselves.

"And what do you recommend?" asked Seth Richardson.

"At present, government control should be by men of the Caucasian race, by men who are not imbued too keenly with the peculiar atmosphere of the Islands or with predominance of inter-family connections, by men without preconceived ideas of the value and success of the melting pot," said the Admiral, adamantly laying both hands flat on his desk and gazing with level blue eyes directly into those of the Justice Department official. He then leaned back in his chair and concluded, "Although there may be no real objection to a considerable measure of self government in purely civil and local affairs, actual control of the laws, their inception, promulgation and enforcement should be by the National Government.

"Should the logic of the situation decide for a government of limited suffrage with a considerable measure of control by the National Government, the constitution of such controlling government, though predominantly civilian, should include an officer of the United States Army and an officer of the United States Navy, specially selected, for the fact must not be lost sight of that the Hawaiian Islands are primarily of national concern, a fortress of vital importance to the United States as a whole." A copy of the Commandant's remarks was given to Richardson and the Assistant Attorney General included them in his report.

Admiral Stirling's statement also voiced the sentiment of many Americans on the mainland and a large segment of the United States Congress, conservative elements whom generations of isolation had made suspicious of races other than Caucasian, of immigrants other than Anglo-Saxon. For these people, the melting pot of the Pacific was, at best, an outpost of civilization, with Honolulu a U. S. military reservation in a foreign country. It would take yet another day of infamy to correct these views and prove to all America that Hawaii and its people were a loyal, integral part of the United States. The wrath of the shark goddess beneath Pearl Harbor had not yet been fully appeased. In exactly a decade other marauders would come across the sea to blast her grotto and threaten the life of the land.

In the context of the times, however, Admiral Stirling's report to the Assistant Attorney General was the sincere expression of an isolationist, innately prejudiced military clique. The Admiral had taken an oath to protect his country. He felt duty-bound to uphold that oath in peace as well as in war, when he considered the security of his country imperiled. "A Naval man is disloyal to his country if he does not reveal acts that are doing harm to his firm conviction that the ship of state could founder on the undermined reefs of the Pacific islands." The old sea dog was not about to give up the ship.

On April 4, the Richardson Report was made public:

> "We found in Hawaii no organized crime, no important criminal class and no criminal rackets.
>
> We found, however, ample evidence of extreme laxity in the administration of law enforcement agencies.
>
> We found in the Territory no present serious racial prejudices, neglectful and unintelligent, with its chief concern political activity.
>
> We recommend appointment by the President, with confirmation by the Senate, of a territorial police head for the entire Territory...to the end that a territorial constabulary may be formed...
>
> We recommend appointment by the President, with the consent of the Senate, of an Attorney General for the Territory, who shall be public prosecutor, and who shall have charge of all prosecution throughout the Territory, superseding all other prosecutors.

We found no serious criticism of the courts...

We found no serious complaints of the jury system.

It is imperative that more parole officers be provided by the Legislature.

We were not impressed with the seriousness of alleged bad conditions at the public beaches.

Our tabulations do not show that crime, including sexual crime, in the Islands can properly be laid at the door of the Hawaiian. The amount of sex crime in the Territory seemed less than reported from many cities and localities of similar population on the mainland...

We found considerable demand for appointive commission government for the Islands...but we are unwilling to agree that local self-government should now be changed.

Something must be done to stop importation into the Territory of any more common laborers."

These highlights from the intensive investigation by the Assistant Attorney General filled two columns of the front pages of the Honolulu newspapers and prompted a twofold reaction: jubilation at the exposure of less crime than in other cities of the same population, and concern for the recommendation that "the federal government assume closer responsibility" for law and order in the Islands. The man in the street rejoiced at the clean bill of crime for Honolulu, but the political solons of Hawaii were less pleased. Richardson's suggestion that Hawaii be put under a territorial police force and the Attorney General of the Islands be made a Presidential appointee were strongly opposed by Governor Judd. He arranged for a transoceanic wireless conference with Delegate Houston in Washington. This caused as much excitement as the report itself.

A battery of twelve receivers and one transmitter was set up in the Senate Chamber of Iolani Palace by the Mutual Telephone Company under the direction of its president and arrangements were made for Houston to be next to his phone 5,000 miles away at exactly the appointed moment.

"Hello, Victor, this is Bob Shingle," said the president of the upper house, as the history-making, long distance parley opened. "We are sitting here in the Senate chamber, the Governor, members of the Senate and House, Princess Kawananakoa, and the Democratic Party of Hawaii in the person of Linc McCandless."

A great precedent was being set in more fields than communication. The Massie tragedy had temporarily bridged the chasm between political parties in Hawaii, and the threat to self-government was healing partisan wounds that had festered for years. For the first time, the Islands' political factions were working together for the preservation of their privileges as self-governing citizens, and a long overdue reassessment of responsibility was being taken.

"We are very much upset over the Richardson Report," continued Senator Robert Shingle. "We appreciate the fact that he gives us a clean bill of health and tells the world there is no serious crime in Hawaii, but we are shocked at some of the recommendations that might take away our rights as citizens."

Roy Vitousek, brilliant and visionary Speaker of the House, who had long advocated police reform, took over the receiver and seconded these sentiments, then handed the phone to Princess Kawananakoa, representing the Republican National Committee.

"Hello, Victor dear," said Princess Abigail, her voice filled with aloha. "Thank Mr. Richardson for the nice things he said about the Hawaiian people. Tell him the rest of the report didn't interest me, but that the whole Territory is seething. Victor, my greatest political enemy is here beside me, Linc McCandless, but he's a delightful enemy today and I'll pass him on to you."

The maverick stallion among warhorses of the Democratic party in Hawaii, freewheeling Linc McCandless had been defeated the year before as Delegate to Washington by Republican Victor Houston, but bygones were bygones with the Islands' exoneration by the Justice Department.

"Hello, Houston. This is your old foe, Linc," shouted McCandless over the phone. "But we're all together today!"

Delegate Houston reassured the politicians in Honolulu that the report was a great vindication for the Hawaiian people and "it is now officially on record that we are not 'different kinds of birds.'" This last remark was a sly dig at the Navy, who had used such an expression in an official communication at the time of Kahahawai's killing.

The conversation lasted fifteen minutes. "It must have cost a tidy figure," reported the evening paper, "but the taxpayers will not have to pay for it. It was a gift of the telephone company."

EIGHTEEN

The Richardson Report would have garnered larger headlines in the Honolulu papers had not the date of its publication, April 4, 1932, coincided with the opening day of the most celebrated trial in Hawaiian history.

Their conscience assuaged by a relatively clean bill of health, the citizenry prepared to turn their full attention to the courtroom drama. Already on the first day, devoted to technicalities of selecting a jury, the defense and prosecution had developed lively differences in questioning jurymen. The problem especially at issue was whether jurors could be questioned regarding the influence of the Ala Moana Rape Case in forming opinions of the murder case now on trial. The wily strategy for the defense soon became apparent: to emphasize the emotional side of the Ala Moana outrage that first stirred the nation, threatened the social and political fabric of the Islands and triggered the events leading up to the killing of Kahahawai. "The law was on the side of the state," Clarence Darrow was to admit later, "but life and all human qualities that are precious, they were with us." He intended to wring these precious human qualities from the testimony of his clients and offer them to the mercy of the court.

Aiding Darrow in the defense would be a line-up of four attorneys from widely diverse regions: Leisure of New York, whom Darrow had personally trained to assist him, Winn and Thompson of Honolulu, and Lieutenant Johnson of the Navy—a formidable array of legal talent. George Leisure had been in Hawaii just the year before, defending a land suit, and was thoroughly familiar with local legal procedure.

Prosecuting Attorney John Kelley, with a mind as orderly as his sharply-creased white linen suits, intended to stick to facts: a man had been murdered and circumstantial evidence could prove the guilt of his murderers. He would be assisted by Barry Ulrich, originally named as special prosecutor and retained by Kelley when recent reforms created the post of Territorial Prosecutor.

Ulrich was an old hand at Hawaiian histrionics. The week before the trial opened he was playing the leading role in the Honolulu Little Theatre's production of *The Night Cap* at Dillingham Hall. He was not a gifted actor, but in the tradition of personality performers he had been blessed with an indefinable ability to capture the imagination, much of the credit going to a low, penetrating voice that had a mesmerizing effect on his audience. "It rolls out in a steady rhythm," wrote the local critic of his latest performance. "There is little inflection in the voice, but it is so carefully modulated that the slightest intonation lends powerful emphasis to what is being said. He is more effective in his pauses than most speakers are in the inflection of their voices."

Slight, intense, balding, with a head almost too large for his body, middle-aged Ulrich was also noteworthy for his sartorial elegance. In the spotlight, he had a cold magnetism that was penetrating. He had been born in Chicago and arrived in Honolulu soon after his graduation from Harvard Law School prior to the World War, in which he had served as an artillery officer with the crack unit known as the "California Grizzlies." When he returned to Hawaii, he became a partner of Frank Thompson, whom he would oppose in the Massie Case. Also facing him across the courtroom would be another familiar opponent, George Leisure, over whom he had triumphed in the Waialua Land Case.

Ulrich's summons back to legal service to assist the prosecution curtailed his career with the Honolulu Footlighters but caused a dramatic flurry as it was whispered that the popular thespian would be a key figure in the trial. "Barry Ulrich," wrote a reporter after Kelley's announcement of his retention, "is the one man in the Territory who can cut like a knife into Darrow's eloquence...cut like a knife, that is exactly what Ulrich does. His words are like a surgeon's scalpel, his poise as deft and restrained as that of a master surgeon in the operating room."

The prosecution was to present the Territory's case before Circuit Judge Charles Skinner Davis. Judge Cristy had been disqualified by a defense affidavit of prejudice after objections to his handling of the grand jury indictment of second degree murder. "Skinner" Davis, popular in all walks of the community, could be counted on to remain impartial in the midst of conflicting passions. He was a dedicated man with a warm, friendly personality that never stood in his way in the pursuit of justice, as had been proven with vigor and resourcefulness in his exposure of graft a few years earlier. Other than his Canadian birth, in New Brunswick forty-two years before the trial, his career paralleled that of the successful haole kamaaina: Punahou for schooling, an Ivy League college education—Cornell, in his case—and graduate work at Harvard. His law degree was from Stanford and, after graduating, he returned to Honolulu to practice, moving immediately into the swing of civic endeavor and winning hands down in his maiden political race at the age of twenty-seven. A dozen years later he was appointed to the circuit bench. His many friends among the Shriners, Elks, Knights of Pythias, Punahou alumni and population at large applauded his choice as the one man who would not let the predicted pyrotechnics get out of hand.

An hour before the opening session, a huge crowd had gathered about the courthouse, and only possessors of passes were permitted within the Judiciary Building. The colorful tapestry of many races unique to Hawaii was spread out on the sunny lawn: haole white-collar workers in short-sleeved shirts and wearing neckties as their badge of respectability mingled with brawny, brown-armed laborers in bright aloha shirts. The pencil-straight silhouettes of society women in the short-skirted latest mainland fashions picked their way among the ample Hawaiian tutus whose high-necked muumuus dotted the grounds like an encampment of calico tents. An occasional monotone kimono of a Japanese mama-san could be seen modestly blending into the background and, even more rarely, a Chinese laborer in faded blue cotton pajamas. Most of the Asians, however, had long since adopted Western dress and already many faces in the crowd had the fused features of an interracial society.

Police at the door carefully checked those entitled to enter the courtroom. The rest of the 200 seats in the small room were given over to the few who were first in line. The scene within befitted the tradition of great legal battles: a row of sixteen newsmen stretched along the length of one entire wall; extra benches had been placed within the enclosure ordinarily reserved for attorneys and officials of the court. Against the rail of the enclosure, separating the court from the visitors' benches, was another row of chairs, occupied by close friends of the defendants and several attorneys, including Attorney General Harry Hewitt.

Mrs. Darrow, youthful and pretty in a black dress, sat with Mrs. Fortescue and her sister, Mrs. Julian Ripley of New York, and Mrs. George Leisure. The strain of three months confinement aboard the Alton and a half-year of overwhelming emotional pressure in the agony of a rape case had taken their toll on Grace Fortescue. Ever-elegant in a matching maroon ensemble, she now seemed more slender than usual and lines of weariness etched her fine, deep-set eyes. With the faded fragility of a rose pressed in the Almanach de Gotha, the aristocratic socialite stood out in the common mass of the courtroom. She nodded to those who spoke to her, many of them leaning over to put a hand on her squared shoulder, but she did not smile. Next to her sat her son-in-law, also silent and unsmiling in dark civilian clothes, and further along were Albert Jones and Edward Lord, also wearing civies and more relaxed than their co-defendants, an occasional laugh punctuating their whispered comments to each other. Beyond them was another figure, serious and motionless during the examination and never taking his eyes from the stage of proceedings. It was Joseph Kahahawai, Sr., father of the slain victim. He did not speak to anyone.

A strange air of detachment seemed to permeate the courtroom. People watched from the wooden benches without the apprehension of sitting on a powder-keg, a mood that had gripped them only a few months before when the killing of Kahahawai had thrown the city into tumult. The medley of faces in the closely packed chamber shared a mutual concentration, as though watching a solemn ceremony. It was the atmosphere of a canonization or a holy ritual, not that of a murder trial.

The low conversational tone of Darrow had set the tempo. Hunched in his chair, with his eyelids half lowered, he gazed with steady attention at each of the potential jurors as they filed into the jury box. For the most part, in the early examination, he spoke in a soft, friendly voice that carried no farther than the juror whom he questioned. He nodded, smiled, purred like an old tabby in a country store—until he was crossed. Then the fur flew as he swung into the arena, shaking off the homespun image.

The first skirmish was inevitably over the issue that would dominate the trial—the Ala Moana rape. Prosecutor Kelley, whom Darrow had already recognized as "the most dangerous kind of prosecutor because he is fair," was examining Kenneth C. Bankston, one of the 26 jury candidates called the first day.

"Are you willing to return a verdict, understanding that the guilt or innocence of Joseph Kahahawai in the Ala Moana Case has nothing to do with this trial?" asked Kelley quietly.

Darrow rose to his feet, his chin thrust forward and his clenched fist shaking.

"If I have anything to do with it, the Ala Moana Case will certainly have something to do with this trial," he growled, his voice deep and vibrant. "I hardly think counsel should ask the jurors to ignore that matter."

Kelley and Ulrich were on their feet together. The battle had been joined.

"As a matter of law, Joseph Kahahawai could be as guilty as any man could be," answered Kelley, his voice also in impassioned control, "but that does not provide an excuse for killing him."

Darrow, standing alone, his head turned squarely facing the prosecuting attorneys, declared that the defense would undoubtedly resist any effort to bar the Ala Moana Case from the present trial. The protagonists glowered at each other. The sharp blow of Judge Davis's gavel shattered the tension.

"The Court rules out the Prosecutor's question. I cannot see how the earlier case can be legally injected into the trial, but the Court will rule on it if the occasion arises."

The examination settled back into humdrum questioning, but blood had been drawn, and as Kelley met and deflected Darrow's skillful thrusts in trying to implant a predominantly haole panel, the battle grew in tension and the temper of the courtroom followed suit. Three jurors of mixed blood were temporarily accepted, although the defense challenged two and entered exceptions to adverse court rulings.

Then came a talesman who had been a former deputy sheriff of Wahiawa, a one-time aide to Governor Judd and a sergeant-at-arms in the Territorial Legislature. He was wearing an orchid in his lapel. The spectators increased their attention.

"Have you formed any opinion as to how Kahahawai was killed?" asked Darrow.

"I have not," said the former sheriff.

The ambling defense attorney led the questioning through a routine series of points as he moved slowly to a position where he was leaning on the rail of the jury box, talking quietly to his subject from only a foot away.

"Are you anxious to sit on this jury?" Darrow suddenly rapped out.

The startled juror said he had had no choice, he had been drawn for jury duty. The counsel for the defense thrust his face within inches of the former sheriff.

"Do you think you know who killed Kahahawai?" he asked clearly.

"The defendants, I guess," said the prospective juror, unguardedly. "I haven't formed any opinion of the matter."

"But you have an impression that he was murdered?"

"Objection," cut in Ulrich. "Under such an interpretation of qualification, everyone in this courtroom would be disqualified. It is only necessary that the impression be not so fixed that it could not be removed."

Darrow turned to the Court.

"We're not called upon to remove impressions by evidence," he declared, his voice ringing out over the stilled courtroom. "We're entitled to a juror who will enter on the case giving the defendants the presumption of innocence!"

He then turned to the subdued sergeant-at-arms, and his deep-set eyes searched those of the talesman. "It would take evidence to remove your impression, wouldn't it?"

The juror nodded.

"You've had that impression for three months, haven't you—ever since the death of Kahahawai?

"No."

"When did you get rid of it?" Darrow snapped, abruptly leaning forward on the jury rail. The prospective juror said again that he hadn't thought much about it one way or the other.

"What do you think now?" Darrow persisted. "Do you think he was killed, or do you think he committed suicide?"

"I think he was murdered."

Darrow turned to the court as the simple statement hung in the air, then ambled back to his seat. "I challenge for cause," he said quietly.

With the technique of courting confidence, then suddenly stripping the unsuspecting juror's opinion to its core of truth, Darrow sought to weed from the jury box every man who seemed to prejudice his case and the unique factors involved in the defense. Just as skillfully, Prosecutor Kelley questioned the prospective jurors on the matter of circumstantial evidence. Over and over again the alert prosecuting attorney asked the same question:

"Will you give due weight and consideration to circumstantial evidence in arriving at your conclusion if the court instructs you that you may?"

Kelley made sure that each of the jurors he passed had answered in the positive.

Between the two, the lion and the wolf, the game was played: Darrow slumped in his seat, his head sunk on his chest, his large hands limp on the arms of the chair; Kelley, younger by nearly three decades, sat erect and leaning tautly forward, his attention riveted on each talesman with the total absorption of a hound on a scent.

The competence of the counsel on both sides of the case seemed to comfort the courtroom and it relaxed sufficiently to enjoy the humor of

many of the examinations. Even the defendants smiled now and then as
a citizen of a community known for its enjoyment of a sunnier side of
life inadvertently vented this spirit. Jones often reacted with open
laughter. The merry sailor sat with his chin on his left hand, his fingers
stroking his lower lip and his mild blue eyes animated beneath a furrowed forehead. Mrs. Fortescue and Lieutenant Massie rose above such
levity, displaying a tense demeanor verging on disinterest. Dressed in
her simple, dark costume, ornamented only with a strand of pearls,
Grace Fortescue did not look at the jurors. Her view was beyond the
white-linened shoulders of the prosecutor, balding despite his youth,
toward the lilting fronds of the royal palms swaying in the courtyard
above the golden statue of Kamehameha.

A story was going the rounds that she was feigning indifference to
mask her reassurance fortified by the arrival of two alienists who would
testify for the defense. The growing rumor that Darrow had called for
support from psychiatrists was greeted by a shrug from the defender, who
kept his full attention directed on the duty at hand. The mélange of
strange races and even stranger language among the veniremen became
a real challenge for the court veteran and left the world's best known
criminal attorney baffled at times; it was one of the most puzzling experiences of his career, he was to admit later.

A young Hawaiian laborer was called from the panel, and as he
arose he told Judge Davis that he didn't understand what was going on
and he therefore didn't think he'd make a good juror.

"Do you understand English.' asked the Judge.

"No."

"Do you know what doubt is?"

"No."

"You're excused."

The next Hawaiian, a youth named Eddie Kaleiwahae, asked if he could
also be excused from jury duty. "I don't know nothing about this case."

"An ideal juror, Your Honor," said Prosecutor Kelley.

Kaleiwahae, however, was excused, and yet another Hawaiian,
William Huihui, was called to replace him in the jury box. He admitted
he'd talked about the case.

"Did you ever tell anyone what you thought should be done with
these people?"

"Yes, sir. I said they ought to be shot."

William Huihui was challenged for cause by the defense.

Walter Kealoha, a stevedore, was called a little later. Darrow questioned him on his understanding of English, asking what "presumption" and "reasonable doubt" meant. The venireman was as puzzled by the lawyer's language as Darrow was by the Hawaiian's pidgin English, and the defense again challenged for cause.

Kelley rose.

"I don't think it is necessary to know what a reasonable doubt is to serve on a jury," said the Irish prosecutor. "I've been practicing law for twelve years and I'm not sure I know what it means."

A twitter swept the gallery and Jones guffawed.

"The question whether a man knows terminology and how well he can express himself about it are not the same," continued Kelley. "I suggest Mr. Darrow ask him questions in Hawaiian."

Judge Davis examined the juror, patiently repeating himself when Kealoha's only response was a quizzical look. "Do you know what 'burden of proof' means?" asked the Court.

"What did you say, Judge?" answered the Hawaiian.

"Don't you know what a burden is?"

"No, sir."

"Then you're one of the few stevedores who doesn't," said the smiling Judge, turning to the prosecution. "The defense is entitled to have men on the jury capable of understanding the questions and phrases of law that may arise," concluded Judge Davis. "I don't think Walter Kealoha qualifies as a juror in this case."

Nor did Ah Loy Chung, a laundryman.

"What does guilty mean?" Judge Davis asked.

"Wrong," said Chung.

"What does innocent mean?"

"I don't use that word very much, Judge," the talesman replied, and was peremptorily excused from service.

Another leery Chinese, whose reluctance to serve was evident, begged to be excused. Robert Kin Heu told the court that he had formed an opinion.

"And when did you form the opinion?" asked the prosecutor.

"Night before last. After being summoned," said the unwilling Mr. Heu, as the courtroom chuckled. Jones and Lord heartily led the laughter.

Johnny Noble, Hawaiian orchestra leader and composer, whose musical ear was paying off well at the moment, had no ear for Judge Davis when he was called to qualify. The Judge asked him why he wanted to be exempted.

"I can't hear you, Judge." said the musician.

"Is your hearing bad?" the judge asked.

"I'm sorry, but I can't hear a word you say." Noble replied. He was excused.

When a tiny Japanese, Eugene J. Mioi, was called to the box he also claimed exemption because of ear trouble, saying that he had been under doctor's care, but that the doctor had not "fixed him up very good."

"I guess he did his best, though," he added generously. When exemption was denied him by the court, Mioi then asked to be excused because of his unfamiliarity with the English language.

"I don't speak it good."

"I don't suppose any of us speak English perfectly," Judge Davis remarked, noting a pattern developing among the reluctant Asians. Patiently, he examined the small Japanese on such words as "guilty" and "innocent," and again denied Mr. Mioi's claim.

"Judge," said the distressed candidate. "Please now I tell the truth. I am a fisherman. Out Waianae way. All my traps are out in the sea. I fear the longer I stay on jury, the longer my fish be dead."

Again the courtroom relaxed with laughter, and the judge rapped his gavel for order. "Well, I guess most of the gentlemen on the panel have pressing business..." said the judge, about to deny Mioi's request for the third time when the worried fisherman interrupted him.

"I swear, Judge, I don't understand lots of legal terms."

"There are lots of lawyers who don't either,' commented Judge Davis. "However the Court agrees to excuse you."

But the fisherman, the stevedore, the musician and the laundryman were exceptions to the general run of jury candidates. So many of them claimed to have open minds on the subject of the case and displayed such eagerness to serve that Darrow began to suspect an ulterior motive. "I think they need work," he confided to Leisure, unaware that the canneries had laid off hundreds of pineapple workers. "I didn't realize at first that some of these answers are probably due to the unemployment problem." The bemused old legal lion smiled.

A jury equally divided between Caucasians and Asians was gradually taking form, and by the fourth and last day of venire sifting it was apparent that for every haole challenged by the prosecution, an Oriental or Hawaiian was thrown out by the defense. Exactly a hundred veniremen had been called.

When the prosecution accepted a young Portuguese named Edward A. Goeas, a billing clerk and graduate of St. Louis College who was currently working for Theo H. Davies & Co., one of the Big Five firms, Darrow brought out that the man had played barefoot football with Benny Ahakuelo, a defendant in the Ala Moana Rape Case. He'd also known Joe Kahahawai when the latter was an athlete at St. Louis.

"Will this impair your ability to give an impartial judgment in the trial?" asked Kelley.

"No, sir," answered the athlete.

Mr. Darrow left him in the box without further question.

The prosecution and defense concurred on three other jurors: Shadford Waterhouse, a teller at the Bishop Bank, a Punahou School graduate and member of an old missionary family; Charles H. Strohlin, a mechanic and pump engineer for the Oahu Sugar Company on their plantation at Waipahu; and Charles Akana, a cost accountant of Chinese and Hawaiian ancestry who was employed by the Hawaiian Contracting Company, Ltd.

This left eight slots on the panel.

Olaf Sorenson, assistant manager of the Oahu Railway and Land Company, a Dillingham corporation, and resident of Pearl City, was called to the jury box. Kelley questioned him.

"You know Walter Dillingham, don't you?" asked the prosecutor, referring to Hawaii's most prominent citizen whose many firms did a large business with the Navy and who had forcefully pressed for a "clean-up" of Honolulu.

"I do."

"You have an opinion about this case?"

"Yes—but not a very strong one."

"Would that opinion embarrass you in any way, sitting as a juror on this case?"

"It would not."

"Have you ever discussed this case with Mr. Dillingham?"

"Never."

"If selected, you won't let any outside influence sway your opinion, will you?"

"No," said the gaunt Swede emphatically. He was passed, and joined the panel.

After an exchange of challenges, Willie B.E. Beyer was summoned for examination. A short, stolid German of hydrant proportions who identified himself in a thick accent as a potato chip manufacturer, he arose with stiff formality and bowed to the court.

"Gentlemen, I am sorry to say that I don't think I should be a juror," he declared. "I am an American but I have been in this country just five years. I don't have much English. I went to the Y.M.C.A. and they learned me arithmetic. Already I learned arithmetic in Germany!"

Everyone in the court smiled but Willy Beyer.

"Do you understand what presumption means?" Judge Davis asked.

"I read it in the paper and tried to find it in the dictionary, but it wasn't in the German-English dictionary and it wasn't in the English-German dictionary."

"Do you know the meaning of doubt" asked the Judge.

"I looked that up too in the dictionary. But I forgot it already."

"Do you know what it is to be guilty?"

"It means you're wrong," said the little German triumphantly. "I was fined once for speeding, and that's how I know."

"I think you are qualified," the Judge said. Kelley passed the talesman, and for the first time in the trial, Darrow passed for cause without asking a question.

George Duncan McIntyre, a dock clerk for the Matson Navigation Company, was called. He said that he was Island-born and that his mother was Hawaiian.

"We're particularly concerned with your frame of mind toward the defendants," Mr. Kelley said. "Have you any opinion as to their guilt or innocence?"

"No, I have not." Mr. McIntyre replied.

"Mr. Winn informs me that his firm is attorney for the Matson Company. Would that bother you?"

"No. I didn't even know that was so," said the clerk as Kelley passed him for cause and Darrow took up the examination.

"Mr. McIntyre did you ever have any opinion on this case?" asked the defense.

"Well, right after the killing, I thought about how it might have happened. That's all."

The rumpled attorney rose from his chair and walked slowly to the jury box. He smiled at the part-Hawaiian, as though asking directions of a friendly native, and turning, pointed to the back of the room. Casually, but with cold purpose in his voice, he asked, "Do you know that officer?"

All eyes turned to the back of the courtroom and focused on a policeman standing at a closed door.

"Yes, sir. He used to work under me before he joined the Police Department."

"Do you know him well?"

"Only through our connections when he was working for me."

"If he should be a witness, how would you weigh his testimony?"

"The same as anyone else's."

Darrow passed the dock clerk for cause. The defense challenged the next witness, a Chinese plumber, and again the sparring was on. It lasted until a stocky middle-aged haole, whose Babbitt appearance seemed to satisfy both sides, entered the jury box.

Theodore B. Bush, retired civil engineer formerly employed by the Bishop Estate and Island resident for twenty years, admitted that he had some opinion about the case, but not a fixed one. The prosecution passed him for cause. Mr. Darrow was also satisfied with the impartiality of the solid citizen.

Henry S.Y. Chang was passed by the prosecution after he said that he had abandoned his opinion when the trial started. The young man resembled a caricature of a Chinese, a comic "Yellow Kid" in Western dress. "Chang has a high pompadour," wrote a reporter during the jury selection, "and there's an extraordinary distance between the edge of his eyelids and his brows which he constantly lifts upward as though making a tremendous effort to pull the lids open and keep awake. His answers, however, are alert enough."

"But you haven't forgotten what you thought about it?" Darrow continued.

"No," said the sleepy-looking youth, who was an employee of the Schuman Carriage Co.

"You have no opinion now as to guilt or innocence of these defendants? Is that right?"

"Yes, I would say no."

"No what?" asked Darrow, feeling he was being again trapped by the mysterious mind of the East.

"No, I have no opinion," said Chang, smiling blandly.

"Have you talked so much about it that it would be hard for you to be fair?"

"Yes."

"Yes. It would be hard?"

"No. It would not."

Henry S.Y. Chang was passed for cause by the defense, who then challenged the next talesman, a Hawaiian laborer. As Darrow excused the dark husky ditchdigger, the last pure Hawaiian was swept from the box.

Theodore C.H. Char was the substitute. A certified accountant, he assured Mr. Kelley that he had no opinion, bias or prejudice in the case and was passed by the prosecution. Char told Darrow that he had graduated from McKinley High School and had attended the University of Chicago, Knox College and the University of Illinois.

"I have no opinion, nor have I ever formed one, although I have taken part in discussions of the case." The defense was as impressed with the accountant's integrity as the prosecution and Theodore Char remained on the panel.

The prosecution challenged the next two members of the venire, both haoles.

John F. Stone, also a haole and secretary to Frank C. Atherton, president of Castle & Cooke, Ltd., leader of the Big Five corporations, was called.

"I feel in a frame of mind to listen to the case impartially," Mr. Stone told the prosecutor, and Kelley believed him. The defense concurred without questioning. Eleven jurors had now been selected; the panel needed only one more.

Walter Napoleon was called. A young meat cutter for a grocery store on Punchbowl Street, Napoleon had his name to distinguish his distant haole ancestry; his Hawaiian inheritance had determined his appearance. There was Polynesian candor in his wide brown eyes and full lips that pursed with almost childish timidity as he told the court that he had not discussed the case because he didn't want to antagonize any of his customers.

"I get a thirty percent commission. That's why I'm not interested," said Walter as the court tittered. "I've met people on both sides of this case and if I formed an opinion it would hurt my business. Frankly, I don't want to serve."

The honesty of the talesman was so patent and naive that both sides smilingly agreed to take him.

"I'm sorry, Judge," objected the butcher, "but I'd better not accept. I can't side with one party or the other, because of my business which is with the Army and my bonus will drop."

Judge Davis gently reminded him of his duties as an American citizen, and young Napoleon agreed that he'd never thought of it like that.

"You served in the Navy during the war, didn't you?" asked Montgomery Winn for the defense.

"Yes, sir, and I've applied to join the Reserve," said the hapa-haole, eager to prove his patriotism.

"You're a member of the Mormon Church, aren't you?"

"Yes, sir."

"There was considerable discussion in your grocery and Piggly Wiggly stores about the case, was there not?" continued Mr. Winn. "And employees were ordered not to discuss the case, were they not?"

"That's right, sir."

"You obeyed that order?"

"Yes. I didn't think I'd get mixed up in the case."

"Have you formed any opinion?"

"No."

"Any impression?"

"Yes. I felt that if anyone wanted to go out and commit a crime, that was their business."

The courtroom gave way to chuckles and the serious part-Hawaiian in the box grinned sheepishly as though caught up in a mood he didn't understand but was willing to join. Mr. Winn then asked the juror if he was interested in athletics. Did he play baseball?

"Not lately. I've been married nine years," said Mr. Napoleon as the court renewed its laughter.

"Do you have any children?"

"Yes. Seven."

"Boys or girls?"

"Half and half," said Mr. Napoleon amid a roar of laughter that brought down the house. The final juror was passed by both sides for cause.

It was apparent that both sides also felt that further shuffling would not improve the character of the jury and that little was to be gained by the use of challenges on either side. Mr. Winn rose and said that the defense would accept the jury as it was, if agreeable to the prosecution.

"Agreed," said Prosecutor Kelley.

The jury was sworn in at noon on Thursday, April 7, 1932, and Judge Davis ordered adjournment until Monday at 9 a.m.

Joseph Kahahawai   Benny Ahakuelo

Horace Ida   Henry Chang   David Takai

The five young men charged with the alleged rape of Thalia Massie on the night of September 12, 1931, in Honolulu. All denied any knowledge of the assault.
Advertiser Library Photos

Thalia and Tommy Massie. *In circle,* Grace Fortescue, mother of Thalia.

The Massie house in Manoa Valley. Few junior Naval officers can afford to live there today, where modest 70-year old bungalows sell for more than half a million dollars.

The car belonging to Horace Ida's sister in which Thalia claimed to have been abducted. She recalled the license number after it was reported over the radio in the police car taking her to the hospital.

The Judiciary Building, scene of the Ala Moana Assault Trial and the Massie Murder Trial, with the gilded statue of Kamehameha the Great in the foreground.

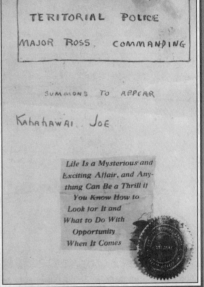

TERITORIAL POLICE

MAJOR ROSS   COMMANDING

SUMMONS TO APPEAR

Kahahawai. Joe

Life Is a Mysterious and Exciting Affair, and Anything Can Be a Thrill if You Know How to Look for It and What to Do With Opportunity When It Comes

Rear Admiral Yates Stirling, Jr., Commandant of the 14th Naval District, Pearl Harbor, Hawai'i.

The false summons, fabricated by Grace Fortescue, with which she and Lt. Thomas Massie and two seamen, A.O. Jones and E.J. Lord, lured Joseph Kahahawai into the car that drove him to the Fortescue cottage for "interrogation."

The defendants in the Kahahawai slaying, as they posed for the first time since their arrest, having spent the night in jail while bond was being arranged, *Left to right:* Lieutenant Thomas H. Massie, Seaman Edward J. Lord, Mrs. Grace Fortescue and Seaman Albert O. Jones.

Inaugural call of transpacific radio telephone service, December 23, 1931, to Delegate Victor Houston in Washington, D.C. Seated before the throne in Iolani Palace, *front row, left to right:* Rear Admiral Yates Stirling, Jr., W.R. Castle, Governor Lawrence Judd, J.A. Balch and Princess Abigail Kawananakoa. *Second row, left to right:* Major General Briant Wells, Ex-Governor Wallace R. Farrington, E.P. Bishop, Kenneth Barnes and Frank Atherton. *Back row:* Staff ushers.

Top left: Clarence Darrow, Chief Defense Counsel; *top right:* John C. "Fighting Jack" Kelley, Prosecuting Attorney; *below left:* Judge Charles S. Davis; *below right:* Lt. Massie, Clarence Darrow and Grace Fortescue confer on leaving the courthouse.

Advertiser Library Photo

Jury of the Massie murder trial, with bailiffs, enjoy a respite from courtroom duties at the Beretania Street tennis courts.

Clarence Darrow is amused at being considered no exception to Judge Davis' order that all those entering the court be frisked by a guard.

The Grand Old Man of the trial relaxes at Waikiki with good friend, Duke Kahanamoku.

The defense party during the "custody" period, outside the Governor's office at Iolani Palace. *Left to right:* Clarence Darrow, Edward Lord, Albert Jones, Sheriff Gordon Ross, Grace Fortescue, Thalia Massie, Tommy Massie and George Leisure of the defense counsel. Mrs. Fortescue is shown holding a copy of Governor Judd's order to commute the guilty slayers' sentences of 10 years of hard labor to one hour served in his office. They got away with murder. Anarchy was avoided.

Right: Thalia Massie in her forties, before her death in 1963.

NINETEEN

"Gentlemen, you will bring your pajamas and toothbrushes with you when the court reconvenes on Monday, as henceforth until the conclusion of the trial you will be segregated incommunicado," said Judge Charles Davis to the newly created jury of the Massie Case.

It was the first time such an order had been given in the history of criminal trials in Hawaii. Another unusual feature of the jury was the high percentage of haoles, out of proportion to their minority ratio in the population. A cross-section of the Islands' racial blend, it was an evenly split mixture of whites and yellow-browns, with six jurors of Caucasian ancestry, two of Chinese, three part-Hawaiian and one Portuguese. Somehow the Japanese had been dealt out in the shuffle.

Admiral Stirling escorted the defendants from the buzzing courtroom. He had been impressed by the procedure. "Each prospective juror had been researched in advance by both the prosecution and the defense, especially with regard to their attitude toward the defendants," he wrote in his journal. "Slouching back in his chair, Darrow was in sharp contrast to John Kelley who was alert, antagonistic, aggressive. He would fight with all weapons on hand. Darrow, his coat hanging loosely on his aging frame, breathed kindliness and sympathy for all. The courtroom seemed pervaded with his gentle old voice. Its soothing effect upon that courtroom was miraculous to see. Slowly, his voice was stamping out all bitterness. Would he be able to persuade the six jurors of mixed blood and cause them to believe that these defendants were not criminals but merely human beings fighting for justice against an inhuman system? A life had been taken, but was it a life worth saving?"

Another staunch supporter of the defense expressed his thoughts on the course of events so far. In New York, still ailing, Major Granville Fortescue stated for Hearst's *New York American*, "I have every confidence that the Territorial Court will render complete justice, as after twenty-two years of married life, I have every confidence in Mrs. Fortescue's complete innocence."

Confidence was also the prevailing spirit of the prosecution as the court adjourned for the long weekend. An amenable and far from antagonistic John Kelley took the arm of his pretty brunette wife, a spectator on the final day of the jury examination, and presented her to his rival, Clarence Darrow.

"Mr. Darrow, I have read every word of your autobiography," beamed Mrs. Kelley. A female bystander gushed that the books were selling like hotcakes in Honolulu.

"You mean they haven't sold out yet?" parried the old charmer.

Captivated, the woman asked how the venerable Chicago lawyer intended to spend his weekend.

"I hope to devote a good share of it to the Kahanamoku boys at Waikiki," said Darrow.

He was in a good mood, mellowed by the first round of the trial. The outcome of the jury selection was to his liking, as was the aloha spirit of the Islands. Basking in a beach chair beneath the hau trees of the Outrigger Canoe Club, Clarence Darrow wondered at his original reluctance to take the case.

He had been following the unfolding situation since the rape trial, but was caught completely off guard when friends of Mrs. Fortescue made the generous overture of a $25,000 fee if he would undertake the defense of the Massie Case.

"I wondered if I could stand the trip," he admitted, "and I was not certain that I could bear the daily routine beginning in court early each day and catching all that goes on in the trial. I was not even sure that my mind would click with its old-time vigor."

He had conveyed his doubts to the Fortescue family, but they would have no part of his refusal. With its racial and military overtones, the case was not the kind he liked and he felt, having retired with sufficient glory to last the remaining years of his life, that he should not get involved in it. He revealed his reluctance to his old friend and confidante, Arthur Spingarn.

"I urged him to go for two reasons," relates Spingarn in Darrow's biography. "One, that he was tired and the trip to Hawaii would do him good, and two, that he needed money so desperately, he was entitled to take on a case that promised a fee, just as other lawyers did, as against the thousands he had tried for nothing."

Darrow accepted the Massie Case. He had always wanted to visit Hawaii and this was a way to kill two birds with one stone— and still have the golden egg, he mused. "Besides, they said I was through as a lawyer, and I wanted to show them that a man in his seventies was keener than a younger man. In addition, Mrs. Massie, as a psychological study, interested me and appealed to my sympathy."

Having decided to undertake the defense, Darrow telephoned a stranger in New York and asked his assistance. There had been a lot of talk lately in legal circles about the young comer George Leisure who had recently formed a partnership with William "Wild Bill" Donovan, the colorful war hero and Assistant Attorney General under Coolidge. Leisure had also already tried a civil suit in Hawaii, and his reputation as a rising defense attorney prompted Darrow to call the Wall Street lawyer himself, although they had never met. He caught Leisure at his office on a late January morning just before lunch.

George Leisure remembered the moment very well: "One day the telephone rang and a voice said, 'Is this George Leisure?' I said, 'Yes.' He said, 'This is Clarence Darrow speaking.' I thought at first that it was one of my good friends inviting me out to lunch and using his name because he knew that I was an admirer of C.D. Since the voice sounded serious, however, I answered, 'Yes sir,' and listened. Mr. Darrow then proceeded to say, 'I am about to try a case in Honolulu and I have been told that you tried a case in Honolulu a year or so ago. I have never tried a case there and I thought that perhaps you would be willing to talk to me and tell me something of the nature of the procedure in that jurisdiction. If you could have lunch with me today I would appreciate it very much.'

"Some years before, while on a steamer going to Europe, I had read Ludwig's *Life of Napoleon*. Upon contemplating the book, I thought how interesting it would be to be able to sit down and talk personally with Napoleon about some of his campaigns. My mind then drifted to the great men of my own profession, and I resolved that when I got back from Europe I would one day go to Chicago and have just such a talk with Clarence Darrow. When I got back to New York the regular demands of courtroom practice kept me at my work, and I never had the opportunity of going to Chicago as I had planned. I now saw Mr. Darrow for luncheon and not only had lunch, but spent the entire afternoon with him, during which time I had precisely the kind of talk with him that I had thought it would be interesting to have had with Napoleon. He seemed surprised to know that I was familiar with many of his cases.

"When I left him at the close of the afternoon he said, 'I have been retired from practice for some time now, and I have not been regularly engaged in courtroom work for several years. I am also getting along in years and I would be very pleased to have a young man accompany me on this trip. I wondered if it would be possible for you to go to Honolulu with me?' Without even checking with my office, I assured him that it was entirely possible and that I was prepared to leave at any time. Soon after that Mrs. Leisure and I joined Mr. and Mrs. Darrow in Chicago. and we proceeded to Honolulu together."

They had worked well as a team in the weeks before the trial and Darrow was pleased with his choice of an assistant. This brief respite at the sun-spangled Outrigger Club, where the lean handsome Kahanamoku brothers caught the waves on their surfboards, would be his last before the concentrated days of the cross-examination. A thrill of anticipation stirred in his sluggish veins. It was true—the courtroom was in his blood, although his humble boyhood had given no hint of an illustrious career at the bar.

"My people were poor but honest," he had said in published recollections. "It may not apply to me, but anyway it applied to my parents." His father had been the first student to graduate from the Meadville Theological School and was a tolerant and profoundly understanding Unitarian. Darrow told of being born in a small country town in Ohio and how he had entered the law by chance.

"I have a theory that whatever is good about me, and whatever is bad—which is plenty—is beyond my control," he had continued.

"Figuring it out biologically, I had one chance in ten thousand in being born on my mother's side and one chance in ten million on my father's side, so you see there wasn't much question about it. Now if we can carry that back to Adam...

"But we won't," he had said, in reference to his most famous case.

"Soon my ambition became to be of service to my fellow man, especially if he was in trouble. It has been my one aim in life ever since. My father was a merchant and across the street was the village tinsmith who was also the Justice of the Peace. I used to hear the lawyers argue and call each other everything in the dictionary and a lot that isn't. I thought that to be a lawyer and call people such names would be great. So I began quite young to study law."

Darrow then told how he had set aside his dream for awhile to help support his family, how he had been sent out to work for a neighboring farmer. It was his first job and his pay was $15 a month and "found," the rural term for room and board.

"The first day I didn't like it pitching hay, but the second day finished me. The farmer put me to work catching potato bugs with a big stick and a basin of kerosene. It was hot and greasy work and mid-afternoon I quit.

"Long years after, I read an interview with a legal highbinder in Chicago in which he said he owed his success to hard work. Now, when newspaper men ask me that question I say the same thing, because that day and a half of hard work drove me to the law profession. I threw away the pan and haven't done a day's work since.

"On Declaration Day and the Fourth of July, the lawyers of the county came to our town to make speeches and in the fall they came around looking for jobs so they wouldn't have to work," Darrow continued.

"Finally I went down to the county seat to see if I couldn't get admitted 'behind the bar,' and I was admitted at Youngstown, Ohio—at the Todd House Bar. The examiners were there and along towards dawn they told me I was admitted. That probably accounts for my love of the bar room and I've even learned to drink your oke since coming here."

The mention of Hawaii's favorite home brew recalled other beverages: "My earliest cases were defending farmers who watered their milk and made hard cider, and sometimes I added to my fortune by playing poker. But once again it was fate that sent me to Chicago. I was going to buy a house in my home town, five hundred dollars down and three thousand dollars the rest of my life, but the next day the man came to me and said he couldn't deliver the deed because his wife wouldn't sign it. I got mad and said I didn't want the darned old house anyway and that I was going away. I didn't know where I was going, but it turned out to be Chicago.

"So you see, I didn't have much to do with it myself. I was born, couldn't help that; got a job on a farm, quit and took to law and then was admitted to the bar. And if it hadn't been for that stubborn woman—I didn't know them then as I do now—I'd still be in the same small town.

"Nobody seemed to notice my arrival in Chicago, nor did I attract notice until I was invited to speak for the single tax. Prior to the auspicious occasion, arranged by fate, I had been invited to speak with Senator Mason, but next day the Senator got all the headlines and the name of 'Darrow' was nowhere to be found in the newspapers.

"Man's life is divided into two parts - trying to get into the papers and then trying to get out of them," said the lawyer who had made more headlines than any other member of his profession since Abraham Lincoln.

"Then Henry George and I were pitted on the same platform with the single tax question at stake. After Henry George got through, the people started to leave and I saw my chance go glimmering. I told the chairman to hurry up and introduce me. I made a pretty good speech and the people sat down again. It was a big hit and the next morning the name Darrow was all over the paper. I read the accounts and read them again. Better reading I have never seen.

"I hurried to the office that morning, and found it no different than before—just single taxers and socialists who came to borrow the telephone," which rang for him.

"Chicago had a new mayor and I got a call to drop down to his office when I had time. When I had time! That was funny. I hurried right down and the next thing, the mayor had offered me a job at three thousand dollars a year. I never dreamed of such a thing, didn't know anything about the job or what was expected of me, but I took it and was put on the payroll before I left the office... Three months later I went up the ladder another rung and became assistant corporation counsel. Then fate stepped in again when the regular counsel became permanently ill with tuberculosis. I was given the job of chief counsel; but it was just an accident, I could have been given tuberculosis instead.

"It all just came along. I had nothing to do with it."

His transition from civil to criminal law he credited to only one thing: "Fate. The great railroad strike of forty years ago happened. Eugene Debs, a fine, active and humane man, was at the head of it. I sort of got my feelings mixed in the strike and then Debs got indicted. Unjustly, I thought. Debs asked me to take his case. I told him I wasn't a criminal lawyer, but a civil counsel. He told me if I lost, he would have to stand for it but he wanted me anyway.

"I took the case and won the jury trial, but Debs went to prison on a contempt finding by the judge. If all the lawyers were held in contempt by the court when they are in contempt, there wouldn't be many of us left.

"After Debs, they kept coming, the poor, the oppressed and unfortunates who had run afoul of the law," continued Darrow, revealing his deep and abiding interest in human beings as individuals and his unceasing efforts to defend them from injustice.

The amazing quality of humanism that canceled ego from the man and left him with a purged love for his fellow man was apparent to all who met him. He radiated an interest in everything about him, his attention always roving outward, seldom introspective. He was not a striking looking man, unkempt, now stooped to medium height, stocky with keen blue eyes and unruly hair. He could have been any kindly old codger approaching his seventy-fifth birthday had not the lines in his face been those of such deep-creased sympathy devoid of weariness that his uniqueness was noticeable at once. Few septuagenarians, too, shared Darrow's extraordinary openness of mind. He accepted the drama of life and its cast of players, from the greatest to the lowest, without preconceived judgment, and what is more, loved them more often than not.

Also he had lived long enough to be considered outdated by his critics, and was wise enough not to care.

"I have visited many jails to see my clients, have seen fathers, mothers, whole families plunged into the abyss, ruined by trying to save the people they knew and loved," he continued, now prophetic.

"To my way of thinking, I have solved the problem of crime. Every man is the product of two things, heredity and environment. He has nothing to do with either. Cure poverty and you will cure most of crime. When men become intelligent and humane, they will study crime as they have studied medicine and disease.

"Punishment only adds to suffering. It is not the cure. Since that day when I defended Debs, I have tried to help others who have been in trouble. I am interested in this above everything else.

"If we can get people to stop hating and to understand each other, if we can stop punishment and try caring, we will get where we want to go."

When asked his frame of mind as he approached his last trial, he replied, "Trials interest me," dodging the loaded question. "The cross examination and the argument both interest me, but there is uncertainty from the instant you step into the courtroom until the jury brings in its verdict. There are no principles governing all cases. Each case has its own peculiar characteristics, just as human beings have. Nothing is certain—especially before a jury. I remember a remark once made by a famous orator—that nothing is ever started until it is finished."

The remark was worth pondering.

TWENTY

Back-lit by dawn, Diamond Head lay silhouetted above the sleeping shoreline that stretched from Waikiki to Honolulu. Beneath its slopes a few roosters crowed but otherwise all was still. In the heart of the city, however, as early as 4 a.m. on the morning of Monday, April 11, there was bustling activity. A crowd was forming on the dark grounds of the courthouse. It was the opening day of the case for the prosecution. By 8:30 a.m., two hundred people were scattered under the statue of Kamehameha, many of whom had been there all night. The lawns were again dappled with the bright muumuus of Hawaiian women carrying lunch boxes of poi, rice and chicken. Prominent military wives had sent their stewards to hold places for them in line, and as the doors to Judge Davis's division of the Circuit Court opened at 9, sleepy gardeners were relieved of their reserve posts by freshly powdered kamaaina haole mistresses. The first person in line for admission was Mrs. Harry Kluegel, of the Citizens' Organization for Good Government. She, too, had come prepared, with a hot thermos. Admiral Stirling arrived in civilian clothes, greeting Mr. and Mrs. Walter Dillingham, who were seated near the door apart from the main body of spectators.

The subdued ambiance was relieved by other counterpoints of color: pink plumeria leis, several wide-brimmed lauhala hats sporting yellow feather bands, a cluster of flower-printed aloha shirts on a trio of Waikiki beachboys, headed by popular "Tough Bill" Keaweamahi, and most brilliant touch of all, the scarlet necktie of the prosecuting attorney.

A pause, as though the packed courthouse had been caught in a picture frame, greeted the four defendants and their attorneys who filed to the front of the court. Outwardly impassive, Grace Fortescue and Tommy Massie, both worn with strain but calm, sat tight-lipped and attentive. Lord and Jones, apparently little concerned and rather curious about court proceedings, gave no outward sign of emotion as Prosecutor Kelley rose and described the circumstances that could put them in prison for the rest of their lives.

Leaning at times on the rail, at times pacing back and forth before the jury box, with one hand in the pocket of his white linen coat, the other weaving in gestures, Kelley addressed the jurors:

"Gentlemen, these defendants are charged with the crime of murder in the second degree," he began, opening his preliminary presentation of the prosecution's case. Five members of the jury were wearing horn-rimmed glasses, which seemed to intensify the utter seriousness of the expressionless panel.

"In order that you may follow the course of the evidence, I will out-line briefly what the Territory will endeavor to prove to you," continued Kelley, speaking deliberately without raising his voice above a conver-sational pitch. "On the eighth of January, 1932, Joseph Kahahawai came to this building to report to probation officers, according to Judge Steadman's order. On that last journey, he was accompanied by his cousin, Edward Ulii. As they approached this building, three persons were outside who were soon to put into action forces that were to end Kahahawai's life." Slowly Kelley turned from the jury and trained his sharp blue eyes on each of the defendants.

"Those persons were Mrs. Fortescue, sitting in an automobile. A second was Albert Jones, lounging by the building. The third was Thomas H. Massie, waiting in a blue sedan. Two of these, Mrs. Fortescue and Jones, were noticed by Edward Ulii. When the two Hawaiian boys had arrived almost to the statue of Kamehameha, under the shadow of its outstretched hand, the finger of doom pointed at one of the members of that King's people!"

Then, directly facing Mrs. Fortescue, Kelley added in the same clear dispassionate voice, as he raised his own hand in the defendant's direc-tion, "And we will prove that it was the finger of Mrs. Grace Fortescue that pointed that doom—that, in the common vernacular of these days, she was the one who put Joseph Kahahawai on the spot."

The tension that had blanketed the room settled heavily on the four defendants as they sat beneath the accusing finger as grim as stone statues.

The prosecutor's was not the only hand that would point at them that day; he had in store half a dozen witnesses who would single them out from the mass of the courtroom, but first he wished to tell the jury the manner in which Kahahawai met his fate.

Calmly, letting the dramatic details speak for themselves, John Kelley described the abduction from the steps of the courthouse to the kidnap car, of the alarm spread by Eddie Ulii, and the subsequent hunt that ended on a barren cliff overlooking the rock rim of Hanuama Bay, where the car was run down and the body of Kahahawai dragged from the back seat.

He traced the thread of the story back to the little bungalow in Manoa Valley, where the killing took place. He described the scene that the police officers found when they entered the hastily tidied house. He told of finding the weapons, the blood spots on the floor, the blood-stained towels in the closet. Quietly, he seemed to take the jury by the hand and lead them to the couch in the living room where a purse was lying, and dramatically told them of opening the purse and finding a photo of all the Ala Moana defendants—"and the picture was so placed in the purse that that of Joseph Kahahawai was uppermost...so that every time that purse was opened, the first thing you would see was the face of Kahahawai."

Then raising his voice for the first time in his address to the motionless jurors, Kelley said, "And the officers found a coil of rope—a coil of rope exactly like that which bound the white sheet about the body of Kahahawai. It had one very distinctive mark, gentlemen of the jury—a purple thread that runs through the center of the rope. There is only one place on Oahu where that kind of rope can be found—and that is the Naval station at Pearl Harbor! And we will further show that it is now in use at the submarine base, where the three male defendants in this case are stationed!"

The prosecutor's only reference to the scene where he contended the crime was actually committed—the bedroom of the Fortescue home—was to deny that there was any evidence of a struggle.

"We will show from physical evidence," he continued, "in Mrs. Fortescue's home—in her own bedroom—that he was shot as he sat on the edge of a large double bed, and that he was carried into the bathroom, where he bled to death...We will show that a more ideal place for a murder could not have been selected...And we will show from physical evidence that there was no struggle in that room that would have justified these people, if they claim self-defense as an extenuation for shooting Joseph Kahahawai..."

The prosecutor walked slowly along the jury rail, looking each juror in the eye. "And when we prove these facts to your satisfaction we will then ask that you return a verdict of guilty as charged against the defendants!" He then swung around abruptly and resumed his chair.

Judge Davis called for a statement from the defense. Darrow rose from his chair. "The defense will reserve its statement until the prosecution has presented its evidence," he said with quiet confidence. Judge Davis ruled that such a decision was satisfactory to the Court.

"Then I would like to call Edward Ulii to the stand," said John Kelley. The courtroom stirred as the solemn young Hawaiian, wearing a blue shirt, green tie and dark blue suit, sat down stiffly in the witness box and took the oath swearing to tell nothing but the truth.

He told again of seeing a woman in a parked roadster "looking at Joe and I," of a man lounging by the building, and another man who drove a Buick sedan up to the curb. He told how the woman pointed to Joe.

"The fellow came up behind and told Joe to get into the Buick and said, 'Major Ross wants to see you, Joe,' and handed Joe a white paper with a gold seal."

"Is this the paper?" asked Kelley, introducing the "summons" as evidence.

"Yes, that's the one, and that's the man who showed it," said the Hawaiian boy, riveting his hard gaze on Jones and slowly raising his arm and pointing a finger at the defendant. "That man, sitting right there."

To make sure, Kelley had Ulii leave the witness chair and walk over to Jones. The latter stood up. "This is the man," repeated the boy, laying his hand on the sailor's shoulder. Lieutenant Massie was identified in the same way. The Hawaiian then turned to Mrs. Fortescue. Darrow forestalled the move to have her singled out so dramatically. The veteran lawyer, who was sitting directly in front of her, leaned back hastily and told his client to stand. Obediently Mrs. Fortescue rose from her chair and, with great composure, stood for a moment, her chin raised, then sat down, resuming her pose of disinterest and never looking at the witness, the jury nor the prosecutor.

"That is the woman," said Ulii.

Kelley unfolded the white paper with the gold seal as the witness returned to the stand and faced the defendants. Enunciating each word, the prosecutor read carefully the false summons. "Life is a mysterious and exciting affair and anything can be a thrill if you know how to look for it and what to do with it when it comes." The words echoed in the quiet courtroom.

Eddie Ulii also identified his cousin Joe's clothing. He told of being brushed from the running board of the car and dashing for help as the Buick sped off. The driver was wearing a false moustache.

"Describe it," said Kelley.

"If it was real, it would stick out, but it lay down flat on his face."

"Did you recognize the man who was wearing the moustache again?"

"Yes. Later, at the attorney's office when they brought him in," said the boy, pointing again at Massie. "He didn't have on the mustache then, but the glue was still on his upper lip."

"Thank you," answered Kelley, turning to Clarence Darrow. "Your witness."

The slouching defender, hands in his pockets, walked to the bar, as all eyes followed him. In a not unfriendly way, he addressed the witness.

"You say Kahahawai was your cousin. Any blood relation?"

"Yes, I'm a related cousin," said the boy. "My sister is married to a cousin of Joe's."

For the first time, the tense courtroom relaxed. Its occupants were well aware of the intricacies involved in trying to explain the relationship of a Hawaiian calabash cousin.

"Let me rephrase my question," said Darrow, asking if the witness was of the same blood of his cousin, being directly related on either his maternal or paternal side.

The equally puzzled Hawaiian shook his head. "I can't understand when you talk like that," he said, affording the spectators a chance to release the charged tension with a ripple of laughter.

Judge Davis came to the rescue, explaining to the defense attorney that Ulii was a cousin-in-law of Kahahawai, a legitimate and frequent relationship in the all-embracing family structure of Hawaiians. Even Darrow smiled as he resumed his cross-examination. He questioned the "cousin" on identification of Kahahawai's abductors, ending with the question of the false moustache.

"Have you ever seen a false moustache before?"

"No."

"That was the first and last one you saw?"

"Yes."

"No more questions," said the defense attorney.

The second witness was the court clerk, who revealed that Mrs. Fortescue had dropped into his office earlier during the week of the murder. "She asked me if it was true that two of the boys in the Ala Moana Case had been arrested in Hilo. I said no, that the boys had been reporting to me regularly."

"Anything else?" asked prosecutor Kelley.

"Yes. I told her myself that the boys were supposed to come every day."

Several police officers testified to the chase. Officer Harbottle telling the court, "We were looking for Daniel Lyman. We had to call in every half hour...At 9:50 I saw a car driving toward Koko Head. A woman was driving and two men were in it. The rear blind was down. That attracted my attention and I drove after the car."

Officer Seymour told of dragging the heavy body, "not quite cold," out of the car. The strapping athlete had weighed close to 200 pounds, and his limp corpse was more than one man could lift. A trusty had

helped Seymour, and the two of them had grabbed the rope that bound
the gory shroud of sheets—"a new Manila rope with purple thread"—
and finally laid the body in a basket.

The purple thread was but one of many in the web of circumstantial evidence being woven by the prosecution to entangle the four
defendants. As testimony on details progressed along the lines laid out
by Prosecutor Kelley in his opening address, loopholes were caught up
and the net was tightened and strengthened. Other police officers corroborated Harbottle's story of the pursuit and capture of the defendants, and each of them was asked by Prosecutor Kelley to get down
from the stand and lay his hand on the abductors of Kahahawai's body.
Each of these dramatic thrusts was in turn parried by Darrow as he
asked Mrs. Fortescue to rise before her accuser could wring the full
drama from his gesture.

There was drama enough in the spellbound courtroom as Kelley
paraded the exhibits of evidence before the jury, turning the solemn
legal chamber into a chamber of horrors. The jurors viewed photographs of the body, before and after the postmortem. A large chart of
the human anatomy was introduced during the testimony of Dr. Faus,
who had performed the autopsy, showing by a scarlet line the course of
the bullet that penetrated vital organs and severed the pulmonary
artery. The prosecutor held aloft the stained sheets, their laundry
marks torn from the corner but the damning spots of blood intact.
The rope was shown, its telltale thread visible to everyone in the
courtroom. The victim's cap, found on the couch at the Fortescue
house, his clothes, wrapped in a wet tarpaulin, his ring and his crushed
watch were held up for view. The rental contract for a Buick sedan
was shown, also a locker receipt and Mrs. Fortescue's purse, buttons,
two guns, cartridges, odds and ends collected in the silent house
behind the drawn shades by detectives on the fatal day—and finally a
single torn towel.

John Kelley snatched it from the table, walked to the jury box, and
with infinite care spread it to its full width, as though he were displaying a symbol of the entire trial. The jurors watched in fascination as
the lawyer smoothed out the terry cloth folds to reveal beneath the
bloody stains the blue initials USN, so boldly outlined that they could
not be overlooked.

With eyes as blue as the incriminating letters, the prosecutor trailed
his gaze across the face of the jury, then turning slowly with his grim tro-
phy raised above his head, looked out over the breathless courtroom.

When he dropped the towel, an audible sigh went up from the gallery. Kelley brushed his hands together in a gesture of ridding them of any distasteful vestige of the brutal crime.

As the courtroom reeled under the impact of the shocking evidence, the prosecutor cleverly called, in quick succession, those witnesses associated with each exhibit whose testimony would add, he hoped, the crushing coup de grace to the defense.

"Will Officer John Cluney take the stand."

The police officer was sworn in, one of half a dozen to identify the defendants, the kidnap car, the blood-soaked sheets. He was shown the coil of rope.

"It resembles the one found on the body," said the patrolman.

"Will Dr. Robert Faus take the stand."

The medical officer sat in the witness chair.

"On January 8, 1932, did you perform an autopsy on the body of a young Hawaiian male?" asked the prosecutor.

"I did."

"Will you describe your findings."

The City and County physician complied in detail. There was muffled weeping in the courtroom, but no other sound.

"Is that the bullet you removed from the body?"

"It is."

John Kelley fastidiously placed the small, lethal pellet in an envelope on the case of exhibits. He took up the rope. "Do you recognize this?"

"Yes. It was around Kahahawai's body."

"Did you notice any identifying marks on it?"

"Yes. Some stains and a purple thread running through it."

"Did you find stains in the Fortescue house?"

"Some stains, which I scraped off the floor. I examined it at Queen's Hospital, and the substance seemed to be human blood. I also found a fresh clot of blood on a towel."

"Did you test it?"

"Yes. It was human blood."

"Where were the spots that you scraped up?"

"In the bedroom with the double bed, opposite the bathroom, on the floor."

"Will Officer Luciano Machado please take the stand."

The officer raised his hand and swore to tell the whole truth. He described the darkened, disheveled house, so ineptly put in order, and the suspicious articles scattered within it: a .45 automatic, torn sheets, a woman's purse, a suitcase full of costumes and make-up, a .32 pistol in an egg basket.

"What kind of bullets did you find on the dining table?"

"A steel jacket .32 caliber bullet."

"Did you find a false moustache?"

"No."

"A length of rope that had been cut?"

"Yes. Like that one there. It was under a cushion of the davenport."

"Mr. Chris Omura please take the stand."

Mr. Omura told the court he was an employee of the Rosecrans Service Station, and that he had rented out a Buick sedan the afternoon of January 7, 1932.

"Do you know the name of the party that rented that car?"

"Yes, Gilkey. He had a friend with him...They wanted to rent a touring car and accepted the sedan. Gilkey came in to sign the contract, but had only twenty dollars; the deposit must be twenty-five dollars. The other party went into the lavatory. Gilkey joined his friend whom I could see washing his hands. He came back with five dollars more, and I made up the contract. Yes, that's it. On January 9, I saw the picture of the defendants in the Hawaii Hochi."

"Did you recognize among them any of those to whom you rented the Buick?"

"Yes, Lieutenant Thomas Massie. He was with Gilkey."

"William Keauough will take the stand."

Mr. Keauough told the court that he was a clerk at the Army and Navy Y.M.C.A. and that he had rented locker 356 to two sailors on the afternoon of January 7, 1932.

"Is this the receipt?"

"It is."

"What are the signatures?"

"A.O. Jones and E.J. Lord."

The prosecutor excused the witness and returned the receipt to its place among the exhibits. Next to it was a box of .32 cartridges. Kelley explained to the court that they were found in locker 356 at the Y.M.C.A.

"Will Mrs. Victoria Akana take the witness stand please."

Portly, part-Hawaiian Mrs. Akana was recognized by many in the courtroom as a police matron at the Honolulu jail.

"Did you search Mrs. Grace Fortescue on the late morning of January 8, this year?"

"I did," she whispered softly, her eyes downcast.

"And what did you find in her coat pocket?"

"A strip of sheeting with a laundry mark. She told me she wanted it back to use as a handkerchief." There were tears in the matron's eyes.

"The next witness was Mrs. Helen B. Stickney, who said that her sister, Mrs. Edna Tarleton, resided on the same street as Mrs. Fortescue.

"I was at her home at about 8 a.m., January 8," she said.

"Did you know who the neighbors were?"

"Yes, I'd been told Mrs. Fortescue lived next door."

"Did anything occur that morning?"

"I heard a noise like a shot around 9 o'clock."

"Could you tell from what direction it came?"

"Yes, mauka; from the direction of the Fortescue house."

"Thank you."

"Will Mrs. Edna Tarleton please take the stand."

Mrs. Tarleton also heard "a report like that of a gunshot about 9 o'clock."

"Were there any existing conditions that made you ladies apprehensive?"

"I noticed the time by the clock shortly after I heard the report. It was a little after 9. I noticed it because the baby cried and I looked at the clock to see whether it was feeding time. My dining room faces the Fortescue living room."

"Can you see the Fortescue yard?"

"On account of an oleander hedge, you can see only the roof of the house."

Concisely, John Kelley presented his witnesses and the trial moved quickly. All indications at the close of the first day of examination pointed to a complete presentation by the prosecution within the next two days. The first day's session ended at noon and the court was adjourned until 9 o'clock the next morning. The gentlemen of the jury were marched out of the building by their bailiff escorts and led through the grounds of Iolani Palace to their quarters in the Alexander Young Hotel.

Vasco Rosa, a serious young man who looked only at his interrogators and avoided the gaze of the jury and the gallery, was called to the stand the next day. He said he was an employee of the sporting goods department of Diamond-Hall Co., and a neighbor of Mrs. Fortescue.

"On the morning of January 8, did you see any cars parked in her driveway?"

"Yes, I did. It was a Buick sedan, blue."

"Had you seen that car in that vicinity before?"

"No."

"Any other cars around there?"

"Yes, I used to see a blue roadster."

"Have you a record of December 16 and 17 from Diamond-Hall with reference to sale of firearms?"

"I have."

"What must a prospective purchaser of a gun do before he can buy it?"

"He must get a police permit; we date and file the permit and issue the gun the following day."

"What name is on your record for the purchase of a gun on that date?"

"Albert O. Jones," said the clerk quietly. He produced the record.

"Have you a record of the sale of ammunition?"

"Yes."

"Did you sell a gun to Jones?"

"Yes, on permit 1810, dated December 16, for one .32 caliber Colt automatic pistol, for twenty-five dollars." Clip and cartridges were already placed in evidence. "Are these the same kind of cartridges as sold in the transaction just related?"

"Yes."

"Did you also sell a gun on December 15, on a permit dated December 14?"

"Yes." The entire courtroom hung on his words.

"To whom?"

"Mrs. Grace Fortescue."

The dramatic moment had been expertly staged. As he questioned the modest clerk, the prosecutor took the death bullet from its envelope and carefully stood it on end in the middle of the table where every member of the jury could see it. Then he removed an exploded cartridge case from the display of exhibits; it was the cartridge case found in Jones's pocket when he was searched by the police. Kelley placed it beside the bullet. He walked around the table, regarding the small objects silently. There was not a sound in the courtroom. Even the sailor Jones stared at the drama in fascination. The prosecutor then placed beside them a cartridge taken from a pistol clip found in Jones's pocket. Eloquently, the bits of steel gave mute evidence as the prosecution pursued its reconstruction of the jigsaw puzzle of Kahahawai's death.

John Kelley, in his skillful weaving of the circumstantial web, manipulated the threads leading to the actual killing, showing in patient detail the facts that traced the outward course of tragedy, but the moment of death was still a mystery known only to the four silent figures sitting behind Clarence Darrow. With infinite pains, the prosecutor picked up the three exhibits and examined them more closely on the flat palm of his hand; then, closing his palm, handled them gently for several moments as his round Irish face and bright blue eyes took on an expression of thoughtful contemplation. In the whole mesh of evidence so ably woven, no moment was more dramatic, and John Kelley played it to the hilt. The silence stretched to the breaking point, until a soft sob snapped its unbearable extenuation. In a corner next to the jury box, where Kelley had placed her in view of all, a dark and portly woman in a pink muumuu raised a handkerchief to her eyes. It was the mother of Kahahawai.

On this unrehearsed but perfectly timed cue, the prosecutor held out the bullet and casing to the young man on the stand and asked him to continue with his description of the gun purchased by Mrs. Fortescue, a gun amazingly enough, that had not yet been found by the police in their thorough search of the defendants, their homes and the kidnap car.

"It was a .32 caliber Iver Johnson revolver," said Rosa. "She also bought a box of cartridges like those," continued the clerk, pointing to the box of cartridges found at the Fortescue address.

"What sort of bullets were bought?"

"Lead bullets."

"Steel jacketed?"

"No."

Mr. Rosa was shown the bullet removed from Kahahawai's body, the shell of an exploded cartridge and a bullet from a clip that was found by police officers on the person of Albert O. Jones. The prosecutor placed the death bullet, the empty shell and a bullet from Jones's pocket in the witness's hand.

"Can you state if the steel jacketed bullets you have in your hand are the same?"

"They are."

"Will you fit the bullet from the body into the empty casing? Could that bullet have been fired out of that casing?"

Carefully, the young man, his face contorted in a frown of concentration, tried to twist the tiny bit of lead into the shell. The courtroom was dead still. Those up front could even hear the faint scrape of metal against metal. The clerk looked at John Kelley and held up the coupled bullet.

"It could fit."

"Call Investigator Arthur H. Stagbar."

The officer from the Public Prosecutor's Office took the stand, and told of searching the Fortescue home after the police officers' investigation.

"Did you find any other evidence?"

"Yes. I found two pearl buttons under the washbowl in the bathroom. They were on the floor." He was shown the buttons and identified them as the ones.

"What about the buttons attracted your attention?"

"Some thread attached to them corresponded with the goods of the shorts found in the bundle of Kahahawai's clothes at Koko Head...The buttons were identical with those remaining on the shorts."

Stagbar was followed on the witness stand by Chief of Detectives John McIntosh who told of going to the Massie home after the kidnapping and seeing Mrs. Massie and Seaman Jones. "Jones had a drink in front of me and seemed drunk."

Later, said McIntosh, he had returned and found them still there with the young sailor, Gilkey, who told of renting a Buick sedan, identified as the death car, and he had arrested Jones. Commander Bates of the Shore Patrol was with the detective and he advised Mrs. Massie to go to the Navy Yard at Pearl Harbor, and she did so, carrying a small bag.

"Was the bag large enough to hide a .32 caliber automatic?"

"Yes."

"Is Toshi Adachi in the court?"

A tiny, doll-like Nisei girl, with black hair cascading to her waist in a swatch of matte velvet, walked shyly to the stand. Under her arm were schoolbooks. She said that she was fifteen years old and had been employed after school as a maid by Mrs. Fortescue. She began working for Mrs. Fortescue on Thanksgiving Day.

"What was the last day you worked for her"

"January 7, 1932."

"Did you see Mrs. Fortescue that afternoon?"

"Yes," whispered the slender little witness, clutching her books to her budding bosom.

"Who was there with her?"

"Lieutenant Massie and two men. Haole men. I'm not sure who they were."

"Where did they go when they came in?"

"To the living room. Mrs. Fortescue and Lieutenant Massie came into the kitchen. Mrs. Fortescue paid me and told me not to come the next day, Friday, but to come Saturday. She said she wouldn't be at home Friday."

Kelley then asked if her mistress was in the habit of giving her days off. On the contrary, only twice before had the young maid been excused from work.

"And what days were these?" asked the Prosecutor.

"Christmas and New Year's."

James Hakuole, interpreter, was called to assist in the testimony of the next witness, Mrs. Shizuko Yamoto, who lived on East Manoa Road. In rapid Japanese she said that her house was about 20 feet from the rear of the Fortescue home. Her house was on higher ground and she could see beyond the hedge.

"Did you see lots of pilikia around there on January 8?" asked Kelley, using the local word for "trouble."

"I did not hear anything unusual, but I went out on the porch with my child at about 9:30 a.m. and saw a boxcar near the garage."

"You're sure you did not see a freight car?" said the prosecutor, smiling. It was a two-edged joke. The defense did not know that the Japanese referred to automobiles as boxcars, and the Japanese woman had no idea what a freight car was. "What else did you see?" he continued, as the spectators shared the wisp of humor.

"I saw a woman in the car, in the driver's seat, reaching back and trying to pull down the shades. I'd seen her frequently on the premises. I'd never seen the big car before. Only a small boxcar. There was also a man in a dark coat sitting in front. The woman finally leaned over the seat and drew the shade in back and then sat down again. I went back to the house."

"Do you see the woman in the courtroom?"

"Yes. There she is," said Mrs. Yamoto, pointing to Mrs. Fortescue.

Grace Fortescue rose without prompting, to be identified.

"Cornelius Gibbs."

Judge Davis reminded the prosecutor that it was close to 12:30 p.m., the hour when the court customarily adjourned. Kelley reassured the court that the testimony from his last witness for the day would be brief.

Mr. Gibbs said that he was employed by the Territorial Board of Health, formerly under Major Gordon Ross of the Territorial Police. He had been making an investigation for the prosecutor's office as to where Manila rope with purple thread through its center might be purchased. "Yes, that is the kind of rope I mean," he continued as he was handed the coil found beneath the cushion in the Fortescue home and the matching stained length of rope from Kahahawai's body.

"Did you find any of this kind of rope in any Honolulu stores?"

"No."

"Did you find any of this kind of rope?"

"Yes. I found this rope and also one of a smaller diameter with a purple thread in it. Such ropes cannot be obtained anywhere except the Submarine Base at Pearl Harbor.'

"That's all."

Throughout the fast-paced session, the defense counsel made little effort to cross examine witnesses, while prosecutor Kelley, confident that he had shown an unbreakable chain of circumstantial evidence, waxed witty and chided the other attorneys as he returned to the table. Darrow had retreated deeper into his rumpled suit, letting his assistants take over most of what cross-examining there was to be done, but when Kelley informed the court that he would close his case within 15 minutes after the opening of the next day's session, the dormant defender boomed from the depth of his chair, "We'll be ready!"

"Darrow has something up his sleeve," was the remark of one veteran of criminal trials, who had often seen the wily Chicago lawyer in action.

Although the cross-examination of the prosecution's witnesses had been played by Clarence Darrow in a minor key—a contrapuntal prelude to a forthcoming crescendo that the defense was keeping in reserve —its effect was not lost on the courtroom, nor had Kelley presented infallible evidence to substantiate the case he had stated with such spectacular assurance. On examining police officers who trapped the Buick sedan at Koko Head, the crafty old defense master created a picture of three dazed occupants, as far removed from life's reality as the corpse discovered with them. Slowly a theme emerged from his questions: that the defense would persistently attempt to bring out the state of mind of the three defendants, Mrs. Fortescue, Lieutenant Massie and sailor Lord, at the time of their apprehension, a state of mind that was not normal.

"Do you recall making a statement that 'Massie was very stern, sitting straight up, and never said a word—just looking straight up?'" asked attorney Montgomery Winn, speaking for Darrow and the defense.

The officer said he did , and that the other two were equally oblivious.

In cross-examining the police matron who had searched Mrs. Fortescue and sympathized with the mother of the battered girl, Winn asked, "Do you recall a few weeks ago telling me something? Did I ask you if Mrs. Fortescue had been nervous when you were with her?"

"Yes, and I said her hand was shaking and she put her finger to her mouth. She said her daughter's face was still disfigured."

Kelley and Ulrich were on their feet, objecting, and a brief, heated exchange ensued, with an accusation of "putting words in the witness's mouth" regarding the condition of Thalia Massie. But the defense had made its point, and in the still courtroom two women wept softly, the matron and mother.

On another occasion, Darrow punctured the prosecution's dramatic dialogue by questioning the exact location of the murder, claimed by Kelley to be Mrs. Fortescue's bed. "Did you find the bloodstains in only one room?" he had asked Dr. Faus.

"Yes. Only in that one bedroom."

"Did you examine the couch or the carpet in the living room for blood"

"No."

"Have you any idea if this was fresh blood?"

"The blood on the towel was fresh; that on the floor was dry.'

It was Darrow who, after police officers sent to search the Fortescue house had drained their memories of every sanguinary detail through the rapid fire of the prosecution interrogation, prompted his assistant to stand and ask a single question.

"Did you have a warrant to enter the house and make a search?" wondered George Leisure.

"No," admitted the officers, deflated and sheepish.

Defense counsel Winn cross-examined the parking attendant at Rosecrans Service Station who had rented the Buick to Gilkey, and discovered that the young man usually talked with "a couple of hundred" customers in one evening, intimating that the attendant's memory might have been refreshed by the Territorial police. "Did any police officers come to see you the day of Kahahawai's death?" asked Winn.

"I don't remember," said Mr. Omura in a sudden lapse of memory.

"After you recognized the picture of Massie on January 9, did you go to the police station?"

"No."

"Are you sure no police officer came to see you?"

"I don't remember."

"How did the police find out about it then? Did you tell anybody?"

"Oh yes," admitted the attendant readily. "The City and County Attorney called me."

"When I say police I mean anybody connected with the Police Department or the City and County Attorney's Office."

"Thanks!" interjected John Kelley. There was laughter in the courtroom, but again the defense had scored.

Wisely, Darrow refrained from cross-examining Mrs. Fortescue's distaff neighbors, the unintelligible lady who had seen the boxcar, the shy little maid, the officer who had found the rope at the Submarine Station, but Vasco Rosa, the young man who had sold the defendants the guns in December, was of great interest to the defense. As the unsmiling clerk fitted the death pellet into the steel casing and compared it with the unexploded steel-jacketed bullet found on the dining room table of the Fortescue house, it was George Leisure's voice that exploded in the courtroom. "Objection!' he shouted.

"Mr. Rosa" said Leisure, adamantly indignant. "You don't mean to say that that bullet was fired from that cartridge!"

"No, only that it might have been."

"About how many pistols did you sell during December?"

"About sixty."

"Was it after the Massie rape?" The single brutal syllable rang out in the courtroom.

"Yes."

"Was it before or after the news of the rape at the airport?"

"I don't remember."

"Was it before or after the escape of Daniel Lyman?"

"I don't remember the date of that."

"Or before or after the Kaikapu rape?" Again the word charged the chamber with danger.

"I don't remember."

"Do you remember," said Leisure, his picture of the panicked period when all of Honolulu was on edge almost complete, "do you remember whether men or women bought most of these guns?"

"Objection!" shouted Kelley. The prosecutor jumped to his feet. "The question is totally irrelevant."

"Then I withdraw it," said Leisure with the trace of a smile. "Witness dismissed."

As the last witness for the prosecution was called, the mother of the assaulted girl and the mother of the murdered boy faced each other across the courtroom.

"Will Mrs. Esther Anito please take the stand."

"Objection!" called out Montgomery Winn promptly, as Joe Kahahawai's mother paused, half-standing in her seat. She clutched her handkerchief and waited, her red-rimmed eyes gazing at the face of the prosecutor and her actions poised for his instructions. She was an ample, kindly woman in a freshly laundered cotton muumuu, and as she stood a murmur of sympathy rose with her.

"The defense is ready to admit as evidence the clothes worn by Kahahawai of the day of his death," said Winn in an effort to avoid the moving scene. "There is no need for identification."

"I prefer to have these clothes identified by the witness," answered Kelley well aware of the dramatic appeal of the moment, and over the objection of the defense, he staged the final scene of his presentation.

In a clear sad voice, Mrs. Anito answered his questions, holding herself with dignity and dabbing her tear-filled eyes with the inadequate square of linen crumpled in her hand. She told of her former marriage to Joseph Kahahawai, Sr., a marriage that had produced four children, only one of whom—a daughter—was now living.

"When did you last see your only son, Joseph Kahahawai, Jr., alive?" asked Kelley gently, close to the witness chair.

"That Friday morning."

"Was Joe in good health that morning when he left you?"

"Yes."

"And when did you see him again?"

"At the undertaker's."

"That was the body of your son, Joe?"

"Yes."

With almost tender care, Prosecutor Kelley picked up the stained and rumpled clothes from the case of evidence and held them before the court. "Are these the clothes Joe wore on Friday, January 8?"

"Yes, that's his shirt." The boy's mother wept openly, the tears rolling down her full brown cheeks and falling into her lap. "I know those clothes, I washed them all. They're Joe's."

"And the watch? And the ring?"

"Yes. Yes."

"Were any buttons missing from the shorts?"

"No." It was a faint wail. The silence in the courtroom seemed to tremble. Tommy Massie kept his eyes on the floor as though deeply moved. Mrs. Fortescue's fingers shook as she touched her pearls, and her sister, Mrs. Ripley, who was sitting at her side, lowered her head into her hand.

"No." said Mrs. Anito softly. "There was no buttons missing. I had washed all the clothes and sewed all the buttons on."

TWENTY-ONE

A week before the prosecution closed its examination of witnesses, on the same sparkling Friday morning, April 8, that the final jury panel had been selected, the Matson liner *Malolo*, out of San Francisco, neared the Aloha Tower at Honolulu Harbor. From its milling rails, the eager passengers smiled down on the bright sails and flower-laden hulls of small craft skirting the ruffled wake of the majestic steamer. The glistening brown bodies of Hawaiian beach boys arched in the sunlight as they dove from outrigger canoes into the faceted depths of the sapphire sea, catching the coins tossed from above.

Four of the passengers wedged at the rail were traveling incognito, and their faces were unfamiliar to their fellow voyagers who had formed the inevitable friendships and fleeting intimacies that the confines of an ocean voyage inspire. More than one passenger remarked that they had never seen the foursome before, and wondered where the two men and their wives had been keeping themselves for the past week. They were recognized, however, by a perceptive reporter who had boarded the ship off Diamond Head from the pilot's boat. The bespectacled face of Dr. James Orbison and the bearded one of Dr. Edward Huntington Williams, the two noted West Coast psychiatrists, were well known to those in the newspaper game. They were among the most reputable men in their profession.

The reporter soon learned that utmost secrecy had surrounded their departure from the West Coast and their arrival in Honolulu. Their names did not appear on the passenger list, although examination revealed that they were listed on the ship's manifest. Officers of the liner professed to know nothing of their presence aboard.

Further inquiry aboard ship revealed that the men were supposed to be Secret Service operatives. They had kept to themselves throughout the voyage, rarely leaving their cabins and taking no part in the ship's activities, but when the persistent journalist approached Dr. Williams, the famous alienist admitted his identity. Although refusing to discuss the case from any angle, he did admit that both he and Dr. Orbison had been invited to come to Honolulu by defense counsel in the Massie Case.

"I have no idea what we are supposed to do," said the doctor. "I cannot say anything until we have conferred with those who sent for us. We may have something to say after that."

When the *Malolo* docked, both men and their wives retired to their cabins and the reporter was informed by the ship's officers that the mysterious passengers would remain aboard until representatives of the defense called for them. It was surmised by the newsman that a conference was to be held aboard that afternoon, but it could not be confirmed. Although the reporter waited until the gangplank was empty, he did not see the doctors leave the ship. Later he conjectured that they must have disembarked on a launch from the far side of the vessel.

Despite the secrecy surrounding the passage of the two doctors, their presence in Honolulu was known in a matter of hours, and a plea of temporary insanity by the defense seemed all but assured. Word of these developments was carried swiftly over the coconut wireless, and the prosecuting attorney was aware of them before the first headlines confirmed the psychiatrists' arrival. Immediately, John Kelley put into motion the machinery of counteraction. He called in Harold T. Kay, Deputy Territorial Attorney General, and asked him to summon Dr. Paul Bowers and Dr. Joseph Catton, both equally eminent alienists in California, and enlist their services for the Territory's case. If they would make plans to leave immediately, they could board the *Malolo* on her next voyage, due to arrive in Honolulu on April 21. Dr. Bowers had been a friend for more than ten years of Dr. Edward Williams, and the two of them had figured prominently in the notorious Ruth Judd murder case.

For several weeks, John Kelley had been pondering the psychological ramifications of the Massie Case, and on more than one evening, musing over a highball, he recalled rumors of Thalia Massie's having had several consultations with a psychologist at the University of Hawaii. As the *Malolo* steamed out of Honolulu harbor without the two defense alienists, he decided that the time had come to track down these rumors. He put in a call to the university and was distressed to learn that the young psychologist with whom Thalia had conferred was out of town, on the island of Maui. Without hesitation, he called on President Crawford of the university, identified himself as Hawaii's prosecuting attorney, currently presenting the Territory's case in the Massie trial, and said that he had good reason to believe that the files of the young psychologist had materials of sufficient relevance to the murder case to warrant their being turned over to the prosecuting attorney's office. The president agreed, reminding Kelley that the contents might be of a confidential nature and any documents could be considered privileged communications, according to law. The prosecutor assured him that they would be treated with appropriate discretion and within legal boundaries. He indicated that the actual contents would not be made public.

When the psychologist returned from Maui, the file was gone. "I never saw the folder or its contents again," Dr. E. Lowell Kelley was later to confide, adding that he had "telephoned her husband, Lt. Massie, advising him that I felt she was in need of medical psychiatric care." He was also to admit that when the murder occurred, its implications had plunged him into deep conflict regarding his responsibilities to Thalia Massie as a student-counselee on the one hand and to society on the other. "In wrestling with this conflict, I decided to ask the advice of the University physician at the time ... I told him of the situation in which I found myself, that of having information of possible relevance to a just decision in the case, and asked his advice as a member of a much older profession as to the proper ethical behavior on my part. I shall never forget his reply. To my consternation, he replied, 'Thank God I don't know what you know!' To this, I immediately responded, 'In that case, please treat our conversation as a privileged communication and I will not mention the matter to anyone else.'"

With the excitement created by the arrival of the defense psychiatrists, the already over-burdened newsmen found themselves working around the clock. The former courtroom of Judge Alva Steadman, scene of the Ala Moana trial, closeby that of Judge Davis, was converted into a press room. The racket emanating from its open doors was in sharp contrast to the sealed silence of the court when in session with the Massie Case. Telegraph machines ticked incessantly as mainland correspondents sent thousands of words out over the air via facilities of two wireless companies. Operators were on duty overtime, handling the mounting backlog. Between deadlines, members of the local newspaper fraternity adopted the former courtroom as an impromptu press club, chatting and drinking coffee at the littered tables. The room took on the air of a convivial retreat. Officials of the wireless companies dropped in from time to time to see how things were going, police officers and court bailiffs briefly enjoyed a smoke , attorneys joked with newsmen to let off steam, and now and then either Jones or Lord, or the two sailors together, would slip into the informal, smoke-filled room and relax over a hand of poker.

One of the typically Hawaiian features of the trial was the absence of obvious guards for the defendants, who were able to enter and leave the courtroom without a bristling escort of armed policemen. During the recesses, the men on trial mingled amiably with newspapermen, attorneys, friends and spectators, smoking and chatting to relieve their nerves. The handcuffs and billy clubs popularly associated with murder trials were nowhere in evidence. Even in the middle of the most horrendous moments of testimony concerning the grisly details of the killing, the stifled air of the courtroom also carried the scent of tropical flowers.

Outside, the clarity of perfect April days bathed the city and a cloudless sun glanced off the gilded statue of the warrior king as the trial progressed into its second week, moving with relentless precision toward its climax.

On the night of Wednesday, April 13, patrons returning home from the late shows at downtown movie houses were startled to see an army of hopeful spectators already camping on the grounds of the Judiciary Building in anticipation of the next day's opening of the case for the defense. It was rumored that one of the defendants would be the first witness. The line for admission to the courtroom, limited to a capacity of 200 seats, only 75 of which were set aside for spectators, had started forming at 11 p.m. At 11:45, the intrepid Mrs. Harry Kluegel, armed this time with a camp stool as well as her customary thermos, settled on the lawn for the night. At midnight, six men in civilian clothes joined the clubwoman and her fellow campers, saying they planned to hold places for Naval officers and their wives, including Mrs. George Pettingill, the Fleet Admiral's wife. Seventeen enlisted men swelled the military ranks. At 3:40 a.m., 75 people, the gallery's capacity, had arrived and no more spectators were allowed on the lanai of the courthouse. The select few all-nighters spread out their pillows and blankets under the arches.

The first streaks of dawn, stage-lighting the scenery of black palms, heralded the breakfast hour, and lunch baskets were unpacked and spread in picnic profusion beneath the statue. As the Hawaiian ladies dipped their fingers in poi and sipped Kona coffee, another member of the Kluegel family arrived to replace thermos bottles with fresh ones and offer hot ham sandwiches, which were shared with other hungry all-night sitters. Many a Honoluluan who had risen before daybreak and rushed downtown to be among the early comers found that they were already too late. Disappointed but determined, they joined the crowd forming across the driveway, where three husky police officers kept them cordoned off from the courthouse entrance. Among the anticipating crowd, women outnumbered men four to one, and when the Judiciary Building was opened by its custodian at 7 a.m., the ladies' restroom was filled with a flurry of powder puffs, washcloths, combs, lipstick and toothbrushes.

"It was, however, a tired, worn-out group who took their seats in the courtroom," commented a reporter as the trial opened its eighth day of session.

"Thomas Massie."

A wave of excitement washed over the gallery as the slender young Naval officer walked to the front of the courtroom to take the stand in his own defense. Clad in a dark blue-gray suit, with a yellow necktie, he stood steadily erect as he took the oath, almost barking out the words, "I do," then sat down with one leg crossed over the knee. His hands lay quietly in his lap, his gaze was fixed on Clarence Darrow who stood facing him. "His face is thin and somewhat sallow, with a pointed chin. His nose is long and sharp and his hair is set far back over a high forehead. He looks much more than his twenty-seven years," wrote Russell Owen of The New York Times.

Pale but composed, the muscles about his jaws twitching slightly, he answered questions rapidly and distinctly in a Southern accent. He said he had been five years in the Navy and was born in Kentucky. He told of his preparatory school training and his graduation from the Naval Academy in 1927, the year of his marriage to teenage Thalia Fortescue. "It was the voice suggesting that of a frightened schoolboy that answered the slow, meditative questions," noted a reporter. Most of the newsmen, however, were impressed by the straightforward and courteous way in which he handled the answers, and considered him a very effective witness.

"I came to Honolulu in June 1930," Lieutenant Massie said.

"Do you remember an incident of going to a dance—" Darrow began.

"I can't forget it." The audience was visibly affected by the emotion in the words.

"That was in September of last year?"

"Yes."

"Where was the party?"

"At the Ala Wai Inn, Honolulu. That afternoon I asked Mrs. Massie if she'd like to go. She said she didn't care much about going, but that she would. We called up some friends to accompany us. After dinner she said she didn't feel like going, but I persuaded her to go."

There was a sudden motion in the quiet courtroom as the prosecutor pushed back his chair. "I'd like to know if counsel intends to go into the Ala Moana Case," said John Kelley in a strident voice. He was dressed in his traditional crisp white suite and scarlet cravat.

"I do so intend,' Darrow replied quietly.

"The prosecution should therefore be allowed to know if an insanity plea is to be used," said the prosecutor.

"We do expect to raise the question of the sanity of the moving one in the last part of this affair, the one who shot the pistol," Darrow said.

"We wish to know if the plea of insanity is to be offered on behalf of Lieutenant Massie," Kelley said.

"I don't think that is necessary," Darrow answered.

His Irish dander up, Kelley thought it was absolutely necessary; he'd like to have the defendant examined by some psychiatrists of his own choosing if there was to be an insanity plea. Darrow said he didn't mind if some psychiatrists heard the testimony, but he might not see fit to submit the defendant to the prosecutor's physicians. Kelley's face turned the color of his tie. "I object!" he shouted. His objection was overruled by Judge Davis.

The prosecutor lowered his voice and continued: "We have a right to know, or feel that we do, that in event the insanity plea is offered, and since we are informed that certain psychiatrists are here, which of the defendants is to be claimed as insane at the time of the killing," said Kelley.

"I'd be perfectly willing to accommodate counsel," Darrow said, "even to the extent of calling another witness, although I'd like to continue with Mr. Massie."

Judge Davis allowed Mr. Darrow to proceed, and he asked Lieutenant Massie to speak up more loudly as his replies lacked volume.

Speaking clearly, Lieutenant Massie told in detail of the party at the Ala Wai Inn, and other events of that fateful night.

People in the court were straining forward, hanging on Tommy Massie's every word. Handkerchiefs began to dot the sea of faces. Even a few men dabbed at their eyes furtively. The jurors heard the defendant's sad story with rapt attention. His voice heightened the effect of his testimony. The first breathless harshness gave way to a soft drawling flow of words that rose and caught suddenly in the more intimate recital of details. He told of his battered young wife, bleeding from the nose and mouth, lying in his arms and sobbing that she'd been raped "over and over." He told of his dazed horror. "I said, 'Oh my God, no!' and sat there stunned while she kept wishing they'd killed her." At such times, Tommy Massie lowered his head and regathered the inner control of his emotions that memory had momentarily snatched from him.

"The next morning I called my commanding officer who came with his wife. I called Dr. Porter and left Mrs. Massie. I went to Captain Wortman, who said he'd do all he could. He took me to a radio office and I wired Mrs. Fortescue what had happened."

Mrs. Fortescue's face twitched as this testimony was given. She fought back the tears, swallowing hard, but they would not be restrained and she let them flow freely down her cheeks, making no effort to hide them.

"Dr. Porter had found my wife in a critical condition from mental and physical shock and possibly a broken jaw. We took her to the hospital. I stayed there until late that night. Then I went home, but I couldn't sleep. The next day or the one following, they brought in four assailants for identification."

"Objection!" shouted the Prosecutor. "We protest to the use of the word, 'assailants.'"

"Objection sustained," said Judge Davis. Tommy rephrased his sentence, using the word 'people' instead.

"Mrs. Massie questioned them all, concentrating on Kahahawai. I was there and later she told me, 'They are the ones.' I said, 'Don't let there be any doubt, darling.' She said, 'Don't you know if there were any doubt I'd never draw another free breath?' The men were Horace Ida, Kahahawai, David Chang and Benny Ahakuelo. The next day they found Mrs. Massie's jaw fractured and that they might have to draw a tooth to allow the bone to heal. They finally found they'd have to draw the tooth. I went with her to the operating room. I held her hand through the whole thing. They had to cut the gums away and she screamed, although they had given her gas. I was sure she felt it, so they gave her ether. She cried all the rest of the next day. I stayed with her every night as long as they'd let me. I went to the police station to learn about these people and the authorities told me that they had criminal records."

"When did you learn just what happened to her?"

"At the hospital, she couldn't talk to the detectives. She told me she had left the dance to walk to Ft. DeRussy. At the turn on John Ena Road, two men jumped out of a car and grabbed her. They hit her to stifle her screams."

Frowning down at the floor, Lieutenant Massie continued his testimony, interrupted briefly by the drone of an airplane passing overhead.

His voice broke as he told the details of the story his wife had told him of the assault. The deeply moved courtroom and each witness of the young husband's agony seemed to share his grief as though it were their own. It was apparent the bowed officer was quietly weeping to himself.

"She offered them money, but they beat her all the more. Every time she spoke, they'd beat her. They laughed when she said that I would give them money. They turned off into the bushes. I asked her who beat her. She said Chang and Kahahawai, but mostly Kahahawai. Kahahawai assaulted her, though she pleaded for mercy. He hit her in the jaw. She has told me this a thousand times."

"Did the police take you to the place?'

"Yes, they did. And told me they had found green beads there. A broken string of such beads was found on her dress, the one she wore that night. After they had taken out the tooth at the hospital, they wired her jaw together and clamped her jaws so she couldn't open them. She'd have to take food through a tube and would scream with pain when she swallowed. Her jaws were wired together for about six weeks...She was running a temperature, and I called Dr. Withington. He told me her condition was critical, so I got a day nurse and acted as night nurse myself. They gave me some clippers and told me that if she should get sick at her stomach to clip the wires or she would strangle.

"One night she rose up in bed and screamed 'Don't let him get me!'" the tormented witness went on. "I said, 'Nobody is here, darling, nobody but me.' 'Yes,' she cried, 'there is Kahahawai, he is there!' Friends advised me to go back to duty to take my mind off it. I went back but every time I was still, the whole thing came back to me and preyed on my mind, and all I could see was the crushed face. I couldn't eat or sleep. I used to get up at night and walk the floor, going over the whole thing again and again."

"Did you ever get it out of your mind?" Darrow asked gently.

"Never," Tommy Massie replied.

"Did her mother come?" Darrow asked.

"That was later. She wanted to go home, where she said she'd feel easier in her mind. We took her home, but kept the nurse. Several nights she called me and said she heard footsteps under the windows. I thought she was imagining things. But one night I heard the steps. I rushed out with a gun and circled the house, but didn't see anyone. But I know someone was there. We kept Dr. Withington for about two months."

"Did he ever treat you?"

"Well, he advised me to get some sleep."

"Did he give you any information as to your wife's condition?"

"At the hospital I was told I'd have to expect two things, disease and conception. After Mrs. Massie's mother came, we knew an abortion would have to be performed. This had a strange effect on my mind. Dr. Withington performed the operation."

"Might that pregnancy have been due to you?"

"No, it couldn't have been."

The exhausted Naval officer had finished his narrative for the day. He stepped down from the stand, his face ashen but his shoulders squared. Mrs. Fortescue rushed forward and wound her arm in his as they left the courtroom.

That night, the full encampment of seventy-five spectators slept on the chilly cement floor of the portico outside the courthouse. At times they stood, chatting in whispers but never forsaking their places in line. Some read the biography of Darrow or the lurid story of Kahahawai's murder in the current issue of a detective magazine. From Manoa and Nuuanu valleys, the usual contingent of yard boys stood as proxy until their sleepy mistresses arrived at dawn to assume their reserved places. After the first day of the defense, the "refugees," as they were dubbed, were offered radio entertainment and the promise of future lanai suppers to be catered by a downtown restaurant. As the doors to Judge Davis's court opened, they filed in, in an orderly line, having survived the earlier stampedes and assumed the privileged distinction of courtroom veterans.

A wail went up and eyes clouded with disappointment as the next morning's session opened with an announcement from Judge Davis: "The court has been informed that Mr. Darrow, chief counsel for the defense, is ill and can not be present. The defense has asked a continuance until 9 a.m. Saturday. This seems a reasonable request, and the court will stand adjourned until that time."

The judge's words had the effect of a sudden drop in an elevator. The shock among the spectators was not one of concern for the aged defense counsel's ailing health but of devastation at having spent a sleepless, hungry night on the hard courthouse lanai in vain. "The audience at today's session of the Fortescue-Massie trial, a disappointingly short session, was a brilliant, almost dazzling, representation of Honolulu society," reported the *Star-Bulletin*, and some of the hollow-eyed ladies in their wrinkled fashions made no effort to hide their indignation at having paid scalpers $5 to $50 for a place that had been reserved since noon the day before.

The defense issued a news release saying "Mr. Darrow's illness, a slight attack of intestinal trouble, is not serious, but sufficient to prevent his appearance in court. He is under the care of Lieutenant Commander J.E. Porter, assistant yard medical officer at Pearl Harbor. Mr. Darrow said that he is feeling much better than he felt last night, and that he expects to resume examination of witnesses Saturday."

Prosecutor Kelley, speaking informally at the conclusion of the brief session, announced his intention of combating further admission of evidence from the Ala Moana Case unless it were shown to be specifically applicable to the person who is shown to be insane.

"If the defense tries to prove that Lieutenant Massie was insane at the time of the shooting, I shall insist that they prove him sane at the present time. If he is still insane, his testimony is not competent."

As the court adjourned, a reporter approached George Leisure and asked if there were any truth to reports that Mrs. Massie would be called to the stand.

"No comment," said the defense counsel.

"One other announcement," said a voice at the courtroom door as the disappointed exodus began. It was Chief of Police Weeber, and he wished to state that "prospective spectators at the Fortescue-Massie murder trial will not be allowed to foregather at the Judiciary Building during business hours. No person will be allowed to loiter about the building until after 6 p.m. Large numbers of loiterers have interfered with the regular business of the courts." The new Police Chief added that all those admitted to the trial would hereafter be searched at the door.

The next day the old court warrior appeared none the worse for his brief bout of "intestinal trouble, brought on by the late night he'd spent with convivial members of the press." He smiled as the bailiff frisked him, there being no exceptions to the strict police ruling. Mr. Darrow had carefully plastered down his hair, but one or two incorrigible locks had freed themselves from their tonic vise and strayed over the heavy brow. He was wearing a coat that would have been described as shapeless had it not assumed the singular form of its owner, as though stuffed at random with bulging objects. In sharp contrast was the immaculate mien of the prosecuting attorney, whose sparse hair was seldom out of place. Within a few minutes, however, of the court's resumption on Saturday, April 16, the grooming of both men was in a state of disarray brought on by a heated argument that preceded the second chapter of Tommy Massie's testimony.

The session had opened calmly enough. Darrow ambled to the bar and addressed the judge in a conversational tone.

"Your honor, there seems to be a little misunderstanding," he said. "The evidence shows that Lieutenant Massie, who is now on the stand, fired the fatal shot. We are willing to state, to avoid conflict in this court, that Lieutenant Massie held the gun when the fatal shot was fired..." Now he turned to his witness. "Lieutenant Massie, let us continue your story. Did you attend the Ala Moana trial?"

"Yes."

"What was the result?"

"Objection!"

Flushed with thwarted fury, the prosecuting attorney leapt to his feet. The creases in his suit seemed to crackle as he strode into the ring with Darrow and raised his arm like a fencer, slicing the air to emphasize the finality of his words. "The only plea on which this testimony is admissible is to show the insanity of Massie or some other one of the defendants. We insist upon knowing this at this time!"

"Your Honor," said Darrow in a purposely purring voice, "I didn't say that Lieutenant Massie killed the man, but that the gun was held in his hand when it was fired, whether or not he knew what he was doing."

"Then we must ask if the defendant is now sane!" Kelley demanded.

"I don't think it is necessary for the Court to rule on this," Judge Davis said sternly. But the prosecutor's trigger temper had been tripped. His florid face knotted in anger as he continued to object. Judge Davis rapped his gavel.

"Then we will presume that Lieutenant Massie was insane," Darrow answered acidly.

It was time for the prosecution to call on the cunning of smooth-talking Barry Ulrich. As Kelley resumed his seat, his assistant coolly asked Darrow to name the type of insanity which he would seek to prove, in order that the state might produce its own medical testimony.

"We are not particular as to the nomenclature of the type of insanity," continued Ulrich in a voice as well-oiled as Darrow's, "but what we want to know is whether the insanity is a species of paranoia or any other definite type of psychosis, so that we may examine the symptoms. We want a statement of the mental condition of the defendant that would bring it into the category of legal insanity."

While this skirmish was going on, Lieutenant Massie sat in the witness chair with lips twitching and eyes blinking occasionally.

"We have two psychiatrists. I do not know whether they will agree on the name or not," Darrow said.

"They are going to try to prove him insane, but don't know how," answered Ulrich in disdain.

"We know exactly how," growled Darrow.

"Then we want to know what it is," said the prosecution.

"Counsel has asked what the result of the trial was," Kelley interrupted, his temper controlled. "That answer will have no bearing on his mental condition. He wasn't asked if the result had any effect on him or what the result was."

Mr. Darrow walked over to Tommy and changed his question.

"Were you in court when the jury returned?"

"No."

"Were you informed what the verdict was?"

"A mistrial."

"I object!" scorned the prosecutor. "The question is immaterial, irrelevant and incompetent!"

"The question has already been answered," the Court informed him.

"I move it be stricken," said Kelley.

"This motion will be denied," said Judge Davis. Darrow continued his examination.

"Did you do anything after you heard the verdict?"

"Yes. I couldn't understand it."

"I object!" said Kelley again. "The question is leading."

"The Court ruled that to save time, leading questions might be allowed as long as the counsel did not put words into the witness' mouth," answered the Judge, indicating the defense continue.

"Whom did you consult afterwards?" questioned Darrow.

"Mr. Beebe. I think he was legal advisor."

"I object to what he thinks," Kelley interrupted.

"Then I know he was!" Lieutenant Massie said.

Judge Davis admonished Lieutenant Massie to withhold his answers when an objection was raised, and not to volunteer answers.

"By whom was Mr. Beebe retained?"

"By me," said Massie referring to Eugene Beebe, attorney with the firm Thompson and Winn.

"You consulted him about a week afterwards."

"Yes."

"What was your physical condition?"

"I couldn't speak much. I was in Dr. Withington's care. The next week I began to hear vile rumors about my wife and myself."

"What were these rumors?"

"One was that I didn't believe my wife's story and was getting a divorce."

"Any truth in it?"

"Certainly not."

"Another was that I had found my wife with a Naval officer, Lieutenant Branson, and that I had beaten her. Lieutenant Branson had been with me all evening." Massie's drawl tightened with indignation. He had been leaning slightly forward in the witness chair, his hands lying loosely in his lap, and his voice had carried the same soft but vibrant inflection of his previous testimony until the mention of the rumors circulated about his wife charged it with tension. Scowling and somber, he gripped the arms of the chair and his slight body stiffened.

"Did you hear any other rumors?"

"I heard that I had left the dance and followed my wife in my car and had beaten her. Then that the assault had been done by a crowd of Naval officers."

"Did you notice any difference in your treatment at the Naval station?"

"Yes. I could not stand being in a crowd. The enlisted men would shun me and avoid me."

"Any other rumors?" coaxed Darrow.

"Yes, the worst one. It was that my wife had not been assaulted at all, and that she was a notoriety seeker trying to get into headlines," said Tommy with such cold contempt that his voice broke.

"Did you hear these rumors often?"

"Yes. They never stop. I could not understand this vile, rotten gossip by people who didn't know us!"

"Did these stories get into the papers?"

"I don't know."

Tommy Massie was permitted to speak freely, using such adjectives as vile and rotten without objections.

"Did you ask Mr. Beebe what could be done?"

"Yes. He said he couldn't understand the rumors, so I asked him if I could get written evidence from one of these people, would it be evidence? He said it would be if no force were used and no marks left on the person. He said the case was in such a condition now that such a confession would be necessary."

"What did he mean by leaving marks?"

"He must have referred to the Ida case.'

"Did you begin thinking about what to do?"

"Yes. I wanted to get an admission to clear my wife's name."

"Do you mean by 'these people' the defendants in the Ala Moana case?"

"Yes."

"Objection!" Again Kelley was on his feet. "I don't want to raise unnecessary objections, but if Mr. Darrow wants to testify in this trial, let him take the witness stand. The witness has not mentioned the name of any of the defendants in the Ala Moana case in his testimony."

"He referred to it in his previous answer," said Mr. Darrow.

"You may proceed," said the Judge to Darrow.

"Did you talk about this to other people?" said Darrow to Massie.

"Yes. I came home from a trip to Hilo. I had asked Captain Wortman to detail a guard while I was away. Jones had been detailed, and I thanked him for taking care of my home while I was at sea. He said he would be glad to help me in any way. Mrs. Fortescue and I talked about how we might stop the rumors. I felt I wanted to cut my brains out so that I wouldn't keep remembering. Then I heard that Kahahawai was getting ready to crack. I told Major Ross about this, and told him who I was. He said he'd be glad to call Kahahawai in, and that he would talk to him as his former battalion commander. He said he would call me in a few days, but he did not. When I didn't hear from him, Mrs. Fortescue went down to learn what time the defendants came to the courthouse every day. We thought we would get one of them and bring him up to the house and scare him into a confession."

"Did you have any intention to kill him?"

Kelley objected but was overruled.

"No," was Massie's answer. "Certainly not."

"Mrs. Fortescue knew about your idea of getting a confession?"

"We figured that we would have to use some sort of a ruse so I took the seal from a diploma of mine and printed matter from the newspaper and fixed up the summons."

"Who furnished the newspaper clipping?"

"Mrs. Fortescue."

"Do you remember the rope that was used in evidence?"

"Yes. It was in my home. Mr. Kelley is right. I got it at the base about six months ago, for a leader rope. I had a wire in the yard between the pear tree and the garage and was going to make a dog run of it until he got used to the place and couldn't get away. One night Mrs.

Fortescue ran into this wire and fell. She suggested I use the rope instead. I got the line from my chief on the boat. When I got it home it seemed pretty large and I never used it..."

Darrow returned to the subject of rumors and asked if they had continued to shatter the young husband's peace of mind.

"Yes. I didn't think I could stand the rumors any longer. About Thursday, January 7, I told Jones that I heard that 'the big one was ready to crack.' Jones agreed to help. I asked him if he knew anyone else he could count on. So he took me up to see Lord, and we drove into town together. And at the Y.M.C.A. they changed to civilian clothes and then went to Mrs. Fortescue's home."

"What investigation was made about getting in contact with the deceased?"

"Mrs. Fortescue did all that."

"Did you arrange to meet the next day?"

"We thought we had better stay together that night so that there would be no hitches."

"Why did you come here?"

"We thought it would be the best place to pick up the big one, Kahahawai. Mrs. Fortescue said he reported here at 8 o'clock."

"Did you get a machine?"

"Yes, all four of us went down the day before in Mrs. Fortescue's car. We ran into Gilkey and Jones and asked them to get us a car. Later that night Jones brought up the Buick and asked if it was all right."

"Were you at the place where the car was hired?"

"No, I wasn't."

"Where did you sleep that night?"

"At home."

"Did Jones and Lord stay there?"

"No, at Mrs. Fortescue's house. I woke them up when I got there at 7 o'clock."

"What room did they sleep in?"

"In the room with the double bed. Mrs. Fortescue was getting them breakfast. After breakfast we went into the living room. I told Jones about the summons idea, but he was uneasy. He wanted to take his gun, but I would not let him. Mr. Beebe had said no force could be used, so he laid the gun down. It was a .32 automatic Colt." Tommy said Jones was worried about Kahahawai being so big.

"What time did you leave that morning?"

"About twenty-five to eight."

"Did you have a gun?"

"I brought my gun over there, but didn't take it to town. That was a .45 service automatic. I think I left it on the settee."

"On the morning of the eighth what time did you start downtown?"

"About 7:35...We got to town before eight. Lord got out to watch the rear entrance."

"How long had you known Lord?"

"One day."

"Who drove on the way downtown?"

"I drove the Buick. I think Mrs. Fortescue drove the roadster." He then told of riding up Kalakaua Avenue. "I remember that we must not use force or any confession would be worthless."

"Did you have on a false moustache?"

"No, sir, I have never worn any kind of moustache. Just dark glasses and gloves, to make me look like a chauffeur. We drove to Mrs. Fortescue's house." The pulse of the courtroom quickened as those present waited to hear what really happened in the bungalow in Manoa Valley.

"When we got into the kitchen, I fixed up a .32 automatic, and called out, 'Come in, Major Ross is here.' I took off the glasses and gloves. Kahahawai was sitting down. Then Mrs. Fortescue and Lord came in. I took the gun and confronted Kahahawai, pulled back the slide and let it slip into place."

In practiced detail Massie told of his interrogation of the terrified Hawaiian who steadfastly maintained his innocence. The Lieutenant's Southern accent lent sympathy to the story of his torment in facing the man whom his young wife accused of brutally raping her.

His knuckles whitened as he gripped the arms of the witness chair and his voice slowly became more strident as his version of events led to the threatening lie that caused the Hawaiian to crack:

"I said, 'You know what Ida got. That's nothing to what you will get.' He refused to talk, so I told Lord to go out and get the boys. He moved forward in his seat. I said, 'Ida talked and he told plenty on you. Those men will beat you to ribbons.' I said, 'you know your gang was there.' He said, 'Yes, we done it.'"

The Naval officer had told his story unsparingly, an appealing and pathetic figure, who, as his lawyer would say later, "has gone through a crucifixion such as come to few men in this world of sorrow." As he neared the end of his ordeal, the slight long-suffering husband carried a larger measure of popular sympathy than ever had been accorded to him before, including that of the Hawaiians. Darrow had also so manipulated his testimony that the clear story of motivation emerged from the cloud of rumors—and it was a sympathetic one. Only the prosecution listened with less than a full cup of charity.

TWENTY-TWO

The most rapid dialogue of the trial was the cross examination of Lieutenant Thomas Massie by Prosecutor John Kelley. It moved with the precision of a duel. Pointed thrusts and responding parries flashed in the courtroom.

"Did you at any time entertain an idea of killing Kahahawai?" Kelley began.

"No, Mr. Kelley."

"Not when your wife identified the men?"

"I might have felt like it. I never thought of it. I knew it wasn't the right way.

"You were born in Kentucky and proud of it?"

"Very proud of it."

"Are you proud of being a Southerner?"

Darrow objected.

"What has being a Southerner got to do with being proud?"

"I don't know, I just want to find out," Kelley answered.

"I do know," Darrow said. "The purpose of the question is evident and has no place in the case."

"Then let Mr. Darrow state what he knows," Kelley said.

"It's irrelevant, immaterial and asked for the purpose of creating prejudice."

"We are confronted here with a man who claims he killed a man through insanity," snapped Kelley. "We've allowed enough latitude to counsel, too much in fact. The question of the motivation of this crime may be traced back to the cradle."

"I do not see that the question of the witness' pride has any bearing," said Judge Davis. "I sustain the objection."

"Mr. Massie, you say you got this rope out at Pearl Harbor six months before Kahahawai was killed?"

"Something like that, Mr. Kelley. It was quite a while ago."

"And you got it to replace the wire stretched in your yard because Mrs. Fortescue walked into the wire?"

"Yes."

"Yet Mrs. Fortescue arrived here only in October."

"I'm not sure about the time."

"It was not six months before you killed Kahahawai that you got the rope?"

"I got it in October, Mr. Kelley."

"Dr. Withington is a very good friend of yours?"

"I hope so."

"You don't know so?"

"I know he's been very kind."

"You knew him non-professionally?"

"Yes. I played water polo with him."

"You have discussed this case with him?"

"I have discussed the Ala Moana case, but not this present case."

"You referred to some other plan to get a confession from Kahahawai. What was that?"

"Sending Lord out for a bunch of boys we pretended were there and threatening him with a beating that would cut him to threads."

"You had no idea of tying him up and torturing him?"

"No, Mr. Kelley."

"How did the rope get to Mrs. Fortescue's house?"

"I only know what I've heard. Jones wanted some shirts and at the same time asked for a rope. Mrs. Fortescue said she remembered seeing the rope at my house."

"As an officer in the Navy, are you accustomed to carrying a sidearm?"

"Yes sir, on duty."

"And you carry a .45 automatic?"

"We carry a sidearm only on patrol duty."

"Your .45 was in the Fortescue house that morning?"

"Yes."

"Why did you bring it over?"

"To scare him."

"A .45 is more impressive than a .32?"

"I don't think so. A gun is a gun to me."

"You intended to get a confession from Kahahawai and prepared this warrant?"

"Yes, sir."

"And you used a seal taken from a diploma?"

"That's right, sir."

"To make it look more official?"

"To make it a warrant."

"On whose suggestion was it that the piece from the newspaper was put on it?"

"Someone said it should have some printed matter on it..."

"Do you remember having your photograph taken out there?"

"I think I do."

A photograph from among the prosecution's exhibits was shown him—one of the photographs taken near Koko Head, when Lieutenant Massie, Mrs. Fortescue and Lord were arrested. The photograph showed Massie shielding his face.

It was shown also to the jury.

"Do you recall hiding your face when it was taken?" Kelley went on.

"No."

"Do you recall the removal of the body from the Buick car?"

"It was all very vague. I remember people around there, but it was all hazy."

"Do you remember Officer Bond talking to Harbottle?"

"No."

"You don't remember congratulating yourself?"

"No, sir."

"Do you remember Mrs. Fortescue telling a newspaperman from New York at Pearl Harbor that her only regret was that the job was bungled? "

"I don't recall that."

He was shown the article by Russell Owen of *The New York Times*. Frowning, he began to read it through. Kelley suggested a recess.

The crossfire was resumed after the recess, Massie having read the clipping.

"Do you recall this conversation?"

"I don't recall the conversation, but afterwards Mrs. Fortescue told me she used the word 'bungled' in reference to the Ala Moana trial."

"Were you present when she was asked if she did not realize the danger of driving the car through the streets with Kahahawai's body in the car, and she replied that she did not know she was being followed and had made the mistake of drawing the shade?"

"No, I'm sure I was not present."

Kelley read from Owen's story, in which he quoted Mrs. Fortescue as saying "we bungled."

"I wasn't present when she made that statement, if she made it," said Massie.

"You know Kahahawai was a boxer?"

"Yes, at the identification. I'd seen him about four times."

"You say the first identification was at the hospital?"

"If I did I was wrong. The first time was at my house."

"You noted he was a big, strong individual?"

"I never thought much about him, Mr. Kelley."

"You referred to what happened to Ida. Were you implicated with that kidnapping?"

"I was not."

"You didn't wear a false moustache that night?"

"I have never worn one."

"You are sure of that?"

"I was never more positive of anything."

"Mr. Beebe, you say, told you not to use force in getting a confession?"

"He particularly said not to beat him. I don't remember anything about not holding a death threat over him."

"Didn't he tell you that a confession obtained under threat of death would be just as inadmissible as if it had been obtained by beating?"

"I don't recall that."

"Did you ever make an effort to run down these rumors?"

"Why should I? I knew they were utterly false. I thought a confession would clear my wife's name."

"Had you heard Ida confessed?"

"I had heard it."

"Did you verify it?"

"No, because I'd been told that a confession gotten by force couldn't be used."

"Did you ever use that purported confession to stop these wagging tongues?"

"No, not that I remember."

"You attended the Ala Moana trial?"

"I was there only once. I was there only ten minutes when Mrs. Massie took the stand."

"What was the last thing Kahahawai said before you had this mental lapse?"

"I'll never forget it." He said 'We done it.'"

"He didn't tell of his part in it?"

"No."

"You were convinced from the beginning of the case that Kahahawai was a principal figure in the assault on your wife?"

"Yes."

"Then all he added to the impression you already had was the words 'We done it?'"

"That's all, Mr. Kelley."

"And then what happened?"

"I don't know."

"Did you ever before have one of these spells?"

"Once I had an operation and bled internally. I told them I could walk downstairs, but fainted in the attempt. The sensation when I came out of the faint was much the same. I couldn't recognize people around me for quite a while, a matter of hours, I guess."

"Will you tell us what was the first thing you recall after the lapse?"

"I can't recall the first thing; it has baffled me. Things would be blurred for a while, then clear. I think I recall being up at the City Attorney's Office. I remember Mrs. Fortescue there. I can't remember what I know for a fact and what was told by me about that period."

"You don't feel that you are in that condition now?"

"My opinion is that I am not."

"You understand the testimony you're giving now?"

"Oh, yes."

"Where was the .32 automatic Colt when you picked it up?"

"In the kitchen, on the sideboard."

"How did you know Jones had the .32?"

"When I told him force must not be used, he mentioned the gun and I took it away from him."

"Did you take your .45 automatic up there to scare Kahahawai?"

"I guess I did."

"Don't you know?"

"Yes."

"Thanks.   And you had never seen the rope around Mrs. Fortescue's house?"

"Never."

"After you got Kahahawai into the car down here, did you or Jones talk to him?"

"Yes, Jones said we were taking him to the home of Major Ross. Once he asked what the idea was, but we told him Major Ross had some questions to ask. We did not cover him with a gun while in the car."

"Was Mrs. Fortescue at the house when you arrived?"

"No, she came afterwards. I was in the front room when Jones brought him in."

"Where did you leave your .45 when you went out?"

"I think I left it on the settee when I came in earlier, but I'm not sure."

"And when Kahahawai came in, where did he sit?"

"In this chair," he said, indicating the position on a chart. Several jurors leaned forward.

"When Mrs. Fortescue came in, did you have him covered with the gun?"

"Either then or shortly after. Lord came in just afterwards, and Jones left when Mrs. Fortescue told him to go outside and see we weren't disturbed. Mrs. Fortescue told Kahahawai to move and he moved to the chaise lounge."

"Did Kahahawai appear frightened?"

"Yes."

"He was trembling?"

"Yes."

"Did he plead for mercy?"

"No."

"Did he beg you not to shoot him, nor beat him?"

"No."

"Was he sitting on the chaise lounge when you shot him?"

"He must have been."

"Did he put up any fight?"

"No."

"Then you got what you wanted out of him?"

"No, I wanted a written confession."

"Did you have any paper and pencils?"

"Mrs. Fortescue was going to take care of that."

"Did you see any writing paper?"

"I don't remember."

"Do you know there was writing material in the house?"

"I know every house in the world had paper in it. But Mrs. Fortescue was to take care of that. I know Mrs. Fortescue writes letters."

"You didn't make any plan, though?"

"On the afternoon of the seventh we talked it over. Mrs. Fortescue, the day before, agreed to write down anything he might say."

"Mrs. Fortescue clipped the piece from the paper?"

"I think so."

"Did you know Mrs. Fortescue had a gun?"

"Yes."

"Did you ever see it?"

"I had seen Mrs. Fortescue with it."

"That is the .32 Ives Johnson in evidence here?"

"It looked like it."

"You didn't see it that day?"

"Not that I recall."

"Who put the rope under the cushion of the davenport?"

"I don't know."

"You didn't put it there?"

"No."

"You're sure you didn't?"

"I'm po...I'm not sure of anything."

"You were going to say you were positive you didn't."

"I was not; I am positive I was not going to say anything of the sort."

Massie bit his lips frequently during cross examination.

"By the way, how were you dressed that morning?"

"I had a sort of gray suit."

John Kelley produced a coat and hat, which Massie identified as those he wore the day of the killing.

"What size shirt do you wear?"

"When I'm up to weight, I wear a 14-1/2."

He was shown a torn white shirt which had been found in the closet, but was unable to identify it as his own.

"Were you in a struggle with anybody in Mrs. Fortescue's house that morning?"

"Not that I remember."

"Do you recall, however, loading that gun, then working the mechanism so a shot went in the magazine?"

"That is when Mrs. Fortescue came in."

"And with an automatic, that same motion cocks a pistol, doesn't it?"

"I think so."

"You know it, don't you? You've handled lots of guns."

"Yes."

"So you were standing there with a gun with the hammer back when you were talking to Kahahawai?"

"I must have been."

"You remember having your finger on the trigger?"

"That's the logical place to have one's finger when threatening a man. I was thinking of only one thing — making that man tell his story."

"And all you got from him was, 'We done it?'"

"Yes, that's all."

Kelley then questioned him as to his general health.

"After September 12, from that time until Kahahawai was killed, you were depressed, weren't you?"

"Yes. Any man would be, Mr. Kelley."

"Did you engage in social activities?"

"I tried to avoid them. One night I went to Waialae on Mrs. Fortescue's suggestion, and spent a miserable evening."

"You take a drink occasionally, don't you?"

"I've been known to."

"Being from Kentucky I would naturally expect you would. You are a drinking man?"

"I don't think so."

"Did you have any drinks on the morning of January 8?"

"Not that I recall."

"On the night or afternoon of January 7?"

"Not that I remember."

"Don't you recall mixing cocktails in a pitcher?"

"No."

"Between September 12 and the day of Kahahawai's death, did you do any extensive drinking?"

"I know one night I did. A friend asked me to come out and have a meal with him. He said I was acting like a fool. I couldn't eat anything. A few other friends were around. I sat around and didn't like to talk to anyone. Felt miserable. He told me to take a few drinks so I could go to sleep. I took them."

"Did you go to sleep?"

"I think so."

"Was Mrs. Massie there?"

"No."

Kelley shifted the questioning to the night of September 12, 1931.

"You say you arrived at the Ala Wai Inn at about 9 o'clock?" the prosecuting attorney asked.

"About 9 or 9:30."

"Lieutenant and Mrs. Branson were with you?"

"Yes."

"Your table was upstairs or downstairs?"

"Downstairs."

"Did Mrs. Massie give any reason for not wanting to go to the party?"

"Only that she did not feel like it."

"Did you bring any liquor with you?"

"I brought about a pint."

"Did Lieutenant Branson or Lieutenant Brown have liquor?"

"Not that I know of."

"Was liquor served?"

"Yes."

"Did everyone have a drink?"

"I don't recall. I poured out one drink below before I went upstairs. Then I gave the remaining liquor to the orchestra with a request that they play 'Pal o' Mine.'"

"How many times did you dance with your wife?"

"I think it was twice."

"Did you see your wife upstairs?"

"Yes."

"About what time was that?"

"I don't recall exactly. I wasn't so interested in the time. I was enjoying myself."

"Did you see Mrs. Massie again at the dance after you saw her upstairs?"

"I don't remember, sir."

"When did you miss her?"

"Between 11:30 and 12, I think."

"At 11:30 that night were you intoxicated?"

"No."

"Was it not a fact that Lieutenant Branson was so drunk that his wife left in disgust and you had to drive him home?"

"It is not a fact."

"Were any of the party drunk?"

"I observed one man who was drunk."

"Was that Branson?"

"No, sir."

"Who was it?"

"I hope I don't have to say that, Mr. Kelley."

"What time did you get to the Rigby's house?"

"It was about fifteen minutes after leaving the dance."

"Do you know it was 1 o'clock?"

"I think it was after that."

"You stated here that your wife had walked out on other parties."

"I said she had excused herself, not walked out."

"She did not leave this party because of your condition?"

"I hope not."

"Did you see Lieutenant Branson after or before you went to Rigby's?"

"I don't remember, Mr. Kelley. That night I would not have recalled an earthquake."

"But you drove him home?"

"I drove him to Rigby's and left him there."

"And you next saw him at the police station?"

"Yes."

"Was he drunk?"

"I don't think so."

"Was he fully dressed?"

"I think he had his coat off."

"How long were you at Rigby's?"

"Not more than a minute. I got home somewhere around 1:30, I think."

"So it was two hours until you saw your wife again at home?"

"I'm not sure. It was, if Mrs. Rainer was correct."

"How long had you had the .45 automatic?"

"I think I had it since—I'd rather find out and be accurate. I've had it quite a long time."

"You said you were at sea over at Hilo when the Ala Moana case terminated?"

"No. I was on my eight-day patrol."

"Had you heard any of these disgusting rumors before you left?"

"I don't know."

"You said you began to hear vile rumors about you and your wife. Was that before or after your patrol?"

"I heard more afterwards than I did before."

"You said these rumors were from people you did not know?"

"I don't think our friends would pass such rumors, but they told us about the rumors and asked what we could do about them."

"These friends were all Navy people?"

"Not entirely."

"You asked Mr. Beebe what you could do about it?"

"Yes, because I heard of the Ida confession. He told me that confession would not be published, but that a confession was necessary."

"Did you ask him if the unwritten law could be invoked in the Territory of Hawaii?"

"I don't think so."

"Will you deny that you did?"

The witness hesitated.

"No, because I am not sure."

"Will you affirm it?"

"I might have, but I don't recall it."

"Did you say, a few days before Kahahawai was killed, that you'd like to take Kahahawai out and shoot him?"

"I want to be accurate, Mr. Kelley. Not that I recall."

"Did you ever say that to Mr. Beebe?"

"Not that I recall."

"There was nothing wrong with your mental setup then?"

"I was never so miserable and upset and nervous and sick at heart in my life."

"Was that a physical or a mental condition?"

Massie answered emphatically: "I don't know."

"Did Jones tell you the morning of January 8 that Kahahawai was pretty big?"

"I don't recall it."

"Saturday you testified that Jones started talking after breakfast and was uneasy about Kahahawai's size when you told him about the plan of using a warrant."

"Yes. I gave that testimony."

"Did you show Jones your gun?"

"Not that I recall, sir."

"Is that the same gun you said you placed on the settee?"

"I believe so."

"Will you indicate where you left your gun?"

"I think I just pitched it on the davenport when I came in the door that morning." He indicated on the chart the place where he left the gun.

"Was there anything to obscure it?"

"Yes, the pillow might have."

He also identified a photograph of the place. He said he didn't specifically remember the pillows being there that day, but thought they must have been because Mrs. Fortescue always used that davenport and liked a lot of pillows.

"When did you next see that gun?"

"I don't remember seeing it again."

"You testified that you were informed by Mrs. Fortescue that Jones wanted to go to your house for shirts and for some rope."

"That's right."

"Where did you keep the rope?"

"Oh, in several places at different times."

"Did she tell you why Jones wanted the shirts?"

"She said he had stains on his cuff and had to tear the sleeve off."

"Were they blood stains?"

"I think so..."

"Do you know who undressed the body?"

"Well, I've heard."

"Do you know who stripped the body of Kahahawai? Were you told?"

"Yes."

"Who told you?"

"Jones."

"What did he tell you?"

"That the stains wouldn't come out, so they took them off. I think that's what he told me."

"Did anyone tell you about washing the clothes in the bathtub?"

"No, I don't think so."

"Did anyone tell you where he died?"

"Yes, Mrs. Fortescue. It was on the chaise lounge."

"Did anyone tell you how long it took him to die?"

"No."

"Did they tell you about taking him to the bathroom?"

"Yes. I think so."

"How long after?"

"I don't remember."

"Were you told how the body was taken to the sedan?"

"Yes."

"And what their purpose was?"

"They said they were all so excited that they were running in circles and shouting. I presumed Lord and Jones carried the body out."

"Kahahawai was a heavy man, wasn't he?"

"Jones and Lord are strong men."

"One of them is a boxer, is he not?"

"Yes, Lord."

"The other is a trainer and second?"

"Yes."

"That's Jones."

"Yes."

"Did they say if Kahahawai struggled after he was shot?"

"No."

"Do you remember getting into the sedan?"

"No, for all I knew I might have gone to China and back. Mrs. Fortescue said Jones pushed me into it."

"Did Jones ever say why he didn't go along?"

"Yes, Mrs. Fortescue had told him to straighten up the house."

"And among the straightening up was to mop the blood off the bathroom floor?"

"You might ask him, Mr. Kelley."

"Did Jones tell you when he got back to your house after the killing?"

"No, sir."

"Did your wife ever tell you?"

"No, sir."

"When Jones told you he was afraid that Kahahawai was too big, was he drunk?"

"No, sober as a judge."

"Did either he or Lord have any drinks there that day?"

"I didn't see them have any."

"Do you want us to understand that Mr. Beebe told you a confession if obtained without force would stop the vile rumors?"

"Practically."

"To use in the next Ala Moana trial?"

"No, to clear my family name. You would have done the same."

"You were worried about the first trial, weren't you?"

"I was worried about my wife's good name."

"Then your attitude was personal?"

Darrow objected.

"The purpose of such a confession was to subdue these rumors and had nothing to do with bringing these alleged defendants to justice?" continued Kelley.

"If it did, I don't know. But I do know what the predominant thing in my mind was."

"You say Jones and Lord were asleep that morning when you arrived and that Mrs. Fortescue was preparing breakfast."

"Yes."

"What time did you leave for town?"

"About 25 to 8."

"Were the shades drawn?"

"I didn't notice."

"It's possible that you were sitting in a house with the windows closed and shades drawn?"

"I don't think so. There was fresh air."

"You noticed that, did you?"

"No, but if there hadn't been, I would have noticed it."

"When did you discuss using a gun to threaten Kahahawai?"

"The day before."

"You felt that it would be more impressive if you went through the motions of loading the gun?"

"I had hoped so."

"When you had him in the car, did he show signs of recognizing you?"

"No."

"Do you remember Mrs. Fortescue putting down the shade when you drove off later?"

"No, sir."

"Then he didn't recognize you until he was in the house?"

"No. I kept my head turned away from him. I made a point of not letting him recognize me. I had that much sense."

"But you didn't go so far as to wear a fake moustache?"

"No. I didn't."

Two jurors smiled.

"When you went in through the back door, you came in through the pantry and kitchen and picked up the .32 Colt automatic."

"Yes."

"Had you put it there before you went out earlier that morning?"

"Yes."

"Did you get to the house first, or did Mrs. Fortescue and Lord?"

"We did."

"When they came in, where was Kahahawai?"

"Sitting on the chair."

"Lieutenant Massie," Kelley continued, "were you ever told by any of the other defendants what happened to the gun you had in your hand?"

"Yes, Jones said he left it at my house."

"Did anyone ever tell you who took it away form your house?"

"No, they wouldn't tell me. Only two people could have, I think."

"Did anyone tell you what you did after the shot was fired?"

"Yes, Mrs. Fortescue said I just stood there like a bump on a log and wouldn't talk. She finally took me into the kitchen and tried to get me to drink some Coke, but I wouldn't take it, and she sat me down on a chair, and I think she said I stayed there."

"What did Jones say?"

"Jones wasn't very complimentary."

"Why? Because you only shot him once?"

"No, he said I acted like a damned fool."

"Jones is an enlisted man, isn't he?"

"Yes, and I resented it just as much as you're going to say I did. Lord didn't say anything. He doesn't talk much. You have to ask him and I never ask him."

"Did Mrs. Fortescue tell you why she took the particular route to Koko Head?"

"I think she's been trying to figure it out for herself ever since ... She said they wanted to go to the sea to dispose of the body."

"Just you and Mrs. Fortescue and Lord were in the car?"

"I don't know."

"You were told that afterwards, weren't you?"

"I don't remember, so I'd answer no, Mr. Kelley."

"You know now that was the situation?"

"I guess it was, I don't know."

"Were you in a condition to be of any help in disposing of the body?"

"I don't see how I could have been. Now, I know why I went along. Jones told Mrs. Fortescue to take me along, so that I'd get fresh air. I recall his saying that."

"When you talked to Mr. Beebe, did you discuss any plans whereby the statement or confession could be secured?"

"No. I just went seeking legal advice."

"Nothing was said about taking Kahahawai for a ride?"

"No."

"Who suggested using Major Ross' name for the kidnapping?"

"Either myself or Mrs. Fortescue."

"Did you have any reason for using his name?"

"It seemed logical. I knew Kahahawai had been in the National Guard under Major Ross."

"When was your interview with Major Ross?"

"On the sixth or seventh."

"Do you recall the time of your interview with Mr. Beebe?"

"It was before the New Year."

"How long after the Ida kidnapping?"

"I don't know how long, but it was after that time."

"Mr. Massie, had you ever been implicated in a kidnapping before?"

"No, sir."

"Quite sure?"

"Quite sure."

Darrow took exception, but was overruled.

"Where were you August 27, 1927?"

"I don't remember."

"Did you ever visit Mrs. Granville Fortescue's house on Long Island when you were at the Naval Academy?"

"Yes."

"The name of the home is Wildhome?"

"Correct."

"Did you not assist in the kidnapping of a baby?"

"I was not implicated in the kidnapping of a baby. Never have been and never will be."

"Were you arrested and charged with kidnapping?"

Darrow was on his feet objecting on the grounds that arrest does not mean anything. His objection was overruled.

"What might have been a charge of kidnapping was later proved to be not that. Miss Fortescue, who later became Mrs. Massie, and I left a dull movie to take a drive. As we came out there was a baby in a carriage, crying. Miss Fortescue said, 'Poor little thing,' and rolled the carriage down the block and back, and as she was doing so, a woman came up screaming and saying we'd kidnapped the child. I think she was an Italian lady. Mrs. Fortescue was called. After some explanation the woman said, 'Give me five dollars and I won't say anything about it.' We refused, and were taken to the station, but the next day the charge was dismissed."

Kelley returned to Massie's earlier testimony.

"You've said that enlisted men had been avoiding you at Pearl Harbor. When did you start to notice that?"

"Along in December."

"You said you discussed the advisability of endeavoring to get a statement from any of the Ala Moana defendants with your friends. Did you?"

"I may have, but I don't recall it at the moment."

"You felt, did you not, that there was an atmosphere of disregard toward you at the Naval Station?"

"I don't know what I felt except—if everyone in the courtroom will pardon me—that I felt like hell."

"Was there not a silence among your fellow officers when you went into the messroom?"

"No."

"And you felt something should be done about the matter?"

"The only thing I had in mind that day or ever was how it was affecting my wife."

"Had you read or heard of a wire sent by Admiral Pratt to Admiral Stirling in which he said..."

Mr. Darrow interrupted with an objection and asked to be allowed to read the message. It was Admiral Pratt's dispatch of December 20 to Admiral Stirling stating that American men will not stand for the violation of their women and have taken matters into their own hands when the law failed to do so. Darrow asked Judge Davis to read the message. The defense attorney said that the cable had no connection with the defendant and that it might be prejudicial. The Judge agreed. He would not permit the message to be read unless sufficient grounds were laid.

Lieutenant Massie was shown the message and read it in silence.

"Did you ever read that message before January 8?"

"Not that I recall. I'm not permitted to read confidential communications."

"Then you never knew of that language being sent out by Admiral Pratt before Kahahawai was murdered?"

Darrow objected to the use of the word "murdered," which Kelley agreed to change to "killed."

"I can't say definitely that I heard about this before, but perhaps I have since."

"Do you deny that you heard it before Kahahawai was killed?"

"If I have to give a yes or no answer, I'll answer, 'Yes, I do deny it.'"

"Did you, before January 8, read the purported text of this message in any papers?"

"I don't think so."

"Did you ever talk about the Ala Moana case with Admiral Stirling?"

"Yes, before the trial."

Kelley abandoned the line of questioning.

"How long did you say you'd known Jones before January 8?"

"I met him one day, about December 20."

"You'd seen him at boxing matches as a trainer at the Yard?"

"No."

"Did you say then that he'd help you out?"

"No, the next time I saw him was January 7 at the Submarine Base. I told him that Kahahawai was shaky and ready to crack and that the rumors were getting as vile as anybody could stand and I wanted to see if I could get a confession out of him."

"Did he say all the fellows should be shot?"

"No. I told him the plan would be better with two men besides myself, and he said he'd get a third man."

"When did you see Lord?"

"That same afternoon. Jones pointed him out to me."

"Did you know them at New London, Connecticut?"

"No."

"You stated that the seal on the warrant was from your diploma at the Edgewood Arsenal."

"Yes."

"What course did you take there?"

"Chemical warfare."

"You also said you were a specialist in gunnery."

"Every Navy man is."

"You said that you entered the aircraft department of the Navy."

"There is a difference between a department and a branch."

"Were you, then, in the gunnery branch?"

"Yes, I had a five-inch anti-aircraft gun under my command."

"Since you came to Honolulu have you engaged in amateur plays?"

"Yes, unfortunately, I was in 'Meet the Wife' once, in which I forgot my lines at an important place. That was a year ago."

"Was that a Naval play?"

"Naval personnel, yes.'

"Do you know Mr. Harry Hayward?"

"Yes."

"You conferred with him when he was at the head of a Chamber of Commerce committee on the Ala Moana case?"

"Yes."

"Did he tell you every effort was being made to have Kahahawai confess?"

"I don't remember."

"Did he say that Kahahawai's attorneys were urging him to confess?"

"I seem to have heard that somewhere."

"Did you talk with Mr. Thompson on this possibility?"

"I don't know."

"Didn't he tell you Kahahawai was about to crack?"

"No. I got that at the Naval Yard from Lieutenant Stickney and another, I think his name was Lieutenant Blake or Blakeley."

"It was based on these statements that you thought you could get a confession from him?"

"Partly, but not solely. It was all around town."

"Weren't you told that Kahahawai had consistently refused to confess?"

"I was usually the last one to get things," said Lieutenant Massie in an ironic tone, "as the husband always is."

Lieutenant Massie was dismissed, his story unshaken. The cross examination was over.

TWENTY-THREE

The trial was two weeks old on Monday, April 18, 1932. The day was also Clarence Darrow's seventy-fifth birthday. It was a long way from the small town of Kinsman, Ohio, to Honolulu, Hawaii, and the greatest of America's criminal lawyers had traveled it by the glory road. None of the old magic had brushed off en route as Darrow celebrated his mid-seventieth anniversary by plunging with renewed vigor into the defense of his last notorious case. Arms folded, his huge shoulders hunched and his head bowed, he continued to dominate the courtroom as master showman of the drama. He had been mobbed by admirers as he made his way from the Alexander Young Hotel to the Judiciary Building. A bailiff had greeted him with a handful of congratulatory cables from all over the world. He sat slumped in his chair, a bemused smile tugging at the corners of his mouth and his bright blue eyes lively in his quilted face, as one by one the members of the press corps reached over their tables to shake his hand.

"I don't feel any older today than I did yesterday when I was only seventy-four," he said to his well-wishers. "When you've had as many birthdays as I have, one more doesn't make much difference."

As Judge Davis called the court to order, the congratulations ceased abruptly and Darrow girded himself for the next crucial round of the trial. The contest had progressed to a pitched battle between the lion and the wolf, as Kelley persisted that the court be told what type of insanity was claimed by the defense so experts from the prosecution could examine the witness and see whether the symptoms were valid. Whereupon the suave old lion said he didn't think anyone on earth knew what the types of insanity were, that doctors disagreed and gave them different names according to their own predilections. All that the statute requires is that insanity be claimed, he continued and, as an inadvertent birthday gift, Judge Davis upheld him. Now he set out to prove that the claim was valid. He called Dr. Paul Withington to the stand.

Dr. Withington, former Harvard crew and football star and a leading physician in the community, had met Tommy Massie when playing water polo a year and a half before. "We played almost weekly," said the doctor.

"How was his health?"

"He was a strong man for his size and in excellent health."

"Were you later called to treat him?"

"Yes, I was called to treat his wife and also gave him medical advice."

"What was his condition?"

"He was under great nervous strain and not sleeping. From September on, he lost weight...I advised him to get rest, as I was afraid he'd crack under his nervous tension... There was no question as to what was bothering him. He discussed the whole situation often..."

"Did you play water polo with him afterwards?"

"Yes, and the difference in his condition was marked. He became one of the weaker players."

All eyes turned to Tommy Massie, where he sat next to his mother-in-law, his back straight but his gaze withdrawn. He was a shadow of the healthy young man the doctor had described earlier. Mrs. Fortescue, immaculate in a print dress, black hat and pearls, also seemed a wraith of the radiant matron who'd danced beneath the White House chandeliers. The haunted pair had retained a strange and compelling dignity in the face of an even stranger fate. No play of Sophocles had more fascinating characters than those in the small Hawaiian courtroom. No Greek tragedy unfurled a more dramatic plot nor foretold a more inevitable doom.

Defense counsel Darrow changed his line of questioning as the handsome, athletic doctor sat in the witness box.

"Do you remember how long it was after the assault that Mrs. Massie came to you?"

"About a week."

"And Mr. Massie?"

"I'd seen him before. I saw him again during that week. I asked him carefully if precautions had been taken against disease and pregnancy. I learned she had taken preliminary precautions after the assault."

"Did you make an examination?"

"Yes, I found that she had a badly smashed and infected jaw, a high temperature, a bone infection, she was extremely nervous, she had bruises on her body and face, and was in a critical condition. She had bruises on the inside of both thighs.'

At the mention of Thalia's injuries, her mother wept. Mrs. Fortescue's thin, proud shoulders shook and tears slid silently down her cheeks.

"Did you learn further about her condition?"

"She did not menstruate when she was supposed to. I took her to the maternity home and performed a curettement." The doctor explained that this was a scraping of the uterus. In response to cross-examination by Kelley, asking if evidence of pregnancy were found, Doctor Withington answered, "in an early stage, one doesn't always find definite evidence of pregnancy." One facet of the lamentable situation, however, was irrefutably evident: "Lieutenant Massie was tremendously worried."

Also among the defense's witnesses was the Chief Quartermaster on Tommy Massie's ship, who said he gave the Lieutenant a rope, with a purple thread through it, in October, for the purpose of making a dog run. Another water polo player, Captain Samuel Stewart, was called to the stand and remarked on the rapid deterioration of Tommy Massie's health.

"He was a strong man for his size, alert, happy and pleasant...his physical ability went down, and what he said showed he was a long way from being level-headed...He looked so worried to me after the assault that I asked him what was the trouble. He said he was frantic because he couldn't get legal counsel. I told him there were plenty of upright lawyers to help him, and he said 'I don't know who they are.' He'd call me up or come over to my house, and I'd tell him everything would come out all right and to hold himself down and take care of himself. I advised him to consult Admiral Stirling and the Commanding General of the Army, and told him they would see that he got justice."

"Was anything said to you about getting confessions?" Darrow asked.

"One night he took me out to the car and said he was frantic. He had a paper in which he said it was stated that a Navy Yard employee had confessed and then repudiated the confession. I told him it was impossible and revolting and advised him to forget it. I never saw anyone so worked up. I told him to forget it, that it was probably all untrue."

"Did he tell you whose confession this was reported to be?" Mr. Kelley asked.

"Yes, but I don't remember it."

"Was it a Japanese name?"

"No."

Mr. Stewart was excused.

Darrow called the next witness, Eugene Beebe, a former partner of Montgomery Winn, and he let his fellow defense counsel conduct the examination:

"When did you first meet Lieutenant Massie?"

"In October..."

"What was his appearance?"

"He seemed nervous and apparently laboring under stress."

"What was your conversation with him?"

"About the Ala Moana case, rumors about his wife."

"Did you discuss these rumors with him?"

"Yes."

"How many times did you see him?"

"About fifteen or eighteen times."

"Do you recall an article in a paper regarding a confession alleged to have been made by Ida?"

"Yes. After that affair, Massie came in much elated. I told him that such a confession would be worthless, and showed him pictures of the man with scars on his body..."

"Later did you notice any change in Massie?"

"Yes, at first he'd sit and talk to me. Later he'd pace up and down and his face would twitch. He seemed to have lost weight."

Next, Prosecutor Kelley cross examined the witness.

"When was the last time you talked with him?"

"I think about Christmas or just before..."

"Do you recall the date of the Ida incident?"

"I remember it was a Saturday."

"After that fact became known, Mr. Massie came to your office, very much elated?"

"Yes."

"And he wanted to know if that confession could be used in court?"

"No. I told him right off that it could not be."

"Did you have subsequent conversations with him?"

"I talked to him about a confession before the Ida case and after the mistrial. As I recall, I was asked by a member of the Chamber of Commerce committee—Mr. Hayward, I believe—if it were true that Mrs. Massie was going to leave the Territory. I called them in and Mrs. Massie said she was going to stick it out. They asked me what I thought of a retrial and I told them their best chance was additional evidence or a confession."

"The purpose of such a confession was to strengthen the case for the Ala Moana retrial?"

"No. I think there was a dual purpose, that and the effect on clearing Mrs. Massie's reputation..."

Kelley completed the cross examination and turned the witness over to Beebe's former law partner, Winn.

"Mr. Beebe, you told them that a conviction in the second trial would be difficult without a confession or new evidence?" said the defense attorney.

"Yes."

"What did you tell Lieutenant Massie?"

"I told him that we couldn't expect any help from the police, with the police divided among themselves and Lau and others reporting to Mr. Heen."

There was a buzz in the courtroom as reference was made to one of the key clues in the muddled mystery of the Ala Moana case. Reporters noted it on their pads and Russell Owen of *The New York Times* wrote perceptively: "That was the first direct testimony in the whole trial of disorganization and mishandling of the Ala Moana case, which has been held to be cause of this entire affair."

The next witness was Major Gordon Ross, High Sheriff, who testified that Tommy Massie had approached him early in January, about a week before the murder, to ask him to question Kahahawai, who had been in Ross's battalion in the Hawaii National Guard, and attempt to obtain a confession.

"He told me Kahahawai was about to crack and wanted me to question him. I told him that my principal duty at the time was to search for the escaped convict Daniel Lyman and attempt to reduce the hysteria that was prevalent at the time. I said, however, that I'd do it if it didn't interfere with the civil authorities. I told him to come back in a few days."

"Did he came back?"

"No."

Darrow then called his two mainland psychiatrists to testify that Lieutenant Thomas Massie was insane at the time the fatal shot was fired, killing Joseph Kahahawai. It was the first time that this type of testimony, from mainland alienists, had been introduced into a Hawaiian criminal case. Dr. Edward H. Williams defined the defendant's affliction as "chemical insanity," caused by abnormal functioning of the adrenal glands when under mental distress. Dr. Thomas J. Orbison called it "delirium with ambulatory automatism." The jury appeared completely mystified by their testimony. One entire morning was devoted to the explanation of psychiatric terminology for the benefit of the twelve puzzled men.

Dr. Orbison, a rotund, rosy physician, wearing bifocals and a hearing aid, took advantage of an opportunity to crack a venerable joke when he was asked about his background. He said he was a native of Pennsylvania, but born in India.

"That doesn't make you an Indian," said the jesting defense lawyer.

The droll psychiatrist chuckled. "No. It's like the cat who had kittens in the oven: they wouldn't be biscuits."

A common smile spread across the jury, an expression that was soon to turn to one of dismay.

Dr. Orbison said he'd begun his practice in Philadelphia as an intern in the Department for the Insane, with about 3,000 patients. After he took up seriously the specialty of mental and nervous diseases, he saw about 300 cases of these diseases a month. Before becoming one of the chiefs of the neurospsychiatric department, Los Angeles General Hospital, he was inspector of prisons of the Latvian government. "At present, I am also a member of the Los Angeles County Lunacy Commission, reaching five thousand cases. I examine about a twelfth of them."

"Did you examine Lieutenant Massie in Honolulu?"

"Yes, at your request and his own."

"And you're familiar with his story on the witness stand. Would you say his mind was diseased when the bullet was fired?"

"It was a typical condition," answered the jolly little psychiatrist, seemingly unable to give a one-syllable answer. "It is defined by law as insanity and by psychiatry as delirium with ambulatory automatism...this man was mentally deranged; he was insane."

"Is this case rare?"

"Oh, no." Again the doctor launched into a dissertation, this time on the common occurrence of such cases, and even straying into a discussion of the prevalence of "post-typhoid psychosis. I've seen cases of mental delirium from typhoid fever..."

As Darrow questioned his witness, the tangle of interrogation became so complicated at one point that Judge Davis felt compelled to intervene: "The questions are becoming interminably long. I wish you would shorten them," he said.

"You are right, Your Honor, but the answers to my questions are getting so long and involved that it is becoming increasingly difficult to ask a simple question."

Darrow returned to the subject at hand. "You've heard of Massie's trouble. What would be the first inducing cause?"

"The ravishing of his wife would be the first."

"What else?"

"Well, he said he carried around this terrible idea for months. His attitude toward rumors, the things he heard on the street. He told me for instance, that the story was around his wife had not been assaulted at all. Tears came to his eyes when he said it was rumored that he himself had struck her in the jaw. Things of that character he was hearing all the time."

"Might this be temporary insanity?"

"Yes, all insanity is. It always ends sometime."

"Is there a known physical basis for insanity?"

This proved to be another cue for a monologue as Dr. Orbison launched into half a dozen aspects of his specialty including "the disease commonly known as softening of the brain." Noticing that pairs of jurors were conferring through his testimony, he sought to enlighten them with a lecture on the physiology of the nervous system, the ductless glands, the voluntary and involuntary muscles, a dissertation that merely increased their bewilderment. Clarence Darrow seemed more interested in this discussion than anyone else—with the possible exception of Barry Ulrich, whose sharp eyes in his large, sleekly brushed head were keenly alert.

"...Fear, hate, rage and stress are known to be due to activity of the suprarenal glands," continued Dr. Orbison. "A protracted worry may bring out an actively irritated condition, resulting in pouring a secretion into the blood which may cause a nervous condition...Lieutenant Massie became insane the moment he heard the last words of Kahahawai. He was under a strain he had never been subjected to before and had been thwarted in his attempts to clear his wife's character. He was agitated daily for months and at times he could scarcely bear it. People had asked him why he didn't kill the assailants. He said to me, 'If I told you why I didn't plan anything of that kind, you wouldn't understand.' I said. 'I am older than you and I think I can understand.'"

The portly doctor paused for a moment and smiled fleetingly at Tommy Massie through his thick glasses. Then he became very serious and turned his full attention to the jury. "There were three things that kept him back, he told me. 'It had been ground into my soul to observe the law ever since I had been in the Navy,' he said. Another thing was that Admiral Stirling had told him to do nothing that might spoil the situation. But his strongest motive was, he said, to get some kind of a confession that could be used to clear up the whole question." The psychiatrist let his words sink in for a moment. Then, still facing the jury, he began again. "I wanted to be sure, to test him, so I said..."

"Objection!" It was Barry Ulrich. He objected to the doctor's addressing the jury in the form of an argument as to the status of Lieutenant Massie's condition.

Judge Davis upheld the objection and asked the rambling witness to proceed by question and answer.

"Was there anything further he said to you of importance?" complied Darrow.

"Yes. The important thing was what happened to him just before the shooting. He told me. 'The last thing that I was conscious of was the image that came to my mind of all that happened to my wife when Kahahawai said "We done it." After that I didn't know a thing'...He told me that later he realized he was sitting with Mrs. Fortescue, who was driving. He said he did not remember the incident of shaking his own hand when a police man approached him. He said, 'That would be the silliest thing I could do.' He asked me, 'What do you think?' and I said..."

"Objection!" Again it was Barry Ulrich, this time complaining that the witness was going outside the bounds of testimony of an expert witness and introducing hearsay.

Darrow realized it was time to close the witness's testimony before the courtroom became a classroom, and wrapped up the doctor's theory with a direct question. "From all Lieutenant Massie told you, you can say he was insane at the time of the shooting?"

"He was insane and didn't know what he was doing," said the doctor, his testimony in a nutshell at last.

Barry Ulrich rose to conduct the cross-examination. Thin and elegantly groomed as a furled umbrella, he stood before the plump psychiatrist and deftly attempted to find out from the witness how much of his opinion was based on observation and how much on what he had been told. "Couldn't Massie's delirium been merely an irresistible impulse?"

"No."

"Can't you understand that a man might kill a man whom he believes to have caused him this worry in a fit of anger?"

"I don't understand," said the psychiatrist.

"You think it is improbable that he killed him in a fit of anger?"

"Yes, because all his plans under this stress led up to his getting a confession, and he killed the very person necessary to this purpose."

For the first time the eminent doctor seemed to be making sense to the jury and they showed far more interest in the cross-examination than in the direct questioning. When Dr. Orbison went on to explain the distinction between true amnesia and an affected state, the tense prosecuting attorney snapped, "The question of the truth or falsity of Lieutenant Massie's testimony is for the jury, not you, to decide. We believe your testimony is based on the assumption of the truth of Lieutenant Massie's story!"

"It is not!" retorted the doctor heatedly. Then realizing he had been caught by a loaded question, he added, "I revise that answer. We learn facts only from what is told us." Dr. Orbison then said, "I doubt that any person could face a case from first to last ... I don't believe that after five hours with me and before this clever District Attorney that Lieutenant Massie could make up a history of typical delirium that the law calls insanity.'

"You recognize that there would be every motive to invent this story?"

"I do, but this man has told the detailed truth, and money wouldn't buy my opinion."

The jury was now fascinated by the session. Ulrich turned to them for a moment before lowering his voice in a casual stage effect and addressing the doctor.

"By the way, how much have you been paid?"

"Thus far not a cent," rapped the doctor. Then, being not totally unfamiliar with courtroom histrionics, he smiled behind his glasses and added, "But I was told that I could not be expected to come so far without compensation."

Ulrich resumed the cross-examination. His well-modulated voice and theatrical timing had turned a pedantic discourse into a hit production.

"During this ambulatory delirium, the man could walk around?"

"Yes. That is what ambulatory means. He does not know what he's doing, but may perform various acts."

"In this case, he automatically fired a gun?"

"I don't think pulling the trigger was automatic. He was in a condition of delirious excitement, and the action was a reflex."

"With a gun in his hand, he was confronting a man whom he despised. You think then his finger just twitched on the trigger?"

"One of the most common manifestations of this form of insanity is muscular contractions."

"Trigger insanity?" Barry Ulrich said in mock amazement. He didn't wait for an answer. "You said a man in such a condition might later shoot again?"

"I think counsel assumed that. I don't think I said that."

"You mean to say," said Ulrich, "that he is a man who would just commit one killing?"

"Depending where you come from," answered the doctor, now on to the prosecuting attorney's tricks. "One killing is generally considered enough."

"Might this necessarily happen again to Massie under the same circumstance?"

"I think it would be difficult to get together a set of similar circumstances."

"Is it possible that this mental 'bomb' might explode when he heard the confession he wanted to hear?"

"That's why I say he was insane."

"Did his emotions rise above his intellect?"

"No. His intellect was out."

"Wasn't it an irresistible impulse?'

"No. He hadn't the ability to resist."

Judge Davis felt the dialogue had gone on long enough and that its main purpose was being obscured by its dramatic effect. "Did I understand that the defendant became insane at the last words of Kahahawai?" asked the Court, getting right to the point.

"No. The mental picture of his wife set him off."

"Before that time he was not insane?"

"No. He was not."

Dr. Orbison was excused.

Dr. Henry Williams, as tall and spare as his colleague was robust, next took the stand. His beard was the only one in the courtroom. He looked every lanky inch the image of an eminent psychiatrist. He crossed his legs with assurance and opened his testimony with biographical exposition, explaining that he, too, was from the East Coast and was now connected with a psychiatric hospital in Los Angeles, where he served on the same lunacy commission as Dr. Orbison. He said he had made a deep study of the relation of physical conditions to mental conditions, and especially of methods of determining whether a patient is really insane or feigning insanity. In modest but protracted prose, he touched on the salient contributions he had made in this field.

"Which briefly brings your work down to the present," said George Leisure.

"Briefly?" interjected John Kelley laconically. The witness had been talking for ten minutes without a pause.

"Have you examined Lieutenant Massie?" asked Leisure.

"Yes."

"Did you form a conclusion as to his mental condition, and if so, what?"

"I based my conclusion on the mass of evidence about the conditions that have existed," began the second psychiatric authority, his opening words already precluding brevity. The jury members leaned back in the box and resigned themselves to another chapter in their introductory course in psychiatry.

"A distressing thing happened and Lieutenant Massie could not get redress. Always before him was the suffering of his wife and the probability that he would not get justice. Then these rumors added to produce a state of mental tension, which is not, however, a whirling of the head. The adrenal glands control the emotions to a great extent. His activity and alertness depend on these glands principally. These glands are strained in time of mental stress, as evidenced by his depleted physical condition and his melancholy. We can test these things and find out through blood tests. If we could have tested Lieutenant Massie's blood at that time we could have confirmed glandular disturbance. This man, becoming more morose, conceived the rather fantastic idea of obtaining a confession. They laid out the plans for getting the confession. He was in a terrific nervous condition, probably not sane.

"His system was set on edge. When the words were spoken, 'Yes, we done it,' I believe that was the breaking point, and the pull of the trigger was a reflex. The prosecution said that he sat by the car looking straight ahead, a natural attitude in a condition of amnesia. His action in shaking hands with himself was not normal. His paleness was evidence of adrenal action. I believe he could not possibly have made up the things and would not have done such things if he had not been in this state. I think he was able to stand because he is a sailor and accustomed to balance himself automatically. If he had been a man accustomed to sitting down, he would have fainted and fallen to the floor. He stood there automatically, it's been shown. Under some conditions of amnesia people do things that seem quite natural. If no crime is committed, little is said about these cases."

Darrow walked over to the bearded psychiatrist, indicating it was time to get down to cases, namely that involving his defendant's mental health at the time of the crime. "What is your opinion of Lieutenant Massie's condition when the shot was fired?" he asked.

"He was legally and actually insane," said the doctor.

"Your witness," said Darrow.

Barry Ulrich also seemed anxious to get directly to the point and wasted no time in leading up to the question of the veracity of Tommy Massie's madness. "You realize, Dr. Williams, that it is important to know if the plea of insanity is being offered in good faith. Isn't it true that this plea is many times offered by defendants who are perfectly sane?"

Darrow rose in objection, saying the question was not relevant to this plea.

Ulrich answered coldly that the question was important to determine the genuineness of such pleas.

Judge Davis sustained Darrow's objection. Ulrich was unfazed and casually picked up a book from the prosecution's table.

"Have you not written a book in which you stated that in most cases insanity pleas are spurious?" asked Ulrich.

"No," said the psychiatrist with remarkable brevity.

"I have a book, entitled 'Crime, Abnormal Minds and the Law,' by Ernest Bryan Hoag, A.M., M.D., and Edward Huntington Williams, M. D. Are you the Dr. Edward Huntington Williams, co-author of this book?"

"Yes."

"Reading from page seventy-four..."

Darrow stepped forward, interrupting the cross-examination. "May I please see the book?" he asked. Ulrich handed it to him. The jury leaned toward the bar as though sharing the defense's curiosity about this surprise tack in the proceedings. Darrow handed back the book without comment.

"On page seventy-four," resumed Barry Ulrich in his low-pitched, sonorous voice, "I read: 'Under the present system in force in most states, Justice Wilbur of the supreme court of California has recently stated, most pleas of insanity are made by sane people, who frequently go free, while most insane criminals make no insanity plea and are duly convicted and sentenced.'"

The doctor shifted uneasily and commented, "As I understand it, that is to introduce testimony that otherwise could not be."

"Then they are faked cases?"

"No. I don't like the word 'fake.' People may think they have been insane," said Dr. Williams testily.

Darrow unfolded from his chair and claimed that the jury should judge on testimony in this trial, "not on whether most pleas of insanity elsewhere are fake or genuine."

"Isn't it true that insanity pleas are interposed to allow counsel to introduce evidence that could not be brought in otherwise?" continued the unperturbed prosecutor, referring to the testimony just offered by Darrow's own witness.

"Objection!" shouted Darrow.

"Overruled," said Judge Davis.

"Yes, it is true," answered Dr. Williams. "By lawyers."

"As in this case," said the assisting prosecutor ruefully.

"This case doesn't come into this argument at all!"

"Didn't you write in your book on page one hundred," continued Ulrich, "'According to our present methods, such testimony is largely unscientific, partisan and undignified, and tends to discredit both the medical and legal professions, and it frequently totally fails to serve the ends of justice, as already indicated.'"

The doctor seemed to flush beneath his beard. Ulrich carried on, reading carefully so each word reached the far corners of the room, and especially that corner in which sat the jury. "'According to methods now in vogue, medical experts are employed both by the prosecution and by the defense, thus, in the very beginning tending to make the whole procedure, from the examination of the patient to the testimony given before the jury, a purely partisan affair rather that an impartial scientific attempt to arrive at a correct diagnosis. This is the antithesis of the method employed by reputable medical men in their usual attempts in the diagnosis of disease.'"

"That was to induce California to introduce the law they now have, allowing the judge to appoint such expert witnesses," explained the medical author.

"That is not the case in Hawaii," said the lawyer dryly.

The courtroom was delighted with this unrehearsed piece of drama and followed the prosecution's further examination with animated interest. Just at this point, too, strains of martial music floated through the windows as the Royal Hawaiian Band struck up its weekly concert in the palace bandstand across the street. *Hail to the Chief* and *The Washington Post March* blended with the testimony. Quickening to response from the gallery and pitching his tempo to the tuba, the prosecutor swung into a fast-paced dialogue, topping the answers to his questions with the adept timing of a veteran thespian.

"...The prosecution witness said nothing about amnesia. The mere fact that he was looking straight ahead does not indicate insanity," pounded Ulrich.

"A man of this type would not do that," answered the doctor with equal alacrity.

"Then he is said to have shaken hands with himself."

"That's good evidence," said Dr. Williams. "It would have been foolish for a normal man to do."

"Can't you imagine a man having been satisfied with what he wanted to do for months, so responding to this congratulations, 'Good work, kid.'?"

"No," said the doctor with disdain. "That was a silly, abnormal action. This is a dignified Naval officer, not a showman." The implication was not lost on Ulrich.

"Then any man to do this would be insane?"

"I didn't say that!"

"Mightn't this show fright?"

"No. It shows he was not in his right mind, but even so, this is only one part of the evidence on which I based my diagnosis."

"How about the fact that he hid his face when they tried to photograph him?" pressed Ulrich, reaching over to the exhibit of evidence and dramatically flourishing the photograph.

"It might or might not be. It has no particular meaning."

"Massie testified, before the county attorney, he was still dazed. It is proved that he was calm and collected and said, 'I do not care to make a statement.' Would that indicate a condition of amnesia?"

"He might have come out of it. The statement is perfectly normal."

"Then he was perfectly normal?" topped the lawyer.

"No, the statement was!" said the witness, eyes flashing.

"Suppose that when he was picked up at Koko Head, he asked an officer for a cigarette," continued Ulrich, letting his voice lapse into a lulling mood of conjecture, "and a light from the stub of the policeman's cigarette? Would that be normal? This was at about 10:30."

"No, that wouldn't indicate either way. Smoking is often an automatic affair, and a person can do such things in a state of automatism."

"But that's a normal act?"

"Yes."

Ulrich's voice became reasonable and conversational as he then asked the psychiatrist, "Now, with this collection of normal acts, haven't you enough of them to outweigh the abnormal?"

"No," answered Dr. Williams, having regained his composure. "Ninety-seven percent of the acts of an insane person are normal. It's the three percent that counts!"

In the press room down the hall, a reporter from the Star-Bulletin typed at the conclusion of his day's story, "Mr. Ulrich...gave Dr. Williams a highly uncomfortable hour on the stand."

A courtroom reporter recorded "Court adjourned at 12:45 on Tuesday. The class in neuropsychiatry was pau for the day."

TWENTY-FOUR

The Massie Case reached its climax on Wednesday, April 20, a moment of supreme human drama on which Clarence Darrow rested his hopes of victory and closed the defense. It was the day that Thalia Massie described to Darrow the ghastly night when she had left the teahouse and a life of personal obscurity, never to return to either. All Hawaii had yet to recover from the stroll, and they listened to the small figure who had uprooted their way of life.

The courtroom was hot and sultry. The windless vacuum of Kona weather had returned and the tropical sun beat down on the city unmercifully. The crowd outside the Judiciary Building had melted to only a few curious stragglers by 8:30 a.m. when the courthouse doors opened and quickly swallowed up the limited number of first-comers whom the small gallery could accommodate. The jury walked across the palace grounds in somber double file and entered the building with closed faces, like monks en route to morning mass. At their entry, the buzzing in the full courtroom dropped to whispers. The first three rows of benches were occupied almost entirely by haole society women whose voices tingled with anticipation as they discussed the prospective testimony of the rape victim. As the rows of faces receded in the room, their complexion darkened and the last seats were filled with Hawaiians, men and women. Several large tutus overlapped metal folding stools and softly joked about their precarious perches. Interest in the awaited testimony was mingled with relief that the trial was nearing its close.

Even the defendants looked more cheerful as they entered. Mrs. Fortescue appeared in the dark red suit and hat with jaunty feather that she wore when arrested. There was a faint smile on her lips. Lieutenant Massie followed, showing frank relief that his testimony was over. Jones and Lord, who had not appeared worried at any time in the trial, assumed characteristic poses, elbow on knees, right hands lifted to the chin, brows furrowed, a gleam of humor in Jones's eye.

But it was on Thalia that all eyes turned. She entered the courtroom for the first time in this second trial, leaning slightly on Tommy's arm. There was a barely audible gasp. People had forgotten how vulnerably young she was, looking much less than her twenty-one years. Her shining blond hair was parted childishly on the side, her round face was slightly flushed, and her pale blue, protruding eyes were wide with

wonder. She was dressed simply in a dark blue dress, and as she sat listening to the preliminary opening remarks of the Court, she placed one
hand in that of her husband, next to her, and in the other she crumpled
a white handkerchief. She had been in the courtroom only a few minutes when she asked for a drink of water.

"The young woman herself is something of a mystery," Philip
Kinsley, of the Chicago Tribune, had written a month earlier when he
called on her at the home of friends in the Navy Yard. "A student who
knows her describes her as neurotic in a broad romantic sense and somewhat unstable. She is described as bovine and calculating at the same
time. Her poise and courage today are excellent. She has suffered no
physical or mental breakdown as a result of her experience, reads a lot,
takes long walks alone with her dog, receives visitors and talks about the
assault as if it happened to someone else. She says she will not let it spoil
her life."

When Darrow called her name, Thalia Massie went forward with
her bright head bowed and groped for the witness chair until the clerk
gently reminded her that she must first stand and take the oath. For the
moment she was proud, with her hand raised. The words sounded
strangely out of context as she swore to tell the truth, then sat dawn
with the prim demeanor of a disciplined child. The scar on her cheek
showed beneath a faint blush. Her eyes brimmed wistfully as she spoke
in a low drawl, slow at times and rising to a note of terror, then subsiding in agony as she recalled the rape, the following nightmares when she
slipped in and out of delirium, of the day Kahahawai was killed. Several
times her head sank in her arms on the rail of the witness box, a few feet
from the jury, as she buried her face between shaking shoulders, then
roused herself and resumed her ordeal.

Her mother, who was not to be called to testify, fortified the
anguished girl, who had become in the eyes of the court no more than a
tender child, by sitting erect and strong twenty feet away.

"She reduced the issue of guilt of the defendants to a simple question of justification," wrote one reporter of Thalia's finest hour, "and
wrought the courtroom crowd to such a pitch that they applauded her.
Superb acting if it was that. But it could not be. There was no reservation of doubt left, in the courtroom at least, that her story of rape by
Kahahawai and the other hoodlums was all true. It was torn from her in
agony as she went to the defense of her mother and husband to save
them from prison."

Thalia did more than this. She embellished her story with such touching details that few could doubt the overwrought condition of her husband when, as he claimed, his mind snapped and he pulled the trigger on the man who had brutally ravaged his wife.

She sat with her feet together, her hands in her lap moving restlessly as she twined and untwined the handkerchief in her fingers. Her large eyes looked up at Darrow as he questioned her in his kind, deliberate way.

"Do you remember the night of the party at the inn?"

"Yes," said Thalia, blinking twice.

"How far do you live from there?"

"We live in Manoa Valley."

"Were you at a party at the inn?"

"Yes, on September 12."

"How long had you known your friends who accompanied you?"

"I had known Lieutenant Branson and his wife more than a year, and Lieutenant and Mrs. Brown six or eight months."

"Did you dance?"

"Yes."

"Did you have anything to drink?"

"I didn't have any except about half of one highball."

Tommy Massie leaned forward, his hand also to his chin as his wife testified. Mrs. Fortescue sat perfectly still. Thalia told of leaving the party about 11:35 p.m. when Tommy was dancing and she was bored. "I wasn't enjoying the party and was tired. I was planning to walk to the corner and back."

"Where were you when something unusual happened?"

John Kelley interrupted. The courtroom stirred as spectators leaned from side to side in an effort to see Thalia behind the hulking form of her lawyer, who blocked their view with arms folded and an expression of undisguised annoyance on his face. The prosecutor was undaunted.

"The only pertinent question is about what she told her husband. We are not retrying the Ala Moana Case." Both counsel were well aware that the soft spot of the murder trial was the rape that had sparked the fatal chain reaction, and Darrow was determined to play on the sympathy of the courtroom and the hearts of the jury. Darrow changed the form of his questions.

"When did you next see Tommy?" he asked Thalia gently. He stepped slightly to one side, reluctant to expose her frailty but careful not to hide her completely.

"Later on that night," she whispered, hiding her face with her hands. When she lifted her head after a moment of silent sobbing, her features were working convulsively. She put her handkerchief to her mouth as though to keep it mute, and the stifled emotion welled up in her eyes and overflowed in tears that ran down her cheeks, but she uttered no sound. George Leisure brought her a paper cup of water. Women among the spectators began to take out their handkerchiefs. A young friend of Thalia's, another Navy wife, bent her head and wept freely. Darrow waited a moment.

Finally Thalia continued in a low monotone. "I saw him about 1 o'clock. He telephoned and I asked him to please come home, something terrible..." She couldn't go on. Darrow waited until she had regained control of herself.

"Did he come?"

"Yes, right away," continued Thalia, her voice trembling but strangely quiet. "I heard him coming to the door and I ran to him and told him something terrible had happened. I wouldn't tell him what because it was so terrible. I sat down on the couch and cried. Finally I told him some men had taken me and beat me up and..." Her face contorted in agony as she struggled to overcome mounting sobs that shook her narrow shoulders. "...and raped me." At this she gave in and buried her head and let the sobs possess her. Tommy covered his eyes with his hand. He furtively reached into a hip pocket and brushed his nose and brow with a handkerchief, which he quickly tucked back out of sight, as though hoping not to have been noticed. The defense again let Thalia rest for a minute as she sipped her water and wiped her eyes.

"Did you tell him who did it?"

"Just some Hawaiian boys ... I didn't know their names."

At the back of the courtroom, a Hawaiian girl began to whimper. Thalia continued. "I told him I had taken medical precautions against disease and pregnancy," she said as the hushed courtroom strained to share the intimacy of events, of her changing into pajamas and lying on the couch, of going to the hospital and the police station, where she recognized one of her assailants who had been brought in at the same time.

"Objection!" declared Kelley, taking exception to Darrow's line of questioning. "He's entitled to ask her only what she said to her husband!" The objection was sustained.

"After I got home I told my husband I had seen one of the men who attacked me, the one who was driving, in the brown coat. Then I told him more or less what happened. A car had stopped and two men jumped out ... Chang and Kahahawai. Kahahawai grabbed me by the arm and struck me and Chang said, 'Come on, baby, you're going for a ride.' They pulled me into the car and Kahahawai struck me again. I screamed." Her voice broke for a moment, as she added, close to hysterics, "They kept beating me all the time."

Mrs. Fortescue asked Leisure to take another cup of water to the stand, and the young attorney promptly complied. Thalia sipped it slowly and looked at her mother, who returned the look with an almost imperceptible raise of her chin, as though commuting courage to her child.

"I told Tommy they had driven down Ala Moana to those bushes. Chang and Kahahawai dragged me out and Kahahawai hit me. They took me into the bushes..." She couldn't go on. The courtroom waited, most of the gallery in tears.

"They wouldn't let me go," she went on. "He hit me as hard as he could; he would not let me pray, and I said, 'Look how you've - you've knocked out some of my teeth,' and Kahahawai said 'What do I care! Shut up!' They were standing around laughing. One was holding my arms and the other one assaulted me, too." The glass-blue eyes glistened under their tears.

In a soft voice she told of the beads being torn from her neck, and of the police finding them later in the car used by her attackers. She told her husband that she'd recognized the boys brought to the house.

"Was anything said about money?"

"I offered to give them money and they just laughed...and one, I think it was Ahakuelo, turned around and took my purse. I told them my husband would give them money if they'd take me back, and they just laughed."

Kelley was on his feet again. "I don't want to keep interjecting objections, but -"

Darrow whirled on him sharply. "You do interject too often!" he said in anger. "You shouldn't."

"I think I should have objected much more," answered Kelley coldly, but Judge Davis asked the defense to continue with the examination of the witness.

"Tommy put me to bed and tried to do something for me, but I couldn't sleep. He couldn't go to bed for a long time and kept walking up and down."

The next day she went to Queen's Hospital. "Tommy went with me." She recognized some of the men who had assaulted her, she told the court, when the police brought them to her bedside. "Tommy asked me if I were sure about that and I said I was positive. I identified four of the five."

Again Kelley objected bitterly. He was overruled.

During all this testimony, the calmest members of the courtroom were the jury who sat back looking serious and refraining from showing any emotion they might have felt. The young Portuguese juror, who wore a crimson tie as bright as the prosecutor's, was chewing gum. Most of them betrayed their uneasiness during the heart-rending testimony by trying to figure out what to do with their hands. Like amateur actors, they self-consciously folded them, cupped them beneath their chins, put them in their pockets, on their knees or clasped them in their laps. They never took their eyes from the tortured face of the witness.

"How often was Tommy there?" continued Darrow.

"Almost all the time."

"Were you treated there?"

"Yes, for my jaw. At first they could not do anything for my jaw because my face was too swollen, but later they put on bands. I tried not to complain but was suffering pretty bad," she said sadly, putting her hands to her throat. The ugly scars were plainly visible now. Finally she was able to be moved to her home, she said, where she would be more comfortable.

"Dr. Withington treated me there. He kept coming all the time from then on...Tommy took care of me at night. He was so tired but never complained about the many times I would wake him at night. He was just wonderful," she said, biting her lip. "He was so fine."

Her weeping overwhelmed her anew and she shook beneath the sobs. Judge Davis called for a recess. Thalia tried to rise, reaching blindly for the railing as Tommy rushed to the stand. She held out her arms to him and fell against his chest. He took her arm, putting his around her wracked shoulders and led her back to the seat beside him. There she lay her smooth blond head on his sleeve and wept as her husband patted her comfortingly. In the next seat, Mrs. Fortescue sat motionless with her eyes blinded by tears.

Thalia was calmer as she resumed the stand, walking up to the chair with her body stooped and her pale hair falling across her cheek. "Tommy was there almost all the time," she continued.

"What was his condition?"

"He wasn't sleeping well or eating hardly anything at all."

"How long did Dr. Withington continue to treat you?"

"All along."

"Did he examine you?"

Thalia looked down at her hands. Her mangled handkerchief was twisted around one finger and the rest had been twirled into a coil. She gazed at it unseeingly, then looked up again and spoke dispassionately.

"Yes," she resumed. "He said I was pregnant and had to have a curettement."

It was during those painful days, she said, that she began hearing rumors, cruel stories that upset Tommy even more than her. "I remember hearing Tommy hadn't believed me and that he was going to get a divorce," she said in a low voice. "I heard I was assaulted by a Naval officer and that Tommy found him in my room and beat him and then beat me up. I heard all kinds of rumors. He used to worry about them and I told him not to. He didn't seem very well anyhow."

"Did you know about his talking to lawyers?"

"Yes, to Mr. Beebe. He said several times it would be wonderful to get a confession. I said there was no use talking about it. He never wanted to go out. He did not sleep, had rings around his eyes, and would get up at night and walk up and down in the living room, smoking cigarettes. When I got so I could cook, I would prepare tempting dishes for him, but he would not eat. He would get up and smoke a cigarette."

Her quiet words tore at the heartstrings of the women in the courtroom, where many of them were now openly weeping and more than one man brushed away a stealthy tear. She then told of Tommy's going to sea and of Albert O. Jones, the enlisted man, being detailed to guard the house while her husband was away. It was Jones who had burst into the house the morning of January 8, at 10 o'clock, after the killing.

"He came in and called me excitedly. He handed me a gun and said, 'Here take this. Kahahawai has been killed!' I said 'Where is Tommy?' and he said 'He's with your mother.' He asked for a drink and I fixed him a highball, but he said 'that's not enough,' so I filled the glass."

"Did Jones bring a gun?"

"Yes."

As the court ruled on an objection the witness drank another cup of water. Darrow's bulky frame leaned over the huddled figure and he smiled with gentle encouragement as he concluded his direct examination. Despite her instability on the stand, or perhaps because of it, she had fulfilled his hopes as a witness who could stir the heart. Thalia Massie's devotion to her husband, who had so tenderly cared for her, neglecting his own progressive deterioration under the strain, had inspired a record number of handkerchiefs to find their way to tear-filled eyes. "He was so kind and attentive and took such good care of me."

"Was he always so kind?"

John Kelley began the cross-examination. There was little sympathy in his voice, and its contrasting acerbity brought the courtroom up short. Handkerchiefs paused in mid-air. In the quiet, condoling courtroom only one person was aware that the climax of the trial was but a few questions away, and that one person was the man who was asking them.

Casually, the prosecutor asked the red-eyed girl if she remembered Jones going to the phone after she had answered it and asked who was calling.

"No," she said, on guard.

"Do you remember that Jones went to the telephone and said 'Leo, cover him up...?'"

"No!" Thalia's voice for the first time struck a sharp note. "I just told Lieutenant Pace to stall them off until I could find Tommy. I don't know what it was all about."

"Did you or did you not hear Jones speak to Lieutenant Pace and say, 'Leo, cover him up.'"

"No. He would not address an officer by his first name," she said disdainfully.

"But he calls your husband 'Massie,'" prodded the prosecutor.

"He certainly does not!" she said, now incensed and her guard down.

Quietly and clearly the prosecutor then asked, "Did you have a psychopathic examination at the University of Hawaii last summer?"

The young wife on the stand bridled at once and her body tensed as she sat erect. Her ice-blue eyes looked straight at John Kelley. Her hands were frozen in her lap. A transformation had come over the pathetic child, now a woman of cold fury.

"I did. I went to see a psychology professor," she answered cautiously, on the brink of open hostility.

"Do you remember the response you made on a chart or graph of questions which you wrote?" said Kelley, taking a folded piece of paper from his pocket.

The girl leaned forward, dangerously aroused. "Do you realize this is a confidential document? This is a matter between a doctor and his patient. You have no right to bring this into the courtroom."

"I'm asking the questions, not answering them," snapped Kelley, stepping forward and handing her the paper. A flush of anger reddened her cheeks. "Is this your handwriting?"

She gasped, then snatched at it and deliberately tore it up, rending the paper over and over, the white flakes falling silently to the floor. She faced her tormentor with flaming defiance.

The stunned courtroom was suspended in a moment of mute fascination, then a wave of applause rose from the benches of spectators. Brown hands and white hands alike clapped in admiration for the heroine of the hour. Tommy Massie, his head reeling for a second as though from a blow, leaned forward and brought his hands together in wide, swift claps.

"Order! Order!" shouted the Judge, pounding his gavel.

The applause stopped instantly. Thalia rose from her chair and rushed to the embrace of her husband. As she ran past John Kelley, the prosecutor said in a low voice, "Thank you, Mrs. Massie, you appear in your true colors at last!"

"That language is objectionable!" said the Court. Lawyers were on their feet in confusion. Thalia threw her arms about her husband. She made no effort to hide her sobs now and they echoed in the spellbound chamber.

"What right had he to say I do not love you? Everyone knows I love you!" This was in a stage whisper that penetrated every corner of the courtroom and abruptly ended the progress of the prosecution.

TWENTY-FIVE

Judge Davis, more incensed than at any time during the trial, reprimanded the spectators. "Such demonstrations constitute a direct contempt of this court...and if there are any more, they will be severely dealt with!"

He adjourned the court for the day, and ordered that the first five rows of spectators' benches be removed.

The defense agreed not to consider the shredded paper a privileged document, inadmissible in court, and the prosecution refrained from objecting to the destruction of state's evidence. The effect on the jury of Thalia's impassioned outburst remained a matter of conjecture. The effect on her husband was witnessed by all.

"Whether Lieutenant Massie was good to her or not a year ago is of small concern now," wrote reporter Kinsley, "as this trouble had thrown them together tenderly and her testimony makes plain his great devotion and care...her action may react in her favor. It was as if she were defying all the Hawaiian world that has put her on secret trial at tea tables and bridge parties these long months, rather than aiding in tracing and convicting her assailants. The scene on the witness stand when the story of her rape by four men was torn from her again will always live in the memories of those in the room, worthy of the efforts of a great tragic actress to emulate. Hawaii, land of beauty, paradise of dreams, was never made for such a record of human woe as has been written in this little courtroom the last few days."

Outside, the shadows of the strange, hot day lengthened and the normally rustling palms were still, as though embedded in the clear plastic air.

The following days of the week were an anticlimax for those in the courthouse. The prosecution called several rebuttal witnesses before the court was adjourned for a long weekend in order for counsel to prepare their closing arguments, which were scheduled to begin Tuesday, the day the last witness would testify.

Prospects of a cool morning, augured by an early breeze blowing down from Manoa Valley, evaporated with the meringue of clouds on the mountains as the rising sun heated the city and cleared the sky. By 9 a.m., Monday, April 25, the close courtroom was already warm. The wind died down. The spectators' seats, now limited to only seventy, had been filled long before the convening hour of court. In the front row, twenty-one of the twenty-three places were occupied by haole women. "They included several of the regular 'sitters' who are maintaining their amateur standing or one might say, their amateur 'sitting,'" mocked a court reporter in his notes. "The relay championship is now definitely conceded to the Kluegel clan, though the individual honors are in dispute, questions of professionalism having been raised."

The front bench also included Mrs. John F. Stone, wife of one of the jurors, who sat where she could see her husband and occasionally exchange a smile, although by the rules of court procedure laid down by Judge Davis, she could not speak to him. This would be the third week that the men of the jury had been sequestered from family and friends.

The twelve jurymen entered refreshed and evidently relieved by the prospect of winding up the testimony before noon, as promised by the prosecutor. John Kelley had called three rebuttal witnesses the previous day of the trial: Dr. Paul Bowers, noted alienist from Los Angeles, Dr. Robert B. Faus of Honolulu and Miss Mapuana Peters of the Prosecuting Attorneys' Office, who had taken down Tommy Massie's first noncommittal statement when he was brought in from Koko Head. "He seemed to know what he was talking about," said the pretty secretary. "He seemed nervous, but we all were." She had not been cross-examined.

The testimony of Dr. Bowers and Dr. Faus was in direct contradiction to that of Drs. Orbison and Williams. They testified that in their opinion the evidence in the trial showed that Lieutenant Massie knew what he was doing when the shot was fired. Bowers, a sturdily built, smooth-faced man in a beige gabardine suit, answered the questions with a brisk professional air, often peering intently at the jury through horn-rimmed glasses as he defined terms in precise and untechnical language. He was an excellent foil for Barry Ulrich, of the prosecution, who rose from his seat at the counsel table and conducted the examination in the smooth, mellifluous voice and scholarly language for which he was famous.

"We have had a diagnosis of delirium with ambulatory automatism," he began.

Several jurors exchanged glances and smiled. Ulrich continued. "Do you believe Massie was suffering from delirium?"

"No, not at the time of the killing or at any time," Dr. Bowers reflected, defining delirium as well as ambulatory automatism and canceling both from the Naval officer's behavior.

"Have you reached an opinion as to whether Massie was sane or insane when Kahahawai was killed?"

"He was, in my opinion, sane," answered the doctor firmly. "The records show no defects in the family tree; he has been through two military schools, has served in the Navy without record of lack of mental capacity. There have been no records of abnormal acts of inefficiency of service to the government. We have learned that his wife suffered a dreadful experience..." Darrow's objection at this point was overruled. "That the memory of this experience preyed on his mind, that the mistrial annoyed Lieutenant Massie, that he heard unpleasant rumors, that he may have felt the law had failed in its duty, and, urged on by the avalanche effect of memory, he deemed it proper to attempt to obtain a confession. And that in the course of trying to obtain this confession and free himself from rumors, he made and executed a deliberate plan to obtain the confession, and that during the course of this execution an individual was killed. The killing was a logical sequence of the plan...At no time in reading the records of this case did I find any evidence of any symptoms of insanity, and I conclude that the individual was in a normal state of consciousness at the time of the crime."

"Is there anything in his condition when he was captured to weaken your opinion?"

"No. His reaction was that of one being surprised at being caught in the commission of a crime."

"Then your opinion is that he was sane."

"It is."

The cross examination by Clarence Darrow took less than ten seconds.

"Dr. Bowers, I assume you have been paid or expect to be paid for coming down here?"

"Yes."

"That's all."

An atmosphere of expectancy without the depressing tension of earlier sessions prevailed in the courtroom on Monday morning as the trial entered its final stages. Flower leis and feather hatbands again lent a festive note to the bleak chamber. The defendants were smiling as they took their places, and when a reporter leaned over and asked Albert Jones how he was feeling, the sailor grinned and said, "In the pink."

John Kelley, who chatted with his pretty wife and friends before taking his place behind the boxes of prosecution exhibits at the front table, had not denied that young Dr. Joseph Catton of Stanford University, one of the rising and most colorful figures in West Coast psychiatric circles, had arrived on the *Malolo* the previous Thursday, and the defense showed no surprise when the tall, sparse, alert-looking professor with a neatly clipped moustache entered the room. He walked over and shook the hand of his senior colleague, Dr. Thomas Orbison, who, having offered testimony for the defense, was now among the spectators. They chatted amiably, although it was not the first time the two alienists had represented opposing sides in a legal battle. There was a stir of anticipation in the courtroom, which was instantly silenced by the entrance of Judge Davis in his black robes.

"Will counsel stipulate the jury is present," said the Judge, bringing the court to order.

"Yes, Your Honor," answered Montgomery Winn.

"Yes, Your Honor," seconded John Kelley.

"The defendants are personally present?"

"Yes, Your Honor," said Winn.

"Very well, proceed."

"At this time, if the Court please," began the prosecutor, "we would like the record to show that we have made a request upon the defense in this case to be permitted to examine the defendant Massie by psychiatrists and experts for the purpose of their testimony in this case and the request was refused. At this time we wish to renew that request."

Darrow boomed out a second refusal.

"Let the record show," continued the Court, "that the defense has refused the request and does so again."

Dr. Catton took the stand. With rapid clarity, as though lecturing one of his classes at Stanford, he answered the examination by Barry Ulrich, informing the Court that for the past dozen years he had limited his medical work to the study of mental and nervous diseases. During the war he had been a major in the Army medical corps. He currently was an associate professor at Stanford Medical School, visiting psychiatrist at the San Francisco County Hospital and in charge of the psychiatric clinic for the San Francisco jail.

"Have you read the records of this case?"

"Yes."

"As a result of your study have you an opinion as to the sanity or insanity of Lieutenant Massie at the time of the time of killing?"

"From the record I learned things that gave me an adequate picture of Lieutenant Massie's mental condition on January 8, and of his mental condition previous to the killing. It is my opinion that Lieutenant Massie was at the time of the killing a man of twenty-seven years of age, who had been to military schools, graduated from the Naval Academy, married Thalia Fortescue when she was sixteen. The last two years of their living together had been in Honolulu." The doctor paused in his rapid-fire recital and asked for a drink of water, while Clarence Darrow suggested he speak more slowly.

"She had gone to the Ala Wai Inn party, more or less reluctantly..." Dr. Catton rattled on, giving a concise but detailed review of events. As he reached the part of his story covering Thalia's disappearance, Mrs. Fortescue again began to weep.

"The jury has heard all this, Your Honor," objected Darrow, on his feet. "Does it have to hear it all again?"

Smoothly, Ulrich explained that the material was necessary to show the basis on which his witness formed his opinion. The relaxed courtroom became restless and the jurors stirred in their seats, some looking at the ceiling, as the doctor proceeded, sparing no sensitive sections in the tragic drama of Thalia's abduction. Grace Fortescue sobbed audibly, and Tommy Massie, sitting at her side, put his arm around the shaking shoulders of his mother-in-law.

"Mrs. Massie was found by her husband to be bruised and bleeding. She had to have medical treatment. He nursed her at the hospital and at home, and was made more nervous and under tension, lost weight. As time went on, he awaited a trial of these alleged assailants."

"I object!" interjected Darrow. His dormant temper was aroused. "I object to the word 'alleged.' Does the witness imply that he doesn't believe the story of the rape?"

"The objection is overruled," said Judge Davis.

"I will amend my reply," said Dr. Catton calmly. "Lieutenant Massie awaited the trial of the men who he believed to be the assailants of his wife. The trial arrived. Lieutenant Massie was sent away on duty and learned of the mistrial. Then he states he discussed with one Admiral Stirling, one Beebe, one Stewart, one Mrs. Fortescue and one Major Ross about getting a confession, and learned from Beebe that a confession would be useless if marks were left on the confessor. He admits that he had felt at one or two times like killing Kahahawai. He gave as restraining factors: his Kentucky birth, his Naval training and Admiral Stirling's advice ..."

The short rapid sentences were interrupted regularly by an increasingly exasperated Darrow, who contended the summary was repetitious and unnecessary. Mrs. Fortescue's sobs subsided as the witness showed signs of coming to the point.

"These are the factors I have used in arriving at my opinion," he concluded, having brought Tommy Massie's pathetic saga to its conclusion at Koko Head.

"And what is that opinion?" asked Ulrich.

"My opinion is, first, that at the time of the killing he was sane in the medical sense; second, that he had no brain disease which might prevent ability to discern the criminality of the transaction; third, that at that time he was in a condition that he could afterward prepare a defense of the crime with which he was charged; fourth, that records explain his mental condition, and the pulling down of his nervous reserve." Darrow again rose and objected, but was overruled.

Undaunted, the psychiatrist then continued to list the reasons for his opinion, telling of Tommy's reaction to rumors. "When the trial fails, he is perplexed. He feels that his theory that Kahahawai assaulted his wife is not the theory of the populace and of the Ala Moana jury."

"Your Honor," countered Darrow again, "he has no right to report the feelings of the populace or of the jury that disagreed!" Barry Ulrich resisted the objection, but the ruffled defense veteran was not to be soothed. His voice rose. "The doctor is testifying about the popular opinion of the assault case. This doctor from California knows no more about that than if he had been in Australia!" Darrow clenched his fists and pounded one on the table. "All he knows is what he has heard since he has been here, from talking with the attorneys for the prosecution."

Dr. Catton turned to the judge. "I asked permission to examine the man whose sanity it is," he reminded the Court, "and that request was refused."

Darrow glared as the doctor continued with his conclusions. The courtroom listened, now alert and delighted with the clash that had made the old lion show his fangs. Grace Fortescue shook her head from side to side repeatedly during the testimony.

"Lieutenant Massie believed he could not depend on the forces of law and order, and at that point as a sane man, makes his first step away from conventional behavior. He makes himself the agency to bring about the results he desires, instead of leaving it to society and the authorities of law and order, and discusses certain plans to get a statement. He feels that he might kill Kahahawai. He is working out a plan for satisfaction to Massie, not for satisfaction of law and order."

Pale but expressionless, Tommy Massie listened to the clinical discourses as though it might have been an anonymous case history. He controlled his own emotions and devoted his concern to Mrs. Fortescue, who seemed to be suffering from the testimony far more than its subject.

"His anger-flight mechanism is in force when he plans this transaction. I see his fear-flight mechanism, as evidenced by his using a car other than his own, the fake summons, the dark goggles and gloves, the hiding of his face from the camera, the refusal to make a statement. All are normal, sane reactions under anger-flight and fear-flight mechanisms. I see no single solitary evidence of insanity..."

The lecturing doctor was not to be stopped. Addressing the jury directly, he went on in the same manner of complete control over the situation at hand. The jury seemed fascinated. "I found no evidence in the record of the presence of delirium, from one end of the record to the other; I found no suspicion of the presence of delirium...not traumatism, alcoholic intoxication, hysterical neurosis or psychosis!"

Irritated to the point of combustion, Darrow exploded. "I object to the manner of the witness! Why can't he sit in a chair like other witnesses instead of making an argument to the jury? He might just as well stand up—this is not the manner of a witness who is trying to give an honest testimony!"

It was Dr. Catton's turn to bristle. "You used the word honesty, and I resent..."

"All right! Come down and resent it!" growled Darrow.

"Cease arguing back and forth," ordered Judge Davis, pounding his gavel for order. "This will accomplish nothing!"

"I'm sorry, Your Honor," said Dr. Catton, continuing as before. "I found no evidence of chemical insanity. I never heard of it..."

"How can he say he found no evidence of chemical insanity and in the next breath say 'I don't know what chemical insanity is?'" demanded the unsubdued Darrow.

"I think we will let the witness finish first, Mr. Darrow," said the Court.

"But will he ever finish?" said Darrow testily. He did not share the smile that flitted across the courtroom.

"I believe there were gland changes from the fear-flight and anger-flight mechanisms," continued the witness, only to be interrupted yet again by Darrow's objection, this time to a resumption of the doctor's "lecture to the jury." The objection was overruled.

"Different people have different mannerisms," placated Judge Davis.

"So I see," said Darrow.

Dr. Catton continued to direct his words to the jury. "It is not my opinion that Lieutenant Massie was insane as evidenced by his acting, as one of the men said, like a damn fool. It is also reasonably certain to me and it is my belief in this case that Lieutenant Massie as a sane man should, following the killing of Kahahawai, go about and act in a manner which might be referred to as acting like a damn fool...for all I have read from the record, on analysis by me, indicated not the actions of an insane man but the actions of a man who was not insane."

Barry Ulrich relinquished the witness to cross-examination.

"How often have you testified in court?" asked Darrow of the doctor.

"Once or twice a month for the last two years," said Dr. Catton. "After the war, I don't think four months have ever elapsed without my being called."

"Where is your practice?"

"In San Francisco. I have gone into other states in consultation, but not as a resident."

Barely hiding the sarcasm in his voice, Darrow asked the witness if he had not traveled widely.

"No. This is the farthest I have been from California."

"You couldn't get much farther away without jumping into the ocean, could you?" asked Darrow. One did not have to be a psychiatrist to catch the innuendo.

"I don't know whether New York is farther away or not," answered Dr. Catton, his trim moustache twitching in a faint smile.

"Neither do I," said Darrow wryly.

It became apparent to the courtroom that both contestants relished the stimulation of battle. The defense asked the doctor to define insanity. Dr. Catton complied and restated that he was of the opinion Lieutenant Massie had not suffered from it.

"You testified for the defense?" Darrow asked the experienced witness, referring to previous cases.

"Yes."

"Are you interested in having Lieutenant Massie convicted?"

"No, only in giving correct medical testimony."

"Can't you depend on the lawyers to bring out these points?"

"No."

A burst of applause rose from a spectator in the back of the room. He clapped alone and no cognizance of the disturbance was taken by the Court. Dr. Catton then admitted he was not always on the winning side, that he had considered the assassin of President Garfield insane, but the jury had voted for conviction. He was excused.

The courtroom rustled as spectators prepared to leave. It was assumed that Dr. Catton was the last witness in the two week's examination. John Kelley, however, had yet another surprise for them. He asked Dr. Robert B. Faus, City and County Physician, to return to the stand. It was Dr. Faus who had performed the autopsy.

"In your opinion, how long after Kahahawai was shot did he die?"

"I believe he retained consciousness from three to five minutes and could have been pronounced dead in about twenty minutes." There was a gasp in the courtroom. "He might have been able to move about for a few minutes."

"Could he struggle?"

"He might have been able to do so."

On this dramatic note Kelley indicated the conclusion of testimony, but Darrow was determined that the defense would have the last word. "But you don't know this," he said to Dr. Faus, "and you don't know if there was a struggle?"

"I don't know because I wasn't there, but it is reasonable to suppose that he could struggle."

"Do you know that counsel said in the beginning that there was no evidence of a struggle?" he asked in a tone of triumph.

"Yes."

The examination of witnesses was over. Both prosecution and defense rested their cases. The next day Barry Ulrich would open the argument for the prosecution, to be followed by George Leisure for the defense. The day after, Clarence Darrow would make the final plea for acquittal while John Kelley would offer the state's closing argument for conviction.

Tommy Massie left the courtroom, holding the arm of Mrs. Fortescue, and paused briefly as he passed Mapuana Stevens, the young secretary who had testified that everyone was confused on the day of Kahahawai's death. He thanked her for being kind.

Dr. Catton was approached by a reporter and chuckled when asked how he'd enjoyed a round in the legal ring with the old champion: "I wish Mr. Darrow had kept up the cross-examination longer."

Mrs. John Kelley took the still-crisp white sleeve of her husband and told the public prosecutor as they walked into the glaring light of noon, "I'm going to take you out to lunch. You know you didn't have any breakfast this morning."

"I'm keeping trim so I'll be in shape for Wednesday," said Kelley, smiling.

Under the statue of the warrior king, Clarence Darrow joked with friends, while well-dressed ladies in spring hats vied for introductions to the celebrated "attorney for the damned."

The sunlit grass, the cool silk dresses, the smiling faces and warm greetings transformed the Judiciary lawn into an after-church social hour.

TWENTY-SIX

"Gentlemen of the jury, we approach the end of this trial, I am sure, with some relief. It has been an ordeal for many of us, particularly you gentlemen who have been held away from your friends and family. But I know you appreciate that you would not have been segregated if your duties were not so vital to the Territory of Hawaii, the most critical of our history.

"The defendants alone are not on trial, but the whole judicial system, the people of Hawaii, charged with inability to maintain law and order. It is in your power to do great good or great harm...perhaps never before has a jury been put to such a severe test, which you must meet unflinchingly."

Thus Barry Ulrich opened the argument for the prosecution on Tuesday, April 26. "You cannot make Hawaii safe against rape by licensing murder!" he told the crowded courtroom.

Stepping before the jury box, the slender, immaculately tailored special prosecutor seemed more at ease than the twelve tense men to whom he directed his words in a vibrant voice. He hooked one thumb in a pocket of his vest, raised a highly polished foot to the edge of the stand, and leaned forward slightly, his face determined beneath silver-grey temples, as he continued in a more sympathetic key.

"We come with no cry for vengeance, no song of hate, but only asking that justice be done. I don't ask you to hate these people. I don't ask you not to sympathize with them. But your sympathy must not sway you.

"The scene of the young woman on the stand was calculated to stir your emotions. We don't dispute her suffering, we don't ask you to minimize this suffering. Any of us would gladly, if we could, turn back the hands of time. But we are faced with things that cannot be undone." The rich melodious voice was that of the classic tragedian. Ulrich saw to it that his lines were conveyed with all their dramatic impact. His motions were minimized to slight but eloquent gestures with his free hand.

"In every case, people brought before the courts have suffered, more or less. But if we are to be so influenced, we might as well close the courts...Never has any case demanded more that a verdict be returned on facts and law. You are the finders of the facts...There must be no question of emotion, sympathy or prejudice. You must hold your trust inviolate. Questions of penalty are for the court. Questions of clemency are for the executive.

"And now gentlemen—" Ulrich leaned even closer to the jury and freed his right hand, raising it in an impressive gesture of admonition. "You will be instructed that no man may take the law into his own hands, and no amount of suffering or injury will justify taking the life of another...The crime charged is second degree murder. Murder in the first degree involves malice and premeditation; the elements of deliberation need not be present in second degree murder...The argument that these people had the right to do these things, that they are creatures of fate...is not the law!"

Barry Ulrich continued to impress upon the jurors the view of the prosecution that there was no justification for the killing of Joseph Kahahawai even if the asserted facts of the Ala Moana rape case were true. "Now let us consider the facts of this case. We have a man whose wife tells him she has been raped..." Once again, the prosecutor proceeded to give masterly summation of the events leading up to the crime. Raising his tone, he challenged the contention that the defendants sought only to obtain a confession. "If you felt you wanted to get a confession without hurting a man or without using physical force, what would you do? And if that man was one you hated, who seared your soul, would you follow this course?" The intense attorney was almost shouting now. "They had a veritable arsenal up there. They had not one, but three guns, all loaded! Kahahawai was confronted with people whose every natural impulse would be to let something happen to him. Don't you think that under those circumstances, not only might you hurt him but probably you would?

"Do you think that Mr. Massie really believed that a confession procured at the point of a gun would allay rumors? Anybody knows the man naturally would say anything he was told to say, to save his life or avoid torture.

"Mr. Massie said he was to have procured a written confession, but nothing in the records shows any preparation for a written confession. Mr. Darrow puts us through a clever line of cross examination and wrings a confession of a fact that Massie already believed. Then when they're just about to get a fuller confession, 'trigger insanity,' 'ambulatory automatism' or 'chemical insanity' intervenes." The shade of irony in the rich voice was not lost on the courtroom. As Ulrich continued, Clarence Darrow leaned forward, arms folded on his chest and jaw firmly set, brows knitted beneath his tousled hair.

"I tell you gentlemen, these people have come before you and practically pleaded guilty...It's true that they plotted a plan that might place a life in jeopardy. They get a rented car, they learn when Kahahawai will be at the courthouse, taking every precaution against detection. It is tragic that they should initiate this undertaking at the very door of the hall of justice. They are posted about the building so that there can be no mistake."

Ulrich walked quickly to the clerk's desk and held up Grace Fortescue's handbag.

"Premeditation is definitely indicated. Here she stood with her purse with the picture of the man on whom sentence of death had been pronounced. He was, as Mr. Kelley has said, 'on the spot.' He was shown this fake warrant."

With a flourish, the associated prosecutor exhibited the warrant.

"There is something peculiar about this warrant," he continued, his voice now sinister. "It is something indicating an unusual state of mind, a state that would not be harbored by those anticipating a quiet conference to get a voluntary confession. We have the suggestion that life was in some way involved—'Life is a mysterious thing'—why did they put that sentiment on it? Isn't there a suggestion that he is to be led where life is indeed mysterious and uncertain?"

There was a pause at the eerie implication. It was merely a prelude to a dramatic dissertation on the mysterious circumstances surrounding the actual moment of Kahahawai's death. "Dr. Faus has testified that Kahahawai probably did not die instantly, that with such a wound a man might be conscious from three to five minutes and able to move about and would remain alive fifteen to twenty minutes. Three to five minutes allow much to happen.

"It is obvious that these defendants, when Kahahawai was shot, had no way of knowing he was going to die. They could not know whether the bullet had pierced a vital spot. If there were honesty in their endeavor to do him no harm, why would they not have taken steps to save his life?" Ulrich threw the question to the entire courtroom where it echoed in the utter silence. Then he turned again to the jury and quickened his timing. "They had a telephone. There are plenty of doctors in town. Why didn't they do something then if they didn't want him to die?

"I say that here is shown that they were willing for him to die, unwilling to save his life for fear their criminal undertaking might be revealed. They let him die because they wanted him to die. Does that not appeal to reason? Other facts bear out this analysis of their state of mind. Gentlemen of the jury—"

The magnetic man before the rail let his voice drop impressively to an intimate tone of persuasion.

"I don't know who killed Kahahawai," he continued confidentially, "but that isn't important. Lieutenant Massie's story cannot be accepted at face value. I can show you he hasn't told you what happened. Let me call your attention to a certain phase of evidence."

Ulrich assumed a pantomime pose, that of a gunman pointing his weapon. "I want you to consider this as how people act under a certain set of circumstances. He has told you of one man confronting another with a gun. The natural impulse would be to face him, not to stand at his side. Yet we know that the shot entered the body from the side, clear over by the left nipple."

The courtroom, caught up in the one-man skit, was startled when Ulrich dropped his "gun" and grabbed the picture of Kahahawai's dead body, flashing it before the jury. "Massie testifies that he went over and sat in the chair at Kahahawai's left and from that position conducted the examination. That places Lieutenant Massie in a sitting position, confronting his victim with a gun. What does the other evidence show?" The prosecuting attorney then held up the chart of the human body, indicating a downward course of the bullet. "Dr. Faus has testified that the bullet passed diagonally...we also know the revolver was held not less than two feet away. So it's conclusively demonstrated that Massie could not have been where he said he was, he could not have been sitting—if he fired that shot!"

Clarence Darrow leaned over and whispered with Tommy Massie at this point in the argument. Mrs. Fortescue looked straight ahead, her face carved from marble. Albert Jones's jaws worked like pistons as he chewed his gum.

"Whoever did fire that shot was someone standing some distance away and to one side...that is consistent with the facts. The defense theory is made to fit certain circumstances but not to fit all the facts. These little impossibilities, these great improbabilities, show that the testimony has been false. The Court will instruct you that you may disregard all uncorroborated evidence of a witness if you doubt his truthfulness, and in this case there is no corroboration!"

This new angle sparked a current of interest in the courtroom and there were a few whispers among the spectators.

"Now let us consider again the plea of insanity," continued Ulrich. "Evidence shows that a man has been killed and these people caught red-handed with his body. In cases of this kind, the defense of insanity is a last resort." Ulrich mocked the defense theory that "shock amnesia and ambulatory automatism conditions arose in a man who had been sane all his life, became insane to kill a man, and regained sanity!" He then asked the jury if a man in a trance would be included on a dangerous mission that entailed lifting a heavy body. "Would they want an automaton in the car and leave an able-bodied man behind? Would you advertise your criminality by foisting on yourselves an automaton?" Continuing to appeal to the jury's common sense, he asked, "Which is more probable—that a man would kill a man he hated or would lapse into trigger insanity?"

It was at this point the special prosecutor, still as cool as the hour before when he had opened his argument, returned to his first premise and prepared to wind up his summation.

"Gentlemen, we agree that rape is terrible...but it does not license murder. Any verdict placing a stamp of approval on any crime is a step in the direction of anarchy. So guard yourselves against such insidious directions. You must not be influenced by expenditures of money, by differences of stations in life. Suppose Kahahawai had taken a person of Massie's station into his poor home and had tried to extort a confession or money, then had lapsed into insanity and killed him, how would he be treated? His plea of insanity would be laughed out of court!

"What case is there in which a man doesn't go through an emotional period, with glandular action, before he commits a murder?...If a man is to be acquitted because he has enough money to hire chemical insanity experts, Hawaii is not safe from crime!

"They say it is a difficult thing to feign. To give a series of 'I don't remembers' to questions...it's the easiest thing in the world.

"As a plain and obvious fact, I state that these defendants are guilty. They proclaim it themselves. In the bright light of the Hawaiian day, at the portals of this building, which is dedicated to justice, they took a boy and with their poisoned minds passed judgment on him and passed the sentence of death for a crime of which, for all they can determine now, he may have been entirely innocent.

"They killed him and wrapped his body in a sheet, a deed that shocked the world and made the dignity of the Hawaiian government and justice in Hawaii a by-word and a reproach. Now they ask you to make Hawaii's shame complete. They have money and one of the greatest attorneys money can obtain...

"In the presence of the representatives of the press, indicating the eyes of the world are on you, I ask you to write a verdict that here in Hawaii, government cannot be defied with impunity, that we can maintain law and order. I ask you, gentlemen of the jury, to find Mrs. Grace Fortescue, Lieutenant Thomas H. Massie, E.J. Lord and A.O. Jones guilty of murder in the second degree!"

As his predecessor had appealed to reason, George S. Leisure, opening the final arguments for the defense, appealed to human sympathy. A relaxed, sophisticated man who spoke quietly with his hands clasped naturally and without self-consciousness behind his back, he addressed the jury with courteous deliberation. Thoughtful pauses punctuated his argument with an effectiveness equal to the dramatic gestures of Barry Ulrich.

"Gentlemen of the jury, the issues you are about to decide are important. My discussion will be brief. I shall not thank you for your attention, because you, like soldiers, give this service without asking for thanks..."

"Misfortune is the sinister guest of every man or woman at some time. Whenever it comes it leaves behind as deep and dark a desolation as can be woven from human souls. This boy, Massie, was overtaken by misfortune before he and his wife were launched on their life. They came here trusting the kindly welcome of this city. It was under these auspices that a calamity blighted the lives of his entire family. This calamity may have happened anywhere. It has happened elsewhere. But this thing did happen to this boy..."

"Not long ago the body identified as that of a man who criminally assaulted the wife of one of your neighbors, was found. His death was as just under the laws of God and as direct a consequence of his own acts, as if he had leaped from your historic Pali. Do you suppose the cruel appetite of this man would have been satiated by one drunken debauch? No. His next victim might have been your wife or sister. I feel confident that every civilized man regards the ravishing of his mother, wife or daughter as the greatest crime that can be perpetrated on a human being. It is a shame, a living death that preys on minds of men..."

"You are to determine if when a man's wife is ravished, that man shall go behind prison bars if the shock is too great for his mind and he kills the man identified as his wife's assailant. Can any of you say that your mind would have survived such a shock if such a thing happened to your wife? Our laws cannot protect us against all things that may befall us. Laws against rape are effective only after the event has occurred. We have to protect ourselves. The law provides for our protection if the strain is too great for our minds."

George Leisure paused, rocking slightly forward on his toes. His simple language, decorated with flights of rhetoric, brought out the atrocity of the crime of which Kahahawai was accused and the feasibility of Tommy Massie's subsequent insanity. He paused as he again asked the jurors to put themselves in the place of the frantic husband, to imagine the effect on their minds if someone near and dear to them had been brutally ravished. He then quoted from the Mosaic law, as found in Chapter 22 of Deuteronomy, verses 25 and 26:

"But if a man find a betrothed damsel in the field, and the man forces her, and lies with her; then the man only who lay with her shall die.

"But unto the damsel thou shalt do nothing; there is in the damsel no sin worthy of death..."

By playing up Christian charity and employing the subtle use of understatement, the defense assistant made clear to the jury that a verdict against the defendants would be merely adding salt to the open wound of the tragedy they had suffered. "Mr. Kelley will probably try to convince you that fate has not been sufficiently cruel to this boy, and that under the dress of duty you must inflict further cruelty on him...

"You gentlemen know that a jury is to protect the weak and unfortunate from the state, and that your duty is as much to the individual as to the state. There may be a difference of opinion as to what one may consider the public good: but when an intelligent jury returns a verdict of not guilty, that is law and order. The prosecution has taken several tacks. When you have a case where the facts prove the case, you don't have to go way back and bring up a trivial incident about a boy and girl wheeling away someone else's baby. This shows their case to be weak."

Clarence Darrow turned from his seat and smiled proudly at Mrs. Leisure, who returned the smile. Mr. Darrow continued smiling as Leisure went on:

"They started on the theory to prove first degree murder, with pictures, ropes, and tarpaulins. Then this boy bares his heart and tells his story. It is proved that the rope was for a different purpose entirely as a runway for a dog. Then there was the sweaty shirt and Jones' gun to fasten it on Jones. Then it developed that pretty near everybody in Honolulu was buying a gun. A man planning first degree murder doesn't take the victim to his own home, or serve a summons in broad daylight before other people. If they had intended to kill Kahahawai it would be much simpler to take him out somewhere along the seashore where they could dispose of the body quickly and easily. The boy's cousin saw a moustache that wasn't there. Then the Japanese boy who rented the car saw Lieutenant Massie when he rented the car, but it was Jones, not Massie who was there. He had not seen Massie at all. Then the learned experts were put on. Dr. Bowers summed up facts that would produce psychosis, but when he got to the fact of psychosis, he stopped. But you don't have to accept this testimony; you know that minds can be deranged.

"Then we had Dr. Catton who, I am afraid, has read more history than medicine, who wanted to be prosecutor himself, who wanted to decide the facts instead of letting the jury decide them. Mrs. Massie may be ravished, but Dr. Catton must be on a winning case, he must bring a conviction."

Dr. Catton, sitting in the front row next to the defendant, Jones, did not change his facial expression as this sarcasm was directed at him.

"He was taking no chances with the jury. His statements were unfair. He tried to displace Mr. Kelley and Mr. Ulrich as prosecutor. He made deliberate miscalculations. He said he's never heard of chemical insanity and then proceeded to tell us that Massie didn't have it, although Drs. Orbison and Williams were practicing when he was in diapers."

A ripple of laughter passed through the spectators. Determined to keep the courtroom's interest and not succumb to the pitfall of an overly lengthy plea, Leisure glanced at the clock on the back wall of the room and tightened his already refreshingly terse summary. "I won't take your time going through all this evidence that you have already heard. As to self-government, I can't see that it's on trial any more than any other case. You're trying this case on the facts and evidence, and you are the judges of what justice is. I have read other charges by this Court and have found them masterpieces of American jurisprudence, and I assume that you will receive instructions of equal high quality. You have been told not to be influenced by sympathy. Of course, sympathy must be evident in your deliberations. A jury must consider everything.

"Mr. Ulrich read certain instructions that should have been left to the judge to read. Among them was one which implies that insanity is no defense. That it is not the law. The part of people on an unlawful enterprise being all guilty if death ensues is a misstatement, for had one of them died by being struck by lightning, there would have been no murder, and Lieutenant Massie's mental disturbance was just as much an act of providence.

"We are making no plea of unwritten law. If he wanted to kill him, why wait three months, why kill the man whose confession was the thing he wanted? Would he spoil what he had been waiting for...by killing the man? Why didn't Massie drive the car if there wasn't something wrong with him instead of letting his mother-in-law do it? Why would he kill the one man in the world who could help him? This was not a normal act. Mr. Ulrich thinks we have pleaded guilty. Well, if we have pleaded guilty of anything we have pleaded guilty to insanity!

"Mr. Ulrich sees sinister ideas in the wording of the warrant. That is ridiculous. The defendants ask the presumption of innocence, Mr. Ulrich says. They are not asking. They are entitled to it by law! The maid was told not to come that day, instead of coming at 3 o'clock. Does that show that they expected to get a confession?"

The improbability intimated in the statement raised another chuckle from the audience. Loudest among those laughing were prosecutors Ulrich and Kelley. The young defense lawyer smiled briefly, but his voice was deadly serious. "Is it reasonable that these men would ask a confession without loading the gun? It was necessary as part of their plan to get a confession to load it in front of him. I believe the gun was held as Lieutenant Massie said it was. Mr. Ulrich said he was sitting, but Massie said he was standing. The whole record should be considered—not just a part of it."

Darrow wrote a note and carried it up to a small table near his assistant. Its contents were not revealed, but George Leisure, with no change in his even voice and poised demeanor, neatly wrapped up his argument. "Mr. Ulrich said that the defense suggested the insanity plea. That is untrue; the act suggested the plea. No normal man would do what was done. The attempt was made to instill a feeling of social position against this boy. I believe that any boy under the same circumstances would receive the same consideration.

"He says that a defense of insanity would always be available in a case of murder. Of course it would under these circumstances. The mention of the cost to the Territory was indelicate. Does not Mrs. Massie face the possibility of having her breadwinner taken away from her?

"I feel satisfied that you will do your duty as just men. I thank you."

Judge Davis reminded the jury that they had been instructed not to discuss the case among themselves until its conclusion, and repeated this instruction. As the twelve men filed from the chamber, it filled with chatter rivaling the raucous mynah birds in the banyans beyond the windows. Beneath the extended boughs trailing tendrils on the palace lawn, the Darrows and Leisures strolled behind the guarded jurymen on the familiar route to the Alexander Young Hotel. Clarence Darrow put a proud paternal arm around the shoulders of his assistant and congratulated him on his opening argument for the defense. The young lawyer said that he was looking forward to the next day's closing argument by the past master of the final plea.

Leisure's remarks were not those of flattery but of truly sincere anticipation. He was interested to know the mechanics of "making a moving address to a jury," he was to remark later when recalling the Massie trial. "Up to the night before Darrow was to argue the case I had observed that he had not made a single mark on paper in preparation for his summation."

The Darrows and Leisures enjoyed a relaxed supper that evening, the senior member of the congenial quartet being the least apprehensive. George Leisure was in the famous lawyer's room after dinner when the phone rang. "...some of the Navy men wanted to call on us that night," remembered Leisure, who was about to tell the party on the other end of the line that he was sorry but Mr. Darrow would be busy. "He interrupted me, however, and told me to tell them to come on over. We sat and talked until 10 o'clock that evening, when Mr. Darrow went to bed."

The dean of defense had not yet taken a single note and court was to convene promptly at 8:30 the next morning. "Mr. Darrow had made no visible preparation up to that time," recorded his amazed assistant. It promised to be a fascinating day.

TWENTY-SEVEN

The city of Honolulu spent a restless night. Not only were the eyes of the world on the small courtroom of the Judiciary Building, but also the ears of the world awaited Clarence Darrow's closing argument, to be broadcast to the mainland. Aware that Wednesday, April 17, was to be the final day of Hawaii's most famous trial, many spectators had reverted to the practice of staying up all night to be assured of admission. Lines were not permitted to form until 4 a.m., but the regulars began arriving in the vicinity before midnight and camped on the grounds of Iolani Palace, across King Street from the courthouse. The moonlit lawn was littered with blankets, camp stools. beach mats and even a card table, which four enterprising ladies had set up under the towering trees. With the aid of flashlights, they whiled away the dark hours playing cards and enjoying a pleasant camaraderie. Parked cars were laden with sleeping passengers.

The day again was devoid of tradewinds. In the still courtroom, the crush of the spectators deprived two of the defendants of their seats: Jones and Lord had to sit at the counsel table. Mrs. Darrow was robbed of her chair and stood until a court officer spotted her and brought her a camp stool. The crowd soon filled the benches and overflowed onto the platform of the jury box itself, where half a dozen people perched precariously, well out of sight of Judge Davis, who looked at the ceiling and drummed his fingers on the bar. As usual white faces predominated, most of them under fashionable ladies' hats. The few males who were brave enough to take front row seats looked sheepishly out of place, as though they'd strayed into a bridge luncheon at the country club. The handful of Hawaiians who were able to find seats edged to the back of the room and sat next to the wall, looking out over the front benches with sad dark eyes.

In the row facing the rail, only a few chairs removed from the defendants, sat the parents of Joseph Kahahawai, Jr. The father bowed his head in his hands and silently wept. At his side, Esther Anito, Joe's mother, sat upright and wiped her eyes with a crumpled handkerchief. In the same row, a dozen seats removed, Grace Fortescue also held a handkerchief, gripped tightly in her lap, as her pale face worked to hold back the tears. Anticipation reached its highest pitch as the hands of the clock above the judge's head jerked visibly to 8:30. At that moment, it was the only movement in the room.

The leading protagonists entered: Clarence Darrow, almost shabby in a gray suit with pockets drooping from the continual burden of fists; John Kelley, immaculate in his uniform of white Palm Beach suit and crimson tie. During the five minutes before Judge Davis called the court to order, Darrow made four or five little half-line notes on a yellow pad, which he proceeded to throw down and leave behind him on the counsel table when the Court announced, "Very well, you may proceed now, Mr. Darrow."

He stepped in front of the jury, a kindly old man who gazed for a brief silent second into the twelve pairs of eyes with an expression of tenderness then, thrusting his hands even deeper into his misshapen jacket, in a low conversational tone began his glorious close of the Massie Case with a sermon on the fallibility of mankind. America's most famous lawyer was aware that this swan song for the defense might well be his own.

"Gentlemen, we are getting close to the end of this case. It has been a long, serious, tedious trial, and you of the jury probably have had the worst of it.

"This case illustrates the working of human destiny more than any other case I have handled. It illustrates the effect of sorrow and mishap on human minds and lives, and shows us how weak and powerless human beings are in the hands of relentless powers. Eight months ago Mrs. Fortescue was in Washington, respected and known like any other woman. Eight months ago Lieutenant Massie worked himself up to the rank of lieutenant in the Navy, respected, courageous and intelligent. His young wife, handsome and attractive, was known and respected and admired by the community. In that short space of time they are in a criminal court and the jury has been asked to send them to prison for life.

"What has happened is a long series of events, beginning at a certain time, ending we don't know where," began Darrow, inadvertently prophesying his own summation.

"A whole family—their life, future, name—bound up in a criminal act committed by someone else in which they had no part. About eight months ago Massie and his wife went to a dance. They were young, happy, he was following the profession he had chosen, and she was the wife of a Navy officer—brave, courageous and fearless.

"Today they are in this court, in the hands of you twelve men, to settle their fate. I ask you gentlemen to consider it carefully, seriously. The power is given to you to do justice in this case.

"We contend that for months Massie's mind had been affected by all that was borne upon him: grief, sorrow, trouble, day after day, week after week, and month after month. What do you think would have happened to any one of you under the same condition? We measure other people by ourselves. We place ourselves in their place and say, 'How would we have acted?' We have no further way of telling, except perhaps from the conditions of the life in which we live." His confiding voice rhythmically rocking his audience in a hammock of commiseration, he paused.

"As to the early history of this case—they went to a dance with their friends. About half-past eleven in the evening, Mrs. Massie, who didn't especially care for these festivities, went out for a walk, intending to go down the street and come back and join her husband again at the dance. It was only a few steps from safety to destruction.

"What did Massie learn from her a few hours later? An unbelievable story—almost—at least an unthinkable one about which even my friend who opened this argument for the state said: It was a terrible story—so terrible that he pitied them. Still, he asked you to send these people to prison.

"She had gone but a short way when four or five men drove up behind her in an automobile, dragged her into it, beat her, and broke her jaw in two places. They were ruffians, unknown to her. And after that they dragged her into the bushes, and she was raped by four or five men.

"Can you imagine anything worse that could have happened or any greater calamity that could have fallen upon that family? They had nothing to do with it—not the slightest.

"She was going on her way as she had a right to go, and in the twinkling of an eye her whole life, the life of the family, was changed and they are now here in this court for you to say whether they will go to prison—for life!

"Is there a more terrible story anywhere in literature? I don't know whether there is—or who it was—or where I can find that sad tale but right here. You and all the other people in the city have been chosen to take care of their fate. I hope you will in kindness and humanity and understanding—no one else but you can do this.

"She was left on that lonely road in pain and agony and suffering. In this, Mrs. Massie suffered the greatest humiliation that a woman can suffer at the hands of man. She had done nothing! Massie had done nothing! So far, suffering has been inflicted on them. Suffering that few people encounter in their lives.

"Massie dances until the dance is nearly over. He is ready to go home. He looks for his wife. She is not there. He goes to a friend's house. She is not there. He calls home, and she isn't there. He looks wherever he can and he calls home again and she sobs out a part of the story over the telephone, part of the story as terrible, as cruel, as any story I ever heard: 'Hurry home, something terrible has happened to me!'...

"Tommy rushes home! She meets him at the door and sobs and tells him this terrible story—isn't that enough to unsettle any man's mind? Suppose you'd heard it then and there—what effect would it have had on your mind—what effect would it have had on anybody's mind!"

The pacing defender, disheveled in his sagging suit, paused to collect his thoughts. "There are few men who would listen to a story like that—" he said, sadly, shaking his large head with its downcast eyes, "a story that came through her sobs and her tears, this harrowing story." He stood still again and faced the jury. His voice rose.

"Shock, grief, and sorrow, at times protracted, sometimes at once, causes a human mind to break down in the end. This was only the beginning—here was his wife: she told him that they had broken her jaw, that they had beaten her, taken her into the machine, dragged her into the bushes, ravished her and left her by the road to find her way home." Unabashed by repetition, Darrow again appealed to the jury.

"Do you remember the subsequent story? The police were called to pick up the trail. No one raised even a doubt about this story, except the originators of a few vile slanders which were carried from tongue to tongue over these fair islands. Has anybody placed their finger upon a single fact to contradict the saddest tale that was ever brought to a husband?

"What did Mrs. Massie do? All of this she told her husband. He had reason to believe and fear infection and that she might be placed in a family way from these men who dragged her into the bushes and ravished her. She took the best precautions she could. She gave her information to the police and they jested and hinted and quarreled and haggled about what should be done.

"Finally an indictment was found. I'll tell you then what happened." Slowly the old weaver spun his web of words, stringing epigrams, platitudes and hyperboles in a skein of sympathy. The audience was caught up more in the cadence than in the content, until Darrow again recalled the harrowing weeks following the fateful night. The courtroom came to life as Thalia's tale of agony was unfolded for the last time by her most ardent defender. "During days and days and nights and nights, she had to take liquid food and suffer extreme pain. Any question about that? This wasn't testified to by the Massies alone. Dr. Withington tells us about it. He said that the inside of her thighs, knees and hips were bruised. Both legs!

"There have been people who spread around in the community stories I don't believe true. They concocted these terrible stories and what effect did they have on the Massies? I ask what effect they would have had on you, and how you would have stood them? Massie attended to his days' duties as best he could. He went back and forth, nursing his wife. working all day and attending her at night for weeks. It was all that any husband could do, or any man could do. He lost sleep. He lost courage. He lost hope. He was distraught, and all the load was on his shoulders!

"Any cause for it? Our insane institutions are filled with men and women who had less cause for insanity than he had. Everyone knows it. The mind isn't t too easy to understand at the best. But what happens to the human mind? It does one thing with one person and another thing with another. You know what it did to Massie's. Do you think he is responsible, or has been, from that terrible night?

"What did he do? Days he worked. At night he nursed his wife. Could anybody do more? The slow, long terrible times. The doctor attending her helped Massie, too. Gentlemen, just think how much is involved here now. Here was the assault, the rape, the days and the nights, and what else? Dr. Withington told them that they must take the greatest pain to guard against disease and pregnancy. So he watched her day by day. Day by day Tommy tended to his duties. He nursed his wife at night. Well, how would it affect you? Finally the doctor said, 'You must have an operation to prevent pregnancy.'

"Here is a man—his wife—she is bearing inside of her the germs of—who? Does anybody know? Not he, but someone of the four ruffians who assaulted her and left a wreck of her. The doctor was not only a physician, but a friend. He asked no questions. He didn't even read the statutes. He wasn't afraid the District Attorney would indict him for abortion. You know what a friend would do, what an intelligent physician did do. So he took away what was there. He did it out of kindness and consideration—and prescribed for Massie, too."

"Now, gentlemen, don't you suppose all this trouble might have been what ailed him? Would you take a chance on your own mind or any other person's, strong or weak?"

He let the question hang in the air as he brushed aside a wanton lock of hair. His keen blue eyes shone behind the sprouting brake of brows and a spark of indignation kindled in their depths as he took up the prosecution's answer. "Dr. Catton said 'No! No, there is nothing to it,' ...I think Dr. Catton is an honorable fellow. He sits at his door as a spider sits in his web, watching for flies. He is impartial. The first one is taken in. He would just as soon swear away a man's life as to deliver it. All that is necessary is to get there first." There was still a sharp bite behind the growl.

"It is almost inconceivable that so much could happen to one family. In time, four men were indicted for the crime. Tommy was away on duty some of the time. Part of the time he was in the courtroom during the trial of the assailants. A strange circumstance, indeed, that the jury disagreed in that case. I don't know, I don't see why. But anyway, after all their work, and all their worry, the jury disagreed. What effect did that have?

"Many have no doubt raised the question that has been raised over and over since man organized courts—'Can't I get justice?' Is there a chance to get any? Months passed and this case still was not retried.

"Then began a campaign such as has been waged against few men and women. Why? Why? I don't know why. Do you know why? Out of the clear air, with nothing on which to rest, strange, slanderous stories were spread over these islands about Lieutenant Massie and his ravished wife. Stories that she had never been raped, or else that she ravished herself. Stories that her husband, whose faithfulness the doctor has related to you, and it has been plainly evident to every person who sat in this courtroom during these long trying days, broke his wife's jaw. Then they spread the rumor that it was some Navy person who had ravished her. This spread all over the islands. Everybody heard it. It came to Tommy, it came to Mrs. Massie. And it came to her mother.

"Gentlemen, I wonder what Fate has against this family, anyhow? And I wonder when it will get through taking its toll and leave them to go in peace, to try and make their own life in comfort for the rest of their days. I wonder!"

Again he paced as he pondered. Then he rose to the full height of his majesty and, without removing his fists from their tweed burrows, managed to pull out the most sentimental stop: motherhood.

"Here is a mother. What about her?" Already handkerchiefs were emerging; eyes were misting as they focused on Grace Fortescue. She sat straight-back and motionless, only the muscles of her jaws moving.

In the baroque style of old-fashioned oratory, the grand old man of the courtroom waxed mellow. "They wired to her and she came. Poems and volumes without end have been written about mothers. I don't want to bring forth further eulogies which are more or less worthwhile, but I want to call your attention to something more primitive than that. Nature. It is not a case of the greatness of a mother. It is the case of what nature has done. I don't care whether it is a human mother, a mother of beasts or birds of the air, they are all alike.

"To them there is one all-important thing and that is a child that they carried in their womb. Without that feeling which is so strong in all life, there would be no life preserved upon this earth. She acted as every mother acts. She felt as your mothers have felt, because the family is the preservation of life. What did she do? Immediately she started on a long trip to her daughter. The daughter was married and a long way off, but she was still her daughter. I don't care if a mother is seventy-five and her daughter fifty, it is still the mother and the child.

"Everything else is forgotten in the emotion that carries her back to the time when this was a little baby in her arms which she bore and loved. Your mother was that way and my mother, and there can be no other way, because life can be preserved in no other way. The mother started on a trip of five thousand miles, over land and sea, to her child. And here she is now in this courtroom waiting to go to the penitentiary.

"Gentlemen, let me say this: If this husband and this mother and these faithful boys go to the penitentiary, it won't be the first time that a penitentiary has been sanctified by its inmates."

Amazingly, Darrow's disorganized circumlocution had the desired effect. No one stirred, nor yawned, nor took his eye from the star performer. The courtroom was adrift in a sea of words, caught in an oratorical riptide beyond its control.

If his associate, Leisure, wondered at the master's modus operandi, the answer was simple: There was none. Darrow was telling a tragic tale of two helpless young lovers entangled in a cruel twist of fate that shattered the lives of all involved.

The direction of his story was unpredictable. Even the storyteller himself did not know it.

"When people come to your beautiful islands, one of the first places that they will wish to see is the prison where the mother and the husband are confined because they moved under emotion," he continued. "If that does happen, that prison will be the most conspicuous building on this Island, and men will wonder how it happened and will marvel at the injustice and cruelty of men and will pity the inmates and blame Fate for the cruelty, persecution and sorrow that has followed this family.

"Gentlemen, you are asked to send these people to the penitentiary. Do you suppose that if you had been caught in the hands of Fate would you have done differently? No, we are not made that way. Life doesn't come that way. It comes from a devotion of mothers, of husbands, loves of men and women, that's where life comes from. Without this love, this devotion, the world will be desolate and cold and will take its lonely course around the sun alone! Without a human heartbeat, there will be nothing except thin air. Every instinct that moves human beings, every feeling that is with you or any of your kin, every feeling that moves in the mother of the animal is with us in this case. You can't fight against it. If you do, you are fighting against nature and life.

"What a theory! What a theory!"

Darrow shook his head, stunned by the magnitude of it all. Many of the spectators wept. He turned to the prosecuting attorney. "My amiable friend who opened this case for the state," he continued in a fresh voice, "wondered why anyone should be taken on the steps of the courthouse." At this point Darrow sought to justify the fact that the defendants kidnapped the victim from the steps of the house of justice by saying that the only people who sanctify the building are lawyers who earn their living within its walls. A new and cynical note colored his remarks.

"My home has been in courthouses for more than fifty years. What have I seen there? I have seen sorrow and distress. I have seen men on the way to the gallows. I have seen them tired and confused, led into...dungeons, and beaten after they got there. Every man who lives and goes on his way passes on the other side of the courthouse. A blind lady holding the scales she can't see doesn't enter into it...A feeling for justice, instinctive since the earliest man, has existed independent of law, or rules that often destroy it.

"Don't you know what justice is, you and you and you and you, just as well as if you had spent four years getting ready to practice law and getting ready to make people pay for an offense? You know why they came to the court house to get this man. They came there because they knew he was one of the four defendants that the jury had disagreed to punish and he had to report to the courthouse...He was taken in front of the courthouse just as well as if he been taken at a church or on a street corner or anywhere else..."

He meandered on, playing on his favorite theme of Fate, the inexorable tide of events that overwhelmed the people he was now defending. Two or three of the ladies who had been up all night now began to doze beneath their nodding coiffures. Enraptured by his own eloquence, at one point Darrow forgot the name of one of his clients... "as for those two boys who were not mentioned by the psychiatrists at all—what is the name of the other one? I remember Jones because he got drunk and somehow that appeals to me, but the other one..."

"Lord," came a whisper from the counsel's table, as Darrow was prompted by the prosecution.

"Oh yes, Lord—I must speak of him now before I forget his name again; it popped right out of my mind..." But such an oversight was a mere trifle in the grand scheme of things. For a few more minutes, he pursued his theory of humanity, then realizing he was caught in something of a current himself, called for a ten-minute recess. When court resumed, Darrow again slouched to the front of the courtroom. He had recaptured the thread of his raveling plea.

"Gentlemen of the jury, this campaign against Massie and Mrs. Massie began very, very early. It was very strong when the jury disagreed. Stories have been peddled all over this town that Massie and his wife were about to get a divorce. They said that another Navy officer was out that night with Mrs. Massie...

"Stories have been peddled up and down in the streets and broadcast against this woman who had been raped, and the husband was doing all he could to help her as any husband would. What effect could it have on the mind of this defendant?

"Gentlemen of the jury, it was bad enough that the wife was raped. These vile stories were circulated and caused great anxiety and agony. All this is bad enough. But now you are asked that they must spend the rest of their lives in prison. All right, gentlemen, you have the power, but let me say to you—that if on top of all else that has been heaped upon the devoted heads of this family, if they should be sent to prison, it would place a blot upon the fair name of these islands that all the Pacific seas would never wash away.

"There is somewhere deep in the feelings and instincts of a man, a yearning for justice, an idea of what is right and wrong, of what is fair between man and man, that came before the first law was written and will abide after the last one is dead. Picture Tommy's and his wife's minds, when he went up and down investigating these stories. He doubted his friends and he thought he heard people's footsteps on the lawn outside in the dead of the night, and he was harassed and worried from the time this happened until now.

"How much could you, how could any human mind stand? Some men have gone insane by a word, by fear, by fright, others by slow degree, by long trouble, by mishap.

"Poor Massie, strong and vigorous, when all of these things were heaped on him. What did he do? He began to rid his mind somewhat of his own troubles and of the persecution of the men who performed his deed. He began to think of vindicating his wife from this slander. She had been lied about, she had been abused with talk."

Again the sly old king of the courtroom jungle faced his adversary. "My amiable friend here," he said, looking at John Kelley, "the prosecutor, I came near saying the persecutor, you are an Irishman—you understand persecution."

Neither man was smiling as Darrow continued. Addressing his words to Kelley, he often glanced beyond the well-tailored, spotless white shoulders of the prosecutor to the spellbound faces of the gallery.

"What is the reason you seek to cause the destruction of these people? Don't you understand? Think what a good fellow this is," he waved his hand at Tommy Massie, sitting nearby. "Five years ago, before Massie and his wife were married, they went down to a theater near their home to a moving picture. They went out and there was a baby in a baby carriage. It was crying. They trundled it down a couple of blocks. They weren't looking for babies; they weren't married." The spectators tittered, but Darrow continued to keep a straight face. "They trundled it down a couple of blocks to give it a little air and someone arrests them for giving it a little air!"

His voice had that 'Now-I-ask-you' tone, tinged with ridicule. "They can't turn around in safety! The safest place for him is in a submarine at the bottom of the sea where they will leave him alone!

"The police court the next morning dismissed the case. My God!" shouted Darrow suddenly, jarring the courtroom and looking directly at Kelley. "What are you thinking of! Mrs. Massie was only then sixteen years old—stealing a newly born baby! There was no argument about it because the case was dismissed as nothing. And yet that prank, or whatever it was, was produced in this court by those who are trying to land

Massie and Mrs. Fortescue in prison. There are some things that even a prosecutor shouldn't do, and this is one of them—one of them...

"Gentlemen, why should it be? Why should any one man in this world be so anxious to accomplish the destruction of some one else?" Suddenly he shouted "My God, gentlemen, am I dreaming?" He swung his right arm in a furious arc. "It is possible that twelve men are deliberating whether they shall put the husband and mother of this afflicted woman in prison for life? I don't believe it! I don't believe anywhere on this wide earth that twelve men would be so lacking in humaneness and kindness to carry our this infamous design!" He breathed deeply, filling the barrel of his chest and releasing a long sigh of compassion before abruptly changing his tone and tack.

"Massie went to Beebe, the lawyer, and tried to interest him in the case. I know only one reason why lawyers don't get interested in cases and I'll give you two guesses. The first guess it that Massie didn't have enough money—and that is the second guess, too. From Beebe's talk we got the first introduction of the word 'confession,' which he said must be obtained without threats or violence. That is not true! The prisons of this country and every other country are filled with persons who have been beaten almost to death in getting confessions from them. Get arrested once—and find out!" This admonition prompted another of the fascinating diversions that punctuated the plea that eventually would spin out into a day-long dissertation. Darrow glanced at the clock and returned to the subject.

"Massie was discouraged. Months of slander since his wife had been dragged into the bushes and raped; months of abuse. He had ideas and fears and delusions. The doctor tried to quiet his fears, but they could not be quieted. He couldn't work—and work has been the first and last aid of many other unfortunates.

"He wanted to get a confession. For what? To get somebody imprisoned? No—that did not concern him. He was concerned with the girl whom he had taken in marriage when she was sixteen—sweet sixteen.

"Mrs. Fortescue was worrying about the delay of what she thought was justice, and what other people thought was justice. I fairly well know what law is, but I don't often know what justice is—it is a pattern according to our own personal conceptions.

"Mrs. Fortescue, too, believed it necessary to get a confession. The last thing they wanted to do was to shoot or kill.

"What did they do? They formed a plan to take Kahahawai to their house and get a confession. They never conceived it to be illegal—it was the ends they thought of—not the means. Are Jones and Lord, two common seamen, bad? There are some human virtues that are not common—loyalty, devotion.

"Jones had been out there to see that the slanderers didn't kill—but slanderers don't kill that way. He was faithful as a dog, he was loyal when a shipmate asked for help. Was he bad? There are so many ways to measure goodness and badness.

"There isn't a single thing that either of these two boys did that should bring censure; they ought not to trouble you.

"I know the state's attorney would rather convict four people instead of two, but I think he should compromise on two—that ought to be enough for one day.

"If you needed a friend, would you take one of these gobs, or would you wait outside prayer meetings on Wednesday night—I guess that's the right night? I say to you I would take one of these, rather than the others.

"Tommy had prepared this warrant or subpoena, woven, like Joseph's coat, of many colors. Jones handed it to the Hawaiian boy and said Major Ross wanted to see him.

"They did not want to kill—they made no plan to kill—they didn't know what to do when it happened. And the house was not a good place to kill—one family thirty feet away, another house twenty-five feet away. A lovely place to kill someone, isn't it?

"Tommy, I say Tommy because he will never be anything else to me. I have not known him long, but I have learned to love him and respect him. Tommy was driving the car when it came to the courthouse—this man got in. Tommy for months had been subjected to delusions and fears that bring insanity.

"There is nothing in this evidence to indicate that they ever meant to kill—there was never any talk about killing, as far as this evidence is concerned.

"I would not want to add to the sorrow of the mother of the boy, Kahahawai, or the father of the boy, or the cousin, who sit here. They have human feelings. I have, too. I want you to have human feelings, too. Any man without human feeling is without life.

"The party entered the house. Tommy had a .45, which is a much surer death that a .32, and this unfortunate boy was killed with a .32.

"It's of no consequence who fired that shot—I am arguing the facts, and the only facts as you get them. Is there any reason in the world why Massie, on top of all these other troubles, should assume the added burden of the responsibility of this killing?

"I haven't always had the highest opinion of the average human being; man is none too great at best. He is moved by everything that reaches him, but I have no reason to think there is anybody on this jury who will disregard the truth for some fantastic, imaginary theory. Tommy has told you the fact that there was no intention of killing.

"When Kahahawai said, 'Yes, I done it,' everything was blotted out—here was the man who had ruined his wife.

"No man can judge another unless he places himself in the position of the other before he pronounces the verdict.

"If you can put yourself in his place, if you can think of his raped wife, of his months of suffering and mental anguish; if you can confront the unjust, cruel fate that unrolled before him, then you can judge—but you cannot judge any man otherwise.

"If you put yourself in Tommy Massie's place, what would you have done?

"How many men would have done the same? How many men would have done anything else?" He pointed to the men in the jury box. "Would you and you and you?" Then spinning with amazing adroitness, Darrow directed his outstretched finger right at John Kelley. "Would you?"

He turned back to the jury. "Ten out of twelve men would do what poor Tommy Massie did, the thing for which you are asked to send him to prison for the rest of his life!"

It was noon. The defense requested a recess, but Judge Davis decided to adjourn for lunch and reconvene at 1:30 p.m. Clarence Darrow and George Leisure walked to their nearby hotel and had a sandwich and coffee. "As soon as we had taken lunch, I walked out of his room" recalled Leisure, "assuming that he would want to jot down a few notes for the remainder of his summation. When I called for him again in ten minutes, I found him asleep. We proceeded immediately to the courtroom, where he continued his summation all afternoon without reference to any notes and without the help of any memoranda of any kind. Just as the long shadows began to fall in the tropical and beautiful setting, Mr. Darrow finished his summation with lines which were almost poetic."

The young Wall Street lawyer continued to be dismayed by Darrow's lack of preparation, and years later was to look back on the hot day in Hawaii as one of the most revealing and rewarding of his life. "At the time I felt that my effort in trying to learn how a great lawyer put together the steelwork of a great summation had been a total failure, but in thinking the matter over, I realized that I had learned a great deal. Mr. Darrow is an insatiable reader. It was almost impossible to mention any book that he had not read and with which he was not thoroughly familiar. His tremendous reading and his tremendous brain power enabled him to dictate these jury addresses. I say dictate, because that is how I discovered what it was that Mr. Darrow did in the preparation of his speeches. When I first got out of law school it was necessary for me to write out in longhand every agreement and every brief before I dictated it from my own notes to a stenographer. Later, when I became sufficiently familiar with the subject matter, I always dictated directly to the stenographer without making notes in advance. I then realized that that was exactly what Mr. Darrow was doing when he summed up to a jury. He knew all the facts of the case thoroughly when he started to sum up, and with his knowledge of those facts he drew upon his tremendous store of knowledge and gave his address just as the atmosphere and character of the courtroom demanded."

Invigorated by his nap and freshly, though temporarily, combed and brushed, Clarence Darrow entered the courtroom at 1:33 p.m. and without pausing at the counsel table walked to the front of the courtroom and resumed his argument. Only a hoarse voice indicated that he had already been talking for more than three hours.

"I shan't detain you much longer. Again I say I cannot understand why the prosecution raises a doubt as to who fired the shot and how. I don't know how many of you know the many directions a bullet may take...There was not much force behind this bullet—it was fired by a .32. Nobody can tell how Massie was standing at the time, how high the gun was—it would be all idle speculation.

"Massie was there! He rose! The picture came before him! He doubtless shot! One bullet was shot and only one—the reaction of rage would have been to empty the gun. He saw the picture of his wife pleading, injured, raped—and he shot. There could have been nobody else. And then what? Had any preparations been made to get rid of this body? In the house, doubtless, were Lord and Jones and Mrs. Fortescue, but what could they do? What would you have done?"

Rambling, repetitive, improvising, the old actor still had the power to hold his audience. He was speaking to the jury as though sincerely asking their advice. His tone was conversational, personal. The very fact that it was unrehearsed reflected his immense appeal.

"What is the first instinct? Flight. It comes to every man the same—with no plan formed—just as you and you and you would do. They got a rope which had been obtained as a line for a dog—what was at hand, what came to them. They placed a tarpaulin over the body and tied it with the rope. They got in the car—what was there to do but flight—to the mountains, to the sea, anywhere but where they were."

"Here was the dead body—they couldn't leave it—perhaps they could get rid of it. There isn't one in ten thousand who wouldn't get away, no matter how. This isn't the conduct of someone who had thought out a definite plan; it is the hasty, half-coordinated instinct of one surprised in a situation.

"This wise man from the East," continued the mellowed phrase-monger, indicating Dr. Catton, "from San Francisco, said Tommy had the emotions of fear or it may have been any one of the emotions which these experts carry around in a valise. He knows that is so because he is paid to know it." The blade of sarcasm cut through his sonorous voice.

"Is Massie the first person who ever fainted or whose consciousness ever lifted? Is anything more common? The inmates of our asylums are being increased all over the world. We are just beginning to understand man's mentality..."

"We are now realizing that many acts have been punished as crimes that are acts of insanity. Why? Because lawyers have been too cruel to look for insanity; because an act is considered as a crime, not as a consequence of causes.

"Observe other people. Observe yourself. Ask for a cigarette. You will see that it is instinctive. It means nothing. Does a man think every time he takes a cigarette? I have been a cigarette smoker and I could ask for a cigarette in my sleep.

"And many in any situation may do it. Neither does turning away from a camera indicate anything; it may be just instinct and means nothing.

"Of course, as time went on, he began to recover. Two hours later he had sufficiently recovered at the City and County Attorney's Office to refuse to answer questions. He had had delusions, had lost flesh, had been ill. Did he have anything to go through? It's a wonder he didn't go crazy that first night. Many men have gone insane on slighter provocation!"

Clarence Darrow again paused and a look of profound wisdom came over the gnarled features in the large head, sunk deep in sloping shoulders. A common homeliness made the old man strangely appealing. There was no artifice about him. He seemed both vulnerable and powerful—indeed an aging lion who had outlived his mastery of the pride but retained the instincts of protection and of battle.

"I believe I have covered this case as far as I care to go." The exhausted courtroom shared his conclusion. "The facts are before you. It was a hard, cruel, fateful episode in the lives of these poor people. Is it possible that anyone should wish to heap more troubles on top of all their suffering? If so, I cannot understand it. There are many things in this world that I cannot understand. Can anyone say that they are of the type on whom prison gates should close. Have they ever stolen, assaulted, forged? Are they of a criminal type?

"They are here because of all the things that have happened to them, and I am asking you gentlemen to take these poor suffering people into your care. Take them not in anger, but in cool judgment, in pity and understanding. Judge them as you yourselves would be judged under these circumstances, and I know what your verdict will be."

There was no other sound in the room as Darrow drew to a close. The lowering sun lit the horizon at the window beyond his head. Shadows traced the lines in his face.

"We live but a short time; it seems only yesterday I was a child. The span of human life is short, but the race goes on. Nature is invincible, in adjusting hostile people to each other and adjusting people to their environment. Hate, laws, make no difference to nature...only time and experience can change these things. The people of the Polynesian islands, if they live, must live in peace and kindness and goodwill. Nature is slowly shaping the mind of man. This peace and goodwill must come, or if it does not, the Pacific Ocean will run red with blood."

The histrionics were curtailed. The fires of spring were long banked in the aged frame, but a spark still smoldered. The heart was speaking. "I have no feeling on account of race against the four or five men who assaulted Mrs. Massie—and my clients knew that when I took this case. There are people of every race and every land, and all are different. Nobody can afford to condemn another on account of his race. The peoples must live with tolerance, kindness and love.

"I have looked at this island, which is a new country to me. I've never had any prejudice against any race on earth. I didn't learn it, and I defy anyone to find any word of mine to contradict what I say. To me these questions of race must be solved by understanding—not by force.

"I put this case, regardless of race or nationality or feelings of any juror, asking them to pass on it as a human case. As it affects the

Massies, it affects you and it affects me." His voice again gentle, confiding.

"Ask yourself what is right, and I'll be content with your verdict.

"Take it broadly.

"Take it kindly.

"Take it humanly—consider the dire disaster of this family, written
all over by the hand of fate. Understand them, that is all that is needed.

"I'd like to think that I had done my small part to bring peace and
justice to an island wracked and worn by strife.

"You hold not only the fate but the life of these four people. What
is there for them if you pronounce a sentence of doom on them? What
have they done?

"You are a people to heal, not to destroy. I place this in your hands,
asking you to be kind and considerate both to the living and the dead."

TWENTY-EIGHT

A long silence followed Clarence Darrrow's last great plea in defense of human frailty, the sanctity of motherhood and the brotherhood of man. The gaunt septuagenarian finally looked his years as he walked slowly, slightly stooped, to his chair and leaning back, again stuffed his huge fists into his pockets. A rueful smile played across his face. He had spoken, with only a brief respite, for more than four hours. The day in court was drawing to a close.

Judge Davis called a ten-minute recess, to be followed by the final argument of the prosecution. Glowing praise for Darrow filled the room. In the halls the costumes of the tragic drama mingled for the last time: bright muumuus and aloha shirts stirred into the crowd of conservative business suits and white Naval uniforms. The straight, sparse figure of Admiral Stirling could be seen cutting through the sea of spectators as he congratulated the defense.

The judge, in his black robe, reentered the courtroom. He called the court to order. John Kelley rose, still crisp in his white suit, and faced the jury.

"Gentlemen of the jury, I would imagine that you are approaching a state of argument amnesia, or verbal psychosis. I will not detain you with a long plea.

"I stand for the law and opposed to those who have violated the law, and ask you to do so. You have been presented with an argument of passion, not reason, a plea of sympathy, not sanity."

Tersely, he began his summation. His argument was as lean as Darrow's was fulsome. A pacing man, he presented the case for the state with alert, precise movements, following each scent to its conclusion. He spoke for less than an hour.

"I submit to you that we have presented only the facts in this case, and those facts lead to the unrefuted fact that the defendants killed Kahahawai. Are you going to decide the case on the plea of a man who for fifty years has stood before the bar of justice which he belittles today, or are you going to decide this case on the law?

"They ask you why should Massie take upon himself the blame for shooting Kahahawai. Because he couldn't hide behind the skirts of his mother-in-law. He couldn't stand up and blame these two men whom he had inveigled into this affair.

"I am going to paint you a conceited, vain, egotistical individual who is responsible for what has happened since September 12, the selfishness of the man who insisted that his wife go to this party when she did not want to go.

"Clarence Darrow tells you he was a brave, frank witness on the stand, but I can show you evasion after evasion in that testimony and in his other testimony before he conveniently got insane. His action is the basis of everything that happened and his action caused the death of Joseph Kahahawai.

"Since the case of Harry Thaw, the defense has been the screen for the rich and influential, so they could get liars and experts to put on a defense of insanity—as it has in this case. The defense is not insanity, but sympathy.

"They tried to keep Mrs. Kahahawai off the stand, but they sacrificed that poor young girl over there, on the altar of ego and made a Roman holiday for the crowd that disgraced this court and the justice of this government.

"Are you going to follow the law of the Territory of Hawaii or the plea of Clarence Darrow and George Leisure?

"The same presumption of innocence that clothes the defendants in this case at this time clothes Joseph Kahahawai way down deep in his grave. They have removed by their act the possibility of his ever being anything but innocent in the Ala Moana case and 'not guilty' on the records of this court.

"When the defendant Massie entered into a plan—the law says they entered a conspiracy—and if the other three defendants entered this plan, and if Massie went insane at the last moment, they are still guilty!"

Kelley ceased his pacing and lowered his voice. He approached the jury rail and spoke directly to the twelve men in the box. He assumed a reasonable approach and slipped one hand casually into a trouser pocket.

"Let us suppose, for the time being, that this defense they offer is an honest defense.

"If Lieutenant Massie went into one of these trances the doctors give such funny names to, where were the officers at the Submarine Base? Did they bring them here to tell you what his condition was? They were conspicuous by their absence.

"Where were these brave and loyal friends of Lieutenant Massie? Why did he have to stoop to get enlisted men in the Navy to carry out this nefarious scheme? Was it solely to get a confession?

"Do any of you think there wasn't any drinking at the Ala Wai party—that Branson wasn't drunk—that Massie himself wasn't high?

"He slipped twice on cross-examination. Once where he said 'I'm pos-' and caught himself before he said 'positive.' And again, for the record, page 478, when he said 'I know why I went now. Jones told Mrs. Fortescue to take me along with the body so I could get some fresh air.' I remember him saying that.

"If he remembers that, he remembers everything that was happening, and their insanity plea, like the dove of peace, flies out the window. That, coupled with what happened, the fear-flight mechanism, Dr. Catton called it.

"He was pale. When I'm mad, I'm red and when I'm afraid, I am pale. I don't know about you gentlemen, but that's the way I am. He hid his face because he was afraid.

"Figure his ego, his conceit. That was what caused him to shake hands with himself. 'Fine work, old boy. Thank you very much.'

"When I asked him about the interview with Mrs. Fortescue by Mr. Owen, in which she said, 'We bungled because we drove with the shade down,' Massie said he didn't remember it.

"They almost got away with it—another five minutes, a shade up in the rear window of the car—and the body of Joseph Kahahawai would have been consigned to the deep forever. But an omnipotent God said, 'Thou shalt not kill' and the hand of fate saved Kahahawai's body from the sea that it might rest in a Christian grave.

"Three able men and a cold, calculating woman let a man bleed to death in front of them, inch by inch.

"They aren't kids! They're brought up in an atmosphere of guns. They're taught the art of killing, also of first aid. But they let him die, dragged him into the bathroom like a dog and let him die..."

Kelley paused again. The only sound in the courtroom was the weeping of Kahahawai's parents.

"There was no right in cutting off his life illegally; no matter how good or bad you may think he was, he was entitled to his life. This was an unjustified killing and under the laws of this Territory, it was murder.

"The defense delighted in jumping on Dr. Catton, saying he was a spider in his web waiting for the first fly. Who was that first fly?

"They said Dr. Catton was wearing diapers when the learned experts from Los Angeles were practicing psychiatry. Well, I was wearing diapers, if any, when Brother Darrow was winning his spurs in Chicago debating for the single tax as a follower of Henry George."

Several people in the courtroom chuckled, among them Clarence Darrow. He leaned over to Mrs. Fortescue's sister, who was sitting next to him, and whispered "That's good."

"Dr. Williams had to swallow a good deal of his book. Dr. Catton will be practicing medicine when Drs. Orbison and Williams are perambulating around in automatism. And I'll be practicing law when Mr. Darrow will have rejoined William Jennings Bryan to discuss fundamentalism in a place where they'll know more about it."

Darrow laughed again appreciatively.

The prosecuting attorney then became vehemently serious as he rendered an excoriating indictment of Tommy Massie's behavior, calling it again that of a "vain, egotistical individual who is responsible for any act" leading up to the murder. It was the Naval officer's selfishness that led his wife to attend the party at the Ala Wai Inn, Kelley reminded the jury, continuing to blast Thalia's husband, her mother, the U.S. Navy, the defense attorneys and their plea of insanity. "We do not ask for vengeance, but for justice!"

When referring to Massie's reluctance to discuss the drunken teahouse party and his fellow officer Branson's condition, Kelley remarked, "The most you can say about Massie is at least he lied like a gentleman!"

The prosecutor pointed out that several doctors testified that the defendant was sane at the time of the crime, including the City and County Physician who was thoroughly familiar with both cases. Kelley had resumed his pacing and suddenly walked with purpose to the case of exhibits. He picked up the service .45 automatic, dramatically he pointed it at the ceiling.

"Lieutenant Massie, if he had taken this gun and mowed these men down in the hospital when his wife identified them, would at least have had the respect of the community, however wrong, by law, that act might have been.

"He waited months and dragged in these enlisted men. But they were free and voluntary parties to the act. and are therefore fully responsible.

"A killing is a killing, and under certain circumstances is murder.

"In the Loeb-Leopold case Darrow said he hated killing, regardless of how it was done, always had and always will.

"And now he comes before you and says a killing is justified and is not murder.

"He told you Dr. Catton's testimony could be summed up in one word. His own plea can be summed up in the same word, 'Pay.' A lawyer doesn't work without something on the line.

"There is no evil that we cannot face or fly from except consciousness of duty. If that consciousness of duty is with you, you cannot escape it by letting sympathy run rampant with judgment.

"Law is the gift of the people, is for the people, created by the state, which is the people. We must abide by law or revert to chaos.

"Hawaii is on trial. Is there to be one law for strangers and another for us?

"Are strangers to come here and take the law in their own hands?" demanded the prosecutor, his voice frosted with scorn. "Are you going to give Lieutenant Massie a walk-away ticket in this case? They'll make him an admiral! They'll make him chief of staff! He and Admiral Pratt are of the same mind, they believe in lynch law!

"If one man is allowed to take the law in his own hands, others will do so. I tell you, if the serpent of lynch law is permitted to raise its head in these islands, watch out—watch out!

"The interests of all the people can be best served by adherence to law, even though some applications may be harsh on the individual.

"As long as the American flag flies on that staff, without an admiral's pennant over it, you must regard the Constitution and the law.

"You have taken an oath to uphold it. Massie took the oath to uphold it, and he is here because he violated that oath."

John Kelley put both hands on the rail of the jury box. "I say to you gentlemen of the jury, to you, Mr. Stone, and you, Mr. Waterhouse, and Mr. Akana, and Mr. Char, "—impressively he addressed each of the jurymen by name. "Each of you has the most vital duty to perform of any twelve men who ever sat in a jury box under the United States flag."

The prosecutor straightened to his full stature.

"Do your duty without being swayed by influences of sympathy. Pay no heed to what the admirals say, because with General Smedley Butler, I say, 'To hell with the admirals!'

"If you do it, you will have nothing to fear. Your loved ones will have nothing to fear. I put this case in your hands fully convinced that you will do your duty.

"Deliberately, calmly, dispassionately reach a verdict not based on color lines. I pray to God you men will not be divided along racial lines because some of you are white and others are not.

"There is no reason on earth why you cannot render a unanimous verdict.

"I have called on no sympathies. Has Mrs. Fortescue lost her daughter, has Massie lost his wife? She sits there. But where is Kahahawai?"

TWENTY-NINE

The trial was over. Under Judge Davis's instructions, three verdicts were possible: guilty as charged; guilty of manslaughter, or not guilty. For Massie the same charges applied, plus not guilty by reason of insanity.

"Gentlemen of the jury," said the Judge in the lull of the let-down, "the defendants in this case, Thomas H. Massie, Grace Fortescue, Edward J. Lord and Albert O. Jones, stand charged in the indictment with the crime of murder in the second degree."

He then read the indictment: "...on the eighth day of January, 1932, with force and arms—to wit: a certain pistol loaded with gunpowder and bullets...held in the hands of them, the said defendants, unlawfully, feloniously, willfully, and with malice aforethought, and without authority and without justification and without extenuation by law, did kill and murder one Joseph Kahahawai, Jr."

Turning to the jurors, Judge Davis spelled out in detail their duties. "To this indictment each of the defendants has entered a plea of 'not guilty.' You are the exclusive judges of the facts in this case and the credibility of the witnesses but it is the law you must take from this court as given you in this charge, not withstanding any opinion you may have as to what the law should be..."

For another hour, he explained the technical terms and legal instruction of the law which the twelve men were to abide by in order to decide the outcome of the titanic struggle that would forever leave its mark on Hawaii's history. At 4:22 p.m. on Wednesday, April 28, 1932, the Massie Case was placed in the hands of the jury.

During the three weeks of the trial, the jury had survived their incommunicado state without complaint, being comfortably housed at the Alexander Young Hotel and sumptuously fed. In the afternoons, when court had recessed for the day, they were taken to the nearby Y.M.C.A., the same one at which Jones and Lord had rented a locker, where they played volleyball and did calisthenics to keep fit. All twelve of them had been seen at the tennis matches on the Beretania Street courts and they became a familiar sight at night when they filed into Honolulu movie theatres under the watchful eyes of their bailiffs. The government paid for the food and lodging, but it was up to the individual jurors to fund the price of a theatre ticket. They'd also been taken to stores and the barber shop by their two faithful guards. Only one of them had suffered ill health in the strange interim, and that was no more than a cold. Now, at last, they were to devote all of their waking hours to the duty for which they were chosen. They walked from the court-room with far graver steps than the four defendants, who would also stay at the Alexander Young Hotel until a verdict was reached.

The general sense of relief was not shared by the Navy. Admiral Stirling and Captain Wortman would have gladly strung John Kelley from the nearest yardarm. They marched, full steam ahead, from the courthouse. The Admiral, his lean face drained of color, and the husky Captain, flushed with resentment, entered their waiting staff car and drove off with the defendants to the hotel to meet with Darrow. Later Admiral Stirling was to record his thoughts on the insulting words that had closed the argument for the prosecution.

"Self-government was on trial!" scoffed Stirling indignantly. "Self-rule everywhere else under our flag has proved itself and is safe. The prosecuting attorney failed to explain why self-government in Hawaii was on trial. He avoided the issue. He did not mention in his eloquent harangue the hideous fact that a woman of his own race and color had been brutally assaulted by five men of the dark-skins; that the Government of Hawaii, which he now claimed was fighting for its life, instead of convicting these criminals and sentencing them to hard labor for life in the Hawaii prison—to show the world that Hawaii was a civilized community and subscribed to civilized ideas of decency and morality—had made heroes of the attackers, had turned its back on white men's ideals of justice, and had adopted those of the Orient, where women are mere chattel for men's use."

The jury was out forty-nine hours. During this time Clarence Darrow enjoyed an occasional respite at Waikiki. Again his companions as he paddled in outrigger canoes were Hawaii's renowned beach-boys, the Kahanamoku brothers. Less relaxed was the rest of Honolulu. Armed forces were held ready at assigned posts; units at Pearl Harbor and Schofield Barracks were put on ready alert to move into the city if necessary. Chief of Police Weeber also held his reserves in readiness. Posted around the courthouse were plain-clothes detectives, while police cars, with riot guns mounted for action, were stationed before the building. Dim lights shone in the deserted corridors, and the only sound was the clatter of wire service tickers in the press room, several doors from the sealed jury chamber. No loiterers were allowed on the streets in the vicinity, and the Judiciary Building was guarded night and day by a cordon of policemen.

Throughout the late hours of Wednesday, according to *The Honolulu Advertiser*, and all day Thursday, balloting stood at seven to five for acquittal, with the haoles, for the most part, voting for acquittal. Their ranks included John F. Stone, Olaf Sorensen, Theodore Bush, Charles Strohlin, Willy Beyer, Shadford Waterhouse and hapa-haole Hawaiian George McIntyre. As they came down the stairs for lunch on Thursday, each distancing himself from the other as though a diversity of opinion had thrown them apart, their faces were scowling and serious. Several of them pushed back their disheveled hair and mopped their faces. It was apparent that the sessions were becoming heated and difficult.

From across the street, on the palace grounds, passersby, pretending to be strolling casually beneath the monkeypod trees, could discern through the open windows of the jury room that the discussion was anything but dispassionate. Men in their shirt sleeves walked up and down, gesticulating and raising their voices, joining in small groups. Now and then, an overheated juror would lean out the window to cool off.

A patrolman kept the pedestrians moving. As Friday lengthened into another day of indecision, one of the weary jurymen was seen beyond the balustrade, chinning himself on a door frame for exercise. Hope began to fade among the observers—attorneys, newsmen and the crowd of curious who ambled past the building and through its court-yard—that a verdict would be reached. Twelve men in a closed room were working to agree. Three men and a woman in a hotel room two blocks away were waiting, all Honolulu was waiting—Washington was waiting, and the world—all for the same decision that would come from the small closed room.

Accompanied by Captain Wortman, Mrs. Fortescue and Tommy Massie left their hotel rooms for their meals in the dining room. Thalia was with them, and the two Navy boys. "Mrs. Massie and Mrs. Fortescue looked sad and forlorn as they glanced toward the jurymen and bailiffs who were having lunch in a far corner of the same dining room," wrote a reporter. They were overhead complaining because they had not been allowed to stay in the Navy Yard. Jones and Lord were less depressed; they made no effort to hide the fact that they were getting a kick out of being guests at an exclusive downtown hotel. Despite reprimanding glances from the submarine commander, they laughed and joked and drew curious stares from other guests at the hotel. Jones wore a rakish turtle-neck sweater and seemed unmindful of the temporary abstinence imposed upon him.

He was also unaware that his name had been the main topic in the jury room Friday morning. Doubt had been expressed by one juror that Tommy Massie had actually fired the fatal shot, and that Jones had held the gun that had ended the life of Kahahawai. A compromise was suggested by another juror on the basis of acquittal for Massie, Mrs. Fortescue and Lord, and "guilty as charged" for the unsuspecting Jones. The suggestion was being made, said the member of the "solid seven" holding out for acquittal, in the hope that a verdict would result in a mistrial on the grounds that it would be contrary to the "law and evidence in the case." The maneuver failed when a member of the minority said he "smelled a rat" and flatly refused such a verdict.

Later in the day defense counsel Winn proposed to the prosecution that they accept a verdict of eleven members of the jury, or even ten. It was the first time that such a stipulation in a criminal case had been proposed in Hawaii, he explained, but it had recently been handed down by the Supreme Court in the case of a deadlocked jury on the mainland. John Kelley rejected the suggestion.

Still later, a cheer went up from the jury room. "Somebody's been won over," said a reporter. A member of the defense team sent for Darrow. "A favorable indication," he said, smiling as he entered the rotunda.

"Well, boys, how does it look to you?" he asked the members of the press who greeted him. "You know," he continued, grinning more broadly. "I wonder if I could get the prosecution to agree to leave the verdict to newspapermen?"

"Would you be satisfied with that?" someone asked.

"Yes, I think I would," said the popular defender.

At 4 p.m., the flurry among court officials and the press was heightened by the arrival of Judge Davis, who called in the jury to ask if they had reached a verdict. The defendants were summoned, Jones and Lord leaping jauntily from the official car and waving to Darrow as they entered the building. Darrow laid an arm around Lord's shoulder in a fatherly manner. Mrs. Fortescue also smiled at the veteran defense attorney as she walked quickly to the courtroom.

"Gentlemen of the jury, you have been out nearly forty-seven hours," said Judge Davis. "Have you reached a verdict?"

"No, Your Honor," replied foreman John F. Stone.

"Are there any prospects of reaching a verdict within a reasonable time?"

"Yes, Your Honor."

"Does the jury need any help from the Court?"

"May I state the situation?" asked the foreman.

"No," said Judge Davis.

"Then there has been no request for further instructions," said juror Stone.

"Very well," said the Judge. "The jury may retire and resume deliberation."

Disappointment drew down the faces of the defendants. As they went out, Mrs. Harry Kluegel, who had heard a rumor that a verdict was imminent and sped to the courthouse, entered the building. Rushing up to Tommy Massie and seaman Lord, she kissed them both. She didn't catch Jones, who was near the pressroom door trying to persuade his attorneys to let him take the newspapermen back to the hotel for a game of poker.

"Give us a break then," pleaded the burly sailor, "and let us stay here. Just a couple of hands of straight stud."

George Leisure smiled and hesitated.

"Come along, Jones!" ordered Captain Wortman.

Jones obeyed, looking wistfully over his shoulder. Lieutenant Johnson, the Navy counsel, said, "Sorry, old chap. You'll have to postpone that game till later."

Lord had slipped away from Mrs. Kluegel, who was commiserating with Thalia and her mother, and walked over to chat with Prosecutor John Kelley. Tommy Massie joined them and, to the surprise of the prosecuting attorney, said with the grace of a Southern gentleman, "I want to thank you for the courtesies you have shown us. I think you are a fine man—and I hope you do not believe I am insincere."

Kelley said, "Lieutenant Massie, I was only doing my duty. I have no hard feeling against you personally."

Thalia was at Tommy's side in a second, her face frozen with anger. She took her husband's arm, drawing him toward the door.

"—or your wife," continued Kelley, making a slight bow to Thalia.

"Oh, no, you haven't!" she said to the prosecutor with sarcastic bitterness. "You haven't acted as if you didn't! You—"

Tommy took her arm and quickly led her away. He patted Kelley's shoulder as he passed.

At 5:30 p.m., the jurors filed in and resumed their places in the jury box. The defendants reentered with Captain Wortman, who had just called Admiral Stirling at Pearl Harbor and informed him that a verdict had been reached and the court was meeting.

"I tore uptown in my car, jubilantly sure that the jury had agreed: it could not be other than an acquittal," recalled the Commandant.

Mrs. Fortescue's shoulders sagged but she managed a slight stoic smile. Thalia wore a pale blue costume with a white cap "that heightened the cold flame of her blond beauty," according to a reporter. Tommy and the two Navy men were seated at attention, Jones being the most shaken, his eyes glassy and wide, his light brown hair ruffled. A hush settled over the courtroom as the strange quartet of accused murderers took their places, white faced and silent, before the Court.

The word had spread magically through the city that a verdict was near, and the room filled rapidly. A reserve squad of police came swiftly from headquarters and formed a patrol through the corridors. Mrs. Kluegel, true to form, was one of the first spectators to enter the courtroom. Reporters clustered near the door, ready to dash to the press room a few doors away with the news flash of the outcome. Only Prosecutor Kelley and Judge Davis were missing from the courtroom. Kelley had returned home after the first false alarm and had been summoned again by telephone. He was rushing downtown as the Judge briefly peered from the door of his chamber, then withdrew until all counsel were present.

The wait was one of agony. Seconds stretched into minutes, straining the nerves of the defendants. The usual pre-session chatter had given way to a palling silence. Thalia linked her arm with Tommy's and clung to him tightly.

Finally John Kelley appeared, immaculate despite his breathless flight to town. The jury filed in just as Judge Davis looked out again from his door behind the bar, then entered and took the bench. The defendants rose. Thalia rose with them. A clerk asked her to sit down, since she was not on trial.

"I won't," said Thalia. And she wouldn't until her husband told her to do so. She continued to hold Tommy's hand.

"Gentlemen, have you agreed upon a verdict?"

"We have, Your Honor," replied foreman Stone.

The verdicts were handed to a clerk who passed them on to Judge Davis. He read them through quickly, with no change of expression, and gave them back to the clerk to read. The clerk's voice was trembling and his hand shook as he read the first one.

"We, the jury, find the defendant, Thomas H. Massie, guilty..."

Guilty!

At the sound of the word, Thalia broke into uncontrollable sobs. Captain Wortman patted her consolingly but she only increased her wails. Massie and Mrs. Fortescue remained motionless, stoic and haggard. The verdict, however, was not one of second degree murder, but of manslaughter. Leniency was recommended. The next verdict found Mrs. Fortescue guilty of the same charge with leniency recommended. Similar verdicts for Jones and Lord followed.

On the first ballot that morning, the seven to five stand for acquittal had remained unchanged. It was then that the leader of the minority had offered the suggestion of a manslaughter charge, and five of the solid seven had swung over to their side, leaving Willy Beyer, the German potato chip manufacturer, and George McIntyre, the hapahaole, holding out for acquittal. After three hours of persuasion, just before noon, Willy Beyer had been worn down and the count stood eleven to one with only McIntyre in disagreement. Just before 4 o'clock, the eleven cheered when McIntyre was persuaded to discuss the manslaughter charge. On the fifteenth ballot, he capitulated. The part-Hawaiian had held out the longest for acquittal of the murderers of the Hawaiian boy.

Jones, who had maintained an air of indifference verging on cheerfulness throughout the trial, was briefly stunned. He gripped his head as his name was read and had to be prodded by Captain Wortman. Lord shrugged slightly. Grace Fortescue held herself in proud control. Thalia continued to cry aloud, and the submarine commander put his arm around her shoulders.

"The defendants may be seated," said Judge Davis.

As soon as Tommy was beside her, Thalia laid her head on his shoulder an threw her arms around his neck, still sobbing desperately. As her tears verged on hysteria, Tommy spoke to her in a low soothing voice and stroked her hair.

"Don't cry, darling."

It was the only sound in the still courtroom and many spectators were weeping with her, even some of the jurors were visibly touched. The wives of Naval officers in the gallery broke into hushed exclamations of fury. Admiral Stirling, who had arrived just after the verdicts were read, stood with clenched fists at the back of the room as rage stiffened his frame.

"I needed only to see the defendants to have my hopes dashed," he said. "Mrs. Massie was in tears; Mrs. Fortescue held her head high, dry-eyed. Guilty of manslaughter, I was told. My God, the penalty can be ten years at hard labor!"

A newsman standing beside him, turned to the livid commandant. "Have you anything to say, Admiral?"

"Not a damned word! What I might say would not pass the censor."

The dean of newsman, Owen, of *The New York Times*, described Darrow's reaction to the outcome of the case in which he had rallied all his remaining strength and full heart: "He seemed quite depressed by the verdict. His whole huge frame was sunk into itself as he slid down in the chair, and his chin fell forward toward his chest. George Leisure, his associate, was equally downcast and sat with a stern look on his face."

The Judge announced that sentence would be passed a week from that day, on Friday, May 6. The matter of custody of the defendants was discussed. Montgomery Winn asked that they be allowed to remain in Naval hands. John Kelley, who had become prosecutor after the agreement on custody had been first made by Judge Cristy, said if there were a Navy officer present who could be responsible for the defendants, he saw no objection, but Barry Ulrich recalled that the agreement was to continue only until sentence.

Ward Wortman was on his feet immediately, his neck like a band of scarlet above his white collar. "That was the arrangement," he sneered, infuriated by what he considered a final indignity to the defendants. "I see no reason why Mr. Kelley and Mr. Ulrich don't know it!"

"I didn't know it," Kelley replied, turning to glare at the Captain.

"You know damned little!" sneered Wortman.

The two tempers clashed like combustible chemicals. The prosecutor objected to the language. Judge Davis rapped for order.

Captain Wortman ignored the objection and rose to escort the departing defendants. As he passed Kelley, he said in a low voice, "Son of a bitch!"

Thalia was still weeping bitterly, one arm around Tommy's neck, as she walked by. She sobbed out some incoherent words to Kelley and was silenced by her husband with a tightening of his embrace around her waist.

"They have no right to question that!" snapped Mrs. Fortescue indignantly.

As the defendants filed from the courtroom, many of those present reached out to press their hands and express their sympathy. Among them, Mrs. Ann Kluegel rose and again kissed the sailors and put a motherly arm around Massie, offering him condolence. Tommy was too busy taking care of his wife to reply. Thalia was more deeply shaken by the verdict than any of the defendants.

Jones had rapidly recovered his cocky equanimity and was smiling with Lord as they waited for the others to enter the staff car beneath the statue of Kamehameha. They stood by as casually as they would have at the parimutuel window of a racetrack. In fact, with a broad grin, Lord passed a folded bill to Jones who took it with a laugh. He'd won the bet they had on the verdict. It is conjecture whether or not he pasted the bill in his scrapbook.

THIRTY

There was little laughter throughout the nation. Public indignation again flamed into wildfire, with the white heat of its core centered in Washington. The verdict was denounced from the floor of the Capitol. A message signed by 106 Congressmen, including powerful committee chairmen, was dispatched immediately to Governor Judd:

> "We, as members of Congress, deeply concerned in the welfare of Hawaii, believe that the prompt and unconditional pardon of Lieutenant Massie and his associates will serve that welfare and the ends of substantial justice. We therefore most earnestly request that such a pardon be granted."

In the House of Representatives, Majority Leader Henry T. Rainey, Democrat from Illinois, urgently endorsed the message, as did Congressman Bertrand Snell, Republican Minority Leader from New York. Democratic Southern Senators Morris Sheppard of Texas, Duncan Fletcher of Florida, and M.M. Logan of Kentucky vehemently demanded action absolving the defendants. The signers of the Senate message stressed that such action would result in the "wisest solution of a most tragic situation, both for the Territory and all concerned." The senators added that they were "deeply solicitous for the best interests of Hawaii and the American flag."

The section of the petition signed by the representatives expressed belief "that the stigma of felony should be removed" as soon as possible.

Senator William King of Utah issued a personal statement: "I cannot help feeling that the verdict was a miscarriage of justice." Representative James E. Rankin was more adamant, and strongly advocated placing Hawaii under direct federal control "until white women are secure from such brutal attacks as that made on Mrs. Massie. That seems to be the only way to put a stop to such mockeries of justice as have grown out of this horrible incident."

The marble halls of the Capitol became heated with debate as other members of Congress branded such action unconstitutional. Senator Henry Ashurst of Arizona said the proposed bill would create a precedent, and that pardons were not within the powers of Congress: "The pardoning power rests with the Governor and the President." Senator Kenneth McKellar of Tennessee was on his feet proposing a bill that the president be given full power to pardon the four defendants at once. "It is an important bill and should be passed immediately!" Senator William E. Borah of Idaho asked to what committee the bill for congressional pardon would be referred. When told it was the Judiciary Committee, of which he was a member, he boomed out "Good!" and sat down.

Already the White House had felt the furious backlash of resentment from across the nation. Within hours after the wire services flashed the word "Guilty!" telegrams poured into the Executive Mansion. A woman's club in Oakland, California, sent an incensed cable demanding pardon. From New York, attorney Dudley Field Malone, intimate of Clarence Darrow, wired the Chief Executive in Washington urging him to place the defendants aboard a warship and ship them immediately to the West Coast of the mainland, "where they can get a fair trial!"

Delegate Victor S.K. Houston, Hawaii's representative in Washington, bore the brunt of Capitol censure as long as he could, then realizing its scope and implications, wired an urgent appeal to Governor Judd:

> "Since justice seems to have been served by recent findings, may I as an individual, urge you to exercise your pardoning power at the appropriate time. I also recommend allowing the present defendants to remain in Navy custody till the matter is finally disposed of. I am convinced that Hawaiian interests will be best served by the suggested action."

Nor was the relentless pressure confined to mainland critics of the verdict. More than a hundred members of the Honolulu Citizens' Organization for Good Government gathered at Queen Emma Square and drew up a petition, under the aegis of Mrs. Harry Kleugel, president, calling for a full and free pardon of Mrs. Fortescue, her son-in-law and the two sailors. Immediately after the meeting, volunteers circulated copies from house to house in the community and left them in the offices of business leaders. Within a few days, 1,781 names of local people had been obtained, and the petition was presented to Governor Lawrence Judd. "Copies of the petition are still coming in," announced Mrs. Kluegel after the petition had reached Iolani Palace.

The majority of clergymen in Honolulu also deplored the verdict. The Reverend Frank T. Carter of Kaimuki Christian Church told newsmen that he thought the jury made a mistake in voting guilty. "I do not believe the defendants were the kind to deliberately kill. There is a higher law than that made by man," he continued, endorsing Darrow's thesis. "It is the law of humanity and protection instilled in all of us. The jury should have obeyed the higher law!"

Reverend A.S. Baker of Kalihi Union Church expressed grave disappointment. "There was ample justice for the killing," he said, despite the Sixth Commandment. "It is my own personal feeling that Lieutenant Massie did perfectly right."

Episcopal minister the Reverend Clyde Boyer said, "I couldn't believe the verdict! I am disappointed ...under the circumstances involved, I don't believe any jury should convict." Pastor Frank Purnell of the First Christian Church admitted that his "profoundest sympathy has always been with the defendants."

Only Dr. Horace H. Leavitt, of Central Union Church, the leading missionary church and seat of religion for the kamaaina haole establishment, said he thought the jury acted wisely, although he approved the plea for leniency. "The verdict serves both ends—justice and mercy. I imagine plenty think these people have been sufficiently punished, but standing as I do for the law versus anarchy, I think the jury has done right."

Among the Hawaiians, there was no comment. Was not their motto, given them by King Kamehameha III nearly a hundred years before, the premise of justice? "Ua Mau Ke Ea O Ka Aina I Ka Pono." The Life of the Land is Preserved in Righteousness.

Rumors came from Navy circles, bitter about the verdict, that they were exerting all possible pressure along political lines in Hawaii and Washington to free the defendants from being jailed. Flag officers on the West Coast expressed varied feelings, keeping their opinions as taut as the ships they ran. "A shame. I didn't believe it was possible," said distinguished Rear Admiral Joseph M. Reeves, whose silver beard was as familiar in American Naval circles as that of King George V on Britain's flagships.

Rear Admiral C.S. Kempf, cruiser division commander, said, "It's only the first round." Vice Admiral William H. Standley, commander of cruisers of the fleet's fighting force, said he was not surprised by the verdict, "but I am sure Lieutenant Massie will have the sympathy of the Navy." The Commandant of the 10th Naval District in San Francisco, Rear Admiral W.C. Cole, personal friend of the Fortescues, remarked tersely, "I feel that justice and law in the abstract has been upheld."

Tommy Massie exclaimed publicly, "The Navy is behind us to a man. Do you wonder that I am proud to be in the Navy!"

Cables of sympathy and encouragement again flooded the signalroom at Pearl Harbor, among them one from Colonel Granville Fortescue, out of the hospital at last and recuperating in New York. "Stand up," he told his wife. "Don't give up hope. The case isn't lost yet."

He had been stunned by the verdict. When a correspondent from the Associated Press had called him, "he received the news at though struck."

"What?" he asked, after the verdict was read to him over the telephone. There was silence on the line. "I have nothing to say now," finally came the dazed voice. "Thanks." The receiver clicked.

Two thousand miles across the Atlantic, in Oxford, England, Thalia's sister, Marion, took the news of their mother's conviction of murder with typical Fortescue fortitude. She told the reporter who had relayed the verdict that she had no intention of leaving England, or discontinuing her studies at Oxford University; however, she intended to spend the day in her room.

Tommy Massie's sister and mother were shattered when they heard the outcome of the trial.

"Convicted of manslaughter? What does that mean?" asked the incredulous mother. It was her only statement to the press. Tommy's sister said they had been confident of acquittal. They had no plans for going to Hawaii; they didn't know what they would do. She put her arm around her mother who was now sobbing.

The major load of the cable line was directed to the governor's office in Iolani Palace. Before the weekend was over, more than a hundred cables urging pardon had been received at the palace. They came from all over the country. Racism was again raising its hydra heads in print. Among the thousands of words damning Hawaii and expressing unfounded scorn of Territorial justice was an editorial signed by the publisher of Paul Block Newspapers that reached nationwide distribution:

DEGRADED HAWAII SPEAKS

Word comes from Honolulu that the most fiendish of all men, those who assault womanhood, those who destroy the purity and sanctity of the home, are to have control of the Islands in the Pacific.

For that is what the verdict against the Fortescue-Massie family means.

Forty women have been attacked in Honolulu during the past year. Convictions have been negligible and thus added encouragement is given to those whose degraded souls permit them to carry on this fiendish practice.

Justice? Yes, there was justice for the fiend who assaulted an American girl, but no justice for decency and purity and sanctity of the home.

Gangsters and racketeers dominate most of our new cities in America and violators of pure women seem now to dominate in Hawaii.

When will all this be stopped? Will Washington close its eyes to this outrage, as it has to so many of our bad laws, or will we now give control of the Islands to a Naval Commission, as should be done?

For the security of our country and for the security of what is dearest to our homes and our womanhood, Congress must act at once.

Lawrence Judd recognized the writing on the wall. The burden of mainland and local pressure, increased by the weight of his responsibility to the laws of the land and the happiness of his people, were forcing Hawaii's greatest hour of decision on the harassed governor. Sleepless nights again ravaged his strength. Briefly, he paused to look out over the tranquil lawns of Iolani Palace, the palace whose name meant "Hawk of Heaven" and signified to the Hawaiians a god on high. It was a sacred name in old Hawaii and Judd considered his obligation as occupant of the palace a sacred trust. Into the night, when only the ornate gate lamps, once lit by gas, gave a ray of life to the deserted grounds, Judd paced his office and pondered the best course to ward off the welling turmoil that again imperiled his island Territory.

Governor Judd reflected on the words of Hawaii's motto. Never had the life of the land been in such drastic jeopardy; the very rights of freedom that his grandfather had helped restore might again be supplanted by military rule. The mounting cables, constant phone calls, bitter editorials and deluge of protests were topped by a long telephone conversation with Secretary of the Interior Ray Lyman Wilbur, calling from Washington and voicing the urgent concern of the nation's highest authority.

Immediate and final action seemed the only solution. That alone could extinguish the spreading blaze of indignation that at any time could burst into a full-blown holocaust of hysteria, exceeding even that sparked by the death of Kahahawai. This time the turmoil could throw Hawaii into its most devastating upheaval since the volcanic violence of its birth.

At 9 o'clock on the morning of May 4, Public Prosecutor John Kelley advised newsmen to stand by for a possible news break. Earlier the Governor had announced that a statement would be made to the press at 11 a.m. The night before he had spent the evening conferring with Clarence Darrow. The latter arrived at the Judiciary Building, telling the newsmen to stick around. Kelley had a 9:30 meeting with Attorney General Harry Hewitt and First Deputy Harold T. Kay. The three of them walked across the palace lawn to the courthouse together. About 10 a.m. an unannounced session of court was called, two days prior to the date set for sentencing. Only a few newsmen in addition to the attorney were in the courtroom. The surprise move was taken as a precaution against mass demonstration and possible violence. The city was unaware of the important action taking place in the near-empty room. The Citizens Organization for Good Government called an emergency meeting to petition for "an immediate, unconditional pardon." Less than two thousand signatures were obtained, more than half of them were haole women, and other than a handful of employees of the Big Five corporations, none of them were Hawaiian.

The four defendants drove up in the customary Navy staff car, accompanied by Captain Wortman, Thalia and Mrs. Fortescue's brother and sister. Sight of them was the first public notice that sentence was to be passed. Calmly, for the last time the defendants faced the bar. Each stood in turn before the Judge as his and her name was called and the Court asked if they had any statement to make before the sentence was pronounced.

"No, sir," said Jones, the first to be called.

He was sentenced to "ten years at hard labor in Oahu prison."

Lord was next. He replied in the same way, and the same sentence was pronounced.

Tommy Massie was more nervous than the two sailors and he moistened his lips before speaking. When his same sentence was read, he said in a low, firm voice, "No, Your Honor."

Mrs. Fortescue whispered the answer, the first and last time that her voice was heard in the trial. She said softly, "No, Your Honor," and listened unmoved as her sentence of "ten years at hard labor" was pronounced.

Prosecutor Kelley then asked that a mittimus be served immediately.

"I don't understand about the mittimus," said Clarence Darrow. He and Kelley went into a huddle and Darrow agreed to the service.

Immediately after sentence was pronounced, Judge Davis cleared the courtroom of all but the defendants, bailiff and their attorneys. The four defendants, accompanied by Attorney General Hewitt and Clarence Darrow, crossed the street to Iolani Palace. They walked casually, as though strolling beneath the sheltering shade trees. The waiting reporters wondered at their unrepressed good humor in the face of imprisonment, and rumors flew as a crowd gathered before the palace balcony. The defendants sat in the Attorney General's office while a petition of clemency was drawn up for the Governor. Mrs. Fortescue signed the document with a brilliant smile on her face, while Clarence Darrow sat on the edge of the desk, swinging one leg. The group then filed into the office of Governor Judd. High Sheriff Ross had been called in the meantime and took them into custody as they entered the high-ceilinged chamber that had once been a royal bedroom.

As the defendants chatted almost gaily, Lord and Jones breaking into real laughter, Governor Judd called his 11 o'clock news conference in the outer office. He read the petition for a commutation of sentence, signed by Grace Fortescue, Thomas H. Massie, Edward J. Lord, Albert O. Jones, Clarence Darrow, George S. Leisure, Montgomery Winn and Lieutenant L.H.G. Johnson:

> "The undersigned, defendants in the matter of the Territory of Hawaii vs. Grace Fortescue, et al, and their attorneys, do hereby respectfully pray that Your Excellency, in the exercise of power of executive clemency in you vested, and further in view of the recommendation of the jury in said matter, do commute the sentences heretofore pronounced in this matter."

Then came the announcement that sentence had been commuted from a maximum sentence of ten years to one hour in the custody of the High Sheriff.

Since the hour had already been served in the Governor's office, nothing more was required of the former defendants than to walk out into the sunlight of freedom.

Except for an hour of retention in a palace, the killers of Kahahawai had gotten away with murder.

The wildfire was extinguished, the holocaust was avoided, but for long years the bitter ashes of the Massie Case would smolder in Hawaii. Although *The Honolulu Advertiser* expressed a prevalent view that mere commutation was not enough and a full pardon including the restoration of civil rights should have been given, and the Governor received the praise of Walter Dillingham and powers of the business community, there was glowering resentment in other quarters. Judd's action was seen as a result of mainland pressure and not local interests.

Speaking for the Hawaiians, Princess Abigail Kawananakoa called it a "travesty and a farce." Scathingly, she pointed out, "the atmosphere has been so permeated with 'laxity of conditions and strict law enforcement' that a belief that justice could only be served by strict adherence to the law has become part of daily existence. With this commutation, the verdict of the jury, composed of men of intelligence, sound judgment and good character, with the facts and law before them, becomes a farce and the truth as brought out by the prosecution becomes a travesty. Are we to infer from the Governor's act that there are two sets of law in Hawaii— one for the favored few and the other for the people in general?"

The Navy in Hawaii was as incensed in the other extreme. Mere commutation they considered a farce. "The right of security for the defenders of the Islands must be given weight!" stormed the stormy petrel from his eyrie at Pearl Harbor. Admiral Stirling, his blue eyes snapping with disdain at what he considered the final slap at military prestige, scorned the Governor's decision. "Here was an officer," he summed up the Navy case, "Lieutenant Massie, ordered to the Islands to serve his government. He is married and brings his wife. She is assaulted by Island citizens. The attackers are tried and convictions found impossible. The hung jury in its effect might as well have been acquittal. The defendants go free. The family of the martyred woman invoke the unwritten law for the crime. They failed to kill all, but succeeded in slaying the most brutal and unfeeling. For this, four people are tried and convicted. They do not serve their sentences because the civil government of Hawaii could not be that crude, and also it knew that the people of the mainland would have torn the Islands' so-called self-government to ribbons if these defenders of white womanhood had been sent to prison!"

These were also the sentiments exactly of Tommy Massie's home state, and the Governor of Kentucky granted him a full pardon.

Another admiral blasted the compromise of commutation by publishing a sensational story that exhumed old skeletons in the case. Rear

Admiral W.C. Cole, Commandant of the 12th Naval District, vouched for the truth of an article that appeared in *The Chronicle* stating that Horace Ida had confessed during his rough ride over the Pali. Attributed only to "friends of Lieutenant Massie," the story reported that December 12, 1931, had been chosen as the night that groups of individuals would "interview" the accused men simultaneously in different places. Ida was picked up first, and denied any knowledge of the attack. He was threatened and asked: "Was the woman in the front seat with you?"

According to the story, the boy replied: "No, she was in the back with Chang and Ka—." The story then said when Ida realized the import of his answer, he immediately reiterated that he had not been there and knew nothing about the case. His interrogators threatened again, asking whether he was the first to attack Mrs. Massie, and this time the boy answered, "Chang was the first and last."

The article said that Ida afterward was "so frightened he nearly collapsed." This, and a desire to learn how the other "interrogators" had made out, led his abductors to abandon him on the mountain slope and speed back to town.

None of the defendants in the Massie trial were involved, emphasized the source.

When news of the Admiral's story reached Hawaii, Prosecutor Kelley said he had no reliable information to substantiate it and besides, "a confession obtained in that way would have no value." A reporter headed for Cunha Lane to get the denial from Ida himself. The Japanese boy was sitting on the front stoop of his house, playing cards. The newspaper carrying Admiral Cole's story lay beside him on the steps.

"Yes, I saw the story. It's all untrue." He declined to say anything more. The reporter persisted.

Ida then called William Pittman, his attorney, and was told it would be all right to talk.

"They say I confessed when that gang of men took me over the Pali and beat me," said the boy emphatically. "This is a lie. I did not confess then or at any time. They said I said Mrs. Massie was in the back with Chang and Kahahawai and Chang was the first and last to assault her. All lies. I made no confession at all. They threatened to kill me if I didn't confess and I told them to go ahead and kill me. I am innocent of the charge against me and I never confessed to anyone."

Most of the press approved Judd's action. Seasoned commentator Heywood Broun admitted that Secretary Wilbur's statement that Governor Judd had found an adequate solution to a difficult question was the first time in many months he was in complete agreement with a member of President Hoover's Cabinet.

The appraisal of *The New York Times* has perhaps best withstood the test of time:

> Honolulu, May 4 - It is generally felt here that what occurred today is the best possible thing that could have happened. The town undoubtedly will be divided for many years but if the Ala Moana Case is not tried—and those who should know predict confidently that it never will be—Honolulu will have opportunity to settle down to problems of reorganization and try to work out some solution of its social and economic difficulties which will tax all the ingenuity and courage of the Islands.
>
> There is general belief that what had focused the criticism of the country on Hawaii has been removed by Governor Judd's action and even the threat of a Congressional investigation does not worry the people nearly so much as the feeling they have had so long of sitting on a volcano of human bitterness.

After releasing the message of the commutation of one hour to the astounded press, Governor Judd told reporters that the Territory was fully prepared to prosecute the Ala Moana Case, which would be scheduled to go before the court in about three weeks.

"We have tried to do what we believe to be right in this case," said the Governor, whose hollow eyes attested to the sleepless soul-searching involved in his decision.

A gust of excitement blew through the office as the door opened and the four smiling defendants walked out. Photographers immediately rushed them to the balcony and posed them leaning on the wrought-iron balustrade of the palace. Friends gathered quickly and Thalia, flushed with animated pleasure, hugged her loyal Navy neighbors. Mrs. Fortescue and her brother and sister willingly posed as an exuberant threesome, and even the stern features of Captain Wortman relaxed in amiability. He told reporters that the mittimus committing the Navy men to the custody of the High Sheriff preserved their Naval standing. If they had been sent to Oahu Prison, even for an hour, federal action would have had to be taken to clear their records and to restore them to their present status in the Navy. He anticipated an early transfer for Lieutenant Massie and the two grinning sailors.

Clarence Darrow was clear-eyed and elated. The valiant old veteran had not only survived his last battle, but in the end, triumphed.

"I am very much gratified," he said in a mellow voice. "This is the way it should be, and I approve what the Governor has done. I appreciate the fact that the newspapers have given this case such wide publicity and that it has gone before a jury of one hundred million people." He spread his arms in a gesture of magnanimity.

"That jury has rendered its verdict, unhampered by foolish and absurd rules of law. They have not placed the statutes above human beings—as if human beings were not made before the law."

The country's most famous trial lawyer sounded more like a fundamentalist preacher than a venerated member of the bar.

Shadows of palms played on the balcony of Iolani Palace as the former defendants and their attorneys and friends celebrated the surprising end of the tragic trial. Tears of relief mingled with smiles of congratulations. Darrow threw an affectionate arm around the shoulders of Attorney General Hewitt and, to the latter's amazement, conceded "that it was a fair trial, and one of the fairest judges I have ever seen. Your law has been upheld—and so has the higher human law." As the party moved into the library of the Attorney General's chambers, Mrs. Fortescue asked if she could send a wire to her mother and husband on the mainland. To Colonel Fortescue, now in Los Angeles on his way to Hawaii, she cabled:

"Free to come home, dearest. Grace."

She also sent a message to her mother, Mrs. Charles Bell, who was with Colonel Fortescue on the West Coast:

"Meet you in California. All love. Grace."

To her daughter, Rion, or Marion, Fortescue, in England at Oxford University, she wired words of encouragement:

"Meet you at Wildhome after college is over.
Love. Mother."

The sailors, Lord and Jones, glowing from the happy outcome of the extraordinary adventure that had spotlighted their lives, also wired their families. Lord sent word to his sister in West Philadelphia:

"We're free. Much love. Eddie."

And Jones, as intoxicated on excitement as he ever was on okolehau, gave the operator the address of his mother in New Bedford, Massachusetts, and conveyed a flippant greeting:

"Dear Moms: Will be home soon. Keep the coffee hot.
Albert."

THIRTY-ONE

The day after the commutation, Lieutenant Thomas Massie received orders to report to San Francisco for reassignment. He was to leave on the *Malolo* on Sunday, May 8. Mrs. Fortescue booked passage on the same ship. Jones and Lord were told they would be transferred to San Diego. Thalia was still subject to appear as witness in the new trial of the Ala Moana Case, but could not be reached for the service of a subpoena.

"Mrs. Massie has told her story twice," commented Clarence Darrow when asked if he'd represent Thalia in the retrial. "She has suffered enough. I don't think she can do any good by telling it a third time. If they ask me, I advise them to drop the case. One jury has disagreed. My experience has been that a case in which there has been a disagreement is seldom settled."

To complete the liberation celebration among the departing defendants aboard the *Malolo*, Darrow revealed that he too had made return reservations on the Matson steamer.

On Saturday morning, Police Officers Arthur Stagbar and Dewey Mookini were instructed by Public Prosecutor Kelley and Chief of Police Weeber to go to Pearl Harbor and serve a subpoena on Thalia Massie. In store for the two policemen was a run-around that rivaled a reel of the Keystone Cops.

They reported to Admiral Stirling, who turned them over to Captain Horne, who said he was powerless until he had spoken to Prosecutor Kelley. The cops cooled their heels outside Stirling's office for close to an hour while the call went through. A young lieutenant then took them in tow and the three of them headed for the *Alton*, where the Naval officer approached the guard at the ship's gangway and asked for the officer in charge.

"No one's in charge, and that includes me," said the warrant officer. He telephoned his superior, another young lieutenant, who arrived and went into a huddle with the policemen's escort. A heated argument ensued, and Detective Stagbar heard the *Alton's* commanding officer angrily demand, "Well, what are you going to do about it?"

"I'm going to get Lieutenant Massie," said his fellow officer, and did so. Tommy Massie came topside and asked the policemen to wait until Clarence Darrow arrived, but that Thalia had left the ship and he would go look for her.

"Mrs. Massie wishes Mr. Darrow to be present while service of the subpoena is being made," explained Tommy, hopping into a waiting car and disappearing into the Navy Yard.

Mrs. Fortescue came on deck, smiling cordially and greeting the police officers like old friends. "I'm sorry, gentlemen, but Mr. Darrow has just telephoned that my daughter is with him in town. Why don't you go to his hotel and serve your subpoena?"

Instead the frustrated servers returned to Admiral Stirling's head-quarters and demanded more efficient cooperation. Again the Commandant called in his executive officer and the two closeted themselves for another lengthy conference. When Captain Horne emerged, cordial and cooperative, he told the officers to wait while the Navy conducted a search of the *Alton*. They'd already been waiting more than four hours.

"Mookini and I decided that we had been kidded enough," wrote Stagbar in his affidavit. "The search would be useless, for Mrs. Massie could have left the ship in the meantime."

Captain Horne assured the thwarted detectives that this was not the case and that a concentrated search would be made. "Whom shall we notify when Mrs. Massie is found?" asked the Naval officer.

"Police headquarters," said Detective Stagbar with irony. He knew when he was licked.

Sunday dawned a glorious day. The lei-sellers in their gaudy muumuus and lauhala hats crowned with wreaths of blossoms strung their wares in a fragrant curtain before their stalls. The leis of plumeria and pikake, of vanda orchids and ginger, carnations, tuberoses, jade vine and rare ilima were still dew-bejeweled from the gardens in the valleys. The huge Hawaiian women, excited anew by each boat day, sat on their buried stools and gossiped jovially. They shouted saucy greetings to the members of the Royal Hawaiian Band, who dismounted from their bus in their starched white uniforms, resplendent with gold braid, and set up their instruments in a dazzling array on the sunlit pier. With them was the traditional hula troupe of slender brown dancers in green ti leaf skirts, each freshly woven that morning by its pretty wearer. The girls waved at their whistling admirers among the *Malolo's* crew and passengers already at the rail, and shook their capelets of glistening long black hair as they teased the hapless departees with inviting hips.

An hour before the noon sailing time, a large crowd already packed the pier, most of them eagerly awaiting the arrival of the leading players in the dramatic trial. A car rolled up, bringing Mr. and Mrs. Darrow and the Leisures. Cheers greeted the beloved lawyer as he stepped from the car, the tradewinds ruffling his mane for the last time. As the old warhorse of the legal profession went up the gangplank into permanent pasture, he could not refrain from a final flourish of oratory.

"I am gratified at the outcome," he said, waving from beneath a heavy ruff of yellow and pink blossoms. "It is as it should be—the best for everybody concerned. I think it's the only way to return to normalcy and good feeling in the community. I want to say that everybody here has been most kind to me. I admire the Hawaiians particularly for their generosity and fair-mindedness. I appreciate what the Governor and the Judge have done." He looked out over the shore of smiling faces and his blue eyes sparkled warmly. "I never met a more kindly and hospitable people anywhere than here in Hawaii," he called to his fans, "and I thoroughly enjoyed my visit!"

The crowd at the rail parted and he disappeared into the ship.

But the drama had not yet been completely played out. Again its leading star, the beautiful blond ingenue just out of her teens who had come close to capsizing the entire Hawaiian ship of state and sending it plunging into chaos, was to create a final scene. A crowd of several thousand people awaited her arrival. Among them was Police Sergeant Dewey Mookini with an unserved subpoena in his hand.

There was a rumor that the defendants were already aboard, although no one had seen them arrive, and the mass of humanity on the pier became more tightly packed.

Pushed to one side, the Royal Hawaiian Band bravely carried on, and the girls danced with flashing smiles in the tiny corner that remained to them. Confetti and bright streamers floated down from the high white sides of the ocean liner.

Unnoticed, on the far side of the ship, a gray submarine tender pulled alongside and a group of waiting seamen on the *Malolo* threw them a line. On the tender deck, reclining in steamer chairs, were the figures of Mrs. Fortescue, Tommy Massie and several friends. The small Navy craft and its passengers seemed to be enjoying a yachting cruise, but the stocky figure of Captain Wortman appeared topside and ordered the lines secured. Mrs. Fortescue's tall, slender figure stooped through the low-cut door as she and Tommy went below for a moment, then reappeared to watch the sailors hoist the trunks aboard and fit a hook to the crate of Thalia and Tommy's setter dog, Chris.

Thalia then emerged, her bright head bowed, and her arm locked in that of Tommy. Supported by her mother and husband, she stepped through the cargo port of the *Malolo*. Standing just inside the hatch was Sergeant Mookini.

Brusquely, Ward Wortman ran interference for his charges. The persistent policeman, pushed to the bulkhead, began reading the subpoena aloud.

"Before I could finish it, Mrs. Massie had quickly passed through a narrow doorway into the adjoining passageway," said the thwarted sergeant. "I was in full uniform with my badge conspicuously showing. I attempted to follow her, whereupon Captain Wortman threw his right arm across the doorway and caught me under the chin with his left forearm, forcing my head back."

"What the hell do you want here?" demanded the tough submarine commander, his perspiring face twisted in anger.

"I'm a Sergeant of Police and I have a subpoena to serve on Mrs. Massie," replied Mookini, his own Hawaiian features set in determination.

"I shall report you to your superior officer," stormed Wortman. "Don't you ever lay hands on me again!"

"I'll report to him myself. You assaulted me," answered the sergeant. He slid under the captain's arm and followed Thalia down the passageway, still reading aloud.

The burly Naval officer, panting, thrust the policeman back against the wall while Thalia slipped into her stateroom, followed by her mother.

"I caught up with her as she approached her stateroom and completed service of the subpoena just before she slammed the door in my face," claimed Mookini.

"Listen here!" barked Wortman, infuriated by the policeman's persistence. "Next time don't you interfere with me!"

"Next time don't you interfere with a police officer in the service of a process of the court," snapped back the undaunted sergeant. "You can't give me orders."

"When you address me, say 'sir!'"

"You say 'sir' to me then. If you want a police officer to respect a commanding officer you should show more respect yourself!"

"You—entitled to respect?" snorted Wortman sarcastically, "To hell!"

Tommy Massie approached the battling officers, one in Navy white, the other in police blue. He extended his hand to Mookini.

"No hard feelings here," said Tommy. The police officer took his hand and wished him a pleasant trip, saying that he'd been merely doing his duty.

"Well, here's to Hawaiian aloha," said the policeman. "I have to obey these orders, just as you must those of your superior officer."

"Well, here's to Southern hospitality," answered a smiling Tommy, offering apologies for the misunderstanding. For a brief moment in the hot, crowded passageway, Hawaiian aloha and Southern hospitality vied to surpass each other in affability. Even Ward Wortman's gruff glare relaxed into a smile.

"I was merely doing what any one hundred percent American citizen should do," explained Sergeant Mookini.

"That's the way!" said Captain Wortman, and the two shook hands.

Sergeant Lono McCallum approached the trio as Captain Wortman volunteered to see if Thalia was ready to receive the officers of the law. He rapped on the stateroom door and entered.

"I want to do some talking in there, too," said McCallum, still hoping for a better service of the subpoena.

"You'll have to do some writing first, old man," said Tommy Massie, in his smooth Southern drawl. He took McCallum by the hand and drew him into the next stateroom, where he had the policeman sign an autographed copy of Clarence Darrow's biography that was being passed around for signatures among attorneys and other friends from the trial who were crowded in the small room.

A bugle sounded on the deck and the first bars of Aloha 'Oe floated through the porthole. Mrs. Fortescue entered the cabin and smiled at the policeman; on her heels came Mrs. Harry Kluegel, breathless after forcing her way through the clogged corridor. A photographer from one of the news services, also returning to the mainland, slipped in and was greeted by Grace Fortescue, whom he had persistently photographed during the past weeks.

"What on earth are you doing here?" asked Mrs. Fortescue.

"I have to go home sometime, too. I didn't come aboard just to pester you."

While Grace Fortescue posed for final pictures, Mrs. Kluegel threw her arms around Tommy and kissed him soundly on both cheeks. Other giggling matrons, all members of the Citizen's Organization for Good Government, followed suit. Tommy maintained an affable demeanor despite has blushing embarrassment. Walter Dillingham charged through the doorway, with Captain T.K. Whitelaw, Chief Officer of the

Malolo. Behind them appeared a beaming Admiral Stirling with final farewell wishes and an armload of leis. The packed stateroom lacked only the Marx Brothers. It was no time for comedy, however, as Darrow stuck his head in the door and announced, "Everything seems to be all right now." The policemen, crushed in the bosom of Honolulu high society, realized that his words meant Thalia had again been spirited away to an inaccessible quarter of the ship. The tinkling scale of chimes filled the corridors.

"All ashore who're going ashore!" sang out a steward. The police officers retreated, friends wept and crushed each other in flower-laden embraces. Mrs. Fortescue's sister and brother came to take her on deck.

"I think Hawaii is a lovely place, except for its politics," she called back to departing newsmen. Last call ashore echoed through the ship.

"How do you feel, Lieutenant Massie?" asked one of the reporters.

"How do I feel?" answered Tommy, dazed by the sudden deluge of well-wishers, but happy. "I'll feel a lot better when Mrs. Massie and I get back to Maple Street in Winchester, Kentucky." Thalia, however, was nowhere in sight. Nor was she seen again before departure.

On deck, Tommy's mother-in-law, with Mrs. Julian Ripley and Robert Bell, smiled gaily as the Darrows approached them with Lieutenant Johnson, the Navy legal officer. They formed a group at the rail, watching the last visitors go ashore as the ship cast off from its mooring of paper streamers. The churning blue water, creamed by the wake of the propellers, widened between the ship and the pier. The hands on the clock of the Aloha Tower pointed to noon and the proud profile of Diamond Head appeared beyond Honolulu harbor.

Faint strains of Aloha 'Oe could still be heard as the *Malolo* headed for the open ocean. From her rails, the lovely leis rained down upon the sea and floated shoreward as passengers cast their farewell aloha on the waters. The only voyagers who did not observe the Hawaiian tradition that promises a return to the Islands were Mrs. Fortescue and her friends.

The *Malolo* was far over the horizon when the sun followed it, leaving the afterglow of the tropics.

The soft sound of cooing doves and rustling palms produced a respite of peace for "Fighting Jack" Kelley as he leaned back in a comfortable chair on the lanai of his home. He picked up the glass at his side and took a deep draught. Despite the smoothness of the liquor, the taste in his throat was bitter. The few good friends who were with him noticed a look of irony that seemed to mock his strong Irish features. He had succumbed to a mixed mood, combining triumph and defeat, rather like the chap, he mused, who in a rival profession remarks that the operation was successful but the patient died. He knew full well that along with the Massies and Mrs. Fortescue sailed the last hope of retrying the Ala Moana Case.

"Have you ever made a study of masks?" the public prosecutor asked aloud, addressing no one in particular, unless it was himself. "The artist Benda depicts them cleverly and grotesquely. I wish he were here. I will set up one for Thalia Massie and proceed with the trial."

Jack Kelley declined to amplify this statement, but all those present knew it to mean that he did not intend to proceed further.

And would Thalia's mask have been the proper one? More appropriate would have been that of Melpomene.

A week after the *Malolo* sailed with the stellar cast of the Massie Case—none of whom would ever return to the scene of one of Hawaii's greatest tragedies—the next steamer carried a confidential letter from the Governor of Hawaii to his superior in Washington. It was Lawrence Judd's final appraisal of facts, and it concluded with an interesting recommendation.

TERRITORY OF HAWAII

Executive Chambers

Honolulu

CONFIDENTIAL

Honorable Ray Lyman Wilbur
Secretary of the Interior
Washington, D. C.

Dear Mr. Secretary:

There are several matters relating to the situation here which, I consider, should be brought to your special attention.

From the night of the Naval party at the Ala Wai Inn, Honolulu, on September 12, 1931, the incidents and nature of which are detailed in the first few pages of my report to you dated January 18, 1932, a series of events has transpired which have done great harm.

Captain Ward Wortman's wire, was, in my opinion, not only unjust to Honolulu but has been proved to be an exaggeration by the reports of incidents upon which it's based. I believe this wire was one of the main bases for the dispatch from Admiral Pratt, which probably did much to incite Lieutenant Massie and his companions to kill Kahahawai.

Various wires and reports were sent to the Navy Department by Rear Admiral Yates Stirling, Jr., Commandant of the Fourteenth Naval District, which are likewise treated in the aforesaid report, in which exaggerated or inaccurate statements of local conditions were made, several of them according to Admiral Stirling's admission to me, being based upon newspaper accounts without proper investigation. His report to the Honorable Seth W. Richardson, Assistant Attorney General of the United States, dealing with the Oriental situation and attitude of the Oriental mind toward the whites in these Islands was to my mind most unfortunate. It is also unfortunate that the report was published. His conclusions are those of a man only recently come to the Islands. The problem is very complex and merits careful study. Certainly his expressed views are not shared by many responsible citizens who have spent years or perhaps a lifetime in these Islands.

The attitudes of Rear Admiral Stirling, Rear Admiral George Pettingill and Captain Ward Wortman have gone far toward creating a condition in the Islands inimical to the welfare of everybody concerned, including the Navy and Federal Government. Certainly the charges then made, that Hawaii was not safe for American womanhood, were entirely disproved by Mr. Richardson's investigation and report.

Throughout the unfortunate events which have transpired in Honolulu during the past few months, other incidents have occurred which indicate disrespect by certain Navy personnel for the constituted civil authority and legal procedure of this Territory:

The kidnapping and violent beating of Horace Ida, one of the Ala Moana defendants, at that time awaiting retrial, was probably the work of Navy personnel, although this is denied by Naval authorities.

The erroneous dispatches by Navy personnel, treated in my report of January 18, are other indications thereof.

This was further evidenced on the last day of the jury's deliberations in the Massie-Fortescue trial when Captain Ward Wortman, in open contempt of the court then in session, made certain statements which are covered by a certified copy of the transcript and an affidavit of Mr. John C. Kelley, Public Prosecutor for the City and County of Honolulu, hereto attached.

As to whether or not Captain Wortman was partially under the influence of liquor upon that occasion, I do not personally know. I have, however, been informed by several persons who were present, that, in their opinion, he was, and that at least one of the defendants, Albert O. Jones, was intoxicated upon that occasion.

Further evidence of this contempt is found in the methods employed by certain Navy personnel to block the service of a subpoena upon Mrs. Thalia Massie, requiring her presence at the proposed retrial of the Ala Moana case.

Although Admiral Stirling, through Lieutenant L.H.C. Johnson, advised the Public Prosecutor that he would permit service of process upon Mrs. Massie at the Pearl Harbor Naval Station, there was withheld the active assistance of Navy officials at the Base in the service of this subpoena.

The attempt to make such service upon Mrs. Massie at the Naval Station on Saturday, May 7, is covered in the affidavit of Detective Arthur H. Stagbar, hereto attached.

The efforts to make such service on the SS "Malolo" on Sunday, May 8, are covered in the affidavit of Sergeant Dewey Mookini, also hereto attached.

I believe it is only fair to say that, in my opinion, the local courts have taken no action regarding the various acts of contempt of court of Captain Wortman because of a desire to avoid any further unpleasantness locally with the Navy.

No one realizes the importance of these Islands to the Federal Government as a major military outpost any more than the citizens of this Territory, but it must be recognized by all that the value of the Islands as such can never be what it should be unless there is harmony and good feeling between the two armed forces of the United States and the residents of the Territory. Such harmony and cooperation do exist in the case of the Army forces located here, and I cannot commend Major General Briant H. Wells, U.S. Army, too highly for his splendid attitude of cooperation since his assignment here.

The attitude of the Navy officials in the recent occurrences has indicated what appears to be a definite attempt to force a "military" form of government upon the Territory.

According to Admiral Stirling's own statement to me, made at his quarters at Pearl Harbor in the presence of the Territorial Attorney General, practically all of the Southern officers of the Navy consider the Hawaiians or any dark-skinned person to be inferior. This is an inaccurate conclusion, as anyone who has come to these Islands with a fair and open mind soon learns. I feel that a tremendous benefit could and would accrue, both to the Federal government and these Islands, if fair and open-minded officers, particularly those in high command, were sent to the Islands. Those in high command could also render a very definite service by endeavoring to inculcate into their subordinates some comprehension of and respect for the Hawaiians and our problems.

To come directly to the point, Mr. Secretary, I feel that the sooner Admiral Stirling and Captain Wortman are assigned to other duties, the better it will be for all concerned...

Sincerely yours,
Lawrence M. Judd

In the days following the Massie-Fortescue departure, Admiral Stirling also had a few personal opinions and fascinating footnotes to contribute to the full story of the case.

"I dwelt upon the fact that discipline is a strong deterrent against men of the armed services seeking a revenge which could take a human life," he wrote in his version of the Massie Case, which was later published in *True Detective Mysteries*.

"I brought this point out purposely, because I have always believed that Mrs. Fortescue, and not Lieutenant Massie, held the revolver that killed Kahahawai."

Yates Stirling, Jr., was more than a commanding officer to Tommy Massie, he was a close and devoted friend of the young man's family, a relationship he shared with another leading citizen of Hawaii's community who also shared his conclusion.

"Ann Kluegel, a splendid type of patriotic woman who was the head of a civic organization for better government, was a great friend of Mrs. Fortescue," wrote the Admiral in his autobiography, "and told me she firmly believed that the mother killed Kahahawai, and not Massie."

It was a theory on which Stirling relished speculating, and his interpretation of the crucial moment of the case afforded a revealing insight into not only the Admiral's prejudiced opinion, but also his personality.

"A mother's love is far stronger, deeper and more self-sacrificing than a lover's or a husband's," said the haughty admiral in the florid tradition of an antebellum Southern gentleman. He shared Darrow's awe of motherhood. "The consciousness of discipline might have stayed Massie's hand, even after hearing the brute boast of his crime. Not so with a woman and a mother. She could see, swimming before her eyes, all the terrible, revolting and degrading experiences forced upon her child by this great athlete and man of dark skin. No idea of abstract justice could soften the hardness in her mother's heart for this confessed criminal as he stood before her , saying 'Yes, I done it.'

"Massie claimed that when he heard those words drop from Kahahawai's lips, everything went black. He said he did not remember firing the shot until afterwards, when he saw the smoking gun in his hand, and Kahahawai's heart had been pierced. In my opinion, when Mrs. Fortescue heard these fatal words, she did not experience the sensation of having everything 'go black,' but saw all the clearer. She saw not a man but a crawling worm, a scorpion, a centipede. Maybe this was the moment for which she had long been waiting—to have the self-confessed ravisher of her baby standing there before her. Did she grab the gun out of Massie's hand and fire the fatal shot?

"I have always hoped so."

Not until years later was it learned that Mrs. Fortescue's own gun, never recovered by the police, had been hidden in a Kotex box in the Massie home in Manoa Valley—presumably taken there from the murder scene by Seaman Jones.

THIRTY-TWO

Gradually the heat of public opinion cooled, and talk of the abolishment of Territorial government and the substitution of commission or Navy rule subsided. It was ended once and for all when Assistant Attorney General Richardson announced that continued self-government was in the best interest of Hawaii.

Nine months after the *Malolo* sailed, a notice appeared in a local paper that a statement signed by the vice president and general manager of Pinkerton's National Detective Agency, addressed to Governor Judd and dated October 8, 1932, was to be filed on February 13, 1933, in the City and County Clerk's Office by John C. Kelley, public prosecutor. The Pinkerton Agency had been engaged to conduct a complete investigation of the Ala Moana Case after Judd had asked the Justice Department for such an inquiry and been refused on the grounds that the case was not within the scope of Federal Government activities.

The Board of Supervisors of Honolulu had appropriated $1,000, during the summer, for Public Prosecutor Kelley to go to New York, San Francisco and Los Angeles to check reports of the private investigators regarding suspects, and to determine whether or not the four remaining youths originally accused would be tried. Kelley said suspects in addition to the original five had fled to the mainland after the alleged attack.

A squad of Pinkerton sleuths, headed by the agency's leading investigator, spent four months tracking down clues and sifting facts from fiction. The first week in October 1932, Governor Lawrence Judd, Attorney General Harry Hewitt and John Kelley met with Pinkerton officials in their New York headquarters and the full report, addressed to the Governor of Hawaii, was read and its conclusion presented:

> In consequence of your instructions to investigate the so-called "Ala Moana Assault Case" to determine, if possible, the true circumstances of the assault upon Mrs. Thalia Massie about midnight Saturday, September 12, 1931, at Honolulu, T.H., and particularly if raped, by whom, we detailed for this purpose our California Division Manager, Mr. J.C. Fraser, a skilled detective of many years experience with this agency throughout the United States and abroad.

> By your instructions Mr. Fraser met you at San Francisco, June 9th, and at the conference which ensued you reviewed the Ala

Moana assault case and instructed Mr. Fraser upon his arrival in Honolulu to call on Attorney General Harry R. Hewitt, Deputy Attorney General Harold T. Kay and Public Prosecutor John C. Kelley; also to meet Acting Governor Raymond C. Brown, who would render all possible assistance. You informed Mr. Fraser that Deputy Attorney General Kay had been assisting the Attorney General in an exhaustive investigation of the Ala Moana case and was in a position to furnish information as to the investigation to date.

Mr. Fraser left San Francisco, June 10, 1932, and arrived at Honolulu at 5 p.m. June 14th.

At this interview you impressed upon Mr. Fraser that the investigation he was to make would be free from interference of any kind and that what was desired were truth and facts, "no matter where it struck..."

An analysis of the reports of our representatives, together with the reports and statements of the Attorney General's office, the office of the Public Prosecutor, and the Police Department, also the testimony at the trial of the defendants, makes it impossible to escape the conviction that the kidnapping and assault were not caused by those accused, with the attendant circumstances alleged by Mrs. Massie. We can only assume that the reason Mrs. Massie did not give to the authorities, immediately after the alleged offense, the same details of information she was able to furnish by her testimony at the trial is because she did not possess it at the time she was questioned by those she came in contact with immediately after the alleged offense.

In other words, concluded Chief Investigator J.C. Fraser, "facts and evidence unearthed have very definite bearing on the probability of the innocence of the accused."

The Pinkerton Report revealed the following facts:

A careful examination into the alibi of the accused failed to discover any important circumstance disproving their statements. The movements of the five boys on the night of September 12, 1931, remained precisely as they were originally accounted for. Five persons saw Benny Ahakuelo, at the dance at Waikiki Park between 11:45 and the last dance just before midnight. "This testimony has not been disproved."

Thalia claimed her assailants were Hawaiian. Only Joe Kahahawai and Benny Ahakuelo were Hawaiian. Henry Chang was Chinese-Hawaiian, and David Takai and Horace Ida were Japanese.

The examining physician, who treated Thalia two-and-a-half hours after the alleged rape, could find no evidence of violent sexual abuse, although he accepted her claim to have been raped six times by five men.

Nurse Agnes Fawcett, who prepared Thalia for the examination at Emergency Hospital at 2:30 a.m., failed to see any indications of rape and stated, "She was clean as a new pin."

Though Thalia was wearing a dress of fragile silk fabric, and claimed to have been dragged thirty feet over rough terrain, "the garments were in perfect condition, no rips or tears." There was no evidence of a struggle, her snakeskin slippers were unscuffed, the only imperfection in her apparel being a run in one stocking. Inspector McIntosh said he had seen no spots on the garments when the dress was brought to the police headquarters by Lieutenant John Jardine the night of the alleged rape, "except grease marks caused when she sat down in the car."

Captain of Records, R.O. Griffin, gave J.C. Fraser a varying report, since he found on Thalia's slip "several stains resembling those of vegetation and a possible blood spot, on her girdle—at back, inner side, which would come just between cheeks of buttock...a smooth, stiff coagulation which might be seminal material," on her garter belt, a stain, "such as might be made by grass." The back of the dress showed water marks, and on the bodice faint smears that appeared to be blood.

Dr. Nils P. Larsen, Medical Director of Queen's Hospital and in charge of the laboratory, made a microscopic examination of Thalia's clothing and found no sperm or blood stains.

Dr. Larsen also gave the Pinkerton investigator an interesting side note: laboratory examination of the scrapings from Thalia's operation in October "disclosed no evidence of pregnancy."

Dr. Thomas M. Mossman, of City and County Emergency Hospital, told one of Fraser's operatives that examination of the boys' clothing and genital organs showed no evidence of their having perpetrated a violent rape.

The time element also negated the possibility of rape as Thalia described it. "It is exceedingly doubtful if Mrs. Massie was assaulted by four or five young men a total of four to six times, with Mrs. Massie resisting with all her strength, or that it was accomplished in twenty minutes." This was the length of time Thalia herself judged to be consumed and also the time worked out in a retracing schedule drawn up by the Pinkerton investigators. Also, pointed out Fraser, it must be borne in mind that the rapists "had no need to complete this multiple rape in the shortest time possible."

Thalia's close and careful observation of details was remarked on by the Pinkerton man: "...her lack of knowledge of these same important details when interviewed immediately after the rape, must of necessity give rise to grave doubt as to their accuracy."

A report made by three sailors, who had hijacked a truck from Ship's Service Stores at the Submarine Base and "gone joyriding in Waikiki," where a Ford touring car passed them on John Ena Road a little after 11 a.m. and the local occupants shouted insults to the Navy men, was brought to F.C. Fraser's attention by the Navy. In the back of the touring car, the sailors had noticed a white woman "in a peculiar position." The investigator interrogated the three men, but the sailor's stories conflicted radically. "These seamen had provided themselves with a bottle of Oke before undertaking the ride and acknowledge to having consumed it while riding about. There is nothing in their statements which would indicate the woman in the car was there by force— also it should be taken into account that they did not disclose to the authorities what they alleged to have seen until seven months after the occurrence. We place no belief or importance in their story."

Fraser reported that during his stay in the Islands he came in contact with many Hawaiians in different walks of life and conversed with many prominent citizens and police officers familiar with Hawaiians, "and without exception the same verdict has been pronounced—that a Hawaiian will talk." Police records showed that confessions had been secured from Hawaiians with no difficulty and if the accused were guilty, this would be practically the first time in their memory that some of a number of accused in the same crime did not talk.

The Pinkerton men also checked out suspicious local gangs, other than the School Street Gang, headed by Joseph Kahahawai. "They are merely groups of local youth who drink beer, fight and may be regarded as a rough element but they are not of the type of mainland gunmen and gangsters." Tinny Tommy's Group and the Crawford Gang were rounded up and questioned. Boys from the latter gang had gone to Maui as a dance band after the assault and stayed with one of the member's sister-in-law, who later circulated the report that the boys were the ones supposed to have committed the rape. Nothing could be proven. Considerable suspicion was directed against the McCabe Gang, caused by an affidavit sworn to by "Tahiti" Kemp, an associate who was serving time in Oahu Prison. Fraser visited "Tahiti" in prison at the request of Princess Kawananakoa, but the criminal could furnish no definite information. Some of McCabe's gang had fled to the mainland after the killing of Kahahawai, and the leader was induced to return to Honolulu by Public Prosecutor Kelley, "but without anything helpful being obtained."

With so little real evidence, concluded Fraser, "it seems fair to assume that the prosecution of the accused was forced upon the Territory by reason of Mrs. Massie's story and her identification of these boys. No other course appears to have been possible in view of the circumstances, than to try the case...that the prosecution failed for want of corroboration of essential parts of Mrs. Massie's story and the alibi of the accused was inevitable.

"There is a preponderance of evidence that Mrs. Massie did in some manner suffer numerous bruises about the head and body but definite proof of actual rape has not in our opinion been found."

Even the most experienced of Pinkerton sleuths had to admit, however, that "although there has been found no corroboration of the statements of Mrs. Massie that the alleged kidnapping and rape occurred...neither has it been proved that the kidnapping and rape did not occur."

Only Thalia knew the truth and she was one person whom the Pinkerton detectives did not interview.

Also in Fraser's summary of his findings was a more positive conclusion than that of what actually occurred the night of September 12. "The manner of procuring the identification of the suspects, the delay in the thorough examination of complainant and suspects for evidence of the offense on their persons, the manner of attempting identification of Ida's automobile, license number, auto tracks at the Quarantine grounds, was not in accordance with best police practices."

On the morning that Investigator Fraser was sailing for the mainland, he was awakened at his hotel by a phone call. It was Andrew Adams, Commissioner of the Board of Equalization. He told the detective that a woman, name unknown, who rented out cottages in the vicinity of the Niumalu Hotel, claimed to have rented a cottage to a Naval officer in the summer of 1931.

"He ceased being her tenant shortly after September 12, 1931," continued the Commissioner, adding "that frequently her tenant's cottage was visited by a young woman, name unknown, who was slender, had a pale face and blond hair and slightly stooped as she walked; that she saw this young woman enter and leave the cottage sometimes at night, sometimes in the daytime and that these visits were rarely brief."

The name of the Naval officer was Lieutenant Branson.

The Pinkerton man jumped from his bed, hurriedly dressed and shaved after placing a call to Lieutenant J.J. Branson at Pearl Harbor. The young Naval officer would be glad to see him immediately. It would be Fraser's third meeting with Jerry Branson. He had thoroughly checked out Branson's story of his actions the night of the Ala Wai Inn party and they had been verified by friends who were with him. Within the hour, the detective was at Pearl Harbor, where he confronted the submarine officer with the information just given to him by Adams.

"Jerry Branson positively denied that he had ever rented a cottage and had a lady caller as described...he consented to face at any time the woman who had rented out this cottage."

J.C. Fraser returned to his hotel to finish packing, stopping en route to report this last lead to Deputy Attorney Harold T. Kay and suggesting he see Commissioner Adams and follow up on the matter.

When the Pinkerton Report was read, Fraser remarked at the close of the section concerning Jerry Branson, "We have been unable to uncover anything that would connect him with the assault of Mrs. Massie."

The complete Pinkerton Report was not made public.

At 11 a.m. on February 13, 1933, soon after it was placed in the hands of the Honolulu County Board of Supervisors, Judge Charles S. Davis granted a motion by Public Prosecutor John Kelley that a nolle prosequi be entered against the four surviving men charged with assaulting Thalia Massie seventeen months before. The proceedings required less than ten minutes.

The boys were free. The court's action also cleared, as far as the Territory was concerned, the name of Kahahawai.

Two days later, on hearing of the Pinkerton Report and the dismissal of the rape charges, Thalia Massie, in Philadelphia where Tommy was currently stationed, told reporters that the Honolulu authorities had offered to commute the sentences of her mother, her husband and the two sailors to one year, if she would agree to leave the Islands immediately. "I refused and the authorities then offered to commute the sentence to one hour." She said she had accepted this offer, thus automatically depriving the state of a complaining witness in the retrial of the Ala Moana Case.

"Pure bunk!" scoffed John Kelley when told of Thalia's remarks. Now that the boys were cleared, he seemed as relieved as the girl who had claimed to suffer so brutally at their hands. "If Mrs. Massie had returned and testified, all the racial animosities that developed during the trial of her husband would be rekindled to set another figurative fire under Honolulu."

The Massie Case was ranked as the ninth most outstanding story of 1932 by Associated Press editors. It was overshadowed by such news-making events as the Lindberg baby kidnapping, the Democratic land-slide that brought Franklin Delano Roosevelt to the Presidency, the bonus army of the Great Depression, the Olympic Games in Los Angeles and Amelia Earhart's solo flight to Europe.

THIRTY-THREE

Tommy and Thalia took a train from the West Coast to Indiana, where they bought a small coupe and were able to slip secretly into Winchester, Kentucky, late one Saturday afternoon two weeks after they had sailed from Honolulu. They enjoyed a quiet home-cooked dinner with Tommy's family before word of their arrival spread through the town and the phone began to ring. The next day they were spotted at the polo matches in Lexington, and hundreds of friends and strangers came to their seats to shake their hands and congratulate them.

A month after the final day of the trial they stopped off in Washington and spent the night with Thalia's relatives, Dr. and Mrs. Gilbert Grosvenor, of the National Geographic Society. While there, Tommy received his orders to report for duty on June 3 aboard the *USS New Mexico* in the Philadelphia Navy Yard. The next day they were reunited with the Fortescues at Wildhome, in Bayport, Long Island. "Changed orders for Lieutenant Massie will not permit Mrs. Massie to be with him," read a brief news item, datelined Bayport. "It is expected that Mrs. Massie will remain with her parents after Lieutenant Massie boards his ship."

Lord and Jones also received orders to the East Coast after they were shipped out from Hawaii on a nitro-transport via the Panama Canal. Lord was sent to the Submarine Base in New London, Connecticut, and Jones was assigned to do experimental submarine work.

Admiral Stirling remained on as Commandant of the 14th Naval District at Pearl Harbor for two more years. It was enough time for the friction between the Navy and the community to be smoothed out, in a new era of mutual respect. As the salty old sea dog's tour of Hawaiian duty drew to a close, there was sincere regret in many parts of the city. The Stormy Petrel, himself, never regretted for a moment his stand in the Massie Case. "Not boastfully, but merely to show that my stand in this baffling case did receive some favorable comment from Hawaiian newspapers of the highest standing, I am quoting two editorials published on my departure from Honolulu," wrote the Admiral in his autobiography. From the pages of the pro-Navy *Honolulu Advertiser*, an editorial went overboard with praise:

> When the liner *Lurline* sails tomorrow, it will carry on its passenger list one of the most popular and able Naval officers ever to

have served in Hawaii: Rear Admiral Yates Stirling, Jr., who for three years has been in command of the 14th Naval District.

During his tour of duty as Commandant, the relationship of the Navy in Hawaii to the civilian community became more firmly cemented, in spite of distressing episodes which, had a less able man been the head of the service in Hawaii, could have brought about an estrangement...

Under Admiral Stirling's administration "Yes" meant yes, and "No" was a decided negative in Navy-civilian contacts. There was never any evasion of any issue...This community regrets the departure of Admiral Stirling and will remember him as an officer - and citizen—who typified all that was best in an officer of the United States Navy and in an American.

The extent to which bygones had become bygones was seconded by *The Honolulu Times*, which reminded its readers that Admiral Stirling was "very much in the spotlight during the unfortunate Ala Moana Case and subsequent Massie trial. Unwaveringly he insisted that Hawaii was a part of the United States and that American standards...must prevail. To him, more than any other man, Hawaii is indebted for the cleaning up of the rotten police situation."

Managing to keep his graying red head afloat despite an inundation of leis, the Admiral looked down from the *Lurline* on the medley of Hawaiian faces, more than ever convinced that "the Islands must be governed in the manner of the mainland and not by the ethics of the Orient. We have taught the dark-skinned races," he mused with a smile of satisfaction, "how far the white man will go to protect his woman."

Governor Judd picked up his duties of running the Territory after they had been so shatteringly disrupted, finding time, however, to give a few speeches on the mainland in an effort to undo the damage that had tarnished the reputation of his beloved and shining Islands.

"Hawaiians are intensely loyal to the United States!" he said to a San Francisco audience. History was to prove him right.

A few years after the bitter dust had settled, Grace Fortescue agreed to do a series of first-person articles on the Massie Case for the weekly magazine *Liberty*. Thalia sought vainly to dissuade her mother, even threatening an injunction to prevent their appearance, and obtained withdrawal of two of the articles. She was powerless to stop publication of the remaining three because her lawyer advised her that the only grounds for injunction were in the first two. Thus Mrs. Fortescue was able to tell the world her version of exactly what happened at 9 a.m. the morning of January 8, 1932, in the Manoa Valley of Hawaii.

After Joseph Kahahawai had blurted out his epitaph "Yes, we done it," Tommy Massie's mother-in-law went into action.

"I turned toward my desk to get paper and a pen. Suddenly the room vibrated with a shot. I wheeled around. Kahahawai was dead and facing him Tommy stood transfixed, the pistol at his feet, staring before him unseeingly, unknowingly. I have seen men die. I have seen dead men in Belgium in the war, but never before had I seen a man motionless, rigid, unconscious on his feet..."

Grace Fortescue said she led the young Naval officer into the kitchen and the necessity for flight overcame her.

"I sincerely regret the death of Kahahawai. I don't believe in lynch law—I can't state that too emphatically and I am opposed to capital punishment. Could I have looked into the future but a few hours, nothing would have persuaded me to go to the courthouse that fatal day."

The law officer on the case with the clearest power of recall was William Seymour, who accompanied Thalia to the hospital after her night of abuse and who later removed the body of Kahahawai from the rented Buick sedan. From retirement in Hilo, the policeman had this to say about Hawaii's most scandalous crime:

"Well, let me tell you, when Detective Jardine interviewed Mrs. Massie at her home, she said she could not remember the car's license plate, make or color. She was later to 'recall' the numbers of the license plate, which led to the arrest of the five Hawaiians. The 'recollection' was due to the fact that while we were driving her from her home to an emergency hospital near Queens Hospital, she overheard a bulletin on the police radio saying the five Hawaiians had smashed their car up on Middle Street in Kalihi and giving the license plate, make and color. It was quite evident she picked up that little piece of information from the police radio and used it later...

Now, about the murder of Joseph Kahahawai...We found the body wedged between the front and the back seat, naked and wrapped in a sheet and bound with new manila rope. His clothes, dripping wet, were on the floor board. Mrs. Fortescue's feet were resting on the clothing...Mrs. Fortescue retained her composure at all times and remained at ease. We made her and Massie walk by and view the body and she was calm as anything. Massie was visibly shaken. Police hauled them off in a paddy wagon.

I think the greatest event of my whole life was being State's witness at the subsequent trial, since the greatest criminal lawyer, Clarence Darrow, was defense attorney, and I had to face up to him. Let me tell you, your knees shake when you're going to be cross-examined by a man like that...

I think some of the violence and riots that took place during the rape-murder cases were due to widespread publicity in detective and other magazines, with pictures of Hawaiian warriors with clubs standing behind trees ready to pounce on innocent haole women. Passions were heated because the Navy was involved, outraged Hawaiians were involved, and in the middle was the white community. It took a long time for things to quiet down."

The corner of John Ena Road and Kalakaua Avenue is now one of the busiest intersections in Waikiki. A steady stream of traffic flows by the bridge over the slower moving water of the Ala Wai Canal, and at night the still surface is bright with reflections of headlights as tourist-laden cars drive to a Mecca of highrise hotels, including the 2,998-room Hilton Hawaiian Village, which soars thirty-five-stories above the beach where the shabby Niumalu cottages once stood. Dominating the intersection at Kapiolani Boulevard is the new Convention Center. Few people in Honolulu know that many years ago the land harbored a booming nightspot, the popular tea house called the Ala Wai Inn.

Manoa remains one of the most desirable neighborhoods in Honolulu. The valley itself is as beautiful as always and rainbows have never ceased to rise each day in the verdant embrace of the Koolau Mountains.

Unchanged also is Puea Cemetery on School Street, where the weeds and keawe brambles grow in even wilder profusion and most of the dead rest in anonymous peace. The sordid slums of Mosquito Flats and Hell's Half Acre and Blood Town have long since been razed. A few Buddhist temples keep solitary watch over the blocks of public housing where street gangs, prostitutes and gamblers once hustled among the teeming streets.

There's a new Police Headquarters, and Hawaii is justly proud of its record of efficient law enforcement. The governor's office was moved from the royal bedchamber in Iolani Palace to a handsome $15-million capitol building, and the quaint palace has been beautifully restored, with a museum. Court is still held in the Judiciary Building, and the golden statue of Kamehameha the Great continues to grace its lawn with indomitable dignity.

In a small, windowless office in downtown Honolulu, a locked file cabinet was opened thirty years after the crime. One drawer contained voluminous folders of notes and transcripts, marked "The Massie Case." Among the papers was a printed test sheet, a psychology test for neurosis. Clipped to its yellowed pages were several pencil-scrawled descriptions of dreams. The childish handwriting was the same as that of the name at the top of the test paper: Thalia H. Massie. Only one person had the key to the file, and the late Detective John Jardine seldom used it. The building is gone now. The cabinet is closed. So is the Massie Case.

What happened to the dramatis personae of this Hawaiian tragedy that starred the namesake of the muse of comedy?

Thalia and Tommy Massie were divorced on February 22, 1934, on grounds of extreme mental cruelty. Thalia stopped off in Chicago en route to Reno and told reporters that she was getting a divorce at the request of her husband and her mother. She said that she still loved Tommy and considered a divorce "very stupid after a couple has been through as much as Thomas and I." Thalia spent only ten minutes with the judge behind locked doors. That night she collapsed in a Reno nightclub with a strange and sudden illness, but suicide rumors were denied.

"This will start a new page in my life," she told newsmen the next day. She was "visibly nervous and depressed." In April of that year, she slashed her wrists and threw herself from the top deck to the deck below of the Italian liner Roma while on a Mediterranean cruise. She was admitted to a clinic in Genoa in a state of severe depression, and released a month later completely recovered. "I wanted to die," she said. "I regretted getting a divorce from my husband."

In 1946, she was arrested in Los Angeles on charges of drunkenness. She had allegedly beaten her pregnant landlady who sued her for $10,000. Five years later she startled family and friends by enrolling at the University of Arizona on her fortieth birthday. Friends were even more stunned when she eloped to Mexico with a fellow student, twenty-one-year-old Robert Uptigrove. They were divorced in 1958 and Thalia took an apartment near her mother in Palm Beach, where she died at the age of fifty-one on July 2, 1963, of an overdose of barbiturates. Medical examiner Hugh Dortsch maintained, "As far as I have been able to determine, the death was accidental."

Lieutenant Thomas H. Massie remarried in 1937. A year later, on sea duty abroad the gunboat Tulsa, in Japanese occupied Tsingtao,

China, the beleaguered officer was again in the news. The Associated Press reported that his wife had been slapped by a Japanese sentry. Returning from her husband's ship to town, Mrs. Massie had not understood the sentry's command in Japanese. An international incident was averted when Secretary of State Cordell Hull was advised by Shanghai officials that "Third power nationals residing in Japanese occupied territory do not enjoy special status because of extrality."

In 1940, Massie was sent for "observation and treatment" to St. Elizabeth Hospital, the mental hospital near Washington, D.C., and was retired with a permanent physical disability the same year. This did not prevent his assuming a second career as a civilian and enjoying many years of relative seclusion before his death at eighty, on January 8, 1987, fifty-five years to the day after Kahahawai was killed.

Former Governor Lawrence M. Judd also lived to be an octogenarian, dying at the distinguished age of eighty-one.

On a Sabbath day in March 1938, just a few weeks short of his eighty-first birthday, Clarence Darrow kept his date with William Jennings Bryan, as prosecutor John C. Kelley predicted.

Kelley, however, had preceded him. He died of a heart attack in January of the same year. He was fifty-two years old. Captain Ward K. Wortman also died prematurely in Brooklyn, New York, in 1943, at the age of fifty-four.

Admiral Yates Stirling, Jr., was buried with full military honors in Arlington National Cemetery on January 29, 1948. Prior to his retirement in 1936, he estimated that his long sea service of forty-four years had taken him 400,000 miles around the world. In 1944, the seventy-two-year old Admiral applied for a return to active duty. Secretary of the Navy James Forrestal replied that it was "regretted that no billet suitable to your rank is available," adding, "the patriotic urge to contribute in greater measure to the war effort is highly appreciated."

The two enlisted men, Jones and Lord, returned to the fleet, both eventually rising to the rank of Chief Petty Officer. Both also reported, years later, that Mrs. Fortescue and Lord did not enter her house until after the shot was fired. Who fired it? Astonishingly, Albert O. Jones said he did. Thirty-five years after the fact, as reviewed in the October 7, 1966, issue of TIME Magazine, the publicity-awed, habitually-drunk seaman claimed to have pulled the trigger. By the time the police were involved in the murder, however, Tommy Massie had assumed full responsibility. The motive was his—to defend the virtue of his wife and the honor of the Navy. In the tradition of a Southern officer and a gentleman, Tommy took the rap.

It's too late now for true confessions or for false ones.

Of the four surviving defendants of the Ala Moana Case, only one had a prison record after the case was dismissed. He became an alcoholic, served time in Oahu Prison, and on December 20, 1965, was arrested again for vagrancy. One became a taxi driver, another was a janitor before retirement and the fourth, Benny Ahakuelo, rose high in the ranks of the Fire Department, a well respected member of the community.

Mrs. Grace Fortescue remained a doyenne of Palm Beach and Long Island society, her pride undiminished, her social standing intact. She seldom returned to Washington. Nor did I. The sloping lawn of our former home was subdivided and a stout fence marked the boundary of the Bell Estate. At Twin Oaks, the children who laughed under the apple trees had yellow skin and almond eyes, for the summer home of Alexander Graham Bell became the Embassy of the Republic of China, Taiwan.

This is an account of actual events. Sources include government documents, trial transcripts, Territorial records, medical and police reports, diaries, contemporary magazine and newspaper articles, letters, and personal interviews. Material has necessarily been edited by the author for brevity and clarity, with the sincere intention of avoiding any distortion of meaning or fact.

ACKNOWLEDGMENTS

I wish to express past gratitude to:

My dear parents, Captain Elwood Alexander Cobey, U.S. Navy, and Margaret Beall Cobey, from whom I first learned of the Massie Case; my husband, Brigadier General Edwin F. Black, U.S. Army, whose access to unclassified documents of the Department of Defense was invaluable and whose devoted support made this book possible; Bennett Cerf and Horace Sutton, who asked me to write the story; editors William Ewing and A.A. (Bud) Smyser, of the *Honolulu Star-Bulletin*, who made the files of their news library available to me; Lou Jo Hollinger, reporter, who covered the trials; Agnes Conrad, Hawaii Archivist, now retired, who guided me through the labyrinth of Massie Case material in the Hawaii Archives; Assistant Police Chief Dewey Moʻokini and Detective John Jardine, of the Honolulu Police Department, for sharing their extensive first-hand knowledge of the case; psychologist Dr. E. Lowell Kelley for his enlightening correspondence; and Pinkerton's National Detective Agency, Inc. for a copy of its report.

Present thanks to:

Justice Samuel P. King, Senior U.S. District Judge, who reviewed my manuscript and made many cogent corrections and wise suggestions; Kenneth Robbins, trial lawyer, for his enthusiastic approval; Attorney Sherman Hee for his seasoned advice; publisher Thurston Twigg-Smith for arranging my access to the photo library of *The Honolulu Advertiser*; Seth Jones, photo editor; Kevin O'Sullivan, of AP/Wide World Photos, for archival newspaper photographs; Vice Admiral Howard Greer and Captain E. Chipman Higgins, both U.S. Navy retired, for their research in the Register of Naval Academy Graduates; Tin Hu Young, Archivist of Kawaiahaʻo Church; fellow columnist Eddie Sherman who has for years encouraged me to publish this story; Madeleine Shaw, of Basic Office Services, for her secretarial and editorial assistance, as well as for her home-baked cookies; publishers Dale and Lynne Madden who have made me welcome at Island Heritage, and Brian Lavelle, of Island Heritage, for his supportive and patient expertise in coordinating production.

Final heartfelt thanks to my six children, Star, Christopher, Noel, Nicholas, Brian and Bruce, who were often lulled to sleep by the tune of my typewriter.